Massachusetts Trail Guide

9th Edition

**AMC's
Comprehensive Guide to Hiking Trails
in Massachusetts**

Compiled and edited by
John S. Burk

Appalachian Mountain Club Books
Boston, Massachusetts

The AMC is a non-profit organization and sales of AMC books fund our mission of protecting the Northeast outdoors. If you appreciate our efforts and would like to make a donation to the AMC, contact us at Appalachian Mountain Club, 5 Joy Street, Boston, MA 02108.

http://www.outdoors.org/publications/books/

Cartography by Larry Garland
Book design by Jennie Sparrow
Front cover photograph © Kindra Clineff
Back cover photographs: left © Jerry and Marcy Monkman,
    middle © William H. Johnson, right © John S. Burk

Library of Congress Cataloging-in-Publication Data

Massachusetts trail guide : AMC's comprehensive guide to hiking trails in Massachusetts / compiled and edited by John S. Burk.—9th ed.
    p. cm.
  Includes index.
  ISBN 978-1-934028-25-4 (alk. paper)
1. Hiking—Massachusetts—Guidebooks. 2. Trails—Massachusetts—Guidebooks.
3. Massachusetts—Guidebooks. I. Burk, John S. II. Appalachian Mountain Club.

  GV199.42.M4M373 2009
  917.4404'4—dc22

                        2008049709

Outdoor recreation activities by their very nature are potentially hazardous. This book is not a substitute for good personal judgment and training in outdoor skills. Due to changes in conditions, use of the information in this book is at the sole risk of the user. The author and the Appalachian Mountain Club assume no liability for accidents happening to, or injuries sustained by, readers who engage in the activities described in this book.

Printed in the United States of America.

⊛ Printed on paper that contains 30 percent post-consumer recycled fiber, using soy-based inks.

10 9 8 7 6 5 4 3 2 1   09 10 11 12 13 14 15 16

Editions of the Massachusetts Trail Guide

First Edition	1964
Second Edition	1967
Third Edition	1972
Fourth Edition	1978
Fifth Edition	1982
Sixth Edition	1989
Seventh Edition	1995
Eighth Edition	2004
Ninth Edition	2009

CONTENTS

KEY TO LOCATOR MAPS

The numbers within the boxes on the locator map at the beginning of each section of this book indicate which maps show trails discussed in that section.

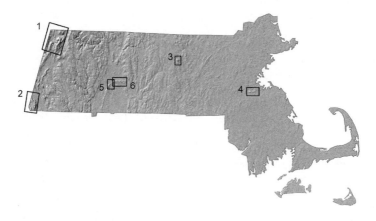

Map 1: Northern Berkshires

Map 2: Southwestern Massachusetts

Map 3: Wachusett Mtn. State Reservation

Map 4: Blue Hills Reservation

Map 5: Mt. Tom State Reservation

Map 6: Mt. Holyoke Range

FOREWORD

As a hiker, outdoor writer, and photographer based in Massachusetts, I've had the good fortune of regularly sampling the fine variety of trails and natural features the state has to offer. Within a matter of days in September 2008 I observed colonies of shorebirds and fiddler crabs along the mudflats of the Wellfleet Bay Wildlife Sanctuary, colorful late-season wildflowers blooming along the Appalachian Trail at Tyringham Cobble in the Berkshire Hills, and four moose in the forests surrounding Quabbin Reservoir.

Indeed, for such a small state, Massachusetts offers a remarkable diversity of habitats and trails, thanks to a host of factors including climate and geology. Those footpaths in turn offer endless opportunities for explorers, whether you're looking for an easy walk around a pond or wildlife sanctuary or a backpacking excursion along the Appalachian Trail.

For this edition, with the assistance of numerous landowners and trail maintenance organizations, we have revised, updated, and expanded many existing trail descriptions, and added a number of new hikes as well. The guide is divided into sections covering each of the state's distinct regions: the Berkshire Hills, the Connecticut River Valley, the Worcester Hills, the North Shore and vicinity, the greater Boston area, and Cape Cod and the islands. Detailed information is provided for the state's ten long-distance trails.

Complementing the hike descriptions are a series of detailed topographic maps, for six popular hiking destinations, such as Mt. Greylock, the Holyoke Range, and Wachusett Mtn. These maps have been updated with distances between trail junctions and other new information. The introduction includes a summary of the state's natural history, as well as safety information for hikers. Finally, the book's easy-to-use format and size make it convenient to carry on every adventure. We hope readers will use this information to enjoy the trails and appreciate the nature of this small but diverse state.

ACKNOWLEDGMENTS

Thanks are due to a number of people for their timely feedback and assistance with verifying and updating material for this edition. From the Appalachian Mountain Club, thanks to Dan Eisner, my editor at AMC Books, for editorial feedback and suggestions for shaping this revised edition, as well as cartographer Larry Garland, publisher Heather Stephenson, production manager Athena Lakri, and the rest of the staff of AMC Books. A multitude of thanks are also due to Charles W.G. Smith, who compiled and edited the eighth edition of the *Massachusetts Trail Guide*, as well as the committee members who worked on the prior editions of the guide.

Don Hoffses of the AMC staff deserves thanks for coordinating the Midstate Trail update. For the Metacomet–Monadnock Trail revision, I received assistance from Mike Gildsesgame of the AMC staff and Berkshire Chapter members Chris Ryan and Pat Fletcher. The following people and organizations provided information about specific places and trails: Tad Ames, Marie Auger, Elwin Bacon, Susan Baeslack, Becky Barnes, Beth Bazler, Rick Blanchette, Ken Brown, Maggi Brown, John Burk, Lale Burk, Nicholas Burk, Jim Caffery, Cosmo Catalano of the AMC Berkshire Chapter, Joe Choinere, Gerry Coffey, Tammis Coffin, Nina Coleman, Cara Criscione, David Dargie, Becky DaSilva, Kristin DeBoer, Brian DeGasperis, Robert Dwyer, Chris Eaton, Dwayne Ericson, Frank Fink, Ellen Fisher, Wendy Fox, Alan French, Jim Goyea, Julian Hadley, Sue Haley, Jennifer Kern, George Kingston, Walker Korby, Luke Labenes, René Laubach, Amanda Lewis, the Massachusetts Audubon Society, the Massachusetts Department of Conservation and Recreation, Brenda McComb, the Midstate Trail Committee, John O'Keefe, Leslie Reed-Evans, Matt Robinson, Beth Rosenblum, Susan Russo, Russ Schott, Suzanne Silveira, Dave Small, Cynthia Sommer, Liz Tentarelli, The Trustees of Reservations, Kate Tonino, Ron Wolanin, and Leigh Youngblood. Thanks also to the Petersham, Athol, and Woods (Barre) Public Libraries, Harvard Forest, and the Mount Grace Land Conservation Trust for a variety of useful resources.

TO THE READER OF THIS BOOK

This book is designed to fulfill the needs of all hikers, from beginners to backcountry experts. To help you prepare, the introduction contains information essential for a safe, responsible hiking experience. First, read and review the section on Safety and Trip Planning. Hikers can learn more about the diverse natural features, flora, and fauna of Massachusetts in the Natural History section. This chapter is also valuable for hikers who have explored one region thoroughly and are interested in finding new areas to visit. Of course all the beauty that you'll encounter on the trail is a resource that every hiker is responsible for maintaining. We go into the wild seeking adventure, but conscious of the fact that we are always stewards of the creation around us. The Stewardship and Conservation section outlines ways to minimize impact on the landscape we all enjoy. After all this careful reading and planning, simply look through the descriptions of each region's parks, forests, preserves, and sanctuaries to locate the perfect destination for your next outdoor adventure.

This guide divides the state into six regions, organized west to east from the Berkshires to Cape Cod and the islands. Each part begins with comprehensive descriptions of that region's long-distance trails. Following are entries that describe trails and trail systems in area parks, forests, and other protected spaces. In general, major trails are described before major paths in the trail system or network.

Massachusetts has a rich tradition in land conservation and as a result contains an extensive number of trails, far more than the size of the state might imply. A description of every one of these trails is beyond the scope of this book. What this guide does provide is a broad selection of the state's best paths and trails. Because of space limitations, some trails that appear on the maps included with this guide do not appear in the text. For information on additional hiking opportunities, many agencies (including The Trustees of Reservations, Massachusetts Audubon Society, and Massachusetts Department of Conservation and Recreation) have literature, maps, and websites that are excellent supplements to this guide. Many parks, forests, and preserves also have booklets or other information on short trails designed as interpretive nature walks. Contact information for these agencies can be found in the appendix at the back of the book.

TRAIL DESCRIPTIONS

Each trail description provides an overview of the route, concise directions for following the trail, and mileage points along the way; many include information on the surrounding natural history. Driving directions to the trailhead are included, usually with the destination introduction. An exclamation point (⚠) in the margin indicates a potentially dangerous area on the trail. Following most trail descriptions, distances and estimated times to key landmarks are listed. Mileage information was obtained from a variety of sources, including ground measurement, computer topographic map programs, and posted trail signs. Hiking times are estimates for an average hiker traveling under normal weather conditions. Your hiking speed may be faster or slower. After you have done a few hikes and compared your hiking times to those listed in the book, you will get a sense for the necessary correction factor for your physical condition. Carrying a heavy pack or traveling in a large group adds time. Remember that going up slows you down, but going down can often slow you down even more, especially in unfavorable conditions.

DISTANCES, TIMES, ELEVATIONS, AND ELEVATION GAINS

The distances and times in the tables at the end of trail descriptions are cumulative from the starting point at the beginning of each table. Elevation gains are included for trails on the maps included with this book. Elevation gains are given for the reverse direction only when they are significant, and they are not cumulative—they apply only to the interval between the current entry and the next one. The following example shows users how to read tables that are at the end of trail descriptions.

Ashley Hill Trail (map 2: D2–E2)

Distances from Mt. Washington State Forest parking area (East St.) (1,660 ft. **[elevation]**) to
  · loop trail (1,850 ft. **[elevation]**): 2.5 mi. **[distance]**, 190 ft. **[elevation gain]** (rev. 150 ft. **[reverse elevation gain]**) , 1 hr. 30 min. **[time]**

Elevation gains are estimated and rounded to the nearest 50 ft.; some elevation gains can be determined almost to the foot, but others, such as where several minor ups and downs are traversed, are only roughly accurate. Elevations are estimated as closely as possible when not given precisely by our source maps. This data was gathered from AMC's maps and Google Earth. Elevation data has been included for other trails throughout the guide where reliable information could be obtained from Google Earth and park maps from The Trustees of Reservations and the Department of Conservation and Recreation.

There is no reliable method for predicting how much time a particular hiker or group of hikers will actually take to complete a particular hike on a particular day. However, to give experienced hikers a rough basis for planning, times have been estimated based on factors including the length of the trail, the elevation gain, and the difficulty of the terrain.

SUGGESTED HIKES

At the end of each section of this guide you will find a list of suggested hikes designed to inform readers of options for easy, moderate, and strenuous hikes within a region. While there are no strict criteria for these classifications, a short (easy) hike generally can be completed in about an hour or less, a moderate hike in one to three hours, and a strenuous hike in three to eight hours. The numbers in brackets indicate distance and estimated time; "ow," "rt," and "lp" mean "one way," "round trip," and "loop," respectively. Remember that the time allowances are merely a rough estimate—many parties will require more time, and many will require less—and they do not include time for extensive stops for scenery appreciation, eating, or rest.

MAPS

The 9th edition of the *Massachusetts Trail Guide* includes six computer-designed topographic maps, created using a variety of digital data to ensure the highest degree of accuracy. They provide coverage of the state's most popular hiking regions, and clearly indicate trails, campgrounds, backcountry shelters and tent sites, parking areas, visitor centers, and other available facilities. Land ownership and general use guidelines are indicated as well, but it is the responsibility of the individual to be aware of current land-use restrictions for both public and private lands. The maps are sufficient for navigation in all of the featured regions.

The regions covered are: the Northern Berkshires, including Mt. Greylock (Map 1); Southwestern Massachusetts and its large complex of interconnected parklands (Map 2); Wachusett Mtn. State Reservation in central Massachusetts (Map 3); Blue Hills Reservation just south of Boston (Map 4); and Mt. Tom State Reservation (Map 5) and the Mt. Holyoke Range (Map 6), both located in the Connecticut River Valley.

Due to the broad distribution of hiking opportunities in Massachusetts, not every trail described in this book appears on these maps. For areas not covered, the U.S. Geological Survey produces a series of detailed topographic maps. Most areas in Massachusetts are now covered by the recent, more detailed 7.5-min. quads, which have largely replaced the old 15-min. quads. While topography on the newer maps is excellent, some are inaccurate in showing the location of trails. These maps, as well as index maps showing the available quads in every state and a pamphlet on how to use them, can be obtained at a number of local outlets and from USGS Map Sales, Federal Center, Box 25286, Denver, CO 80255 (800-USA-MAPS, www.usgs.gov). USGS maps are now also available on compact disc from a number of sources, including TOPO USA and Maptech.

Many state parks and forests also provide useful trail maps; they may be more accurate than the USGS quad for the area. They are usually available at park entrance stations and visitor centers, or can be downloaded from the Department of Conservation and Recreation website (www.state.ma.us/dem/forparks.htm). Lastly, many of the organizations listed in the back of the book produce maps for their respective areas; contact information is provided.

CAMPING

Overnight trips are as much a part of hiking in Massachusetts as day hikes. Some locations offer backcountry camping, but most overnight opportunities involve staying at one of the dozens of designated campgrounds found across the state. Some drive-in campgrounds require reservations, while space in others is on a first-come, first-served basis. Massachusetts state parks and forests provide the most campgrounds, but nearly every land-management agency offers at least one campground somewhere in the state. For in-depth information on camping opportunities, use the appendix to locate contact information for the appropriate management agency. Their websites are usually loaded with updated information for all types of camping, from extremely rustic to drive-it-up-and-plug-it-in RV camping sites.

Backcountry camping is mostly limited to the Berkshires region in the western part of the state. Overnight shelters and camping areas are established along the length of the Appalachian Trail, and several other parks provide excellent backpacking opportunities. Parks and forests that offer backcountry camping include Mt. Washington State Forest, Mt. Everett State Reservation, October Mtn. State Forest, Mt. Greylock State Reservation, Monroe State Forest, and Dubuque Memorial State Forest.

OTHER RECREATIONAL OPPORTUNITIES

The trails in this guide are first and foremost hiking trails, yet many of them are also open to other recreational opportunities such as cross-country skiing, mountain biking, and horseback riding. What types of recreation a trail is open for often changes, and these changes may occur frequently. When in doubt about the legal uses of a trail, check with the managing agency either via the Internet, by phone, or by visiting the property headquarters. Some trails provide excellent opportunities for mountain biking, yet hiking and mountain biking are different enough to demand the tolerance and patience of both bikers and hikers. Mountain bikers must observe trail-use restrictions. Where biking is permitted, riders should yield to hikers on the trail, and suspend biking during wet weather in areas where trail erosion is a problem.

Lately much debate has centered on the use of all-terrain vehicles (ATVs) and dirt bikes on forest trails. At present the solution has been to open selected areas of some state forests to motorized recreation. This limits erosion and other damage to the environment but also concentrates the machines in a smaller area, and thus increases the environmental damage in those areas. Trails that have been designated as ATV and dirt bike trails are largely not compatible with a pleasant hiking experience. In some areas, hikers are specifically requested not to use these multiuse trails at all. As a result, trails that are open to motorized recreational use are not described in this guide.

ACRONYMS

The following acronyms are used for the major conservation and trail maintenance organizations in this region.

AMC	Appalachian Mountain Club	**LHA**	Laurel Hill Association
ATC	Appalachian Trail Conference	**MAS**	Massachusetts Audubon Society
AVIS	Andover Village Improvement Society	**NETC**	New England Trail Conference
		PAOC	Phillips Academy Outing Club
BCAMC	Berkshire Chapter, Appalachian Mountain Club	**THC**	Taconic Hiking Club (Troy, N.Y.)
		TTOR	The Trustees of Reservations
BNRC	Berkshire Natural Resources Council	**WCAMC**	Worcester Chapter, Appalachian Mountain Club
DCR	Massachusetts Department of Conservation and Recreation	**WOC**	Williams Outing Club
FOW	Friends of the Wapack	**WRLF**	Williamstown Rural Lands Foundation
HVA	Housatonic Valley Association		

ABBREVIATIONS

ft.	foot, feet	**rd.**	road
lp	loop	**rev.**	reverse elevation
mi.	mile(s)	**rt**	round trip
min.	minute(s)		
Mt.	Mount		
mtn.	mountain		
ow	one way		

LONG-DISTANCE TRAILS

This book provides comprehensive coverage of the ten major long-distance trail systems found in Massachusetts. Most travel through several of the state's ecoregions.

Appalachian Trail

Perhaps the nation's most famous footpath, the AT travels more than 2,100 mi. from Springer Mtn. in Georgia to Katahdin in Maine; 85 mi. of the trail are located in Massachusetts, running north–south through the Berkshires. The AT crosses many of the state's highest summits, including Mt. Everett and Mt. Greylock, the highest point in Massachusetts.

South Taconic Trail

The 16-mi. South Taconic Trail and a network of connecting trails provide access to the southern end of the Taconic Range in the southwest corner of Massachusetts. These trails extend into New York and Connecticut.

Taconic Crest Trail

The northern end of the Taconic Range, straddling the Massachusetts–New York border, has a network of more than 100 mi. of hiking trails, including the 29-mi. Taconic Crest Trail.

Metacomet–Monadnock Trail

This 114-mi. trail follows the ridges bordering the Connecticut River Valley, including the exceptionally scenic ranges of Mt. Holyoke and Mt. Tom. It begins on the Connecticut state line, where it connects with the Metacomet Trail, and ends on the summit of Mt. Monadnock in southern New Hampshire, where it connects with the Monadnock–Sunapee Greenway Trail.

Midstate Trail

The 92-mi. Midstate Trail runs north–south across Massachusetts through the woodlands, open fields, and isolated hills of Worcester County. It traverses Wachusett Mtn., the highest peak in eastern Massachusetts. At its northern terminus near Mt. Watatic in Ashburnham, it connects with the Wapack Trail, which traverses the Wapack Range in southern New Hampshire.

Robert Frost Trail

A scenic trail stretching over 40 mi. of countryside from Mt. Holyoke Range State Park in Granby to Wendell State Forest in Wendell, the path coincides with the Metacomet–Monadnock Trail over some portions of its route.

Pocumtuck Ridge Trail

One of the newest additions to the Massachusetts trail system, the Pocumtuck Ridge Trail follows the Connecticut River Valley from Mt. Sugarloaf Reservation to the Poet's Seat Tower, a distance of about 15 mi.

Warner Trail

The 30-mi. Warner Trail stretches from Canton, Mass., just south of Boston, through the woodlands of Norfolk County to Diamond Hill State Park in Rhode Island.

Tully Trail

This 18-mi. loop trail in north-central Massachusetts was completed in 2001 and is maintained by The Trustees of Reservations. It connects three Trustees properties—Doane's Falls, Jacob's Hill, and Royalston Falls—as well as Tully Lake Campground and a portion of the lake's shore. It also travels through both the Tully Mtn. and Fish Brook Wildlife Management Areas, both of which are managed by MassWildlife.

Bay Circuit Trail

Still under construction, the Bay Circuit Trail will eventually extend in a 200-mi. arc around the Boston metropolitan area, from Newbury and Ipswich on the North Shore to Duxbury and Kingston on the South Shore. Presently about 150 mi. of trail are open. It is possible (with appropriate detours) for hikers to traverse the entire 200-mi. route.

TRIP PLANNING AND SAFETY

Hiking is a sport of self-reliance. A hiker relies on physical ability, unaided by motorized or non-motorized technology, to reach the goal and return. This aspect of the sport often provides as much satisfaction as the beautiful views or visions of wildlife encountered along the way. As with any worthwhile skill, learning self-reliant hiking takes time and experience. Part of that process is proper preparation.

Plan your trip schedule with safety in mind. Consider the strength of your party and the general strenuousness of the trip: the overall distance, the amount of climbing, and the roughness of the terrain. Knowing the latest weather information is essential to safe hiking. Get a weather report, but be aware that most forecasts are not intended to apply to higher elevations; a day that is sunny and pleasant in the lowlands may well be inclement higher up. Keeping in mind the vagaries of New England weather ("if you don't like the weather, wait a minute"), prepare for the worst possible conditions. During your hike, constantly reassess the weather forecast by observing clouds and wind, and be prepared to change the itinerary as necessary.

Plan to start your hike as early in the day as possible. Know what time sunset will be, and start early enough to allow for a return while there is still plenty of daylight. Remember that dusk and darkness come quickly in the woods, and seem to descend even faster in winter. Hiking after dark, even with flashlights or headlamps (which may fail), makes finding trails more difficult and crossing streams hazardous. For longer hikes in more remote areas, it is also important to let someone know your route and when you expect to be back.

With appropriate clothing you can hike all the trails in this book safely and comfortably during spring, summer, and fall. For spring hikes be alert for lingering patches of ice and to the possibility of difficult brook crossings due to runoff from melting snow. In fall the trail may be covered with fallen leaves that can be slippery or hide rocks, roots, or other impediments that can trip you up. Winter hiking, with the additional hazards of snow and extreme cold, requires special skills and preparation (see Winter Concerns, later in this section). Under such conditions novice hikers should always hike with more experienced trekkers.

Backcountry Hazards

Safe hiking means knowing how to avoid dangerous situations as well as being prepared to deal with problems if they do occur. The following section outlines the common hazards encountered in the Massachusetts outdoors and discusses how to approach them.

Falls and Injuries

The remoteness of the backcountry makes any injury a potentially serious matter. Be alert to places where the footing might be poor, especially on steep or wet sections of trail. In autumn wet leaves are a particular hazard. Remember that carrying a heavy pack can affect your balance. Rock climbing should be attempted only in areas where it is permitted and only with proper training and equipment.

In case of serious injury, apply first aid and keep the injured hiker warm and comfortable. Then take a minute to assess the situation before going for help. Backcountry evacuation is usually measured in hours, not minutes, so don't rush. Write down your location, the condition of the injured person, and any other pertinent facts. At least one person should stay with the injured hiker while two others go for help. (For this reason it is safest to hike in the backcountry in groups of four or more.)

Hypothermia

Hypothermia is the loss of ability to preserve body heat because of injury, exhaustion, lack of sufficient food, or inadequate or wet clothing. The result is a dangerous lowering of the body's core temperature. Our bodies lose heat all the time, but we don't suffer hypothermia because the loss of heat is buffered by insulation. Most often this comes in the form of clothing made of fabrics that help retain body heat. Many fabrics are good insulators when dry, but when some get wet the insulating ability drops so drastically that they become very efficient at cooling the body just when you need warmth. In hiking circles the phrase *Cotton kills* is as accurate as it is serious. Most cases of hypothermia occur in temperatures above freezing (between 32 and 50 degrees F) on windy, rainy days. Some fabrics, such as wool, polypropylene, and polyester fleece, retain much of their insulating ability even when wet. Others, most notably cotton, do not. Even in dry weather, cotton clothing can become quickly saturated with perspiration, which at the least is uncomfortable and at the worst can lead to hypothermia in cooler conditions.

Symptoms of hypothermia include uncontrolled shivering, impaired speech and movement, lowered body temperature, and drowsiness. The ultimate result is death, unless the victim (who may not understand the situation, due to impaired mental function) is warmed up. In mild cases, the victim should be given dry clothing and placed in a sleeping bag if available (perhaps with someone else in it to provide body heat), then provided quick-energy food and something warm (not hot) to drink. In severe cases, only prompt hospitalization offers reasonable hope for recovery. It is not unusual for a victim to resist treatment and even combat rescuers. Therefore prevention of hypothermia is the only truly practical course. Uncontrollable shivering should be regarded as a sure sign of hypothermia; this shivering will eventually cease on its own, but that is merely the sign that the body has given up the struggle and is sinking toward death.

For those interested in more information, a thorough treatment of the subject is contained in *Hypothermia Frostbite And Other Cold Injuries: Prevention, Recognition, Rescue, and Treatment* by Gordon G. Giesbrecht, Ph.D and James. A. Wilkderson, M.D. (2006, Mountaineers Books).

Heatstroke

The opposite of hypothermia, heatstroke occurs when the body is unable to control its internal temperature and overheats. Usually brought on by excessive exposure to the sun and accompanying dehydration, symptoms include cramping, headache, and mental confusion. In Massachusetts the hot, humid days of summer pose the greatest risk of heatstroke, because the high humidity reduces the amount of sweat that can evaporate from the skin. This consequently limits the body's ability to cool itself through evaporative heat loss and can lead to a dangerous rise in core body temperature. Treatment entails rapid, aggressive cooling of the body through whatever means are available—cooling the head and torso is the most important—and drinking lots of fluids.

Stay hydrated and have some type of sun protection for your head if you expect to travel a hot section of trail that lacks shade.

Lightning

Lightning can be a serious hazard in open areas, particularly on any bare ridge or summit. The best course of action is to avoid dangerous exposed places when thunderstorms are likely, and to seek shelter in thick woods as quickly as possible if an unexpected "thumper" is detected. Most thunderstorms occur when a cold front passes, or on very warm days; those produced by cold fronts are typically more sudden and violent. Weather forecasts that mention cold fronts or predict temperatures much above 80 degrees in the lowlands and valleys should arouse concern.

Brook Crossings

Rivers and brooks are often crossed without bridges, and it is usually possible to jump from rock to rock; a hiking staff or stick is a great aid to balance. Use caution; several fatalities have resulted from hikers (particularly solo hikers) falling on slippery rocks and suffering an injury that rendered them unconscious, causing them to drown in relatively shallow streams. If you're wearing a pack with a waist belt, unbuckle the strap so you can get out of it easily if you do fall. If you need to wade across (often the safer course), wearing boots, but not necessarily socks, is recommended. Note that many crossings that may be only a nuisance in summer may become a serious obstacle in cold weather when feet and boots must be kept dry. Higher waters, which can turn innocuous brooks into torrents that almost certainly cannot be crossed, come in spring as snow melts, or after heavy rainstorms, particularly in fall when trees drop their leaves and take up less water.

Avoid trails with potentially dangerous stream crossings during these high-water periods. If you are cut off from roads by swollen streams, it is better to make a long detour, even if you need to wait and spend a night in the woods. Rushing current can make wading extremely hazardous, and several deaths have resulted. Floodwaters may subside within a few hours, especially in small brooks. It is particularly important not to camp on the far side of a brook from your exit point if the crossing is difficult and heavy rain is predicted.

Wildlife

Black bears have made a strong comeback after having been nearly eradicated from Massachusetts by the mid-nineteenth century. In recent decades the state's black bear population has been increasing at a rate of nearly 8 percent per year, and today an estimated 2,000 bears roam the state's forests. They can be found nearly everywhere west of the Connecticut River (approximately one bear per square mile of forest), but are less common in central Massachusetts and rare in the eastern part of the state. Black bears live mostly on nuts, berries, other plants, and dead animals, and rarely kill anything larger than a mouse. They almost never attack humans and will usually flee at the first sight of an approaching hiker. Nevertheless, the black bear is a large and unpredictable animal that must be treated with respect. Several serious incidents have been unnecessarily provoked by deliberate feeding of bears or by harassment by a dog.

The philosophy of dealing with bears has undergone some modification in recent years. Formerly the usual advice was that, if approached by a bear, you should throw down your pack and back away slowly. This advice works, but unfortunately it teaches the bear that people have food and that very little effort or risk is required to make them part with it. The result is a bear that is likely to be more aggressive toward the next visitor, which may result in injury to the human (who may be you) and frequently results in a death sentence for the bear. Many hikers regard bears as an indispensable feature of wild country in New England, and preservation of the bears requires us to make sure that they remain wild, so feeding them either deliberately or through carelessness should be regarded as having potentially fatal consequences for the animal.

Thus the current advice is that a hiker confronted by a bear should attempt to appear neither threatening nor frightened, and should back off slowly but not abandon food unless the bear appears irresistibly aggressive. A loud noise, such as one made by a whistle or by banging metal pots, is often useful. Careful protection of food at campsites is mandatory; it must never be kept overnight in a tent, but should be hung between trees as high as possible (10 to 12 ft. off the ground is optimal) in a bear-proof container; if you don't have one plastic is recommended to mask.

The state's moose population also has been on the increase in recent years, and today numbers between 500 and 1,000 animals. This has added a significant new hazard for hikers driving to the trailhead. Indeed, the state's first-ever moose–car fatality occurred in the summer of 2003, when a driver was killed in a collision on the Mass Pike. Motorists need to be aware of the seriousness of the problem, particularly at night when these huge, dark-colored animals are both active and very difficult to see. Instinct often causes them to face an auto rather than run from it, and they are also apt to cross the road unpredictably as a car approaches. It is thus safest to assume that moose will behave in the most inconvenient manner possible. Moose will generally flee from humans, but hikers should use extreme caution when encountering a mother moose with her young or a bull during the fall mating season. Both bears and moose are most active in the hours around dawn and dusk; pay particular attention when driving during this time.

Two poisonous types of snake exist in Massachusetts—the timber rattlesnake and northern copperhead—but they are extremely rare and infrequently encountered by hikers. Although once widespread across the region, both snakes today are found only in isolated locations, including rocky hillsides in the southern Berkshires, Hampden County, and the Blue Hills. If threatened, the two species can deliver painful, but nonfatal, bites. If bitten, try to remain calm, and remove any constricting items (rings, watches, etc.) from the soon-to-be-swollen extremity. Do not apply ice to the bite; this can cause further damage to the surrounding tissue. Seek medical attention as quickly as possible.

Mosquitoes, blackflies, and deer flies are the woodland residents most frequently encountered by hikers. Mosquitoes are worst throughout the summer in low, wet areas, and blackflies are most bloodthirsty in June and early July; at times these winged pests can make life in the woods virtually unbearable. Head nets can be useful for maintaining sanity at these times. The most effective repellents are based on the active ingredient diethyl-meta-toluamide, generally known as DEET, but there are concerns about its safety. Hikers should probably apply repellents with DEET to clothing rather than skin where possible, and avoid using them on small children. There are other effective, skin-friendly repellents available as well. There is also a good deal of folklore and tradition on the subject: people who seek true solitude in the woods often employ the traditional creosote-scented recipes, reasoning that anything that repels fellow humans might have the same effect on insects.

Ticks, which are common in woods and grassy or brushy areas at lower elevations, present a potentially serious hazard if not detected. Countermeasures include using insect repellent, wearing light-colored long pants tucked into socks, and making frequent visual checks of clothing and skin. Ticks wander for several hours before settling on a spot to bite, so they can be removed easily if found promptly. If you find a tick attached to you, do not try to pull it out with your fingers or pinch the body; this can inject tick juices under your skin and increase the risk of infection. Using an appropriate tool, such as tweezers or a small V-cut in the side of a credit card, gently pull the tick out by lifting upward from the base of the body where it is attached to the skin. Pull straight out until the tick releases; do not twist or jerk, which may break the mouthparts off under your skin.

Lyme disease is present throughout Massachusetts, but only one species of tick is capable of transmitting it—the diminutive black-legged tick (also known as the deer tick). Caused by a spirochete, this potentially life-threatening disease can be hard to diagnose in its early phases. Common early symptoms include fatigue, chills and fever, headache, muscle and joint pain, swollen lymph nodes, and a blotchy skin rash around the bite site that clears centrally to produce a characteristic ring shape 3 to 30 days after exposure. If you fear that you have been exposed to Lyme disease, consult a doctor immediately; it can be easily treated in its early stages. When the tick is extracted, make sure to save as much of it as possible, as it may serve as an important part of the diagnosis.

Poison Ivy

If you learn only one plant in Massachusetts, it had better be this one. Easily recognized by its characteristic clusters of three shiny leaves, poison ivy can appear either as a low-lying shrub or a climbing vine. It can be seen winding up trees in open woodlands, or growing close to the ground along fencerows, in thickets, and in disturbed areas. Yellowish white clusters of flowers appear in late spring and early summer, and the leaves turn red in fall. When not eaten by birds, the plant's small white fruit can remain through winter. Both the leaves and stems contain an oil that causes a strong allergic reaction in most people, creating a maddening and long-lived rash that can spread across the body. Wash thoroughly after any exposure. Avoidance is of course the best form of prevention: "Leaves of three: let them be."

Hunting Season

Hunting is permitted in season in all state wildlife management areas, as well as in most state parks and forests. Most hunters stay fairly close to roads, and, in general, the harder it would be to haul an animal out of a given area, the lower the probability that a hiker will encounter hunters there. During hunting season avoid wearing brown or anything that might give a hunter the impression of the white flash of a white-tailed deer running away. Wearing blaze-orange clothing is recommended.

Various hunting seasons occur from September through the winter months. In Massachusetts the primary deer-hunting season (with guns) does not occur until late November or early December, but archery hunting is permitted beginning in mid-October. Bear hunting is permitted in the eastern regions of the state for a few weeks in September and then again in November. The main hunting season for birds (pheasant, quail, and grouse) runs from mid-October through November. Hunting is prohibited on Sunday and at night from half an hour after sunset until half an hour before sunrise. Exact dates and regulations vary from year to year. Contact the Massachusetts Department of Fish and Game for current information (617-626-1590; www.state.ma.us/dfwele).

Winter Concerns

Snowshoeing and cross-country skiing have steadily become more popular in the last decade. Increasing numbers of hikers have discovered the beauty of the woods in winter, and advances in clothing and equipment have made it possible for experienced winter travelers to enjoy greater comfort and safety. The greatest danger is that it begins to look too easy and too safe, while snow, ice, and weather conditions are constantly changing, and a relatively trivial error of judgment may have grave, even fatal, consequences. Conditions can vary greatly from day to day, and from trail to trail; therefore, much more experience is required to foresee and avoid dangerous situations in winter than in summer. Days are very short, particularly in early winter when darkness falls shortly after 4 p.m. Trails are frequently difficult or impossible to follow, and navigation skills are hard to learn in adverse weather conditions (as anyone who has tried to read a map in a blizzard can attest). "Breaking trail" on snowshoes through new snow can be strenuous and exhausting work. The most dangerous aspect of winter in New England, however, is the extreme variability of the weather: It is not unusual for a cold, penetrating, wind-driven rain to be followed within a few hours by a cold front that brings subfreezing temperatures and strong winds.

Winter on most Massachusetts trails may require only snowshoes or skis and some warm clothing. Even so, summer hiking boots are usually inadequate, flashlight batteries fail quickly (a headlamp with battery pack works better), and water in canteens freezes unless carried in an insulated container or wrapped in a sock or sweater. The winter hiker needs good physical conditioning from regular exercise, and must dress carefully in order to avoid overheating and excessive perspiration, which soaks clothing and soon leads to chilling. Cotton clothes are not useful because they cannot be kept perfectly dry; only wool and synthetics retain insulating value when wet. Fluid intake must increase, because dehydration can be a serious problem in the dry winter air.

No book can begin to impart all the knowledge necessary to cope safely with the potential for such brutal conditions, but helpful information can be found in *AMC Guide to Winter Hiking and Camping* by Yemaya Maurer and Lucas St. Clair (2008, AMC Books). Hikers who are interested in extending their activities into the winter season are strongly advised to seek out organized parties with leaders who have extensive winter experience. The AMC and several of its chapters sponsor numerous workshops on winter hiking and camping, in addition to introductory winter hikes. Information on such activities can be obtained from the AMC at 5 Joy St., Boston, MA 02108 (617-523-0655; www.outdoors.org).

Drinking Water

The pleasure of quaffing a cup of water fresh from a pure mountain spring is one of the traditional attractions of the outdoors. Unfortunately the presence of cysts of the intestinal parasite *Giardia lamblia* in water sources throughout the region is probably pervasive. It is impossible to be completely sure whether a given source is safe, no matter how clear the water or remote the location. The symptoms of giardiasis are severe intestinal distress and diarrhea, but such discomforts can have many other causes, making the disease difficult to diagnose accurately. The safest course for day hikers is to carry their own water, allowing 2 quarts per person for a full-day hike, more in hot weather. If it is necessary to use sources in the woods, the water must be treated. The traditional methods of boiling or treating water with iodine are effective but somewhat inconvenient. A popular choice today is one of the newer, lightweight filtering units, which produce tasty, safe drinking water. Although somewhat expensive, these filters are durable and easy to use.

Dogs

Dogs are permitted on many of the trails described in this book, but regulations vary widely by region and managing agency. Dogs are permitted in Massachusetts state parks and forests but must be leashed at all times; they are prohibited at Walden Pond State Reservation and Boston Harbor Islands State Park. In state wildlife management areas dogs may run unleashed but must be under voice control at all times. In order to protect wildlife, dogs are prohibited in all national wildlife refuges and Massachusetts Audubon Society locations. For other areas, call beforehand to check regulations.

When hiking with your dog, please respect other visitors. Barking dogs disrupt the peacefulness of the forest and detract from the wilderness experience—keep your pet quiet or leave it at home. Clean up after your dog and do not leave unpleasant surprises on the trail for the next hiker. Carry out your dog's waste in a plastic bag or bury it as you would your own (refer to the Leave No Trace summary on page 45). When another hiker approaches, keep your dog close and do not let it go bounding toward the other person; some people may misinterpret the dog's behavior as aggressive, while others may be uncomfortable with dogs in general (no matter how friendly). And always, both for its safety (animals such as porcupines and skunks are ever-present) and for the comfort and safety of others, keep your dog under control at all times.

Private Property
Some trails described in this book cross private property and exist only with the consent of the landowners. Hikers must respect the rights of these owners and observe all the customary rules of courtesy if the privilege of trail walking on private property is to continue. In particular, respect No Trespassing signs, do not bend or break fences, and leave gates open or closed as you found them. Never camp on private land without permission.

What to Carry
Adequate equipment for a hike varies greatly according to the length of the trip and the difficulty of getting to the nearest trailhead if trouble arises. If you are only strolling to a pond or waterfall a mile or so from the road in good weather, then perhaps a light jacket, a candy bar, and a bottle of water will suffice. If, however, you are going on an extended hike, you will need a good pack filled with plenty of warm clothing, food for emergency use, and other equipment. No determination of what should be taken along can be made without considering the length of a trip and the hazards of the terrain it will cross.

Good things to have in your pack for a day hike include guidebook, maps, water bottle (ordinary plastic soft-drink bottles, with or without original contents, work well), compass, pocketknife, rain gear, windbreaker, a warm synthetic or wool pullover, wool hat and mittens, waterproof matches, enough food for your usual needs plus high-energy foods (such as dried fruit or candy) in reserve, first-aid supplies (including personal medicines; a nonprescription painkiller such as aspirin, acetaminophen, or ibuprofen; adhesive bandages; gauze; and antiseptic), lightweight plastic tarp, whistle, sunscreen, sunglasses, insect repellent, needle and thread, safety pins, nylon cord, trash bag, toilet paper, a flashlight or headlamp with extra batteries and a spare bulb, and a mobile phone for emergency use. For groups hiking on longer day trips in remote areas, one sleeping bag can provide an additional element of safety, as it can be used to keep an injured hiker warm while awaiting assistance.

For all but the shortest hikes, hiking boots are much preferred over sneakers or walking shoes, because they provide better traction and ankle support and help reduce foot fatigue. Both leather and synthetic boots are available. Leather boots must be properly broken in before being worn on an extended hike. For younger children, hiking boots are not always practical for financial reasons. If it is necessary for children to hike in sneakers, choose shorter trails with smoother footing.

Blue jeans, sweatshirts, and other cotton clothes are popular but, once wet, dry very slowly and may be uncomfortable; in adverse weather conditions they often seriously drain a cold and tired hiker's heat reserves. While such clothes are worn by many hikers on summer trips, people who are planning to travel to remote places or on exposed summits should seriously consider wearing (or at least carrying) wool or synthetics (such as fleece) instead. These fabrics keep much of their insulation value even when wet, and are indispensable for hikers who want to visit places from which return to civilization might require substantial time and effort if conditions turn bad. Not only do hats, mittens, and other such gear provide safety in adverse conditions, but they also allow you to enjoy the summits in comfort on those occasional crisp, clear days when the views are particularly fine, when the other hikers who snickered at your bulging pack are driven from the magnificent vistas with terse greetings forced through chattering teeth.

Following Trails

Getting lost is probably the novice hiker's single greatest fear. Basic navigational skills are not difficult to learn, and with them even the beginning hiker should have the confidence to complete a hike successfully. But to be a true expert requires not only learned skills but also a "woods sense" that can be acquired only through experience.

Most of the time a trail can be followed simply by alert observation. Look for worn footing or footprints, evidence of trail maintenance (such as water bars or sawn logs), or gaps in the undergrowth. But keep in mind that many of the trails described in this book are not heavily traveled or regularly maintained, so the pathway may not always be obvious. At unmarked junctions it helps to know the general direction in which the trail should be heading.

Blazes, typically geometric shapes painted on trees, are used to mark some trails. In some cases the blaze might be a metal cutout attached to a tree or a mark painted on the rocks underfoot. If you have been following a well-blazed trail and the blazes suddenly stop or change color, you might have taken a wrong turn. Stop walking and look all around. If you cannot see a blaze, mark the spot with something obvious that you'll easily recognize—a rock or a stick stuck in the ground. Now retrace your steps to the last blaze you saw and look around again. Trails are usually marked so that three blazes can be seen at all times: the immediate blaze, one up the trail, and one down the trail. Not every path conforms to this pattern, but most do. Pay particular attention to a double blaze mark, which indicates a change in trail direction. Trail descriptions in a guidebook are an important source of information, but they are not perfect. Trails may be rerouted, abandoned, or closed by landowners; signs may be stolen or fall from their posts; bridges can get washed away; beavers may flood trails near wetlands, and storms may cause blowdowns or landslides, which can obliterate a trail for an entire hiking season or longer. Trail guides are an aid to planning, not a substitute for careful observation and good judgment.

Maps are another important navigational tool, but as with trail guide descriptions, they cannot be relied upon exclusively. They are especially useful in trip planning and in visualizing the overall lay of the land. Be prepared to find discrepancies between a trail's plotted location and its actual location. This book includes trail maps for some of the major hiking areas in the region. A compass, and knowledge of how to use it, are important complements to trail maps. The best compass for hiking is the protractor type: a circular, liquid-filled compass that turns on a rectangular, clear plastic base. Excellent compasses of this type, with leaflets that give ample instructions for their use, are available for about $10. Novice hikers in the woods sometimes forget which end is the north end of the compass needle. It is therefore helpful to scratch a reminder somewhere on the case. If in doubt remember that the sun in Massachusetts runs from east to west along the southern portion of the sky, so if your compass needle is pointing at the sun it is the south end of the needle you're looking at, not the north. Compass directions in the text and on the maps give true north rather than magnetic north. On most hikes in Massachusetts the difference, or declination, in these two values isn't enough to make a difference in your hike. In Massachusetts the compass will point about 13 degrees west of true north.

One common source of confusion in trail navigation arises from crossings of other trails and streams. Because most of this region was settled at one time, many old paths and woods roads cross current hiking trails. There are also many old logging roads, and new ones can appear at any time. Many of these are not documented in trail descriptions or on maps. Conversely, intersecting paths that are mentioned may become so overgrown as to be missed entirely. A brook crossing might be deemed too small to be mentioned in the trail guide. At the same time, a documented watercourse might happen to be dry and therefore go unnoticed by the hiker.

The careful hiker will use all sources of information—visual observation, guidebook descriptions, and maps—to chart progress. Try at all times to have at least a general sense of your location, which can be confirmed or corrected when reaching major, unmistakable landmarks such as bridges, signed trail junctions, or summits.

If You're Lost

Even the most experienced hiker will occasionally lose a trail. This is not necessarily a serious matter, even in remote areas. First, stop. Go back over your route slowly, marking it clearly, until you pick up a sure indication of the trail. The point of your first mistake will usually be evident then. If, after a careful and deliberate search, you are still unable to find the trail, your course of action will depend on whether you are on a mountain. If so, you can usually reach a road in a few hours or less simply by going downhill until you reach a brook or stream and then following it downward. If you are in comparatively level woodland, you can take a compass bearing and follow it until you reach a road. If you know your general position on the map, your selection of the direction to travel will be easier.

When traveling with a group on a hard-to-follow trail, each hiker should stay within sight of the next person. If the group becomes too spread out, it is almost inevitable that at least one person will take a wrong turn. In no event should slower hikers be allowed to lag behind. If you do become separated from your group, do not wander. Stay in one place and signal your location from time to time by three blasts on a whistle or three loud shouts.

Natural History of Massachusetts

Geology

As you hike across Massachusetts, the diverse landscape that surrounds you is the product of a continuous process that has been molding and forming this area for the last half-billion years. Over that time the region has undergone scores of changes, going from tropical island to ice cap, from mountain range to ocean floor to volcano. Every transformation has built on the previous manifestation until today we walk upon a conglomerate of different histories stratified in rock and glacial drift.

Human history spans only a small fraction of this time. To illustrate, if a book that represented this span of time contained 100,000 pages, the entire account of human history would cover just a single page. But do we need to know about things that happened even before people were here? Does it matter if Massachusetts was the seabed of a tropical ocean hundreds of millions of years ago? It matters because the rocks that formed from the sediment on that seafloor turned into the limestone that is now the bedrock of a river. And that bedrock makes the water of the river more alkaline, and alkaline water allows the soil of the riverbank to release just the right combination of nutrients to support rare plants. And those unusual plants are growing beside the interpretive trail at the wildlife sanctuary. Everything, even something as seemingly remote as a long-extinct ocean, has an effect on the landscape today. Change doesn't stop, and to appreciate the landscape we hike over, neither should our curiosity.

Geology is often defined as the study of rocks. But geological history isn't just about rocks, but about how they got here and what happened to them after they arrived. It is one thing to know that the Taconic Mtns. were once a great range 15,000 ft. high, but another to ask, Where did the mountains go? The current working theory in geology is called plate tectonics. Most of the Earth is molten rock and minerals, with only the top few miles cooled rock. This zone of cool rock is called the earth's crust and is where we live. The crust is cracked into dozens of pieces, called plates, that float on the hot rock layer (called the mantle) beneath. The plates are of two basic varieties, continental and oceanic crust. Continents are typically formed from the less dense continental crust; ocean beds and some islands are made of more dense oceanic rock. The hot rock of the mantle flows in currents, and the currents move the plates above them. As the plates move slowly over geological time, collisions occur between them and cause mountain-building events called orogenies. Elsewhere plates are split apart; this is known as rifting. Evidence of past orogenic and rifting events can be seen in the rocks of New England. The practical geological history of Massachusetts begins at the bottom of a warm tropical ocean 500 million years ago. The only nearby land was a large island with its western shore consisting of what are now the Adirondack Mtns. and Hudson Highlands. Because of plate tectonics this island and seabed weren't anywhere near present-day New England at this time, but rather in the Southern Hemisphere where Brazil now lies. Sediments from the land settled to the bottom of the sea, as did the remains of sea creatures such as trilobites and small aquatic arthropods. Over millions of years this ocean began to shrink, and there occurred the first major event whose remnants are still visible today.

While the shores of what would become North America and Europe drew closer, an island arc of tall volcanoes formed near shore and lifted the seabed around them. As the tectonic plates continued to collide, this arc of islands was joined to the shore and the surrounding land uplifted into a range of mountains perhaps 15,000 ft. high. Today the remains of this range are found in the Taconic Mtns. along the border of New York and Massachusetts. This was not one event, but rather a series of mountain-building episodes that started about 460 million years ago, ended about 440 million years ago, and coincided with appearance of the first land plants.

The upper portions of the mountains were sedimentary rocks (sandstones and shale), while the core of the mountains was composed of metamorphic rocks (schist and gneiss) formed miles below the surface by immense pressures and temperatures.

For the next 40 million years rain and wind wore down the Taconics until Massachusetts was reduced to one great plain. Approximately 400 million years ago another major event began—the Acadian Orogeny. As this event unfolded, another island mass off the coast, called Avalonia, advanced toward and then collided with the continent. The geological remains of Avalonia can be found today from southeastern Connecticut, Rhode Island, and southeastern Massachusetts northward into coastal Maine and Newfoundland. These unusual remains also appear in the Carolinas and parts of England and Wales, but nowhere else in the world. Geologists call Avalonia a "suspect terrane," a term that means its geographic origins prior to collision are unknown.

As the closing continents finally crushed into each other, much of what is now western Massachusetts heaved skyward to create yet another mountain range, this one east of the Taconics. Intense metamorphism occurred, creating high-temperature rocks in the western region and granite intrusions elsewhere. The sea, which until now had still covered portions of the land, drained away as the land rose. The roots of this great range are now the mountains of the Berkshire Plateau. Many of New England's granites were formed as compressed rocks deep beneath the surface melted under the extreme heat and pressure.

Another equally immense erosion of the landscape followed this mountain-building event. A huge fan of eroded sediment, called the Catskill Delta, formed to the west of the mountains. East of the mountains in Massachusetts, other smaller deltas formed. A number of specialized plants thrived in these flat, swampy deltas. From approximately 360 to 290 million years ago swamplands covered much of the region. Immense lycophyte trees, giant horsetails, ferns, and conifers dominated the swamps. Flowering plants evolved during this period. As swampland plants died and decayed, thick deposits of organic material accumulated.

The region's final mountain-building event, the Allegheny Orogeny, had minimal impact on Massachusetts but was felt much more intensely elsewhere in the East. Beginning about 290 million years ago, it created the folded ridges and mountains typical of the central Appalachian Range farther south. Among its effects in Massachusetts were granite intrusions in the southeast. It also helped turn the swamp sediments into beds of coal; a few small coal deposits can be found today in southeastern Massachusetts and the southern Berkshires. At the end of the Allegheny Orogeny, sediments carried down from the towering mountains in the west to the lowland swamps were buried, and eventually formed the rocks that we see in these areas today.

By the late Triassic and middle Jurassic periods of the Mesozoic era (220 to 180 million years ago) the continents of the world had collected together into one supercontinent called Pangea. They then began to break up, creating the present-day Atlantic Ocean as the plates separated. As the land pulled itself apart, great wounds in the crust, called rifts, opened up and allowed molten rock to rise toward the surface. One such tear in the earth created the Connecticut Valley, pulling apart the bedrock as it formed and causing massive faulting. Molten rock poured outward from these fissures and formed distinctive basaltic lava flows. The traprock cliffs of Mt. Tom and the Mt. Holyoke Range are spectacular remnants of these flows. Other rocks of the Connecticut Valley have a very different origin. The characteristic red sedimentary rocks of the region, often seen interbedded between the lava flows, are a result of erosion from other rocks that created sand beds across flat areas. These sandstones have a rich red color, are often high in feldspar, and contain dinosaur footprints and other fossils that can be observed at many locations along the Connecticut River.

After the catastrophic episodes of volcanic activity and faulting during the Triassic and Jurassic periods, New England entered a period of relative quiescence. Significant tectonic activity ceased and erosional forces began to dominate, a state of geological affairs that continues to this day. The towering mountains of earlier times have been mostly eroded away to a relatively flat plain, while more resistant rocks—such as those of Mt. Greylock and Wachusett Mtn.—form the highlands of today.

The last major geological event to shape the landscape of southern New England began approximately 3 million years ago, during a time of global climate change. Around the world temperatures dropped, precipitation patterns changed, and a long cycle of glaciation began. Glaciers and ice sheets have since advanced and retreated across Massachusetts 18 to 20 times. In New England the last and greatest glacial advance began about 70,000 years ago, reached its greatest extent approximately 20,000 years ago, and ended abruptly, sometimes catastrophically, 10,000 years ago. At the peak of this ice age 5 million sq. mi. of ice covered Canada, much of the Northeast, and large areas of the Plains and Northwest. So much of the earth's water was locked up in the glaciers that the sea level in northern Europe and North America was at least 350 ft. below present levels.

A glacier changes the landscape in many ways. The enormous weight of a mile-thick continental ice sheet presses the earth downward, causing the land to sink. As the glaciers retreat in warmer times, seas and lakes inundate the depressed land. Gradually the land rebounds upward, draining the water away and creating earthquakes as it rises. Evidence of the glaciers' advance and retreat can be seen throughout New England. Existing valleys were widened by the glaciers and became U-shaped. Scouring of the bedrock left linear marks—called striations—throughout the region. Formed as the glaciers dragged rocks beneath it over the bedrock surface, striations are indicators of the localized flow direction of the ice. Rocks fell from the downslope side of hills and mountains as the glaciers overrode them. This can be seen in the asymmetrical profile of bedrock hills. Many hills and mountains in New England have gradual, smooth sides facing north-northwest and steep rugged sides to the south-southeast. The immense weight of glaciers keeps their bases above freezing, and streams of meltwater run under the ice. These streams travel through tunnels beneath the glacial ice, depositing long, sinuous lines of gravel and cobbles. Once the glacier melts, these lines form distinctive raised landforms known as eskers. Eskers are common in much of eastern and central New England, but rare in Connecticut and Rhode Island. In the Boston area you can see esker deposits in the Auburndale section of Newton, to the east of the Charles River near the intersection of the Massachusetts Turnpike and MA 128. The tons of soil and rock left behind as a glacier melts are called till. If the soil and rock is washed down streams and deposited in layers, the result is stratified till. As the glaciers overrode the countryside they deposited streamlined, oblong hills of till known as drumlins. These hills are common in Massachusetts; notable examples include Bunker Hill, Breed's Hill, Dorchester Heights, and many of the Boston Harbor islands. Generally drumlins are aligned in the same direction (often northwest to southeast) and indicate the local direction of ice flow.

Beyond the glacier's edge stretched the outwash plain where streams of water carried finer-grained materials from the melting ice. Often, large chunks of ice would break off as the glacier retreated and become buried in the outwash. As these isolated chunks melted they formed holes called kettles. Today kettles typically remain as ponds or bogs. They are particularly common on Cape Cod and in southeastern Massachusetts. One well-known example is Thoreau's Walden Pond in Concord, Mass.

Boulders that were left behind as the glaciers melted and receded are known as glacial erratics. It is important to realize that glaciers advanced as the weight of additional ice and snow pushed them downhill and southward. They retreated by merely melting away as the climate began to warm. Some erratics traveled hundreds of miles, carried by the glaciers. These boulders are common throughout New England. Well-known examples include Plymouth Rock; Cradle Rock in Barre, Mass.; Doane Rock near Eastham on Cape Cod; and the boulder fields of Cape Ann.

Moraines are piles of boulders and debris deposited at a glacier's edge. Terminal moraines mark the farthest extent of glaciation. Southeastern New England provides classic examples of terminal moraines. The glaciers' farthest extent is marked by an undulating line of moraine deposits running east to west through Nantucket, Martha's Vineyard, and Long Island. From this line an unbroken sheet of ice extended 2,000 mi. northward. As the glaciers retreated they stopped temporarily, forming a second line located farther north through Cape Cod, the south side of Buzzards Bay, and westward through southwestern Rhode Island. The Mid-Cape Highway (US 6) follows the crest of the Sandwich Moraine from Sagamore to Dennis. As the ice receded, moraines often functioned as dams, and temporary lakes formed. One of the largest in New England was Lake Hitchcock, which lasted about 4,000 years. Lake Hitchcock filled the Connecticut River Valley from Rocky Hill, Conn., northward well into Vermont and New Hampshire. Over the millennia deep beds of glacial sediment accumulated at the bottom of Lake Hitchcock. When the spillway at Rocky Hill finally eroded and the lake drained away, the present Connecticut River took form. Over the years it has carved the river channel through old lakebeds, the layered soils still evident in the riverbanks along many locations. Many other locations also hosted glacial lakes, including the Housatonic Valley and Lake Bascom in the Hoosic River Valley.

How quickly the ice receded is still in question, but there seems to be growing evidence that the retreat was faster than first supposed. Evidence of great floods implying rapid melting have come to light, but just when or how powerful these floods were is still a mystery.

Geography

All of these geologic processes have blessed present-day Massachusetts with a wonderfully diverse geography that belies its diminutive size. The variety of terrain not only is exciting to hike, but also holds exceptional biodiversity. The six parts in this guide encompass thirteen distinct regions, called ecoregions, that take into account the area's topography, climate, and biology.

Part I: The Berkshires

The Berkshires is a largely mountainous region located at the extreme western edge of the state. It is bounded by Connecticut to the south, New York to the west, Vermont to the north, and the Pioneer Valley to the east. The Berkshires contains four ecoregions: the Taconic Mtns., the Western New England Marble Valleys, the Lower Berkshire Hills, and the Berkshire Highlands. Three long-distance trails cross the region: the Appalachian Trail (AT), South Taconic Trail (STT), and Taconic Crest Trail (TCT). In addition, a large trail network (including portions of the AT) covers the Mt. Greylock massif.

The Taconic Mountain ecoregion largely follows the Massachusetts and New York border, including Mt. Greylock (at 3,491 ft., the tallest peak in the state). Elevations from 1,500 to more than 2,000 ft. are common. Weather conditions in the higher elevations can be severe. This area has abundant swift-running streams and an array of interesting plants and animals that live in the cool forests cloaking the mountains. Notable habitats include the pitch pine–scrub oak plant community of the southern Taconics, seen along the AT and the STT; and the spruce-fir plant community, seen along the AT in the Mt. Greylock area.

The Western New England Marble Valleys ecoregion is sandwiched between the Taconic Mtns. to the west and the Berkshire Highlands to the east, and contains the watersheds of the Housatonic and Hoosic Rivers. The area is underlain with limestone and marble bedrock, which creates one of the most unusual natural regions in the northeastern United States. Calcareous fens, rare in New England, host more than 30 rare species. Lakes, rivers, and streams are plentiful and support species such as bald eagles and ospreys. Elevations are often well below 1,000 ft. The AT passes through many miles of these marble valleys.

The Lower Berkshire Hills ecoregion consists of forested hills ranging from 1,000 to about 1,700 ft. in the southeastern Berkshires. The area offers numerous lakes, streams, and hiking trails scattered throughout state forests and parks. The terrain is usually fairly level, but often covered with hummocks that inhibit drainage and create numerous wetlands and vernal pools. The AT passes through the northern edge of this region. When compared to the Berkshire Highlands just to the north, the Lower Berkshire Hills are lower in elevation and have a slightly less severe climate. Northern hardwood forests and cool upland hemlock forests are common.

The Berkshire Highlands ecoregion contains the southernmost spur of Vermont's Green Mtns. where they creep over the border into Massachusetts as a high-elevation plateau. The high average elevation (approximately 2,000 ft.) helps produce a cool climate more like northern New England, which is evident in the abundance of transition forest (hardwoods with balsam fir and red and black spruce) and spruce-fir forests. The forests are often extensive and unbroken, allowing for large populations of animals such as black bears.

Part II: Pioneer Valley and Vicinity
This large area is a grab bag of climates and terrain, and one of the state's most diverse and beautiful regions. The area runs from the Berkshires on the west to the Worcester Highlands to the east, and from the Vermont and New Hampshire borders to the Connecticut line. Within the Pioneer Valley and Vicinity region are three ecoregions: the Vermont Piedmont, the Berkshire Transition, and the Connecticut Valley. Three long-distance trails are found here: the Metacomet–Monadnock Trail, Robert Frost Trail, and Pocumtuck Ridge Trail.

The Vermont Piedmont ecoregion is found along the Vermont border, between the Berkshire Highlands and the Connecticut Valley, and is typified by hilly terrain from about 500 to 1,500 ft. in elevation. The area sports energetic streams and rivers (such as the Deerfield River) as well as a few ponds and lakes. The bedrock is a mix of many rock types that produce rich, deep soils. The soils in turn support a wonderfully rich array of wildflowers, ferns, shrubs, and trees. The forest primarily consists of northern hardwoods, including sugar maple, basswood, hickory, and elm. Many forests, parks, and preserves are in the area, though no long-distance trails pass through this region.

The Berkshire Transition acts as a buffer between the harsh, high-elevation Berkshire Hills and the milder, lower-elevation Connecticut Valley. It is bounded to the south by the Connecticut border near Southwick and extends north to include the DAR State Forest in Goshen. The eastern boundary runs roughly north-northeast following the western edge of the flat Connecticut Valley plain. This area has a lower elevation than the Vermont Piedmont to the north, and similar geology allows forests of northern hardwoods to mix with warmer-climate hickories and oaks. One notable feature of the Berkshire Transition is the abundance of high-energy rivers and streams. These have flow rates that rise quickly in storms and during spring thaws—stream crossings can be difficult and dangerous during these times. Portions of the Metacomet–Monadnock Trail pass through this region.

The Connecticut River Valley follows the magnificent Connecticut River from the Connecticut line near Springfield to the Vermont border near the Vernon Dam. In shape the region is triangular, with a broad base to the south that tapers to a sharp point in the north. The Connecticut River Valley typically has flat topography and fertile, deep soils. In certain areas, notably the south, a number of basalt hills (including the Mt. Holyoke Range and Mt. Tom) jut up from the plains and offer excellent hiking. Portions of the Metacomet–Monadnock Trail, the Robert Frost Trail, and the Pocumtuck Ridge Trail pass through this region.

Part III: Central Massachusetts

This large region runs from the New Hampshire border south to Rhode Island and Connecticut, and is largely defined by the borders of Worcester County. The area is roughly divided into two ecoregions: the Worcester-Monadnock Plateau and the Lower Worcester Plateau. The area has three long-distance trails: the Tully Trail, the Wapack Trail, and the Midstate Trail. The dominant feature is 2,006-ft. Wachusett Mtn., which is crossed by the Midstate Trail.

The Worcester-Monadnock Plateau, which is lightly populated, covers the area south of the New Hampshire border and north of the Quabbin Reservoir. It incorporates areas just east of the Connecticut Valley, including Mt. Grace. The region is very hilly and ranges in elevation from about 500 ft. to more than 1,800 ft. atop Mt. Watatic. The climate is cool, though not as severe as in the mountains of the Berkshires. Expansive tracts of forests and wetlands, including Quabbin Reservoir, provide habitat for wildlife such as moose, bald eagles, and common loons; this area boasts the state's highest moose population density. The Metacomet–Monadnock Trail, the Wapack Trail, and the Tully Trail pass through this region.

The lower Worcester-Monadnock Plateau is southern sibling to the Worcester-Monadnock Plateau and extends from the Connecticut border north and east of the Quabbin Reservoir area. It is less hilly than the Worcester Plateau and has a milder climate. There are many streams and rivers, such as the Brookfield and Quaboag, and abundant swamps, marshes, and bogs. The Midstate Trail runs through a portion of this region.

Part IV: North and West of Boston

This area consists of low rolling hills interspersed with wide, flat wetlands. It runs from the Atlantic coast north of Boston west along the New Hampshire border to the Worcester-Monadnock Plateau. There are many hiking opportunities, as the region contains an abundance of forests, parks, and preserves with a wide range of habitats. The proximity of this area to metropolitan Boston makes it easily accessible for many residents.

With miles of salt marsh, protected beach environments, and woodlands, the Southern New England Coastal Plains and Hills offer many hiking opportunities. Portions of the Bay Circuit Trail pass through this region. The area has generally acidic soils that support thickets of highbush blueberry and a wide array of plant and animal species. Notable destinations include Parker River National Wildlife Refuge and Crane Beach Reservation.

Part V: Boston and Vicinity

This area encompasses metropolitan Boston and the off-shore waters near the city, including Boston Harbor. The Boston Basin ecoregion comprises most of the area.

The Boston Basin doesn't have vast acres of protected space, but its parklands host a variety of plants and animals, some found nowhere else in Massachusetts. Within its borders the Blue Hills Reservation trail network offers a seemingly endless variety of routes within easy access of Boston. The Boston Harbor Islands are another special treasure

Part VI: Southeastern Massachusetts and the Islands

This region covers the large area south of Boston and offers a nearly unequalled variety of habitats and terrain. Glacial features make up a large portion of the landscape in places, from moraines to kettle ponds. The variety of trails here includes challenging walks through miles of loose sand. The Warner Trail and the Bay Circuit Trail run through this region. Cape Cod National Seashore, Cape Poge Wildlife Refuge, and Sandy Neck Barrier Beach can all be found in this area.

The last two ecoregions—Bristol Lowlands and Cape Cod—incorporate all the area east of Rhode Island, including Cape Cod and the islands of Martha's Vineyard and Nantucket. Created largely during the last ice age, the landscape is a mix of wide outwash plains, moraines, and other glacial features. The dry, largely infertile soils support large tracts of pitch pine–scrub oak forests. Cranberry bogs are common, as are extensive tidal flats and marshes. This area has long been recognized as an area of global ecological importance and offers a number of exciting recreational opportunities.

Climate and Seasons

The ever-changing seasons are part of the beauty and charm of Massachusetts. They rejuvenate any trail you choose to walk, making a familiar path new and different each time you visit. Radiant spring wildflowers, the lush green of a summer forest, the brilliant mosaic of changing autumn leaves, and the beauty of freshly-fallen snow provide myriad backdrops for the hiking experience. The seasons produce spectacular sights, but they also produce weather conditions that can make trails more challenging and sometimes hazardous.

Rain

On average, 41.7 in. of rain falls on the eastern and central portions of the state each year, while a little more, about 44.6 in., falls in the Berkshires.

A very wet year may have 10 in. more than the average, while a dry year might have 10 in. less. Annual precipitation is remarkably even throughout the year, with 3 to 4 in. of (melted) precipitation falling each month across the state.

Snow

Snowfall is fairly uniform across the state, with most regions averaging somewhere between 76 and 115 in. per year. Regions closer to the ocean—and its warming effect—receive less annual snowfall. The southeast region receives only 38 in. on average, while the Cape and the islands get even less (0 to 38 in.). The golden shovel award, however, goes to the northern Berkshires, where 115 to 153 in. fall each year. The earliest snow on record fell on July 10, 1955, while the latest occurred on December 16, 1973. On average the first flakes fall in the first week of November. The last snowfall in spring can occur at any time from late March to mid-June, with the average being April 20. The year with the most snowfall, as recorded at the Boston station, was 1995–1996, with nearly 108 in.

While rain can make the trail slick, snow and ice make it even more dangerous. On many trails in winter, snowshoes, crampons, and other winter equipment will be necessary for a safe trip. South-facing slopes melt out earliest in spring, with north slopes and areas shaded by pines and other evergreens the last to warm up. Exactly when a snow-free hike can be undertaken varies considerably from year to year and location to location. Generally March is the month when the weather transitions from winter to spring, and snow and ice melt from all but the coolest places. In the high country, such as the Worcester Plateau, the Berkshires, and the Taconics, a storm will dump heavier amounts of precipitation on the upwind slopes. For example, a winter storm approaching from the coast with strong easterly winds will drop more snow on the eastern slopes as it is forced up and over the mountains. The western slopes will receive less snow and be somewhat easier for traveling.

Temperature

Massachusetts temperatures run from summer highs in the upper 90s to winter lows reaching −30 degrees. Generally spring is cool and moist, summer warm to hot, and fall pleasantly cool and dry. Freezing temperatures can be encountered as early as late August in the highest elevations, but will generally hold off until late October to early November in most other locations. Winter is frustratingly variable, with some winters being warm and others bone chilling—expect anything from arctic cold and blizzards to mild snow-free conditions.

Storms
In Massachusetts, thunderstorms—affectionately called "boomers" or "thumpers"—are most often associated with cold fronts, but do occur occasionally with warm fronts. Thunderstorms can occur during any month of the year but are most numerous from April to October. The months to be extra alert are May, June, and July. Fronts most often move in from the west to northwest, but also can come from the southwest, north, or south. Thunderstorms can drop a torrential amount of precipitation in a short period, but are usually short lived and pass through quickly. In late summer and autumn, tropical storms (or their remnants) periodically affect the region, and can cause extensive flooding.

Weather Reports
For the most up-to-date weather information, log onto the website of the National Weather Service (National Oceanic and Atmospheric Administration) at www.weather.gov. Reports are available for anywhere in the state—when the map of the United States appears select the portion of Massachusetts you are interested in. NOAA weather radios, special radios that broadcast transmissions from the agency's regional transmitters, also provide automated, regularly updated forecasts.

Civilization and Its Impacts
People began making a marked impact on the environment during the Woodland Period, from about 3,000 years ago to the time of European colonization. During this period there was great diversification among native cultures. People established semi-permanent villages and developed both pottery and agriculture. They used fire to clear the fields, and cultivated corn, beans, squash, and gourds. They gathered roots, herbs, berries, and nuts. They developed trade routes between the highlands and coast. During this period the postglacial coastlines stabilized, and shellfish beds became another food resource.

Woodland Native Americans were the first to encounter the Europeans as they reached the eastern shores of North America. Europeans were first drawn to the Grand Banks fisheries in the early sixteenth century. Then came the fur traders, whose influence had devastating effects on the native populations, bringing disease as well as economic and cultural changes and challenges. Although the indigenous peoples had cleared some land for planting, the European colonists, who rapidly settled the region following the establishment of Plymouth Plantation in 1620, greatly accelerated the agricultural process. When agriculture reached its peak in the mid-nineteenth century, approximately 23 million acres (slightly more than half) of New England's land area was cleared.

By the late 1800s demographics began to shift as the Industrial Revolution attracted more people to the cities and towns. In 1840 less than one-fifth of New England's population resided in towns; by 1880 more than half of the population lived in towns and cities of 2,500 or more people. The great economic depression in the last half of the nineteenth century caused the rocky New England fields to be largely abandoned. Slowly these fields and pastures began to grow back to forest again, with white pines and other pioneer species predominating. It will take hundreds of years for the previously cleared forests to reach full maturity, and in some areas, such as the moorland of Nantucket, the forest has not yet returned.

Clearing of the forests resulted in the destruction of one habitat and the creation of another. At one point, many of the species we take for granted today, such as white-tailed deer, black bears, and wild turkeys, were nearly wiped out of Massachusetts, while wolves and cougars were permanently removed. Bounties on most predators left humans as the only significant predator by the early twentieth century. The settlers altered the landscape not only by clearing trees, but also by introducing nonnative species of plants, animals, and disease. Although the introduced species included cultivated plants and domesticated animals that provided some benefit to the people of New England, the introduction of diseases such as smallpox, typhoid fever, diphtheria, measles, tuberculosis, and chicken pox devastated indigenous populations. Until the early 1900s the American chestnut was a dominant tree species in southern New England, composing up to 25 percent of the forest. Beginning in 1904 the effects of a fungal disease accidentally brought into New York started a blight that destroyed all the big trees. But the American chestnut isn't completely gone from the woods—it survives as stump sprouts. Other introduced pests include the gypsy moth, which seriously threatens the white oak, and the hemlock woolly adelgid, an aphid which blew into southern New England on the winds of Hurricane Gloria in 1985 and has subsequently devastated many hemlock forests. The adelgid is slowly spreading north; when on the trails watch for clusters of tiny white egg sacks on the evergreen needles.

The latest chapter is still being written. The pressures of suburban sprawl and unchecked development in the late twentieth and early twenty-first centuries have fragmented blocks of previously unbroken forest and caused the loss of open space throughout the region. At the same time, more than a century of industrial and postindustrial pollution has taken its toll on the health of the region's natural resources. The future holds promise for the Massachusetts outdoors, but careful stewardship and conservation efforts are required to protect the state's natural places for future generations.

Stewardship and Conservation

It is part of human nature to one day admire and cherish something that is the next day taken for granted. A trail through the woods allows us the freedom to explore the natural areas where we live, but is also representative of our responsibility to care for these places and paths. Hikers are by nature independent, relying completely on their own ability to walk their chosen path and reach their goals. This produces a sense of accomplishment and confidence that is different from any other outdoor pursuit. An even greater feeling, richer and more lasting, comes from building and maintaining the paths others walk.

Think about getting more involved in caring for trails near you. There are many organizations that are presently doing a huge amount of work maintaining trails with very few hands. When you help build a bog bridge or install rock cribbing on a trail that slabs a ridge, you not only improve the trail, but also protect the environment and strengthen yourself physically and emotionally. Volunteering is a wonderfully unselfish way to make a positive difference to something you already love—the outdoors. Many of the organizations mentioned in this book, including the AMC, need your help and will welcome you as a volunteer. For information about getting involved with the AMC, refer to the back of this book.

Hiking Ethics

Every hiker has an obligation to respect and care for the outdoor environment, so that it may be enjoyed by all who follow. As you hike, try to adhere to these rules of the outdoors:

- Carry out everything you carry in. Go a step further: Carry out any litter that you find.

- Don't pick flowers, and avoid gathering wood. Even dead trees have their place in the ecosystem and should be left undisturbed. Do not light a campfire unless it is an emergency. If you are using a backpacking stove, do not leave it unattended.

- Stay on the trail, and try to avoid muddy places where foot traffic can cause erosion.

- Bury human waste at least 200 ft. from the trail and any water sources. The careless disposal of human waste is probably the principal cause of the spread of giardiasis.

- If you wish to listen to music, wear headphones. But it's much more interesting to listen to the sounds of the forest. Preserve the forest sounds for others to enjoy.

- Where dogs are permitted it is often with the stipulation they be leashed at all times. Respect and follow the rules regarding pets when hiking and be sure to control your pet so it won't be a nuisance to other hikers.

- On overnight trips, travel in small groups and practice low-impact camping. Use established campsites if available; if not, camp well away from trails and streams and avoid using sites that have been used previously by campers.

- Respect wildlife. Never feed a wild animal, use binoculars or telephoto lens for closer looks, and leave baby animals alone—their mother is often close by and watching.

Leave No Trace

The Appalachian Mountain Club is a national educational partner of Leave No Trace, a nonprofit organization dedicated to promoting and inspiring responsible outdoor recreation through education, research, and partnerships. The Leave No Trace Program seeks to develop wildland ethics—ways in which people think and act in the outdoors to minimize their impacts on the areas they visit and to protect our natural resources for future enjoyment. Leave No Trace unites four federal land management agencies—the U.S. Forest Service, National Park Service, Bureau of Land Management, and U.S. Fish and Wildlife Service—with manufacturers, outdoor retailers, user groups, educators, organizations such as the AMC and the National Outdoor Leadership School (NOLS), and individuals.

The Leave No Trace ethic is guided by these seven principles:

- Plan ahead and prepare
- Travel and camp on durable surfaces
- Dispose of waste properly
- Leave what you find
- Minimize campfire impacts
- Respect wildlife
- Be considerate of other visitors

For Leave No Trace information and materials, contact:

Leave No Trace Center for Outdoor Ethics, P.O. Box 997, Boulder, CO 80306
Toll Free: 800-332-4100, or locally, 303-442-8222; Fax: 303-442-8217
www.lnt.org

PART ONE
The Berkshires

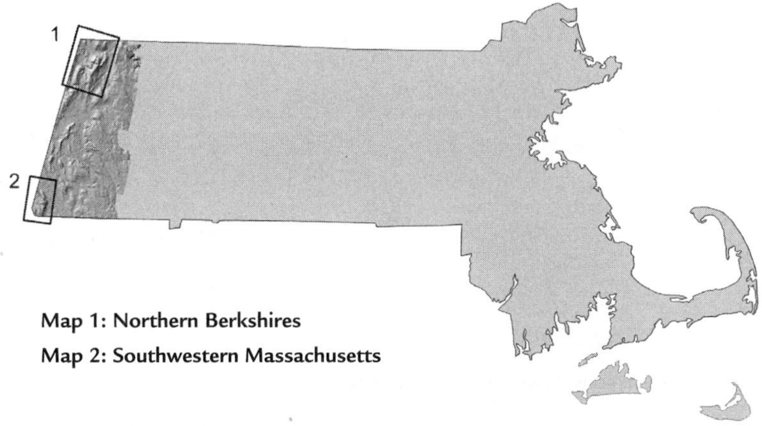

Map 1: Northern Berkshires
Map 2: Southwestern Massachusetts

This part includes Berkshire County, which offers some of the best scenery and views in Massachusetts. Mt. Greylock, the state's highest peak at an elevation of 3,491 ft., is located near the northwest corner of the county, between Williamstown and Adams. Bash Bish Falls, one of the most recognizable water features in the state, is located close to the New York border in Mt. Washington.

The trail system is highly developed in the Berkshires, with many hiking opportunities throughout the region. Mt. Greylock State Reservation offers an abundant number of trails to help you reach the summit. The Taconic Crest Trail runs 35 mi. along the New York–Massachusetts border into Vermont.

TRAIL DESCRIPTIONS

Appalachian Trail (BCAMC, DCR)

In 1676, at the close of King Philip's War, Major John Talcott led his company of Connecticut Militia into the Berkshires in pursuit of Native American refugees. The major was one of the first Europeans to see the westernmost region of Massachusetts now called the Berkshires. And he despised the place. It was a land of wild animals, rugged mountains, raging rivers, and steep ravines draped in impenetrable forest. However, all the things that Talcott scorned make the Berkshires a paradise for today's hikers. The tallest mountains in the Commonwealth, from Mt. Everett in the south to Mt. Greylock in the north, overlook unique marble river valleys that host some of the most treasured ecosystems in the nation. Many long-distance trails, including the Appalachian Trail, weave past the majesty of waterfalls and ridgetop views, ravines, river walks, and woodland ponds.

Approximately 90 mi. of the 2,175-mi. Appalachian Trail (AT) are located in Berkshire County. The trail enters Massachusetts from Connecticut near Sages Ravine, passes over Mt. Race, Mt. Everett, and Mt. Bushnell, and then goes east across the Housatonic Valley. Passing over June Mtn., the trail climbs steeply to East Mtn. State Forest, and descends to MA 23. After skirting Benedict Pond in Beartown State Forest it ascends to the headwaters of Swan Brook and descends through Tyringham Valley. Beyond Tyringham the trail skirts the eastern edge of Upper Goose Pond, crosses the Massachusetts Turnpike (I-90) at Greenwater Pond, and enters October Mtn. State Forest, where it leads over Becket Mtn. and Bald Top. After climbing Warner Hill the trail runs through continuous woods, except for the towns of Dalton and Cheshire, ascends Saddle Ball Mtn. and Mt. Greylock, passes over Mt. Fitch and Mt. Williams, and again descends. After crossing the Hoosic Valley at North Adams, the AT reaches the Vermont line, where it continues north as both the AT and the Long Trail.

For day hikers the AT serves as an access route to a number of Berkshire summits. It can be entered at numerous highway crossings, usually marked with signs. There are parking areas at most of the high-use trail crossings. Long-distance hikers should consult the Appalachian Trail Conference's *Appalachian Trail Guide to Massachusetts–Connecticut.* A number of shelters are located on or near the trail, between 7 and 10 mi. apart. Off-trail accommodations are within easy reach. Note that the times indicated in the mileage summaries are approximate and your hiking time may vary from them—especially on the longer sections. If you are new to hiking or backpacking, be conservative in your time estimates until you have a better idea of your actual pace.

The AT Committee of the Appalachian Mountain Club's Berkshire Chapter maintains the Appalachian Trail in Massachusetts. Hikers interested in participating in these maintenance efforts are always welcome; contact the Berkshire Chapter for more information. White rectangular paint blazes, 2 in. by 6 in., indicate the trail route; double blazes warn of abrupt changes in direction. Most side trails are blue blazed. The exact trail routing is always subject to change as a result of ongoing efforts to run the trail through protected corridors and to avoid paved road sections. Relocations are always well marked in the field.

Section 1. Massachusetts–Connecticut Line to Jug End Rd. (11.9 mi.)

The southern end of the Massachusetts section of the AT, about 0.7 mi. south of Sages Ravine, is accessible by side trails from the east and west. On CT 41 just south of the Connecticut–Massachusetts border is the heavily used parking area for the blue-blazed Undermountain Trail. Follow the Undermountain Trail 0.9 mi. to the intersection with the blue-blazed Paradise Lane Trail. Turn onto the Paradise Lane Trail, constructed in 1954 by the AMC, and hike 2.1 mi. to the intersection with the AT. The west access is from East St. (seasonal) in the town of Mt. Washington. A pull-off is just south of a stone state boundary marker. From the pull-out an unmarked woods road travels east 1.0 mi. to the AT.

Immediately north of Bear Mtn. the AT crosses into Massachusetts and begins the descent into scenic Sages Ravine. The trail follows the south side of Sawmill Brook, passing Sages Ravine Campsite on the left. (A caretaker is on duty May to October; tent platforms, privy, spring except in dry times.)

At 1.0 mi. north of the state line, the trail turns sharp left, crosses the brook (high water, most often in spring, can make crossing difficult), and begins a gradual ascent up the ridge leading to Mt. Everett. At the output from a spring, and before crossing Bear Rock Stream, a sign and path on the left lead to Laurel Ridge Campsite (five dirt tent pads, three tent platforms, a water source, and a composting privy—read the instructions). The trail continues north through an open hemlock grove in a gradual ascent of the ridge.

Emerging from the woods, the trail traverses open cliffs of Race Mtn. that offer outstanding views sweeping from northeast to southeast. For 0.3 mi. the trail closely follows the edge of the cliff and reaches the summit of Race Mtn. (2,365 ft.). From the summit the trail traces the backbone of the ridge past many great views before dropping to the saddle between Race Mtn. and Mt. Everett. Here the blue-blazed Race Brook Falls Trail enters on the right. (The Race Brook Falls Trail leads east about 0.4 mi. to Race Brook Falls Campsite with tent platforms and privy, and then continues another 1.5 mi. to MA 41 and the parking area.) *Caution: Access to MA 41 from the AT as it traverses the southern Taconics is limited to the Undermountain/Paradise Lane Trails, Race Brook Falls Trail, and Elbow Trail. Several hikers have lost their lives, and others have been seriously injured, attempting to bushwhack down the cliffs to the highway. Stay on the trail!*

From the Race Brook Falls Trail junction the AT begins to ascend the south slope of Mt. Everett. This ascent is rocky and fairly steep, climbing into a pitch pine–scrub oak plant community that contains some of the largest unbroken tracts of old-growth forest in Massachusetts. The summit of Mt. Everett (2,602 ft.) offers extensive views in all directions: Monument Mtn. and Mt. Greylock to the north, and East Mtn., Warner Mtn., and the Housatonic Valley to the east. To the south are Race Mtn. and Bear Mtn., while to the west are Mt. Frissell, Alander Mtn., Mt. Darby, and, in the distance, the Catskills.

The fire tower that was atop the summit for many years was removed in May 2003. Near the concrete footings of the old fire tower the AT turns sharp right and begins to descend on a narrow path that widens into an abandoned service road. The trail quickly leaves the road and continues straight ahead down an embankment, and into the woods. About 100 yd. down the service road is a recently renovated stone shelter and parking area. The service/access road was closed in 2001 due to poor conditions, but is now open to the picnic area during summer months (day use only). Camping is not permitted at the shelter. The AT continues through woods and briefly follows a gravel road before turning right and reentering the woods.

As the descent moderates, the trail enters Guilder Pond picnic area (2,042 ft.). The trail bears right at the picnic area past an outhouse. This picnic area is accessible on foot via the access road from the gate on Mt. Washington Rd. (approx. 1 mi.). The AT crosses a small stream, and then the blue-blazed Guilder Pond Loop Trail enters from the left. The AT descends a short pitch, crosses another small brook, and turns left, descending on log steps. A side trail on the right leads 0.1 mi. to Hemlocks Shelter (privy and water source). The shelter area also has a composting privy— read the directions before using. At 100 ft. after the Hemlocks side trail, a brook is crossed, and then a side trail to Glen Brook Shelter and Campsite (privy and water source) exits to the right.

Continuing north, the AT begins a gentle descent along the east slope of Mt. Undine (2,203 ft.) and then snakes sharp right, then left. At this point the blue-blazed Elbow Trail intersects from the right. The Elbow Trail, the last access to MA 41, leads 1.5 mi. southeast to the Berkshire School and MA 41. Soon the AT begins a gradual ascent to reach the wooded summit of Mt. Bushnell (1,834 ft.). The trail crosses two intermediate peaks and reaches Jug End summit at the north end of the ridge, where there is a spectacular view. After a gradual descent from Jug End summit, the AT reaches a crest of rock, the "jug's end," with steep outcrops and extensive open views to the northwest and southeast. Mt. Greylock is clearly visible on the horizon to the north. The trail turns sharp right and shortly begins a steep zigzag descent over rock ledges. Use caution when the trail is wet. The descent moderates as the trail approaches Jug End Rd. (a.k.a. Curtiss Rd.), where there is parking space for one to two cars. *(Note: This road is labeled Guilder Hollow Rd. off of MA 41 and is often a point of confusion for drivers looking for Jug End Rd.)* A spring is located on the south side of the road, approximately 0.1 mi. east of the trail; the piping was removed in 2004, but it is still usable.

Appalachian Trail: Massachusetts–Connecticut Line to Jug End Rd. (map 2: E3–B3)

Distances from the Undermountain Rd. parking area in Connecticut (790 ft.) to
- Sages Ravine and Campsite (1,500 ft.): 2.2 mi., 700 ft., 1 hr. 15 min.
- Laurel Ridge Campsite (1,600 ft.) : 4.1 mi., 800 ft., 2 hr.
- Race Brook Falls Trail (1,900 ft.): 7 mi., 1,500 ft. (rev. 450 ft.), 3 hr. 30 min.
- summit of Mt. Everett (2,602 ft.): 7.4 mi., 2,200 ft., 4 hr.
- Hemlocks Shelter and Glen Brook Shelter and Campsite (1,900 ft.): 8.5 mi., 2,200 ft. (rev. 700 ft.), 4 hr. 45 min.
- Elbow Trail (1,750 ft.): 9.1 mi., 2,200 ft. (rev. 150 ft.), 5 hr. 15 min.
- summit of Jug End (1,600 ft.): 10.8 mi., 2,200 ft. (rev. 150 ft.), 6 hr. 15 min.
- Jug End Rd. (890 ft): 11.9 mi., 2,200 ft. (rev. 300 ft.), 7 hr. 15 min.

Section 2. Jug End Rd. to US 7 (4.5 mi.)

To reach the south trailhead, from the junction of MA 41 and 23 take MA 41 south to Jug End Rd. (a.k.a. Curtiss Rd.) on the right. The trail crosses Jug End Rd. at a small roadside turnout. At 0.1 mi. east of the trail crossing of Jug End Rd., a spring is piped to the roadside.

Proceeding north of Jug End Rd., the AT soon crosses a stone wall in the middle of a mature white pine forest. Upon reaching an open pasture, the trail crosses another stone wall and traverses 100 yd. of wet pasture before coming to MA 41. At 1.1 mi. the trail passes along a fenced pasture and crosses a farm brook. A gradual ascent brings the trail into the trees along a woods road atop a ridge. It crosses a series of bog bridges at 1.6 mi. on the way to higher ground and another ridge. The trail drops off this hemlock ridge to the east and travels through the next swampy area on bog bridging (bring the bug spray). At 2.4 mi. it crosses Hubbard Brook on a large bridge, then arrives at South Egremont Rd., a small parking area, kiosk, and across the street a stone monument commemorating the last battle of Shays' Rebellion in 1798.

Passing the monument on the left, the trail travels on a grassy farm road through active farm fields, then enters the woods to climb a small hill. Descending the hill and crossing West Sheffield Rd. at 3.9 mi., the trail follows the edge of a swamp along the side of the hill, then crosses the swamp on a long set of bog bridges and at 4.4 mi. crosses railroad tracks. Use caution approaching and crossing this active railway. Descend the embankment and cross the field to US 7 at 4.5 mi.

Appalachian Trail: Jug End Rd. to US 7

Distances from Jug End Rd. (870 ft.) to
- MA 41 (818 ft.): 0.9 mi., (rev. 50 ft.), 20 min.
- US 7 (682 ft.): 4.5 mi. (rev. 150 ft.), 2 hr.

Section 3. US 7 to MA 23 (8.4 mi.)

The trail crosses US 7 about 3 mi. south of Great Barrington. (Parking is not allowed on US 7.) Leaving the east side of the highway, the trail follows a grassy trail through an overgrown field; it soon curves right past a small pond and over a stream on a bridge at 0.2 mi. The trail immediately enters an active farm field and goes left, then right, along the bank of the Housatonic River. The trail follows the river south through a series of fields and open woodlands. At 0.9 mi. the trail takes a left onto Kellogg Rd. The AT follows the road across the Housatonic, turns left into the woods for 200 yd., then bears sharply right, emerging at another active farm field at 1.1 mi. The trail skirts the edge of the field to the left, following Kellogg Rd. to its intersection with Boardman St. at 1.3 mi. Crossing Boardman St., the AT enters the woods and begins to ascend June Mtn. (1,206 ft.). Coming off the height-of-land, at 2.9 mi. the trail crosses Holmes Rd. (Brush Hill Rd.). Reentering the woods, the trail reaches a rounded rock ledge at 3.3 mi., then crosses a deep fissure in the rock spanned by a wooden bridge at 3.6 mi. The trail then descends sharp around a split glacial boulder before beginning a moderate-to-steep ascent to attain the top of a ridge.

The AT then runs along the edge of East Mtn. and for the next 0.4 mi. passes several exposed ledges that afford fine views to the south and west. The Catskills are clearly visible, and the Taconic Range, with Mt. Everett (2,602 ft.) dominating, lies west across the Housatonic Valley.

The trail passes a small spring in a gully at 4.2 mi. and, climbing again, soon reaches a viewpoint among large boulders at the south end of East Mtn. This exposed location offers more good views, especially to the south. At the viewpoint the AT makes a sharp turn left, passing an obscure woods road leading left. At 5.8 mi. the northern end of the Bad Weather Bypass is reached on the left in an area that is often wet. The AT continues over undulating terrain, never getting far from the rim of a steep slope on the right. At 6.4 mi. a short side trail leads to Tom Leonard Shelter (shelter, privy, and one tent platform). Water is available from a small creek in the ravine below the shelter area.

The trail then follows along the edge of ledges with views into Ice Gulch, a rocky chasm of boulders and a buried stream. The path snakes through hemlocks as it descends to flatter land, crossing paved Lake Buel Rd. at 7.5 mi. A signed parking area with a kiosk is located 50 yd. west of the trail crossing. From Lake Buel Rd. the walking is easy as the trail crosses numerous horse trails and Shore Camp Rd. The path crosses a broken dam across an outlet of Lake Buel Swamp at 8.0 mi., then passes through an area ravaged by the Memorial Day tornado of 1995. MA 23 and a fairly large parking area are reached at 8.4 mi.

Appalachian Trail: US 7 to MA 23

Distances from US 7 to
- Boardman St. (712 ft.): 1.3 mi., 30 min.
- Holmes Rd. (1,155 ft.): 2.9 mi., 1 hr. 30 min.
- Tom Leonard Shelter: 6.4 mi., 4 hr.
- MA 23 (1,043 ft.): 8.4 mi., 5 hr. 30 min.

Section 4. MA 23 to Tyringham (12.1 mi.)

To reach the MA 23 trailhead, follow US 7 to the north intersection with MA 23 at Belcher Square. Take MA 23 east 5.0 mi. toward Monterey. The parking area is on the left and very close to the Monterey town line. The northern trailhead pull-off (parking for two to three cars) is on Tyringham

Main Rd., approximately 5 mi. south of the MA 102 and 23 junction in Lee, very close to Exit 2 of the Massachusetts Turnpike.

From MA 23 on the Monterey–Great Barrington line the trail crosses an open field and parking area, then enters the woods and climbs steeply to the top of a height-of-land. The trail now gradually descends to a red maple swamp at 1 mi., crosses the wetland on bog bridges and steppingstones, and arrives at Blue Hill Rd. (Stony Brook Rd.). From the road the path steeply weaves up rock outcrops and boulders to the top of a cliff in Beartown State Forest. Crossing through open woods, the trail soon crosses a paved service road, then a blue-blazed side trail left (Benedict Pond Loop Trail) that leads to the Benedict Pond boat launch, parking area, phone, privies, public camping area, and showers (use fee required). These facilities are part of Beartown State Forest. The AT continues and skirts the eastern end of Benedict Pond on bog bridging. At 2.2 mi. it crosses a stone bridge, then turns right onto a wide trail and begins a sharp ascent of stone steps to a formation known as The Ledges and turns sharp right to cross below the outlet of a beaver dam.

The trail follows along The Ledges, a run of exposed cliffs that offer fine views of East Mtn., Warner Mtn., Mt. Everett, and the distant Catskills. The path turns left away from the ridge and begins a moderate-to-sharp descent, crossing a series of brooks and a woods road before climbing again at a powerline crossing. At 3.3 mi. a side path (on the right) leads uphill 200 ft. to the recently renovated Mt. Wilcox South Shelter. Water can be obtained from a spring off the shelter access trail. The AT continues sharp uphill and after a steady climb reaches a plateau with open woods at 4 mi. At 4.5 mi. the trail crosses the outlet to an abandoned (2003) beaver pond before coming to the blue-blazed, 0.25-mi. access trail to Mt. Wilcox North Shelter. Water can be obtained from the brook at the shelter, though this source is uncertain during dry periods.

At the Wilcox North junction the trail turns sharp left and heads north, descending steadily off the ridge to Beartown Mtn. Rd. at 5.8 mi. The trail crosses Beartown Mtn. Rd. (dirt), passes through some swampy areas, and ascends a ridge of white pine. From the ridge crest the path makes a steep zigzag descent and meets Fernside Rd. (dirt) at 8.5 mi. The trail continues across the road and reaches Shaker Campsite on the right at 9.2 mi. Water is located at a stream crossing 0.1 mi. beyond the camp-site. At 9.5 mi. the AT crosses an open field at a buried gas pipeline and continues along the edge of other open fields. It follows Hop Brook for a short distance before crossing a barbed-wire fence onto the Tyringham Cobble Reservation (The Trustees of Reservations). The trail, which for-merly followed the south slopes of the cobble, was rerouted in 2008 to fol-low the TTOR trail to the summit, which offers a fine view across the val-ley. The AT then descends Cobble Hill through woods and scrubby open fields, crossing Jerusalem Rd. at 11 mi. After crossing an active pasture, the AT enters hemlock woods, crosses Braided Brook at 11.3 mi. and shortly thereafter crosses the pipeline right of way again. The trail follows hedge-rows and a boardwalk around a wet field, crosses Hop Brook, and reaches Tyringham Main Rd. at 12.1 mi.

Appalachian Trail: MA 23 to Tyringham

Distances from MA 23 (1,043 ft.) to
- Benedict Pond (1,580 ft.) : 2 mi., 1 hr. 15 min.
- The Ledges: 2.6 mi., 1 hr. 30 min.
- Mt. Wilcox South Shelter: 3.3 mi., 2 hr. 15 min.
- Mt. Wilcox North Shelter: 5.1 mi., 3 hr. 30 min.
- Beartown Mtn. Rd. (1,804 ft.): 5.7 mi., 4 hr. 45 min.
- Shaker Campsite: 9.2 mi., 5 hr. 30 min.
- Cobble Hill side trail: 10.7 mi., 6 hr. 15 min.
- Tyringham (974 ft.): 12.1 mi., 7 hr.

Section 5. Tyringham to US 20 (Jacob's Ladder Highway) (8.6 mi.)

From Tyringham Main Rd. in Tyringham (0.9 mi. east of the village cen-ter) the trail climbs, steeply at times, over a knoll and through an over-grown field near the wooded summit of Baldy Mtn. At 1.9 mi. it descends steeply over cobbles to unpaved Webster Rd. Continuing across the road, the trail crosses an inlet to Knee Deep Pond at 2.2 mi. After going through a hemlock grove, pass a short side trail at 3.4 mi. (this side trail leads 0.1 mi. to a spring). At 4.3 mi. the trail crosses Goose Pond Rd., where an un-marked parking area 50 yd. east (right) of the trail crossing has room for three to four cars. MA 8 can be reached by following Goose Pond Rd. east 3.0 mi. US 20 is 3.0 mi. to the west in Lee, Mass.

Crossing Goose Pond Rd., the AT passes by a stone wall and soon crosses a small brook. The trail parallels another stone wall with abundant ferns and ground pines, leading to a marsh and pond on the right. The path enters a stand of hemlock, crosses a long bridge over the outlet of the pond, and moderately ascends through a deciduous forest. It climbs over some large rocks and at 5.4 mi. reaches a sign marking the boundary of the Upper Goose Pond Management Area (no fires, no camping except at the Upper Goose Pond Cabin area). Paralleling the ridge top to the right, the trail turns left and descends a series of stone steps, then continues easily down slope, passing the narrow east end of Upper Goose Pond, which is intermittently visible through the trees. A spring, accessed via a short unmarked side trail, is reached at 5.9 mi. The trail now bears left at a double blaze (do not walk straight up the hill) and crosses the inlet to Upper Goose Pond at 6.2 mi. At 6.7 mi. the path passes an old chimney, all that remains of the old Mohhekennuck fishing and hunting club. The club sold its land to the National Park Service, a transaction that protected much of the shoreline of Upper Goose Pond.

At 7.0 mi. the trail turns sharp right and briefly ascends to the junction with a blue-blazed side trail left that leads in 0.5 mi. to the Upper Goose Pond Cabin and Campsite. A caretaker is on duty, and the cabin is open from Memorial Day to mid-October. After passing the side trail the path soon steeply descends through attractive woods and crosses the Massachusetts Turnpike (I-90) on a skywalk footbridge at 8.2 mi. After a short, level walk US 20 is reached at 8.6 mi. Lee, Mass., and Exit 2 of the Massachusetts Turnpike (I-90) can be reached by traveling 5.0 mi. west. Bus connections to Boston, Pittsfield, and other destinations are available there. The parking area 0.2 mi. west of the US 20 crossing has plenty of spaces and an information kiosk. Please do not park on the adjacent private property.

Appalachian Trail: Tyringham to US 20 (Jacob's Ladder Highway)
Distances from Tyringham (974 ft.) to
- trailhead on Goose Pond Rd. (1,676 ft.): 4.2 mi., 2 hr. 30 min.
- side trail to Upper Goose Pond Cabin and Campsite: 7.0 mi., 3 hr. 45 min.
- US 20 (1,387 ft.): 8.6 mi., 4 hr. 45 min.

Section 6. US 20 to Pittsfield Rd. (9.4 mi.)

The trailhead is located on US 20, 5.0 mi. east of Exit 2 of the Massachusetts Turnpike and the town of Lee. Limited parking can be found on the south side of US 20 approximately 0.2 mi. west of the trail crossing. Please respect the adjacent private property.

From the north side of US 20 the trail climbs steeply, passing under a high-tension line at 0.2 mi. The trail briefly levels off, turns right, and continues to ascend, passing some all-terrain vehicle trails along the way. At 0.7 mi. it crosses paved Tyne Rd., which leads in 3.5 mi. to Becket (right) and in 0.9 mi. to US 20 (left). The trail now climbs to the wooded summit of Becket Mtn. (2,187 ft.), where a register box (1.3 mi.) is nailed to a tree. The concrete footings are all that remains of the tower that once stood here. From Becket Mtn. the AT descends to a col before climbing to the crest of Walling Mtn. (2,220 ft.) at 2.3 mi. After a moderate descent via some switchbacks, the descent steepens over rocky trail. After crossing another all-terrain vehicle trail the western shore of Finerty Pond (in October Mtn. State Forest) is reached at 3.1 mi. The trail skirts the pond, then turns north away from the water and moderately ascends through open woods, crossing several small streams.

At 4.4 mi. the trail passes close by a fast-moving brook on the right that often makes the trail bed wet. Skirting some beaver ponds and squeezing through some rocky clefts, the AT then intersects unpaved County Rd. at 5.4 mi. This road is rough, but passable by automobile. There is some limited space for day-use parking. Overnight parking is not recommended. (A right turn leads 5.0 mi. to Becket and MA 8.) The trail turns right, briefly follows the road, and then heads left into the woods. It begins a steep ascent of a washed-out trail to the overgrown summit of Bald Top Mtn. (2,040 ft.) at 5.6 mi. The trail soon crosses another ATV trail, and at 6.9 mi. it crosses an underground cable right of way. After crossing a small brook, there is a short side trail to the left for October Mtn. Shelter at 7.2 mi.

West Branch Rd. is crossed at 7.9 mi. adjacent to another beaver pond. (Right leads 0.6 mi. to Pittsfield Rd. and old Washington Town Hall.) From here to Pittsfield Rd. the trail is mostly level. At 9.3 mi. the trail intersects an unpaved service road for the Pittsfield Water Company, turns right, and travels on the road a short distance to Pittsfield Rd. (paved). Pittsfield is 8 .0 mi. down the road to the left. Cars can be parked along Pittsfield Rd.

Appalachian Trail: US 20 to Pittsfield Rd.

Distances from US 20 (1,387 ft.) to
- Tyne Rd. (1,886 ft.): 0.7 mi., 30 min.
- summit of Becket Mtn. (2,187 ft.): 1.3 mi., 1 hr.
- summit of Walling Mtn. (2,220 ft.): 2.3 mi., 1 hr. 30 min.
- Finerty Pond (1,930 ft.): 3.1 mi., 1 hr. 45 min.
- County Rd. (1,883 ft.): 5.4 mi., 3 hr. 15 min.
- summit of Bald Top Mtn. (2,040 ft.): 5.6 mi., 3 hr. 30 min.
- October Mtn. Shelter: 7.2 mi., 4 hr. 30 min.
- Pittsfield Rd. (2,021 ft.): 9.4 mi., 5 hr. 45 min.

Section 7. Pittsfield Rd. to Dalton (9.6 mi.)

The trail begins on Pittsfield Rd., 5 mi. from Becket and 8 mi. from Pittsfield. From Pittsfield Rd. the trail enters the woods. The terrain is generally flat with long runs of bog bridges that pass through a boggy transitional forest of balsam fir and red spruce. This land is part of the Pittsfield Watershed Lands, and the trail crosses on a 50-ft.-wide easement. No camping or fires are permitted. The AT crosses a small stream at 0.6 mi. At 1.6 mi. it passes over a stone wall to cross a bridge over a sandy stream at 2.1 mi. Descending gradually, the trail comes to an active beaver pond and crosses the outlet stream below several beaver dams. After ascending beside an impressive overhanging 30-ft. cliff, the trail turns sharp left at the top. At 3.0 mi. it crosses Blotz Rd. (Left leads 6 mi. to Pittsfield; right leads 1.3 mi. to MA 8.) Parking for three to four cars can be found in a small lot. Overnight parking is not recommended.

From Blotz Rd. the trail continues to the top of Warner Hill (2,050 ft.) at 3.9 mi., with views to the west and north, including Mt. Greylock. The AT now turns sharp left, passing the summit, which is a rock outcrop a few feet off the path to the right. The trail then descends through a beautiful area of ferns and reenters the forest. Turning left, it traverses an abandoned woods road for a short distance, then at 6.5 mi. crosses under high-tension lines, where there is a view to the west. The AT now passes over rocky terrain and reaches the side trail to the Kay Wood Shelter at 6.6 mi.

At 6.9 mi. the trail crosses Grange Hall Rd., follows a stream, then crosses it before ascending steeply to the summit of Day Mtn. at 7.7 mi. The subsequent descent begins steeply, following along a mossy ledge before becoming more gradual as it proceeds through open woods. Railroad tracks are reached at 9.0 mi. Use caution crossing as these are active tracks, there is limited sight distance, and trains approach quickly. Follow the trail down the dirt driveway with a lumberyard to the right. Cross Housatonic St. and continue down Depot St. to the intersection with MA 8 at 9.4 mi. Turn left onto MA 8 and at 9.6 mi. reach the junction of MA 8 and 9.

Appalachian Trail: Pittsfield Rd. to Dalton
Distances from Pittsfield Rd. (2,021 ft.) to
- Blotz Rd. (1,886 ft.): 3 mi., 1 hr. 30 min.
- summit of Warner Hill (2,050 ft.): 3.9 mi., 2 hr.
- Grange Hall Rd. (1,683 ft.): 6.9 mi., 3 hr. 30 min.
- MA 8–MA 9 (Dalton) (1,174 ft.): 9.6 mi., 5 hr. 15 min.

Section 8. Dalton to Cheshire (9.3 mi.)

Cross MA 9 and follow High St. west 0.9 mi. to Park Ave. Cross the street onto Gulf Rd. At 1.0 mi. reach a parking area and kiosk. The trail now continues straight past the kiosk parallel to Gulf Rd. for about 100 yd. before turning right into the woods away from the road and ascending ridges as it follows along the Dalton–Lanesboro line. It passes beneath a power line at 4.3 mi., then at 4.7 mi. meets a blue-blazed side trail that leads to Crystal Mtn. Campsite, with an outhouse. The trail comes to a hemlock grove on the west side of Gore Pond, where significant illegal all-terrain vehicle activity is common. At 5.6 mi. the AT passes over the outlet of Gore Pond and ascends to an overgrown summit pasture. After crossing a number of old logging roads, the trail passes near the Dalton–Cheshire granite boundary marker on the left. The path climbs gently and at 7.5 mi. reaches a USGS bronze marker on Cheshire South Cobble. From here the trail briefly descends steeply over rocks before intersecting a blue-blazed side trail that presses through dense mountain laurel to the North Cobble, a rocky overlook with a dramatic view of Mt. Greylock.

From the side trail the AT descends somewhat steeply, crossing more old woods roads before leveling out and reaching Furnace Hill Rd. The trail turns right and follows the road downhill to a T-intersection at the bottom of the hill. The trail turns left, soon crossing the Hoosic River and the paved recreational Ashuwillticook Rail Trail. Hikers may park in the rail-trail parking lot. Parking is not permitted on Furnace Hill Rd.

Continue from the railtrail toward the center of Cheshire, then turn right onto School St., directly across from the post office. On the corner there is a concrete replica of the giant press used to make the famous "Cheshire Cheese" sent to Thomas Jefferson in the early 1800s. Continuing along School St., turn left just past the senior citizens center onto a grassy path leading across active farm fields and MA 8 at 9.3 mi.

Appalachian Trail: Dalton to Cheshire

Distances from MA 8–MA 9 (Dalton) (1,174 ft.) to
- Gulf Rd. (1,184 ft.): 1.0 mi., 30 min.
- Gore Pond (2,015 ft.): 5.6 mi., 2 hr. 45 min.
- side trail to North Cobble: 7.6 mi., 3 hr. 45 min.
- Furnace Hill Rd. (1,050 ft.): 8.4 mi., 4 hr. 15 min.
- MA 8 (Cheshire) (1,010 ft.): 9.3 mi., 4 hr. 30 min.

Section 9. Cheshire to MA 2 (North Adams) (12.5 mi.)

This section traverses the Mt. Greylock Reservation and the summits of the two highest mountains in Massachusetts. There is significant elevation gain and loss. Weather on the summits can be significantly more severe than weather in the valleys. Be prepared with proper clothing, footwear, and plenty of water. Bascom Lodge on the summit of Mt. Greylock was closed at press time. Day parking at the summit is available for a $2 fee. *(Note: The reservation auto roads were closed for construction in 2007 but are scheduled to reopen in spring 2009. Contact the Mt. Greylock State Reservation at 413-499-4263 for updates.)*

From a small parking area on MA 8, the trail ascends to open fields with views of Cheshire. It soon enters the woods and at 0.6 mi. crosses a stile over barbed wire into an active pasture. At 0.8 mi. Outlook Ave. is crossed just north of the interesting rock formation called Reynolds Rock. Another stile crosses the fence adjacent to Outlook Ave. (no parking available). The AT enters a field beside a stone wall and follows hedgerows and fence lines into the woods. Crossing a muddy area, the trail begins to ascend, soon crossing a power line. Climbing steeply along the north side of the Kitchen Brook ravine, the path offers occasional views down into the ravine. The trail now turns away from the brook and travels through mixed woods often on a rocky surface. At 3.3 mi. the trail crosses unpaved Old Adams Rd. in a grove of red spruce.

Leaving the spruce grove, the trail weaves between some huge boulders and arrives at the bottom of a steep, short pitch of stone steps. At the top of the steps a short side trail offers a view back down Kitchen Brook ravine. Use caution, as the ground is steeply sloped. At 4.1 mi. a blue-blazed side trail leads 0.2 mi. right to Mark Noepel Shelter, where water, tent sites, and an outhouse are available.

From the shelter the AT gradually ascends through a beech forest and passes another short side trail to a small viewpoint on the right. At 5.0 mi. the AT meets the blue-blazed Jones Nose Trail, where the path enters the cool balsam forest that caps the ridges of Saddle Ball Mtn. The Jones Nose Trail leads 1 mi. down the south side of Saddle Ball Mtn. to the Jones Nose day-use parking area on Rockwell Rd. Some excellent southerly views are 0.3 mi. down the Jones Nose Trail. The AT then turns right, bypassing a balsam swamp, and comes to a small view to the east from a knoll on Saddle Ball Ridge. Continuing to traverse the ridge through dense balsam and spruce, the trail passes over beautiful, undulating terrain. Leaving Saddle Ball Ridge, the AT descends toward the topmost hairpin curve on Rockwell Rd., the southern access road up Mt. Greylock. From here is a fine view of the Mt. Greylock summit on the right.

At 6.7 mi. the AT crosses Rockwell Rd. and intersects two side trails, the blue-blazed Cheshire Harbor Trail that leads 6 mi. east (right) to Adams, and the Hopper Trail (also blue-blazed) that leads 1.1 mi. west (left) to a campground and then continues down the mountain to Hopper Rd. in Williamstown. The trail joins the Hopper Trail and climbs easily past a small pond to the junction of Notch Rd., Summit Rd., and Rockwell Rd. The Gould Trail leaves this intersection to the east and descends steeply for 1.0 mi. to Peck's Brook Shelter and Falls. The AT crosses the intersection and climbs over ledge and stunted conifers toward the summit, emerging into the open in a parking lot by a communications tower (restrooms on the right here), then proceeds to the open summit area. A bronze model of the Greylock Range is passed as the trail approaches the War Memorial Tower on the crest of the summit. The summit of Mt. Greylock (3,491 ft.) is the highest point in Massachusetts. Bascom Lodge, also on the summit, was closed at press time. During winter there are no services at the summit.

Continuing north from the tower, the trail skirts the far end of the parking area and passes a winter ski shelter before dropping sharply and crossing Summit Rd. The AT levels off as it begins to trace the ridgeline. The blue-blazed Robinson's Point Trail leaves left, crossing Notch Rd. and descending about 0.75 mi. to a spectacular western view of the Hopper. Immediately after the Robinson's Point junction, two other side trails go off to the east (right). The first side trail is the blue-blazed Thunderbolt Trail, once used for Olympic training in the 1930s. The second path is the blue-blazed Bellows Pipe Trail that leads steeply down about 1 mi. to Bellows Pipe Shelter. The AT passes an outcrop of milky quartz, coming to the tree-covered top of Mt. Fitch (3,110 ft.). Along the way a few short side trails offer views of the Bellows Pipe and Ragged Mtn.

Descending from Mt. Fitch, a four-way intersection is reached at 9.0 mi. To the right (east) the blue-blazed Bernard Farm Trail descends about 3 mi. to Notch Rd. To the west (left) the blue-blazed Old Summit Rd. Trail bypasses the Mt. Williams summit and rejoins the AT near Notch Rd. After the junction the AT climbs briefly and reaches the register box on top of Mt. Williams (2,951 ft.) at 9.4 mi. Turning sharp left, the trail descends via switchbacks, passing over a badly eroded surface to meet Notch Rd at 9.9 mi. Just before reaching Notch Rd. a side trail leaves left to a day-use parking area and kiosk. From Notch Rd., the parking area is about 200 yd. down the road to the left (south).

The AT passes through spruce forest and bears right as the blue-blazed Money Brook Trail bears left (0.3 mi. to Wilbur Clearing Shelter: tent platforms, privy, and water supply). The Money Brook Trail continues down to the Hopper Rd. trailhead and the beginning of the Hopper Trail. Leaving the red spruce grove, the AT ascends steeply over ledge to a spectacular view of Williamstown, the Taconic Range, and the southern Green Mtns. The blue-blazed Mt. Prospect Trail leaves south for 2.0 mi. to its junction with the Money Brook Trail in the Hopper.

The AT turns sharp right at the overlook and descends very steeply at times through a northern hardwood forest. The slope moderates as the trail leaves Mt. Greylock Reservation and crosses a logging road. There is a police firing range to the left of the trail, and although gunfire may be heard, there is no danger to hikers. After passing through a spruce plantation and over a bridge, the trail reaches Pattison Rd. at 11.7 mi. Parking is available for three to four cars but is recommended for day use only. The trail descends through the woods past the North Adams Water Treatment Plant to the Phelps Ave. extension. It then goes left downhill, crosses Catherine St., and continues along sidewalks on Phelps Ave. until it reaches MA 2 at 12.5 mi. Long-term and overnight parking is available at the Greylock Community Club approx. 0.1 mi. east (right) of the trail crossing. Park near the AT signboard behind the building. A small donation is requested.

Appalachian Trail: Cheshire to MA 2 (North Adams) (map 1: G5–A4)

Distances from MA 8 (Cheshire) (1,010 ft.) to
- Outlook Ave. (1,381 ft.): 0.8 mi., 350 ft., 30 min.
- Old Adams Rd. (2,378 ft.): 3.3 mi., 1,350 ft., 2 hr.
- side trail to Mark Noepel Shelter and outhouse (2,800 ft.): 4.1 mi., 1,850 ft., 3 hr.
- Saddle Ball Mtn. and side trail to Jones Nose (3,257 ft.): 4.6 mi., 2,300 ft., 3 hr. 15 min.
- Notch Rd.–Rockwell Rd. junction (3,200 ft.): 6.7 mi., 2,550 ft. (rev. 250 ft.), 4 hr. 15 min.
- summit of Mt. Greylock (3,491 ft.): 7.1 mi., 2,850 ft., 4 hr. 30 min.
- summit of Mt. Williams (2,951 ft.): 9.4 mi., 3,150 ft. (rev. 850 ft.), 5 hr. 30 min.
- Notch Rd. (2,348 ft.): 9.9 mi., 3,150 ft. (rev. 600 ft.), 6 hr.
- Mt. Prospect Trail (2,500 ft.): 10.3 mi., 3,350 ft. (rev 50 ft.), 6 hr. 30 min.
- Pattison Rd. (1,030 ft.): 11.7 mi., 3,350 ft. (rev. 1,450 ft.), 7 hr. 30 min.
- MA 2 (North Adams) (643 ft.): 12.5 mi. (rev. 400 ft.), 3,350 ft., 8 hr.

Section 10. MA 2 (North Adams) to the Massachusetts–Vermont Line (3.5 mi.)

North Adams offers gas stations and fast-food outlets just 0.7 mi. east of the MA 2 trailhead; all-night supermarkets are located 0.7 mi. east and west of the trailhead.

On the north side of MA 2, by the traffic light, a steel-and-concrete footbridge passes over the B&M Railroad and the Hoosic River to Massachusetts Ave., where the trail turns right (east). Just before Sherman Brook goes under Massachusetts Ave. through a stone culvert, the trail departs the paved road and turns north (left) up a driveway along the west side of Sherman Brook, following it for 50 yd. Please respect the private property of trail abutters in this area. At 0.4 mi. the trail enters the woods at the end of the driveway, passes over two well-built footbridges, then runs along an old spillway from the city of North Adams' waterworks. A high-voltage power line crosses the trail at 0.6 mi.

The trail climbs steadily through separate hemlock groves for the next 0.4 mi., then zigzags left then quickly right on and off a logging road. At 1.2 mi. Pete's Spring is reached and a blue-blazed side trail leads left to Sherman Brook Campsite, with tent platforms and an outhouse. The campsite access trail rejoins the AT about 0.25 mi. farther along as the AT ascends a long, gradual ridge covered with patches of laurel. The trail turns sharp toward the west and travels on an old roadbed until it heads steeply uphill through a rockfall of granite, marble, and quartz. A blue-blazed bad-weather bypass trail branches off on the left just before the rockfall and rejoins the AT at the top of the cliff.

After climbing the rockfall and a couple of steep, narrow switchbacks, the trail tops an eastern-facing bluff overlooking the Hoosac Range. On a wide section of East Mtn. ridge, the trail passes around the north side of a fragile mossy pond and arrives at an area of quartzite cobbles. A short distance across the cobbles at 2.2 mi. is the intersection of the Pine Cobble Trail (blue blazes). The Pine Cobble Trail descends 0.5 mi. to an overlook of Williamstown to the west and North Adams to the east. Mt. Prospect and Mt. Williams dominate the horizon directly south. Turning right just before the overlook, the Pine Cobble Trail descends somewhat steeply at times 2.1 mi. to Cole Ave. in Williamstown. Limited parking is available at the trailhead.

Turning right at the junction with the Pine Cobble Trail, the AT goes up through azalea, sheep laurel, and pink lady's slipper. Out of the woods again, the trail passes the Class of '98 Trail, which descends to join the Pine Cobble Trail farther down the mountain. The AT comes to the overgrown

Eph's Lookout at approximately 2.7 mi. Off the trail to the east about 0.3 mi. is Bear Swamp Brook in Clarksburg State Forest. The AT rises sharply, then travels partly on an old woods road to the Massachusetts–Vermont line and the Long Trail register at 4.1 mi. The next trail junction is with the Broad Brook Trail, which makes several crossings of the brook, some of which may be difficult in spring. Go left on County Rd. (dirt) for approx. 0.25 mi. to blue blazes leading left 4.1 mi. back to White Oaks Rd. in Williamstown. County Rd. is just before the Seth Warner Shelter at 2.8 mi.

This is the end of the Massachusetts section. The trail continues into Vermont, where it is maintained by the Green Mountain Club. (See the *Guide to the Appalachian Trail in New Hampshire and Vermont*, published by the Appalachian Trail Conference.)

Appalachian Trail: MA 2 (North Adams) to the Massachusetts–Vermont Line (map 1: B4–A4)

Distances from MA 2 (North Adams) (643 ft.) to
- Sherman Brook Campsite (1,400 ft.): 1.2 mi., 750 ft., 50 min.
- Pine Cobble Trail (2,100 ft.): 2.2 mi., 1,450 ft.,1 hr. 35 min.
- Eph's Lookout (2,200 ft.): 2.7 mi., 1,550 ft., 1 hr. 50 min,
- Massachusetts–Vermont line (2,300 ft.): 3.5 mi., 1,650 ft., 2 hr. 5 min.

Jug End Reservation

Jug End Reservation and Wildlife Management Area covers 1,158 acres in Egremont. It is a joint acquisition of the Massachusetts Department of Conservation and Recreation and the Massachusetts Department of Fisheries and Wildlife. The reservation is on the site of an old resort; the foundations and landscaping are still present around the trailhead on Jug End Rd. The trail that leaves from the parking area on Jug End Rd. is 2.0 mi. long, forming an elongated north-south loop that explores the Fenton Brook ravine sandwiched between Mt. Bushnell (1,834 ft.) to the east and Mt. Darby (2,030 ft.) to the west.

To reach Jug End Reservation from MA 23 in Egremont, turn onto MA 41 south, skirt Mill Pond on the right, then turn immediately right (west) onto Mt. Washington Rd. Travel west 1.7 mi. and turn left (south) onto Jug End Rd. Drive past the brown Jug End sign at about 0.3 mi., cross Fenton Brook, and turn right into the parking area 0.8 mi. from Mt. Washington Rd.

Jug End Loop Trail (DCR)

At the south end of the parking area is a kiosk. The trail (marked by DCR brown trail stakes) leaves from the eastern end of the parking lot, passing through an overgrown field and into the woods. The trail continues south and ascends the lower slopes of Jug End, keeping roughly parallel to Fenton Brook. At about 1 mi. the path bends west and descends to the brook. Crossing the brook, the trail now swings north along the western bank of Fenton Brook Ravine. The trail then begins to closely parallel the brook at 1.6 mi. for about 0.2 mi. before crossing the stream and returning to the parking area.

Jug End Loop Trail (map 2: B3)
Distance from parking area (870 ft.) to
• parking area (circuit): 2.0 mi., 350 ft., 55 min.

Mt. Everett State Reservation

To reach Mt. Everett State Reservation, from the intersection of MA 23 and 41 in South Egremont follow MA 41 south 0.2 mi. Turn right onto Mt. Washington Rd. (this becomes East St.) and travel 7.4 mi. to the reservation entrance on the left. The auto access road from the parking facility on East St. in Mt. Washington to Guilder Pond and other areas of the mountain was closed in 2001 for repair, but is now open to the picnic area during summer months for day use only.

Mt. Everett (2,602 ft.) is the highest mountain in the southern Berkshires but has earned rank and status for much more than its height. The mountain, as well as many other areas along the south Taconic Ridge, is home to uncommon and fragile ecosystems. Along the ridge, traversed by the Appalachian Trail, are pitch pine and scrub oak plant communities that harbor old-growth forests sheltering rare plant and animal species. In spring 2003 the fire tower was removed from the summit, restoring the mountain's natural profile. From the rounded, breezy summit, distant peaks are visible, from Mt. Race and Bear Mtn. to the south to the rugged Catskills to the west.

Guilder Pond Trail (DCR)

On the north shoulder of Mt. Everett is picturesque Guilder Pond (2,042 ft.) surrounded by mountain laurel and hemlock. The blue-blazed Guilder Pond Trail traces a course around the western, northern, and eastern shores of this scenic mountain pond, joining the AT briefly before ending at a picnic area near the south side of the pond. From the southern trailhead on the auto access road, the path crosses the outlet to the pond on a wooden bridge and enters a hemlock grove. It then wanders through thick laurel that blooms in June. Winding around the sometimes wet northern shore, the path goes through brushy spots and joins the AT near a picnic area and privy.

Guilder Pond Trail (map 2: C3)

Distances from East St. parking area (1,700 ft.) to
- southern trailhead along access road (2,042 ft.): 0.8 mi., 350 ft., 30 min.
- AT junction (2,140 ft.): 1.5 mi., 450 ft., 50 min.
- Mt. Everett summit via AT (2,602 ft.): 2.2 mi., 1 hr. 20 min.

Elbow Trail (Berkshire School)

From the intersection of MA 23 and 41 in South Egremont, travel south on MA 41 for 3.5 mi. Turn right onto the paved entry road to Berkshire School and travel west along the road through the school's broad lawn. Take the first right, then turn left and pass between Memorial Hall on the left and Stanley Hall on the right. Bear right, traveling uphill past a house and onto a dirt road (200 yd.). Park behind the gymnasium.

From the parking area the blue-blazed Elbow Trail makes an initially steep ascent up the eastern flank of Mt. Everett. Soon the grade of the well-worn path moderates and the trail becomes a moderately easy hike up the forested mountain. A small brook is crossed on rocks before reaching the junction with the white-blazed AT at 1.5 mi. From the AT junction the summit of Mt. Everett can be reached by following the AT approximately 1.8 mi. south, while the summit of Mt. Bushnell (1,834 ft.) is about 0.5 mi. north on the AT.

Elbow Trail (Berkshire School) (map 2: C3)

Distances from Berkshire School parking area (860 ft.) to
- AT junction (1,750 ft.): 1.5 mi., 900 ft., 1 hr.
- summit of Mt. Everett (via AT) (2,602 ft.): 3.3 mi., 1,750 ft., 2 hr. 45 min.

Appalachian Trail (BCAMC, DCR)

See Section 1, Appalachian Trail, Massachusetts–Connecticut Line to Jug End Rd., on page 3 for a complete description.

Race Brook Falls Trail (BCAMC, DCR)

From the junction of MA 41 and Berkshire School Rd. continue south on MA 41 for 1.4 mi. to a parking area on the right. Traveling north from the Massachusetts–Connecticut state line, the parking area is 2.9 mi. north of the border.

The Race Brook Falls Trail is a rugged, spectacular path that accesses the AT in the saddle between Mt. Race and Mt. Everett. Along the way this blue-blazed trail passes some excellent views as well as the five cataracts that make up Race Brook Falls. From the parking area the path immediately crosses a small stream, skirts a field, and enters hemlock woods. At a junction (signed AT 2 Miles) turn left into thick laurel and reach the brook at 0.4 mi. *Caution: At high water this crossing can be difficult.* The path now begins a steep ascent along Race Brook, passing a side trail to an overlook atop the lower falls at 0.6 mi. The base of another waterfall is reached ⚠ at 0.8 mi. as the trail crosses the brook and continues steeply up the mountain. *Caution: At high water this crossing can be difficult!* The path reaches the ridge crest and easily descends to the brook, which it crosses on a log bridge and follows upstream through flat open woods. After passing many bedrock outcrops, at 1.6 mi. the trail reaches the Race Brook Falls Campsite, with tent platforms and privy. The junction with the white-blazed AT is at 1.9 mi. From here the summit of Mt. Everett is 0.8 mi. north along the AT. To the south 1.1 mi. on the AT is the narrow summit ridge of Mt. Race (2,365 ft.), from which there are fine views.

Race Brook Falls Trail (map 2: C3)

Distances from MA 41 trailhead (740 ft.) to
- first brook crossing (1,100 ft.): 0.4 mi., 350 ft., 15 min.
- second brook crossing (1,400 ft.): 0.8 mi., 650 ft., 45 min.
- Race Brook Falls Campsite (1,800 ft.): 1.6 mi., 1,050 ft., 1 hr. 5 min.
- AT (1,900 ft.): 1.9 mi., 1,150 ft., 1 hr. 30 min.
- summit of Mt. Everett (2,602 ft.): 2.7 mi., 1,850 ft., 2 hr. 15 min.

Mt. Washington State Forest

Mt. Washington State Forest and adjacent Bash Bish Falls State Park protect about 3,300 acres of mountains, valleys, wilderness, and waterfalls in the rugged southwestern corner of the state. Taconic State Park in New York borders this area and adds additional hiking opportunities. Principal summits include Mt. Frissell (2,453 ft.) and Alander Mtn. (2,239 ft.). Just to the east of the state forest are Mt. Ashley (2,390 ft.) and Mt. Plantain (2,088 ft.). Bash Bish Falls, the signature cascade of the Berkshires, is another well-known landmark.

Backcountry camping opportunities are available; it's a 1.5-mi. hike from the park headquarters. Overnight campers must register at the Mt. Washington State Forest headquarters on West St. in Mt. Washington. Reach the area via Mt. Washington Rd., off MA 41 in the village of South Egremont near the junction of MA 23 and MA 41. Mt. Washington Rd. becomes West St. in the town of Mt. Washington and passes the forest headquarters, where trail information is available.

Mt. Frissell Trail (DCR)

Part of the South Taconic Highlands, Mt. Frissell has the unique distinction of hosting the highest point of Connecticut on its southern slope, even though its 2,453-ft. summit is across the state line in Massachusetts. The scenic Mt. Frissell Trail, lying in three states and marked with red-painted blazes, travels over the mountain. It extends 2.2 mi. from Mt. Washington Rd. on the Massachusetts–Connecticut line to the South Taconic Trail.

The trailhead is on East St. in Mt. Washington (on the Massachusetts-Connecticut state line). From the road the red-blazed path briefly heads northwest on a woods road and turns left up a narrow path through dense growth. The path then travels into Connecticut, climbing moderately then steeply up Round Mtn. The trail reaches Round Mtn.'s broad, open summit (2,296 ft.) at 0.7 mi., then descends northwest, reentering Massachusetts and reaching a notch where a side path descends right to a shallow pond (dry in summer). The trail now enters Mt. Washington State Forest and begins to ascend the very steep east face of Mt. Frissell. At 1.2 mi. the trail reaches a stone pile at the summit and a register box maintained by the New Haven Hiking Club.

From the summit the path heads south down the brushy ridge to an overlook, then turns right into dense laurel and a nearly anonymous pile of rock and a survey marker designating the highest point in Connecticut. The trail then continues over rocky terrain to a stone post that marks the tri-state boundary of New York, Massachusetts, and Connecticut. At the time the boundary was set, Connecticut didn't agree with the survey line, and so the marker only has MA and NY chiseled into the stone. The blue-blazed Ashley Hill Trail enters right (1.9 mi.) in a flat spot before the Mt. Frissell Trail scrambles the short distance to its junction with the white-blazed South Taconic Trail at 2.2 mi.

Mt. Frissell Trail (map 2: E2)
Distances from East St. trailhead (1,840 ft.) to
  • summit of Round Mtn. (2,296 ft.): 0.3 mi., 350 ft., 45 min.
  • summit of Mt. Frissell (2,453 ft.): 0.8 mi., 500 ft., 1 hr., 15 min.
  • CT high point (2,400 ft.): 0.9 mi., 500 ft. (rev. 50 ft.), 1 hr. 25 min.
  • tri-state marker (2,150 ft.): 1.4 mi., 500 ft. (rev. 250 ft.) 1 hr. 45 min.
  • Ashley Hill Trail (2,150 ft.) : 1.5 mi., 500 ft., 1 hr. 50 min.
  • South Taconic Trail (2,250 ft.): 1.8 mi., 600 ft., 2 hr. 10 min.

Alander Brook Trail (Taconic State Park, N.Y.)

To reach the trailhead of this strenuous trail, located in the area of Boston Corners in New York's Harlem Valley, take NY 344 to NY 22 in Copake Falls. Follow NY 22 south about 4 mi. to unpaved Undermountain Rd. Drive on this road 0.8 mi. to the blue-blazed Alander Brook Trail, which exits left as a woods road. Park at the trailhead.

The trail goes north past the intersection of the red-blazed Robert Brook Trail, which exits right (east). At 0.8 mi. the trail crosses Alander Brook, turns right, and ascends through mountain laurel. It then turns right again onto another woods road. The trail ascends east and northeast along the deep, hemlock-clad ravine of Alander Brook to where the blue blazes end (this is the end of the Alander Brook Trail) and the white blazes of the South Taconic Trail begin. To ascend Alander Mtn., turn left onto the South Taconic Trail, which climbs steeply north up the mountain to the western summit of Alander Mtn.

Alander Brook Trail (map 2: D1)
Distances from Undermountain Rd. (800 ft.) to
- South Taconic Trail (1,450 ft.): 1.4 mi., 650 ft., 1 hr.
- western summit of Alander Mtn. via STT (2,239 ft.): 2.2 mi., 1,450 ft., 2 hr.

Robert Brook Trail (Taconic State Park, N.Y.)

Follow the Alander Brook Trail from its trailhead north about 150 yd. The strenuous red-blazed Robert Brook Trail, a woods road, turns right and ascends rather steeply along the Robert Brook ravine. The trail reaches an 1898 New York–Massachusetts boundary monument and climbs north as a footpath along the state line to a second such monument. It continues north to the junction with the white-blazed South Taconic Trail, where the Robert Brook Trail ends.

Going left (north) on the South Taconic Trail, proceed to the intersection of the blue-blazed Alander Loop Trail at 0.5 mi. Hikers can continue along the South Taconic Trail another 0.2 mi. to the upper end of the blue-blazed Alander Brook Trail, then follow the white-blazed South Taconic Trail up Alander Mtn. as described in the preceding section. Alternately, ascend the blue-blazed Alander Loop Trail northeast into Massachusetts to a notch at the height-of-land, then follow the trail north along the crest as a narrow path through thick scrub growth, with good views over the highland from open areas, to the eastern summit of Alander Mtn. This has the same elevation as the western summit (2,240 ft.) and has a nice view eastward over the highland in Massachusetts. The Alander Loop Trail continues a short distance west, climbing over a small intervening rise and descending into a final small notch in which a state forest cabin is on the right. It then merges with the Alander Mtn. Trail immediately prior to reaching just north of the summit and old fire tower footings.

Robert Brook Trail (map 2: D1)

Distances from Undermountain Rd. (800 ft.) to
- South Taconic Trail (1,800 ft.): 1.1 mi., 1,000 ft., 1 hr.
- Alander Loop Trail via STT (1,700 ft.): 1.6 mi., 1,000 ft. (rev. 100 ft.), 1 hr. 20 min.
- summit of Alander Mtn. via Alander Loop and Alander Mtn. Trails and STT (2,239 ft.): 2.8 mi., 1,550 ft., 2 hr. 10 min.

Ashley Hill Trail (DCR)

This moderate blue-blazed trail leads to the heart of Mt. Washington State Forest. The trail starts with the Alander Mtn. Trail at the trailhead from the Mt. Washington State Forest parking area on East St. in Mt. Washington, Mass. It leads west across a field and into the forest and soon emerges into another field. The trail descends past a ruined house on the right and crosses Lee Pond Brook on a wooden bridge. The Charcoal Pit Trail, a short blue-blazed connector trail that rejoins the Ashley Hill Trail, leaves left at 0.6 mi. Following a woods road for about 0.3 mi., the Ashley Hill Trail branches left at the intersection with the blue-blazed Alander Mtn. Trail. The Ashley Hill Trail ascends gradually along a woods road and always keeps Ashley Hill Brook to the right, never crossing the brook.

After about 2.5 mi. of easy climbing, the Ashley Hill Trail exits the woods road on the left and continues as a less well-defined trail uphill at a slightly steeper grade. (A blue-blazed connector trail continues straight through this intersection, crosses Ashley Hill Brook, and ascends on a less well-defined path for about 1 mi. to intersect with the white-blazed South Taconic Trail.) The Ashley Hill Trail is well marked and generally follows another woods road to the Massachusetts–New York line, where it intersects and ends at the red-blazed Mt. Frissell Trail (see the description of the Mt. Frissell Trail from the west). Straight ahead the path continues onto private land.

Ashley Hill Trail (map 2: D2–E2)

Distances from Mt. Washington State Forest parking area (East St.) (1,660 ft.) to
- loop trail (1,850 ft.): 2.5 mi., 350 ft. (rev. 150 ft.), 1 hr. 30 min.
- Mt. Frissell Trail (2,150 ft.): 3.9 mi., 650 ft., 2 hr. 10 min.

Alander Mtn. Trail (DCR)

Alander Mtn. (2,239 ft.), with its twin summits, stands on the western escarpment of the Southern Taconic Highland. The blue-blazed trail starts in conjunction with the Ashley Hill Trail at the Mt. Washington State Forest parking area on the western side of East St. in the town of Mt. Washington, Mass. The trail proceeds west across a field and then through the woods. It descends through another field, crosses a brook by a vacant house (do not turn left on the woods road before the brook), and at 0.6 mi. intersects the blue-blazed Charcoal Pit Trail, which branches left. At 0.8 mi. the blue-blazed Ashley Hill Trail forks left. The Alander Mtn. Trail forks right, first descending to cross Ashley Hill Brook and then climbing westward. At 1.5 mi. a side trail ascends left to a primitive camping area of the state forest. The main trail continues west and southwest, ascending as it narrows, and reaches a state forest cabin in a small notch just below the summit of Alander Mtn. The cabin has wooden bunks and a wood stove, and backpackers can stay here overnight at no charge on a first-come, first-served basis. The nearest water supply is back down the Alander Mtn. Trail about 400 yd. A few yards beyond the cabin the blue-blazed Alander Loop Trail enters left. The Alander Mtn. Trail quickly joins the white-blazed South Taconic Trail a short distance north of the summit and old fire tower footings.

Alander Mtn. Trail (map 2: D2)

Distances from Mt. Washington State Forest parking area (East St.) (1,660 ft.) to
- side trail to primitive camping area (1,650 ft.): 1.3 mi., 150 ft. (rev. 150 ft.), 45 min.
- western summit of Alander Mtn. (2,239 ft.): 2.5 mi., 750 ft., 1 hr. 35 min.

Alander Loop Trail (DCR)

This short, 0.9-mi.-long, blue-blazed trail functions as a bypass of the South Taconic Trail on Alander Mtn. and provides a faster means of ascent from the south than following the South Taconic Trail exclusively. The south trailhead is 0.5 mi. north of the junction of the Robert Brook Trail at an elevation of about 1,700 ft. It climbs moderately up a swale before angling northwest through thick scrub. The trail joins the Alander Mtn. Trail about 200 ft. before the intersection with the South Taconic Trail just north of the summit and old fire tower footings.

Alander Loop Trail (map 2: D1)
Distance from south trailhead (1,700 ft.) to
  • junction with South Taconic Trail (2,300 ft.): 0.9 mi., 600 ft., 40 min.

Bash Bish Falls State Park

The centerpiece for this 200-acre state park is the magnificent gorge and waterfall created by Bash Bish Brook. The clear waters of the stream tumble down almost 150 vertical ft. through a dizzying chasm of cliffs with whitewater cascades on the canyon floor. The gorge abruptly ends at a waterfall where the waters drop from an 80-ft.-tall cliff in an unforgettable waterfall into the pool below. The falls have long been known as a signature landmark of the Berkshires.

Bash Bish Falls State Park is within Mt. Washington State Forest, a preserve of 4,169 acres offering 30 mi. of trails and wilderness camping experiences. Trails along the rim of the gorge offer spectacular views, but the gorge itself is a restricted area and entrance is not permitted. Swimming in the pool beneath the falls and rock climbing are also not permitted. Leashed pets are allowed. To reach the park, from the intersection of MA 41 and MA 23 turn onto MA 41 South and travel 0.2 mi. to Mt. Washington Rd. Turn right (west) onto Mt. Washington Rd. and proceed 7.7 mi. to Cross Rd. (Mt. Washington Rd. becomes East St. upon entering Mt. Washington). Turn right onto Cross Rd. and follow Cross Rd. then West St. a total of 3.2 mi. to the Upper Bash Bish Falls parking area on the left.

Bash Bish Gorge Trail (DCR)

This short but rugged blue-blazed trail begins at the gate at the south end of the parking area on Falls Rd. in Mt. Washington. The trail descends easily along a gravel road, then follows Bash Bish Brook the short distance to the mouth of the gorge and crosses the brook. *Caution: This crossing can be dangerous. Cross as far upstream of the gorge as possible. Avoid crossing when current is strong!* The trail climbs extremely steeply along the metal fence to an overlook above the gorge. It then heads away from the gorge, climbing steeply through hemlocks to the junction with the white-blazed South Taconic Trail (STT) at 0.6 mi. From here Alander Mtn. is about a 2.2-mi.-long hike southbound (left and uphill). A loop hike back to the upper parking area can be made by turning northbound (right and down-hill) and descending to the parking area on NY 344. Walk the gravel road back into Massachusetts and the Bash Bish Falls parking area, then con-tinue up the wide gravel road to the falls viewing area. The Bash Bish Falls Trail leaves from the grassy area near the viewing area and climbs to the upper lot. Total mileage for loop is 2.6 mi.

Bash Bish Gorge Trail (map 2: C1)
Distances from Bash Bish Falls upper lot (1,244 ft.) to
 • junction with South Taconic Trail (1,675 ft.): 0.6 mi., 45 min.
 • summit of Alander Mtn. via STT (2,239 ft.): 2.8 mi., 3 hr.

Bash Bish Falls Trail (DCR)

To reach the trailhead, follow the directions to the Bash Bish Gorge Trail. The blue-blazed Bash Bish Falls Trail leaves the parking area near the north side of the paved lot (signed), descending in a serpentine pattern steeply down the ravine. The path passes numerous boulders and ferns, emerging from the woods a few yards from the viewing area for Bash Bish Falls.

Bash Bish Falls Trail (map 2: C1)
Distances from Bash Bish Falls upper lot (1,244 ft.) to
 • falls viewing area (900 ft.): 0.3 mi., 20 min.

South Taconic Trail (BCAMC, DCR, TSP)

The white-blazed South Taconic Trail (STT) runs 15.7 mi. in a north-south direction along the western escarpment of the South Taconic Mtns., a range that roughly follows the border of New York and Massachusetts in the southern Berkshires. The trail traverses portions of Taconic State Park (N.Y.), Mt. Washington State Forest (Mass.), and Bash Bish Falls State Park (Mass.). The nearby Appalachian Trail (AT) runs atop the eastern range of the southern Taconics about 4 mi. away.

The STT runs the western ridge of the southern Taconics, an area that is distinctly more remote and lesser known than its twin range to the east (traversed by the AT) but arguably has a greater abundance of spectacular views. The STT is especially scenic because it runs over large areas of open ridges and summits, such as South Brace Mtn., Brace Mtn., and the nearly 0.8 mi. of almost continuous open ridge on Alander Mtn. The views over New York's Harlem Valley and on to the Catskills are stunning and unobstructed. A public campground accessed by the STT is located in Taconic State Park (N.Y.) at the Copake Falls Campground, very near the lower Bash Bish Falls parking area on NY 344.

The trail's southern trailhead is at Rudd Pond Farms off Rudd Pond Rd. just north of Millerton in New York's Harlem Valley. The northern end is at the Catamount Ski Area on MA 23 in Egremont, Mass., just east of the New York–Massachusetts line. Thru-hikers can traverse the trail in a weekend using the state forest cabin at Alander Mtn. as an overnight stop. The cabin is located at about the halfway point, can accommodate 12 persons, and is open free of charge on a first-come, first-served, basis.

Section 1. Rudd Pond Farms to NY 344 (8.9 mi.)

To reach the southern end of the trail, drive 5.5 mi. north on NY 22 from the traffic light at Millerton. Take a right onto White House Crossing Rd. and follow it to the end. Turn left onto Rudd Pond Rd. for 0.3 mi., then right (east) onto Deer Run Rd.; this road enters Rudd Pond Farms, a residential development. Take a left onto Quarry Hill Rd. and follow it about 0.5 mi. as it loops around to the eastern side of the development, where there is a small parking area at the edge of the woods. Look for the Taconic State Park sign about 75 ft. east of the road.

From the parking area at an elevation of 950 ft., the South Taconic Trail (STT) travels east along the edge of field, enters the woods, and starts to ascend the western escarpment of the Southern Taconic Highland. A steep, rough section begins at 0.4 mi. where the trail parallels a brook, passing a high waterfall. The grade is eased a little by switchbacks that offer repeated open views to the west over the Harlem Valley. At about 0.8 mi. a red-blazed side trail leads south (right) 0.3 mi. to an overlook. Here the STT turns sharp left (north).

The STT proceeds north along the escarpment, with more views to the west, traversing the flank of South Brace Mtn. and staying west of the summit. The path climbs steeply and reaches an open area with an excellent southerly view into Connecticut of the Riga Plateau and Riga Lake. The trail passes west of the summit of South Brace Mtn. (2,304 ft.) and descends moderately to the saddle between South Brace and Brace Mtns., then ascends the attractive open ridge of Brace Mtn. to its summit (2,311 ft.) at 1.9 mi. The summit (the STT's highest point) is a grassy bald marked by a loose cairn of stones with wonderful views of Bear Mtn. to the east and Mt. Frissell to the northeast.

The trail continues north, descending the mountain on a wide, easy path to the plateau. Here, at 2.2 mi., the trail reaches the junction with a side trail (right) that enters from private land. About 200 yd. farther along the ridge, the trail junction (signed) with the Mt. Frissell Trail is reached. The red-blazed Mt. Frissell Trail leaves right (east) into thick, wind-stunted woods.

The STT proceeds from the Mt. Frissell Trail junction along an open crest with fine views and enters Mt. Washington State Forest (Massachusetts) at 2.3 mi. The trail widens into a woods road and at 3.1 mi. a blue-blazed side trail proceeds right (northeast) about 1.0 mi. and connects to the Ashley Hill Trail. The trail proceeds moderately over undulating terrain, reentering New York just before reaching the junction with the Robert Brook Trail at 4.5 mi. (The red-blazed Robert Brook Trail exits left and steeply descends the ravine of Robert Brook in New York. In 1.1 mi. it reaches the Alander Brook Trail near Undermountain Rd. off NY 22.)

The STT continues north, reenters Massachusetts, and reaches the Alander Loop Trail at 5.0 mi. The STT curves left while the Alander Loop Trail forks right. (This blue-blazed trail, more than 1 mi. long with fine views, climbs roughly north up to and along the height-of-land to the eastern summit of Alander Mtn., at 2,239 ft. It then leads a short distance west over an intervening knob, through a notch, and past the state forest cabin to meet the Alander Mtn. Trail a short distance from the summit. Continue to the summit by turning left onto the Alander Mtn. Trail.) The Alander Loop Trail is a quicker route to Alander Mtn. and the cabin. From the junction with the Alander Loop Trail, the South Taconic Trail descends into New York from Massachusetts, crosses a bridge over Alander Brook, and 60 yd. beyond, at 5.2 mi., climbs steeply right. (The blue-blazed 1.5-mi.-long Alander Brook Trail continues straight ahead on a woods road, descending south along the ravine of Alander Brook and making left turns at junctions, crossing Alander Brook, and proceeding on level terrain to Undermountain Rd. in Harlem Valley, N.Y.)

The STT now climbs gradually, then steeply up the southwestern shoulder of Alander Mtn., reaching an open crest at 5.7 mi. The trail then reenters Massachusetts at a boundary marker and goes northeast, ascending along the open shoulder with fine views. The trail reaches the western summit of Alander Mtn. (2,239 ft.) at 6.0 mi., where the foundation of a former fire tower is located. On the summit a nest of signs to the west of the tower footings provides distances to locations along the trail. Just north of the summit the Alander Mtn. Trail enters right (east). The Alander Mtn. Trail descends to a small notch, where it goes straight ahead to the state forest cabin. The Alander Loop Trail goes first east, then south, eventually to rejoin the STT.

The STT goes north, descending gradually along the remainder of Alander's open crest, a splendidly scenic section. To the east is Mt. Everett (2,602 ft.), the dominant feature on the eastern escarpment. At 6.4 mi. the trail descends into woods and continues north along the ridge. At 6.8 mi. there is a view of a beautiful secluded valley to the west, with Mt. Washburn beyond. After passing through a beautiful woodland savanna of oaks and grasses the trail reaches a lookout on the northern shoulder of Bash Bish Mtn. at 7.9 mi. It then makes a quick descent to the junction of the blue-blazed Bash Bish Gorge Trail, which leaves right from a small, level terrace.

The STT turns left (south) and soon reenters New York, where a short spur trail continues west to a rock outcrop with beautiful views down the valley of Bash Bish Brook and beyond to the village of Copake Falls, N.Y. The path weaves through rock outcrops and open woods, descending to the unpaved road of Taconic State Park along a brook and shower house on the right. The trail turns left off the road, crosses a bridge over Bash Bish Brook, and comes out near the lower Bash Bish parking area on the right. Here the northern section of the South Taconic Trail begins.

South Taconic Trail: Southern Section (Rudd Pond Farms to NY 344) (map 2: E2–C1)

Distances from Rudd Pond Farms (950 ft.) to

- summit of South Brace Mtn. (2,304 ft.): 0.6 mi., 1,350 ft., 1 hr. 15 min.
- summit of Brace Mtn. (2,311 ft.): 1.9 mi., 1,350 ft., 1 hr. 30 min.
- Mt. Frissell Trail (2,200 ft.): 2.1 mi., 1,350 ft. (rev. 100 ft.), 1 hr. 50 min.
- Ashley Hill Trail connector (2,050 ft.): 2.9 mi., 1,350 ft. (rev. 150 ft.), 2 hr. 20 min.
- Robert Brook Trail (1,800 ft.): 4.4 mi., 1,350 ft. (rev. 250 ft.), 3 hr. 15 min.
- Alander Loop Trail (1,700 ft.): 4.9 mi., 1,350 ft. (rev. 100 ft.), 3 hr. 30 min.
- Alander Brook Trail (1,450 ft.): 5.1 mi., 1,350 ft. (rev. 250 ft.), 3 hr. 45 min.
- western summit of Alander Mtn. and cabin (2,239 ft.): 5.9 mi., 2,150 ft., 4 hr. 30 min.
- Bash Bish Gorge Trail (1,675 ft.): 7.9 mi., 2,150 ft. (rev. 550 ft.), 6 hr. 15 min.
- lower Bash Bish parking area (746 ft.): 8.9 mi., 2,150 ft. (rev. 900 ft.), 7 hr. 30 min.

Section 2. NY 344 to MA 23 (5.6 mi.)

From the entrance to the lower Bash Bish parking area on NY 344 (about 1.2 mi. east of NY 22), the STT angles west proceeding up the western ridge of Cedar Brook Ravine, while Cedar Brook Trail heads straight ahead generally following the brook. For about the next mile the trail climbs steeply and steadily up Cedar Mtn. passing the Blue and Yellow Trails on the left along the way.

After passing the Yellow Trail, the STT coincides with Sunset Rock Trail and the climb relaxes as the path slabs the ridge. At 1.4 mi. the Cedar Brook Trail enters right (south) and the path ascends moderately to an open shelf at 1.8 mi. A short red-blazed spur trail leads from here west to Sunset Rock (1,788 ft.) with wonderful views to the west.

The STT continues northeast on a wide path through thick scrub growth. Here it has yellow state-park markers in addition to its white blazes. At 2.1 mi. the trail forks from the STT, turning sharp left off the wide path, soon reaching Sunset Rock Rd. (unpaved, seasonal) just west of the Massachusetts–New York line. The right fork is a dead-end path that heads a short distance east to Sunset Rock Rd. near the Massachusetts side of the state line. (This unpaved road runs eastward into Mt. Washington, Mass., as part of West St., and westward it descends steeply into North Mountain Rd. in Harlem Valley, N.Y.)

The trail crosses the dirt road and at 2.4 mi. turns right onto a foot-path that crosses a brook by an old springhouse. It climbs Prospect Hill northeast through dense scrub oak and mountain laurel and at 2.7 mi. reaches the open summit area (1,919 ft.), with good views. It turns left at the Massachusetts–New York boundary monument and reaches an open ledge with outstanding views north, west, and south; the views of Harlem Valley and the town of Hillsdale, N.Y., are especially lovely.

As the trail descends Prospect Hill it reenters Massachusetts and reaches a good northerly view at 3.0 mi., while it follows the north shoulder. Bending back into New York, it reaches an open area at 3.7 mi. along the edge of an escarpment, with pleasant views of a valley to the southwest. The trail continues to Mt. Fray and parallels its crest, turning right at 4.1 mi. and climbing the short distance to the crest, with a fine view from the open ridge. The trail then goes north along the broad summit area of Mt. Fray (1,900 ft.), where open areas in the scrub growth offer distant views, as far as Mt. Greylock about 50 mi. to the northeast. The STT now enters the privately held property of the Catamount Ski Area.

At 4.3 mi. the trail turns right onto Ridge Run, the first ski trail en-countered, which descends east along the ridge just below and to the right of the ski lift apparatus on the summit. (A short distance to the left, or west, is an area with splendid views, including the two upper chairlift ter-minals of the ski area.) The trail follows Ridge Run east (downhill) for 1.0 mi., reentering Massachusetts. Near the end it climbs right a few yards to a pleasant view of Jug End valley and ridge. At the end of Ridge Run, at the top of the ski slope, is a view of the ski area.

The trail then climbs steeply east for a short stretch and continues along a wooded crest, turning north and descending. It enters a driveway at 5.7 mi., follows it downhill, then follows a dirt road coming in from the left, and finally turns left for 65 yd. to reach MA 23, where it crosses the height-of-land and ends. This is the northern terminus of the South Taconic Trail at 6.0 mi. (15.7 mi. from its southern end). (*Note: If the trail is lost at this point, simply follow any ski run down to the base lodge. MA 23 is a short distance away on the ski area access road.*)

A parking area is located on the south side of MA 23; 150 yd. to the left (west) of MA 23 is Hillsdale, N.Y. and to the east is South Egremont, Mass. Overnight and day parking is allowed in the ski area parking lot. Hikers should ask permission at the ski area office to park. Be advised that the parking lot is locked at dusk and vehicles not removed by then must remain overnight.

South Taconic Trail: Northern Section (NY 344 to MA 23) (map 2: C1–A2)

Distances from NY 344 (766 ft.) to
- Cedar Brook Trail (1,400 ft.): 1.4 mi., 650 ft., 1 hr.
- Sunset Rock (1,750 ft.): 1.8 mi., 1,000 ft., 1 hr. 15 min.
- Sunset Rock Rd. (1,700 ft.): 2.1 mi., 1,000 ft. (rev. 50 ft.), 1 hr. 25 min.
- summit of Prospect Hill (1,919 ft.): 2.4 mi., 1,200 ft., 1 hr. 45 min.
- summit of Mt. Fray (1,900 ft.): 3.7 mi., 1,500 ft. (rev. 300 ft.), 2 hr. 30 min.
- MA 23 (1,050 ft.): 5.6 mi., 1,500 ft. (rev. 850 ft.), 3 hr. 45 min.

Yokun Ridge

Yokun Ridge is the name for a section of the central Taconic Range that broadly includes West Stockbridge Mtn. and Lenox Mtn. The ridge is a mix of private and public lands with some excellent public access trails. The primary protective agency for the area is the Berkshires Natural Resources Council (BNRC). The trails constructed and maintained by BNRC have a reputation for being environmentally responsible, well maintained, and logical. The ridge owes its name to a Hudson River Mohican named Jehoiakim Yokun, who owned much of this land around 1740.

Walsh Trail Loop (BNRC)

This short, mostly flat path follows the crest of a portion of Lenox Mtn. high above Stockbridge Bowl. The ridge has many overlooks that peer east, south, and west, depending on where hikers are on the route. It is one of those rare mountaintop hikes that doesn't require climbing the mountain, making this easy hike a nice choice for those not able to manage more difficult trips.

To reach the trailhead from Lenox follow MA 183 south 1.6 mi. to Richmond-Lenox Rd. (just past Tanglewood). Travel up Richmond-Lenox Rd. 1.4 mi. to a gated parking area (Olivia's Overlook) on the left.

From the parking area at Olivia's Overlook the red-blazed Walsh Trail heads through open space to a small bridge. The path then follows the eastern edge of the ridge, passing a knobby overlook before coming to an end at a bench with a fine southerly view of Monument Mtn. The blue-blazed Ridge Trail now begins and traces a path along the western ridge. The Ridge Trail has a number of excellent overlooks as it passes through pine and mountain ash. There are a number of short connector paths that join the Walsh and Ridge Trails, making a hike between the ridges easy. After the Ridge Trail ends, near the communications tower, follow the red blazes back to the parking area.

Walsh Trail Loop

Distances from Olivia's Overlook to
- south end of ridge via Walsh Trail: 0.5 mi., 15 min.
- communications tower via Ridge Trail: 0.9 mi., 30 min.
- parking area: 1.0 mi., 35 min.

Burbank Trail Loop (BNRC)

This red-blazed easy trail begins directly across the road from the parking area for Olivia's Overlook. The path enters the woods near a sign briefly describing the trail (maps are usually available here) and continues along the rocky footway to a junction at 0.1 mi. The loop trail begins here. Continuing left (north) along the ridge, the path cruises through open woods. The forest is thick enough to allow hints of a view without ever actually providing one. At 0.6 mi. the path swings south and tops a craggy summit

(1,630 ft.), runs up and over another minor peak (1,775 ft.), before heading to a sag and a narrow view through the pines at 1.1 mi. The trail then easily continues to the junction with Old Baldhead Rd. (Old Baldhead Rd. is a woods road that continues north 0.4 mi. to Reservoir Rd. in Lenox. It also runs south, then southeast just south of Shadowbrook Pond to meet Richmond-Lenox Rd. about 0.6 mi. east of Olivia's Overlook.)

Turn right and head downhill on the combined Burbank Trail/Old Baldhead Rd. The ruins of the old John Gorman homestead are on the right. In a shrubby overgrown area the Burbank Trail turns right and traces a narrow path through brambles and wet spots, reaching Shadowbrook Pond at 2.3 mi. A path near the dam leads to Old Baldhead Rd. The Burbank Trail heads easily uphill past a long run of rock cribbing, reaching the parking area at 3.0 mi.

Burbank Trail Loop

Distances from Olivia's Overlook (1,385 ft.) to
- first summit (1,630 ft.): 0.6 mi., 20 min.
- overlook: 1.1 mi., 45 min.
- Shadowbrook Pond: 2.3 mi., 1 hr. 35 min.

Stevens Glen (BRNC)

This short, easy loop trail has its trailhead on Lenox St. on the western side of Yokun Ridge. To reach the parking area from Lenox follow MA 183 south 1.3 mi. to Richmond-Lenox Rd. Turn right and follow Richmond-Lenox Rd. 1.6 mi., then turn left onto Branch Rd. Follow Branch Rd. 0.6 mi. to a pull-off (4 cars) on the right.

The trail descends steps and soon reaches a metal post with trail maps. The loop begins here, heading into a plantation of fragrant fir trees. The trail crosses a power line at 0.4 mi. and then crosses a brook on a bridge at 0.5 mi. before the loop trails join again high on a forested slope. A single trail descends the hillside and crosses two bridges, the second a one a long span over Lenox Mtn. Brook. The path now scrambles up a steep slope to the steel viewing platform (0.9 mi.) perched over the cascades of Stevens Glen. Return to where the trails split (1.2 mi.) and take the right branch, which returns to the information area and reaches the roadside parking area at 1.4 mi.

Stevens Glen

Distances from Lenox St. trailhead to
- bridge over Lenox Mtn. Brook: 0.7 mi., 25 min.
- viewing deck over Stevens Glen: 0.9 mi., 35 min.
- parking area: 1.4 mi., 50 min.

Mt. Greylock

In the northwest corner of Massachusetts is the state's highest summit, 3,491-ft. Mt. Greylock. Running slightly more than 11 mi. in length from north to south, the Greylock Range is bordered on the west by the Taconic Range and on the east by the Hoosac Range. To the north lies the Hoosic River Valley, beyond which lie the Green Mtns. of Vermont. The area encompasses parts of six towns: Adams, North Adams, Williamstown, New Ashford, Lanesborough, and Cheshire.

The principal summits of the main ridge, from south to north, include Rounds Rock (2,581 ft.), the three peaks of Saddle Ball Mtn. (3,257, 3,234, and 3,218 ft., respectively), Mt. Greylock, Mt. Fitch (3,110 ft.), and Mt. Williams (2,951 ft.) On a spur ridge leading east from the summit are the twin peaks of Ragged Mtn. (2,528 and 2,451 ft.). On the northwest side of the summit is a deep glacial ravine known as the Hopper. Mt. Prospect (2,690 ft.) is the high point of the spur ridge on the far side of the Hopper.

An extensive trail network offers a variety of hikes ranging from easy to strenuous. Many of the trails have outstanding viewpoints over the surrounding countryside. The broad, open summit offers panoramic views extending over three states. Principal landmarks at the summit include Bascom Lodge, a radio tower, and a 180-ft.-high granite war memorial.

Efforts to preserve the Mt. Greylock area began during the late 1800s, in a reaction to the devastation caused by logging, mining, and other 19th-century industrial activities. Today more than 12,000 acres are protected as part of the Massachusetts Department of Conservation and Recreation's Mt. Greylock State Reservation.

The summit and several trailheads can be reached via two paved roads extending through the reservation—Rockwell Rd. from the south and Notch Rd. from the north. To reach Rockwell Rd. from Lanesborough center, head north on US 7, bear right onto North Main St., then take the first right at Greylock Rd. (also called Quarry Rd.) and the first left onto Rockwell Rd. Notch Rd. begins on Main St. (MA 2) in North Adams, just east of the middle bridge over the Hoosic River. The two roads meet just below the summit and run together for the last 0.5 mi. as Summit Rd. to the summit. Total distance to the summit via either road is about 9 mi. Neither road is plowed in winter. *(Note: The reservation auto roads were closed for construction in 2007 but are scheduled to reopen in spring 2009. Contact the Mt. Greylock State Reservation at 413-499-4263 for updates.)*

The Mt. Greylock Visitor Center, operated by DCR, is located near the lower end of Rockwell Rd. in Lanesborough. At press time, Bascom Lodge was closed, although the Massachusetts Department of Conservation and Recreation was in the process of seeking an organization to rehabilitate and reopen it. Trail information is available at the visitor center. Sperry Campground, on the west slope of the mountain at 2,400 ft., has facilities for individual and group camping. The campground is located on Sperry Rd. (dirt; passable by car), which leads north off Rockwell Rd. about 3 mi. below the summit. Camping at the Sperry Rd. campground is by reservation (877-422-6762). There are also several shelters and lean-tos on the trails that are available for backpackers on a first-come, first-served basis. Camping is not permitted on the summit at any time. Refer to the North Berkshire map included with this trail guide.

Appalachian Trail (DCR)

The Appalachian Trail traverses Mt. Greylock, following the crest of the ridge for most of its route. Road access is at Main St. (MA 2) in North Adams, the Greylock summit road, and Outlook Ave. in Cheshire. For a description of the trail route, see Appalachian Trail, Section 9, Cheshire to MA 2 (North Adams) on page 15.

Roaring Brook Trail (DCR)

This moderate trail is the shortest route to Mt. Greylock from the west. The trailhead is located on Roaring Brook Rd. off US 7 in South Williamstown. Roaring Brook Rd. is 1.5 mi. south of the five-corners (junction of US 7 and MA 43) and 4 mi. north of the Springs Restaurant near Brodie Mtn. Ski Area. Travel down Roaring Brook Rd. about 0.5 mi. to a day-use parking area on the left. From the road the blue-blazed trail follows Roaring Brook, crossing it several times, and reaches the junction with the Stony Ledge Trail (sign) at 0.4 mi. The trail bears right and ascends steeply through birch and spruce woods. At a footbridge crossing Roaring Brook the trail crosses the Deer Hill Trail and the Circle Trail, both blue-blazed. At 1.9 mi. it bears left over a second bridge and enters Sperry Campground.

Roaring Brook Trail (map 1: E3)

Distances from Roaring Brook Rd. (1,100 ft.) to

- Stony Ledge Trail (1,200 ft.): 0.4 mi. 100 ft., 30 min.
- Sperry Campground (2,400 ft.): 1.9 mi., 1,300 ft., 1 hr. 45 min.
- summit of Mt. Greylock (via Hopper Trail and AT) (3,491 ft.): 3.5 mi., 2,400 ft., 3 hr. 20 min.

Deer Hill Trail (DCR)

This strenuous blue-blazed loop trail starts from the Roaring Brook Trail a short walk southwest of Sperry Campground. It descends steeply to the cascades on the left, following rock steps in places. After the falls it continues to descend steeply until crossing a bridge over the stream. It then climbs past Deer Hill Shelter at 0.5 mi. and continues upslope to a sharp left turn. A side trail leaves right that reaches Rockwell Rd. in about 0.4 mi., just 0.1 mi. north of a day-use parking area. The Deer Hill Trail continues to the blue-blazed Hopper Trail at 1.0 mi. To return to the campground follow the Hopper Trail downhill (west), reaching the campground at 2.0 mi.

Deer Hill Trail (map 1: E3)

Distances from Roaring Brook Trail (2,300 ft.) to

- Deer Hill Shelter (2,000 ft.): 0.5 mi. (rev. 300 ft.), 25 min.
- Hopper Trail (2,450 ft.): 1.0 mi., 750 ft., 1 hr.

Circle Trail (DCR)

Circle Trail is a strenuous 0.9-mi.-long blue-blazed loop path that makes a circuit through the beautiful Roaring Brook Gorge. From the parking area at Sperry Campground the trail heads south, crossing several small brooks. The path now turns west, following and then crossing a stream. Heading north, the trail traces the steep face of the ravine, crossing more streams before reaching the blue-blazed Roaring Brook Trail near a footbridge. Follow the Roaring Brook Trail 0.1 mi. to Sperry Rd. and Campground.

Circle Trail (map 1: E4)

Distance from Sperry Campground parking area (2,400 ft.) to
- Campground via Roaring Brook Trail (circuit): 0.9 mi., 200 ft., 45 min.

Stony Ledge Trail (DCR)

This strenuous blue-blazed trail, originally cleared as a ski trail, is now a popular mountain biking path. From the trailhead on the blue-blazed Roaring Brook Trail the path heads north to a ravine carved by a tributary of Roaring Brook. The trail now follows along a spur of the ravine, climbing about 1,000 ft. in about 0.6 mi. The path reaches Stony Ledge, with magnificent views, at 1.5 mi. The trail ends here at the north terminus of Sperry Rd.

Stony Ledge Trail (map 1: D3–E3)

Distances from Roaring Brook trailhead on Roaring Brook Rd. (1,100 ft.) to
- Stony Ledge Trail (1,200 ft.): 0.4 mi., 100 ft., 15 min.
- Stony Ledge (2,500 ft.): 1.5 mi., 1,400 ft., 1 hr. 20 min.

Hopper Trail (DCR)

The Hopper Trail is a strenuous, beautiful path passing through the Bacon Ravine portion of this immense glacial gorge and reaching the summit via the AT in 1.7 mi. To reach the trailhead, turn off MA 43 onto Hopper Rd. 2.5 mi. south of Williamstown at a stone gate. Hopper Rd. crosses the Green River and proceeds about 1.5 mi. to a parking area at Haley Farm on the right near a kiosk. Hike the short distance to the end of the road and the trailhead. The blue-blazed trail soon splits, with the blue-blazed Money Brook Trail leaving left and the Hopper Trail continuing right.

It passes through fields and then steeply ascends the wooded buttress of Stony Ledge, where many unusual plants can be found. The trail levels off just before reaching Sperry Rd. at 2.3 mi.

The trail bears left and follows Sperry Rd. for about 0.1 mi. before leaving the road to the left just past the contact station and heading steeply uphill. The trail passes the blue-blazed Deer Hill Trail on the right. The Hopper Trail continues uphill, meeting the Overlook Trail (also blue-blazed), then turning sharp right and reaching Rockwell Rd. at the hairpin turn. The trail then ascends steeply to a junction with Rockwell Rd., the Cheshire Harbor Trail (again, marked in blue), and the AT. Turn left (north) and follow the white-blazed AT to the summit.

Hopper Trail (map 1: D3)

Distances from Haley Farm trailhead (1,100 ft.) to
- Money Brook Trail (1,100 ft.): 0.4 mi., 10 min.
- Sperry Rd. (2,300 ft.): 2.3 mi., 1,200 ft., 2 hr.
- Appalachian Trail (3,000 ft.): 3.4 mi., 1,900 ft., 3 hr.
- summit of Mt. Greylock via AT (3,491 ft.): 4.1 mi., 2,400 ft., 3 hr. 25 min.

March Cataract Trail (DCR)

This short and moderately easy blue-blazed trail begins at a parking area on Sperry Rd. in Sperry Campground and heads northeast to the scenic March Cataract Falls on Bacon Brook.

March Cataract Trail (map 1: E4)

Distances from Sperry Rd. (2,400 ft.) to
- March Cataract Falls (2,300 ft.): 0.5 mi., 100 ft. (rev. 200 ft.), 45 min.

Overlook Trail (DCR)

The Overlook Trail is a moderate path that runs from the summit area of Mt. Greylock to the Hopper Trail near Rockwell Rd. south of the summit. The path roughly follows the 3,000-ft. contour for much of its length, passing through beech and spruce forest. The trail begins near the radio tower at the western end of the summit, where this blue-blazed trail enters the forest. The path descends and crosses Notch Rd. at 0.5 mi., then traces the contour of the mountain on the edge of the Hopper Ravine to a short side trail that leads to an overlook at 1.1 mi. The view peers down into the Hopper with Mt. Prospect beyond. The Overlook Trail then crosses Bacon Brook (from this crossing the brook falls about 600 vertical ft. in slightly over 1,000 ft. of distance to create the March Cataract waterfall) and ends at the junction with the Hopper Trail, which enters from the right. To continue to the summit, follow the Hopper Trail to the AT, then continue north on the AT to the summit.

Overlook Trail (map 1: E4)
Distances from summit area (3,491 ft.) to
- Notch Rd. (3,100 ft.): 0.5 mi. (rev. 400 ft.), 15 min.
- overlook (2,900 ft.): 1.1 mi. (rev. 200 ft.), 45 min.
- junction with Hopper Trail (2,900 ft.): 1.6 mi., 1 hr.
- summit via Hopper and Appalachian Trails (circuit) (3,491 ft.): 2.2 mi., 600 ft., 1 hr. 15 min.

Robinson's Point Trail (DCR)

Robinson's Point Trail begins on Notch Rd. just north of a day-use parking area. Many people reach the trailhead from the summit area, hiking north on the AT from the eastern end of the parking facility and the ski hut. The white-blazed AT descends a rocky path, crosses Summit Rd., and continues to descend to a blue-blazed side trail on the left at about 0.4 mi. The side path quickly reaches Notch Rd. and a parking area. The blue-blazed Robinson's Point Trail begins a few yards north of the parking area. From Notch Rd. the path descends through a boggy area to a perch at the edge of the Hopper (0.8 mi.) with a view that makes you feel as if you were soaring. The hike back is strenuous.

Robinson's Point Trail (map 1: E4)
Distances from summit (3,491 ft.) to
- Notch Rd. via AT (3,100 ft.): 0.4 mi. (rev. 400 ft.), 10 min.
- overlook (2,800 ft.): 0.6 mi., (rev. 300 ft.), 30 min.
- summit (circuit): 1.2 mi., 700 ft., 1 hr. 15 min.

Money Brook Trail (DCR)

This strenuous blue-blazed trail, in connection with the AT from the north, provides access to Mt. Williams and the Mt. Greylock summit. It is especially attractive in spring because of the number and variety of wild-flowers that grow along it as it weaves through the Hopper. To reach the trailhead, turn off MA 43 onto Hopper Rd. 2.5 mi. south of Williamstown at a stone gate. Hopper Rd. crosses the Green River and proceeds about 1.5 mi. to a parking area on the right near a kiosk. Hike the short distance to the end of the road and the trailhead. Follow the blue-blazed Hopper Trail 0.3 mi. to where the Money Brook Trail leaves left. The trail passes a camping area and follows Hopper Brook into the Hopper. The trail now turns to the north, following Money Brook past the blue-blazed Mt. Prospect Trail, which leaves left. The path traces a course deep into the ravine of Money Brook, a favorite haunt of barred owls and once the hideout of counterfeiters whose illegal craftsmanship gave the stream its name.

The trail swings northeast and follows the brook to a dead-end side trail that leads in 0.1 mi. to the base of Money Brook Falls. The main trail ascends steeply, moderating where a connector trail leaves right for Notch Rd. and a day-use parking area (the one-way hike from this parking area to the falls is approximately 0.8 mi. and takes 40 min.). The Money Brook Trail continues north, passing the access trail for Wilbur Clearing Shelter on the left before reaching the AT about 0.2 mi. west of Notch Rd.

Money Brook Trail (map 1: D3–D4)

Distances from Haley Farm trailhead (1,100 ft.) to
- Mt. Prospect Trail (1,500 ft.): 1.7 mi., 400 ft., 55 min.
- side trail to Money Brook Falls (2,000 ft.): 2.7 mi., 900 ft., 1 hr. 35 min.
- Wilbur Clearing Shelter (2,200 ft.): 3.3 mi., 1,100 ft., 2 hr. 5 min.
- AT (2,300 ft.): 3.5 mi., 1,200 ft., 2 hr. 15 min.

Mt. Prospect Trail (DCR)

Mt. Prospect (2,690 ft.) is a steep-sided wooded ridge on the northwest side of the Greylock Range. The blue-blazed Mt. Prospect Trail is a very strenuous 2.0-mi.-long trail that begins on the Money Brook Trail deep in the Money Brook Ravine and ends at the north end of the mountain where the path meets the AT. The southern trailhead can be reached by following the Hopper and Money Brook Trails from the Haley Farm trailhead 1.7 mi. to the trailhead on the left. The northern trailhead, and a spectacular overlook, can be reached by following the AT 0.3 mi. north from where it crosses Notch Rd. From the AT the trail traces a course atop the attractive wooded ridge of Mt. Prospect, with glimpses of the wide valley to the west. At the south end of the ridge is a rock cairn marking the wooded summit. The trail then descends very steeply, dropping about 1,300 ft. in the next mile before reaching the Money Brook Trail.

Mt. Prospect Trail (map 1: D4)

Distances from AT (2,500 ft.) to
- summit of Mt. Prospect (2,690 ft.): 0.9 mi., 200 ft., 30 min.
- Money Brook Trail (1,500 ft.): 1.8 mi., 200 ft. (rev. 1,200 ft.), 1 hr. 10 min.

Bellows Pipe Trail (DCR)

The blue-blazed Bellows Pipe Trail is open to both hiking and mountain biking. The trail begins as an easy walk and ends as a strenuous climb. The trailhead is on the south side of Notch Rd. where the road takes a sharp turn before it enters the reservation from North Adams. Parking is available at the Notch Rd. gate parking area 500 ft. from the trailhead. From the trailhead the trail heads south along a level dirt access road for Notch Reservoir. Soon the path begins to climb along the flanks of Mt. Williams and Mt. Fitch, with Ragged Mtn. to the east across Notch Brook Ravine. The grade increases, and at 2.2 mi. the blue-blazed Ragged Mtn. Trail leaves left for the top of Ragged Mtn.

Just beyond a grove of red spruce and red pine and after crossing a deep ravine, the trail turns sharp right (northwest) and heads steeply up-slope. A wide path continues straight ahead and intersects the blue-blazed Thunderbolt Trail before descending toward Greylock Glen.

The Bellows Pipe Trail (so named for the winds that blow between Mt. Greylock and Ragged Mtn.) resumes its climb, passing Bellows Pipe Shelter on the right at 2.5 mi. and turning southwest for a level stretch. At 3.2 mi. the trail again turns northwest onto a woods road, ascending the ridge in a series of switchbacks. At the fourth switchback the trail turns northwest off the woods road, which continues south to the Thunderbolt Trail. At 3.5 mi. the Bellows Pipe Trail ends at the white-blazed AT. The summit of Mt. Greylock is about 0.4 mi. south (left).

Bellows Pipe Trail (map 1: C4–D4)

Distances from Notch Rd. trailhead (1,300 ft.) to
- Ragged Mtn. Trail (2,200 ft.): 2.2 mi., 900 ft., 1 hr. 10 min.
- Bellows Pipe Shelter (2,200 ft.): 2.5 mi., 900 ft., 1 hr. 35 min.
- AT (3,100 ft.): 3.5 mi., 1,800 ft., 2 hr. 15 min.
- Mt. Greylock summit via AT (3,491 ft.): 3.9 mi., 2,200 ft., 2 hr. 45 min.

Thunderbolt Trail (DCR)

One of the steepest trails on Mt. Greylock, the Thunderbolt was constructed by the Civilian Conservation Corps (CCC) in 1934 as a championship ski trail. From the summit, it drops 2,260 vertical ft. on its 2.0 mi. descent of the mountain. This blue-blazed, very rugged and strenuous trail was named for the old roller coaster at Revere Beach near Boston because each trip down the mountain was an unforgettable ride.

The Thunderbolt Trail is accessed via the Appalachian Trail from the summit of Mt. Greylock, 0.4 mi. north of the summit parking area. The trail drops very steeply off the ridge on the wide, overgrown ski trail, crossing numerous woods roads on the lower reaches until reaching Thiel Rd. at Greylock Glen at 1.6 mi.

To reach the Thiel Rd. trailhead in Greylock Glen from the McKinley Monument in Adams, follow Maple St. to West Rd. Turn left and in 0.4 mi. turn right onto Gould Rd. and climb past orchards. At the intersection bear right onto Thiel Rd. and follow it to the day-use parking area on the left. The trailhead is a few yards farther up the road on the left just before Hoxie Brook.

Thunderbolt Trail (map 1: D4–D5)

Distances from Thiel Rd. trailhead (1,200 ft.) to
- summit of Mt. Greylock via AT (3,491 ft.): 2 mi., 2,300 ft., 2 hr. 5 min.

Cheshire Harbor Trail (DCR)

The blue-blazed Cheshire Harbor Trail is open to hiking and mountain biking. To reach the trail, follow MA 8 to the McKinley Monument in Adams center. Maple St. exits right (west) at the monument. Follow Maple St. to West Rd. Turn left (south) onto West Rd., cross Pecks Brook, and take an immediate right onto West Mtn. Rd. Continue 1.5 mi. to the end of the road and the day-use parking area and trailhead.

From West Mtn. Rd. the trail zigzags steeply up the south bluff of Pecks Brook ravine, reaching the junction with Old Adams Rd.—an old stage road—at 1.0 mi. The Cheshire Harbor Trail continues climbing, though less aggressively, reaching the connector path to the Gould Trail at 1.5 mi. Resuming a steep climb, the trail reaches Rockwell Rd. at its junction with the white-blazed AT at 2.5 mi. From Rockwell Rd. follow the AT northbound to the summit, which is reached at 3.1 mi.

Cheshire Harbor Trail (map 1: E4)

Distances from West Mtn. Rd. (Adams) trailhead (1,400 ft.) to
- Old Adams Rd. (2,000 ft.): 0.8 mi., 600 ft., 40 min.
- Gould Trail connector (2,250 ft.): 1.5 mi., 850 ft., 1 hr. 10 min.
- Rockwell Rd. (3,100 ft.): 2.5 mi., 1,700 ft., 2 hr. 50 min.
- summit of Mt. Greylock (via AT) (3,491 ft.): 3.1 mi., 2,100 ft., 3 hr. 20 min.

CCC Dynamite Trail (DCR)

This moderate blue-blazed connector trail runs along a fairly level terrace, roughly tracing the 2,500-ft. contour of Saddle Ball Mtn. from the blue-blazed Jones Nose Trail to the junction of Rockwell and Sperry Rds. It begins 0.3 mi. from the Jones Nose parking area and heads north 1.3 mi. to its end. On the way it passes the location where CCC crews stored explosives used to build Rockwell Rd. in the 1930s.

CCC Dynamite Trail (map 1: E4)

Distances from Jones Nose parking area (2,400 ft.) to
- CCC Dynamite Trail via Jones Nose Trail (2,790 ft.): 0.3 mi., 400 ft., 20 min.
- Rockwell Rd. (at Sperry Rd.) (2,600 ft.): 1.3 mi., 400 ft. (rev. 200 ft.), 45 min.

Jones Nose Trail (DCR)

This strenuous blue-blazed trail scales the steep feature called Jones Nose (named for a local farmer with a nose not quite as large but of similar shape) that marks the south slope of Saddle Ball Mtn. This trail offers numerous fine views as it climbs to the cool boreal forest along the summit ridge. The trail begins at the Jones Nose day-use parking area on Rockwell Rd. about 3.7 mi. north of the Mt. Greylock Visitor Center. The trail heads through open areas locally famous for blueberries before entering the woods and beginning a steep ascent. It climbs steeply to a terrace where the blue-blazed CCC Dynamite Trail leaves left at 0.5 mi. The path soon resumes climbing steeply past ledges to a short side trail leading west with fantastic views of the Taconics and Catskills from a rocky ledge. The trail becomes steeper, passing between ledges and conifers to reach the southern summit of Saddle Ball Mtn. (3,238 ft.) and the junction with the white-blazed AT at 1.0 mi. To continue on to the summit of Mt. Greylock, hike northbound on the AT 3.6 mi.

Jones Nose Trail (map 1: F4–E4)

Distances from Jones Nose parking area (2,400 ft.) to
- CCC Dynamite Trail (2,790 ft.): 0.5 mi., 400 ft., 20 min.
- Saddle Ball Mtn. (3,238 ft.) and AT: 1.0 mi., 850 ft., 45 min.

Rounds Rock Trail (DCR)

This blue-blazed 0.9-mi.-long, easy loop trail leaves the western side of Rockwell Rd. 3.0 mi. north of the Mt. Greylock Visitor Center and 0.7 mi. south of the Jones Nose parking area. Park off the road in the designated pull-off. The trail gradually ascends through mature woods to open ledges and blueberry barrens. A short side trail leads to a cliff with outstanding views to the south. At the edge of the barrens a second outlook trail is passed, followed shortly by the Northrup Trail entering from the left. In a beech grove the trail passes a rock cairn and the remains of a twin-engine Cessna aircraft that crashed here in August 1948 during a flight from New Jersey to Albany. The trail continues through mixed hardwoods and curves back northwesterly to the start.

Rounds Rock Trail (map 1: F4)
Distance from Rockwell Rd. parking area (2,430 ft.) to
• trailhead (circuit): 0.9 mi., 50 ft., 40 min.

Gould Trail (DCR)

The strenuous blue-blazed Gould Trail can be accessed from the trailhead near the end of Gould Rd. in Greylock Glen and from the day-use parking area about 1 mi. from the West St. intersection. (See the directions to the Cheshire Harbor Trail on page 48.) The trail ascends the southeast face of Mt. Greylock, tracing a route along the north side of Pecks Brook ravine, passing a connector trail at 1.9 mi. that leads to the Cheshire Harbor Trail, then reaching a side trail to Pecks Brook Falls. At 2.1 mi. Pecks Brook Shelter is passed on the left. The path becomes quite steep as it climbs to the tri-junction with Notch, Rockwell, and Summit Rds. at 2.9 mi. Follow the AT northbound for about 0.5 mi. to the summit.

Gould Trail (map 1: E5)
Distances from Gould Rd. trailhead (1,250 ft.) to
• connector trail to Cheshire Harbor Trail (2,350 ft.): 1.9 mi., 1,100 ft., 1 hr. 10 min.
• Pecks Brook Shelter (2,500 ft.): 2.1 mi., 1,250 ft., 2 hr. 10 min.
• tri-junction (3,200 ft.): 2.9 mi., 1,950 ft., 3 hr. 10 min.
• summit via AT (3,491 ft.): 3.4 mi., 2,250 ft., 3 hr. 25 min.

Ragged Mtn. Trail (DCR)

Ragged Mtn. (2,528 ft.) is a jagged spur forming one wall of Notch Brook ravine on the eastern side of Mt. Greylock. The Ragged Mtn. Trail accesses the rocky peak that stands about 1,000 ft. lower than its towering neighbor. The path is lightly used and offers solitude amid the croaks of ravens that nest among the crags.

To reach the blue-blazed Ragged Mtn. Trail follow the Bellows Pipe Trail south 2.2 mi. from the Notch Rd. trailhead. The Ragged Mtn. Trail leaves left and quickly begins a fairly steep ascent of the mountain. The path weaves through outcrops and forest, reaching a rocky clearing marking the summit at 2.6 mi.

Ragged Mtn. Trail (map 1: D4–D5)
Distance from Notch Rd. trailhead (1,300 ft.) to
- Ragged Mtn. trail via Bellows Pipe Trail (2,200 ft.): 2.2 mi., 900 ft., 1 hr. 10 min.
- Ragged Mtn. summit (2,528 ft.): 2.6 mi., 1,200 ft., 1 hr. 40 min.

Old Summit Rd. (DCR)

From the parking area on Notch Rd. the blue-blazed trail enters the woods and quickly comes to a junction. Continuing straight a few yards leads to the AT; the Old Summit Rd. leaves right, heading easily uphill. The path climbs to the roadbed of the long-abandoned Old Summit Rd. and follows it south. At the burned ruins of an old cabin a connector path leads to Notch Rd. and the blue-blazed Money Brook Trail. Continuing south, the trail swings uphill, passing some ski trails and in part following a streambed to the junction with the white-blazed AT and the blue-blazed Bernard Farm Trail in the saddle between Mt. Williams and Mt. Fitch at 0.7 mi.

To reach the trailhead drive 2.25 mi. up Notch Rd. from the gated entrance of Mt. Greylock Reservation in North Adams. A day-use parking area is on the left 0.1 mi. beyond the point where the AT crosses the road.

Old Summit Rd. (map 1: D4)
Distance from Notch Rd. parking area (2,300 ft.) to
- junction with AT and Bernard Farm Trails (2,800 ft.): 0.7 mi., 500 ft., 40 min.

Bernard Farm Trail (DCR)

This strenuous blue-blazed trail runs about 3.0 mi. from Notch Rd. at the reservation entrance in North Adams (near the old Bernard Farm) to the AT in the saddle between Mt. Williams and Mt. Fitch. The trail was named for Harry Bernard, who ran a dairy farm on this site in the early 20th century. He also drove children to school with his "school team" before buses, extracted timber used for construction of Bascom Lodge in the 1930s, and operated a small ski area in the 1940s and 1950s.

From the farm and Mt. Greylock Reservation boundary follow an old woods road to the northwest. A series of trails and woods roads link up the mountainside, cross Notch Rd., then traverse the eastern side of Mt.

Williams before climbing steeply to the white-blazed AT just south of Mt. Williams.

> **Bernard Farm Trail (map 1: C4–D4)**
> Distance from Notch Rd. trailhead (1,350 ft.) to
> • AT (2,800 ft.): 2.1 mi., 1,450 ft., 1 hr. 50 min.

Haley Farm Trail (DCR)

This strenuous blue-blazed trail begins at the day-use parking area on Hopper Rd. (see Hopper Trail on page 42 for directions). The Haley Farm Trail heads south, then southwest to the base of the western spur of Stony Ledge. The path then makes a very steep ascent that moderates briefly before continuing up to the Stony Ledge Trail, also blue-blazed, which it then follows a few hundred feet to Stony Ledge at 2.1 mi.

> **Haley Farm Trail (map 1: D3)**
> Distance from Hopper Rd. parking area (1,100 ft.) to
> • Stoney Ledge (2,500 ft.): 2.1 mi., 1,400 ft., 2 hr.

Stage Trail (DCR)

The Stage Trail is a moderate 0.8-mi.-long blue-blazed connector path that links the Jones Nose parking area on Rockwell Rd. with Greylock Rd.

> **Stage Trail (map 1: F3)**
> Distance from Jones Nose parking area (2,350 ft.) to
> • Greylock Rd. (2,200 ft.): 0.7 mi., (rev. 150 ft.), 45 min.

Northrup Trail (DCR)

The Northrup Trail is a generally easy hiking trail that runs from its trailhead on Rockwell Rd. 2.0 mi. north of the Mt. Greylock Visitor Center to the Jones Nose parking area, also on Rockwell Rd. Along the way the Northrup Trail provides a connecting route to the Rounds Rock Trail from the west.

From the visitor center a road walk of 2.0 mi. on Rockwell Rd. is needed to reach the trailhead on the left. From the trailhead the path proceeds easily to the Rounds Rock Trail on the right (3.7 mi.). From Rounds Rock the trail descends and reaches Rockwell Rd. opposite the Jones Nose parking area at 4.2 mi.

Northrup Trail (map 1: G4–F4)

Distance from Mt. Greylock Visitor Center (1,660 ft.) to
- Northrup Trail trailhead on Rockwell Rd. (2,200 ft.).: 2.0 mi., 550 ft., 1 hr. 15 min.
- Rounds Rock Trail junction (2,300 ft.): 3.7 mi., 650 ft, 2 hr. 30 min.
- Rockwell Rd. at Jones Nose parking area (2,400 ft.): 4.2 mi., 750 ft., 3 hr.

Brook and Berry Trail (DCR)

The Mt. Greylock Visitor Center serves as the trailhead for several easy to moderate paths, including the Brook and Berry Trail, which is an easy 1.0-mi. walk through nearby woods and open areas. It connects the Visitor Center to Rockwell Rd.

Brook and Berry Trail (map 1: G4)

Distance from Mt. Greylock Visitor Center (1,660 ft.) to
- trailhead (circuit): 1.0 mi., 300 ft. (rev. 300 ft.), 35 min.

Cliff Loop Trail (DCR)

The Cliff Loop Trail is a moderate 0.8-mi.-long hike through some attractive open woods that offer glimpses of the surrounding Berkshire Hills. It connects Rockwell Rd. to the Visitor Center.

Cliff Loop Trail (map 1: G4)

Distance from Mt. Greylock Visitor Center (1660 ft.) to
- trailhead (circuit): 0.8 mi., 100 ft. (rev. 100 ft.), 30 min.

Bradley Farm Interpretive Trail (DCR)

The Bradley Farm Interpretive Trail is an easy 1.8-mi. walk filled with nature and history. Interpretive trail maps and brochures are available at the Mt. Greylock Visitor Center on Rockwell Rd. The trail loops through the site of Ephraim Bradley's eighteenth century farm, passing stone walls that mark old pastures, mixed woodlands, and quartzite rocks. Though much of New England is forested now, farms like this were widespread across the region through the nineteenth century, even on rocky hills and mountains such as Greylock.

Bradley Farm Interpretive Trail (map 1: G4)
Distance from Mt. Greylock Visitor Center (1,660 ft.) to
  • trailhead (circuit): 1.8 mi., 400 ft. (rev. 400 ft.), 1 hr.

Ice Glen Trail System

The forested hills and ravines south of Stockbridge are protected in part by the efforts of the Laurel Hill Association (LHA). Founded in 1853, the LHA has the distinction of being the oldest civic improvement association in the country. The acreage around Ice Glen and Laura's Rest contains some of the oldest trees in Massachusetts and is traced by three trails. To reach the trails take US 7 south from the center of Stockbridge and its junction with MA 102. Proceed 0.2 mi. to Park St. on the left. Turn left (Town Park is now on the right) and drive to the end of Park St. Cross over the Housatonic River on the Memorial Footbridge to the far bank, where the trails begin.

Mary Flynn Trail (LHA)

The Mary Flynn Trail begins just beyond the Memorial Bridge and heads north between the Housatonic River and the railroad tracks. The path follows the river north along a narrow floodplain for about 0.2 mi., then turns east. At about 0.4 mi. the steep slopes of the hill topped by Laura's Tower crowd the riverbank. The trail turns south to its end at about 0.6 mi, making this a 1.2-mi. round-trip.

Mary Flynn Trail
Distance from Memorial Bridge to
  • northern terminus (one way): 0.6 mi., 25 min.

Ice Glen and Laura's Tower Trails (LHA)

The combined Ice Glen and Laura's Tower Trails leave Memorial Bridge and head east, crossing the (active) railroad tracks and entering deep piney woods. The trail meanders up the hill, weaving around boulders and through ancient tall pines to a T-intersection (0.4 mi.), where the trails split.

Ice Glen and Laura's Tower Trails
Distance from Memorial Bridge to
  • split of Ice Glen and Laura's Tower Trails: 0.4 mi., 15 min.

Ice Glen Trail (LHA)

From the trail junction the Ice Glen Trail heads south, reaching the V-cleft entrance to the ravine at 0.5 mi. For the next 0.2 mi. the path weaves through the chilly boulder caves of the glen, which is home to one of the region's most easily viewed old-growth forests, with many old white pines and hemlocks. The path exits the ravine near a 150-ft.-tall, 300-year-old white pine. The path proceeds a short way to a gravel road that leads in about 0.2 mi. to Ice Glen Rd. To return to Park St. via the road follow Ice Glen Rd. 0.6 mi. to US 7. Turn right onto US 7 and walk 0.25 mi. to Park St., then another 0.25 mi. to the parking area.

Ice Glen Trail
Distances from Memorial Bridge to
  • junction with Laura's Tower Trail: 0.4 mi., 15 min.
  • Ice Glen: 0.5 mi., 25 min.
  • white pine: 0.7 mi., 40 min.
  • Ice Glen Rd.: 0.9 mi., 50 min.
  • parking area via US 7 and Park St.: 2.0 mi., 1 hr. 20 min.

Laura's Tower Trail (LHA)

From the junction with the Ice Glen Trail, the moderate Laura's Tower Trail heads left along the contour of the ridge, crossing a small brook before turning and ascending the hill at a moderate grade. The top of the hill is managed to keep the trees from interfering with the view from the steel observation tower at its summit (1,465 ft.). The tower's incline and small steps make climbing the tower a cautious endeavor, but the view is wonderful, reaching to the Catskills in the west, Mt. Greylock in the north, and Monument Mtn. to the south. Laura's Tower and Laura's Rest are named for Laura Belden, the daughter-in-law of David Dudley Field. She came to the hilltop to find refuge from her life's many tragedies.

Laura's Tower Trail
Distances from Memorial Bridge (822 ft.) to
- Ice Glen Trail junction: 0.4 mi., 15 min.
- Laura's Tower (1,465 ft.): 0.8 mi., 45 min.

Questing Reservation

This 438-acre property of The Trustees of Reservations sits astride the rolling landscape of Leffingwell Hill in New Marlborough. The hilltop was one of the first places settled by Europeans in the early 1700s, and is where twin girls were born; according to some sources these were the first non-Native American children born in Berkshire County. The reservation holds old stone foundations and cellar holes, several hundred acres of forest, and a 17-acre upland field that attracts butterflies and birds.

To reach Questing take MA 23 east from Great Barrington to the junction with MA 57. Follow MA 57 for 5.0 mi. and turn right onto New Marlborough Hill Rd. Travel 0.6 mi. along the road to the parking area and kiosk on the left.

Questing Trail (TTOR)

The reservation's easy white-blazed trail begins at the parking area and heads uphill on an old woods road to the field. The path then forks and loops along the hillside, with the left trail entering the woods and passing by stone walls and the settlement ruins before descending through open woods to a field where a mowed path returns to the fork. The circuit can also be done in reverse. Up and back from the parking area is about 2 mi. and takes about 1.5 hr.

Questing Trail
Distance from parking area trailhead to
• parking area (circuit): 2.0 mi., 1 hr. 30 min.

Dry Hill

Dry Hill is a 206-acre property of The Trustees of Reservations that protects a significant portion of the eponymous New Marlborough landmark, so named for the distinct lack of water on the ridge. Dry Hill is a wild place that provides habitat for diverse wildlife, including black bears, bobcats, scarlet tanagers, and butterflies.

To reach the reservation, take MA 23 east from Great Barrington to the junction with MA 57. Follow MA 57 for 5.5 mi. to the New Marlborough town green and turn left onto New Marlborough-Monterey Rd. Continue for 0.7 mi. and turn left onto North Rd. The parking area is on the left about 0.2 mi. down the road.

Dry Hill Trail (TTOR)

The white-blazed, 1.5-mi. trail begins at the information kiosk near the parking area and loops along a shallow drainage that includes hemlock and red maple swamps. A variety of wildflowers and woodland shrubs grow in the rich soils here.

Dry Hill Trail
Distance from parking area trailhead to
• trailhead (circuit): 1.5 mi., 1 hr.

Bartholomew's Cobble

Bartholomew's Cobble in Ashley Falls is one of the most treasured natural areas in Massachusetts. More than 800 species of vascular plants and over 240 species of birds have been recorded on its 329 acres. Four miles of trails weave through craggy limestone hills, called cobbles, along the banks of the Housatonic River, and through open fields. Bartholomew's Cobble is a National Natural Landmark. A small museum and nature center with restrooms is located off Weatogue Rd. To reach Bartholomew's Cobble follow US 7 in Sheffield south and turn right onto MA 7A. Continue south on MA 7A for 0.5 mi. and turn right onto Rannapo Rd. Travel 1.5 mi. and turn right onto Weatogue Rd. The nature center is a few yards ahead on the left.

Ledges Interpretive Trail (TTOR)

An interpretive brochure describing the 20 points along this fascinating path is available at the nature center to aid in the enjoyment of the white-blazed Ledges Trail. This easy 0.5-mi. path begins at the nature center and enters the hemlock woods near the kiosk. It descends through cool hemlocks to the riverside at the beginning of the large meander called Corbin's Neck. This area is usually ice-free in winter and attracts hundreds of geese. The path passes limestone outcrops climbing to a bench (0.2 mi.) overlooking the pasture and river. The trail then continues past a rock face before turning west, passing the junction with the Bailey Trail (0.25 mi.), cedars, and more ledges. The trail parallels the road briefly, then passes a cave on the right before ending at the nature center.

Ledges Interpretive Trail

Distances from nature center trailhead to
- bench: 0.2 mi., 10 min.
- Bailey Trail: 0.3 mi., 15 min.
- nature center: 0.5 mi., 30 min.

Tractor Path (TTOR)

This somewhat unappealingly named trail leads from the edge of Ashley Field opposite the nature center and leads to an overlook at a large field atop Hurlburt's Hill with a view that covers most of the southern Berkshires. From the trailhead the path follows a mowed trail parallel to the road before turning right along the fence line. The path passes an apple tree and begins to easily climb into a second field. The Hal Borland Trail leaves right and travels the short distance to the Col. Ashley House, the oldest house in Berkshire County. The path continues to climb, briefly entering the woods before passing through another field. At the top of this field the trail passes through more woods to reach the Tulip Tree Trail on the left. The Tractor Path jogs right and enters an expansive, 20-acre field that is home to tree swallows, bluebirds, and bobolinks. From the top of the field, the spectacular view encompasses the southern Taconics all the way (on a clear day) to Mt. Greylock.

Tractor Path

Distances from Ashley Field trailhead (670 ft.) to
- Hal Borland Trail: 0.3 mi., 10 min.
- Tulip Tree Trail: 0.7 mi., 20 min.
- hilltop bench and overlook (1,050 ft.): 0.9 mi., 30 min.

Beartown State Forest

Beartown State Forest in Monterey contains 10,879 acres of largely undeveloped forest, mountains, and wetlands. The Appalachian Trail passes through the preserve, which is crossed by many gravel service roads. The highest point is Mt. Wilcox at 2,155 ft. Two shelters serving the AT are found in Beartown State Forest. Wilcox South is southeast of Mt. Wilcox, and Wilcox North is northeast of the mountain. A campground with twelve sites is located on the shore of Benedict Pond, which sits at an elevation of 1,580 ft., just northwest of the dam, and a swimming area (restrooms available) is located a few yards southeast of the dam. Leashed pets are permitted.

Pond Loop Trail (DCR)

This easy blue-blazed 1.5-mi.-long path circles the shore of Benedict Pond in the south portion of Beartown State Forest. To reach the trailhead, from the junction of MA 23 and MA 57, follow MA 23 east for 1.8 mi. and turn north on Blue Hill Rd. Follow Blue Hill Rd. for 1.5 miles past the forest headquarters and a crossing of the Appalachian Trail, then turn right on Benedict Pond Rd. (may be labeled Beartown Rd. on park maps). Follow signs to the parking area and trailhead.

From the trailhead at the public boat launch, the trail heads southeast through tangles of laurel and azalea that bloom in early June. The path then descends easily to a wet, swampy area where the white-blazed

AT enters from the right. The AT and Pond Loop Trails combine briefly, crossing a small stream on bog bridging before crossing a larger stream on a stone bridge. The AT now leaves right; the Pond Loop Trail stays left. (For a nice side trip trek up the AT about 0.4 mi. to the Ledges, an area of open cliffs with great views to the west; there are good views of a large beaver wetland at the top of the climb.) The Pond Loop Trail briefly follows a wide woods road, then descends to the shore, wandering along the edge of the lake and past a marshy area near the north bay. The path then skirts the campground before crossing the dam and swimming area and returning to the parking area by the boat launch.

Pond Loop Trail

Distances from trailhead at Benedict Pond boat launch and parking area to
- south junction with AT: 0.4 mi., 10 min.
- north junction with AT at stone bridge: 0.6 mi., 15 min.
- campground: 1.1 mi., 30 min.
- boat launch (circuit): 1.5 mi., 45 min.

Monument Mtn. Reservation

Monument Mtn. Reservation in Great Barrington is one of the most popular hiking destinations in the Berkshires, drawing more than 20,000 visitors annually. The mountain, an isolated outcrop hummock of pure white quartzite, was sacred to the Stockbridge native, inspired the poetry of William Cullen Bryant, and was the place where Nathaniel Hawthorne gave Herman Melville advice on writing *Moby Dick*. The depth of history here is equaled by the natural wonders of these stunning cliffs. Wildlife abounds in the forests, and the updrafts that sweep up the cliffs are sought out by many species of raptors that routinely soar close to the rocks.

There are many significant features along this beautiful ridge, including Squaw Peak (1,640 ft.), a ragged crest of rock atop the vertical cliffs. Devil's Pulpit is a dramatic, freestanding pinnacle of rock south of Squaw Peak. *(Note: Rock climbing is prohibited throughout the reservation.)*

Parking is available at a picnic area located at the base of Squaw Peak on US 7, 3.0 mi. south of Stockbridge and the intersection of US 7 and MA 102. From Great Barrington travel north 3.0 mi. from the north junction with MA 23 in Great Barrington. A trail map and other information is displayed at the kiosk near the trailhead for Hickey Trail.

Indian Monument Trail (TTOR)

This trail begins at the south end of the parking area and parallels US 7 for roughly 0.3 mi. before joining a wide woods road. The trail follows the woods road, swinging sharp right, reaching a stone wall at 0.5 mi.

The path continues along the level woods road and gradually becomes steeper in grade, reaching the junction with the Squaw Peak Trail (right) in a woodland clearing at 0.75 mi. The Indian Monument Trail continues easily through the woods, the cliffs and boulders of the mountain ever present on the right. The path swings south as it climbs to the junction with the Hickey Trail at Inscription Rock at 1.5 mi.

Indian Monument Trail

Distances from parking area on US 7 (946 ft.) to
- Indian Monument: 0.5 mi., 20 min.
- Squaw Peak Trail: 0.8 mi., 25 min.
- Inscription Rock: 1.5 mi., 45 min.
- summit (about 0.1 mi. north of Squaw Peak) (1,642 ft.): 1.6 mi., 55 min.

Hickey Trail (TTOR)

This heavily used trail is the quickest way to the summit and leaves the Monument Mtn. Reservation picnic area on US 7 near the kiosk. It proceeds easily north through open woods, with the bouldered slopes of the mountain on the left. It passes a small wet area before beginning a steady, moderate climb, passing a huge boulder on the left. The path now crosses a brook on a log bridge, then passes a cave behind a waterfall on the left. Climbing up a gully, the path turns left, crosses the brook on another bridge, and scrambles over a boulder area to reach Inscription Rock and the Indian Monument Trail at 0.75 mi.

Hickey Trail

Distances from parking area on US 7 (946 ft.) to
- Inscription Rock: 0.8 mi., 45 min.
- summit (about 0.1 mi. north of Squaw Peak) (1,642 ft.): 0.9 mi., 55 min.

Squaw Peak Trail (TTOR)

Squaw Peak Trail begins at Inscription Rock at the junction of the Hickey and Indian Monument Trails on the far eastern end of the mountain. The trail then runs across the spine of the ridge, crossing the summit of Squaw Peak before angling down the slope to join the Indian Monument Trail 0.75 mi. from the parking area.

From Inscription Rock the trail climbs steeply up stone steps to the quartzite outcrops that mark the true summit of Monument Mtn. (1,642 ft.). The path weaves among the boulders, pines, and azaleas before descending into a small saddle between the two peaks. The path then climbs up to the ragged sheer cliffs of Squaw Peak (1,640 ft.). The path now begins a small loop, with one fork descending along the rocks to Devil's Pulpit. The other loop descends, steeply at first, joins the other loop descending from the Pulpit, then traverses the ridge to end at the Indian Monument Trail.

Squaw Peak Trail

Distances from Inscription Rock to
- true summit (1,642 ft.): 0.1 mi., 10 min.
- Squaw Peak (1,640 ft.): 0.3 mi., 15 min.
- Indian Monument Trail: 0.7 mi., 35 min.

Tyringham Cobble

Tyringham Cobble is a prominent hill high above Tyringham village. The storied location once served as pastureland for the livestock of the Tyringham Shaker community. Today the hillside is traversed by the Appalachian Trail and is covered with forest and pastures that give the "cobble" a unique, inviting feeling. A touch of mystery was added to the place by geologist Daniel Clark, who ascertained that the oldest rocks were at the top of the cobble and the youngest at the bottom, just the reverse of what should be. He concluded that the cobble was dislodged from a nearby mountain and was flipped upside down during a catastrophe of mind-boggling intensity. The open meadows on the cobble's slopes come alive in late summer and autumn with the blooms of colorful wildflowers including asters and uncommon fringed gentians.

To reach the cobble from the Massachusetts Turnpike (I-90) in Lee (Exit 2) head east on US 20, then turn quickly right onto MA 102, followed in a few yards by a left turn onto Tyringham Main Rd. Travel 4.2 mi. to Tyringham village, take a right onto Jerusalem Rd., and proceed about 0.2 mi. to a parking area on the right. Information and the trailhead are near the big red barn.

Tyringham Cobble Loop Trail (TTOR)

The 1.9-mi.-long white-blazed Tyringham Cobble Loop Trail runs from the red barn near the parking area and follows the fence line to the fork in the loop. Following the trail clockwise—as is most popular—the path heads easily uphill through open fields to its union with the AT, also white-blazed. The AT, which formerly passed over the south slope of the cobble, has been recently rerouted to follow the Loop Trail over the 1,250-ft. summit. The trail bears right and climbs through patches of field and forest to the overlook atop the cobble. The path next descends past a field with wide views of the village below and enters the woods. The descent of the cobble is easy, passing along old woods roads some of the way. The path now enters a pasture and easily descends to the loop junction and parking area.

Tyringham Cobble Loop Trail
Distance from parking area trailhead (972 ft.) to
  • summit of cobble (1,250 ft.): 0.9 mi., 45 min.
  • trailhead (circuit): 1.9 mi., 1 hr. 10 min.

McClennan Reservation

McClennan Reservation protects 491 acres of wild forest and swampland surrounding Round Mtn. (1,517 ft.). The white-blazed foot trail loops around the foot of the mountain, visiting cellar holes, waterfalls, and Hale Pond Meadow along the way. Tradition has it that centuries ago, the Mohican Nation had a sugar camp on the banks of Camp Brook where they lived while making maple sugar each spring. Later the land became tended fields, but a few isolated old trees remain to this day. The property is crossed by old road lines, with stone walls and many stone foundations of forgotten homes and barns. It was one of three farms that were part of Ashintully, a large estate owned by an area family.

To reach McClennan Reservation from the I-90 (Massachusetts Turnpike) and US 20 junction (Exit 2) take MA 102 west for a few yards, then turn left onto Tyringham Main Rd. Proceed to Tyringham village and continue south 2.0 mi. to Fenn Rd. on the left. Park along the side of the road and walk up the dirt road 0.4 mi. to the trailhead.

Round Mtn. Trail (TTOR)

From the trailhead the easy white-blazed trail soon reaches the foot of Round Mtn. and begins to trace a course along the southern slope. The trail reaches a cluster of foundations and stone walls at 0.6 mi. and enters a dark evergreen forest. At 1.0 mi. the trail splits, the right fork making a straight course to Hale Pond Meadow and the left path following along the cascades of Camp Brook. Bear right to reach Hale Meadow at 1.3 mi. The trail then follows along the edge of the meadow, passing more ruins at 1.5 mi. The trail now joins an old woods road that descends to the trailhead at 2.0 mi.

Round Mtn. Trail

Distances from Fenn Rd. trailhead to
- trailhead: 0.4 mi., 20 min.
- ruins: 0.6 mi., 30 min.
- trail split: 1.0 mi., 45 min.
- Hale Meadow: 1.3 mi., 55 min.
- trailhead (circuit): 2.0 mi., 1 hr. 20 min.
- Fenn Rd.: 2.4 mi., 1 hr. 40 min.

Pittsfield State Forest

Pittsfield State Forest contains about 10,000 acres of forests, ponds, and mountains in the central Taconics. There are numerous peaks, including Berry Mtn. (2,182 ft.), Tower Mtn. (2,175 ft.), and Pine Mtn. (2,221 ft.). Berry Mtn. has 65 acres of wild azaleas, near the Taconic Crest Trail, that bloom in June. Berry Pond, on the flank of Berry Mtn., is one of the highest-elevation ponds in Massachusetts. There are two camping areas with a combined 31 sites. Berry Pond Campground has 13 sites; Parker Brook has 18. Universal-access restrooms and a universal-access trail are available near the forest headquarters.

Hawthorne Trail (DCR)

This narrow, strenuous trail, steep in places, leads up the eastern slope of Pine Mtn. and serves as a link to the Pine Mtn. Trail. It is open to multiuse, non-motorized activities. From Pittsfield, at the junction of Routes 20 and 7 south of the city center, turn onto Rte. 20 west (West Housatonic St.). Travel 2.6 mi. to Hungerford St., turn right onto Hungerford St., and drive to the intersection with West St. Turn left on West St. and continue 1.2 mi. to Churchill St. Take a right onto Churchill St. and drive 1.7 mi. to Cascade St. Turn left onto Cascade St. and follow to the state forest entrance. After crossing the footbridge, the Tranquility Trail, a paved universal-access path, is passed on the right. The trail continues straight, passing many side trails, then swings right and ascends the hillside with Hawthorne Brook and its ravine to the left. The ascent is steep at the start, moderates as the path passes through thick laurel, then becomes steeper again. The path crosses the brook, now just a trickle, a few yards before reaching the junction with the Pine Mtn. Trail. It continues past a stone boundary marker on Pine Mtn. and descends to Tilden Pond. At the trail junction, a left leads to Tower Mtn. via a fire road and a right leads to Tilden Pond Dam and to Berry Pond via the same fire road.

Hawthorne Trail

Distances from Pittsfield State Forest ski lodge and parking area (1,172 ft.) to
- Pine Mtn. Trail: 0.9 mi., 50 min.
- Pine Mtn. (2,220 ft.) via Pine Mtn. Trail.: 1.4 mi., 1 hr. 15 min.
- Tilden Pond via Pine Mtn. Trail (1,982 ft.): 2.0 mi., 1 hr. 35 min.

Tranquility Trail (DCR)

This very easy 0.75-mi.-long universal-access trail begins a few yards west of the wooden footbridge opposite the parking area and ski lodge. The smooth paved loop path passes along the bank of Parker Brook, then loops back through cool forest to the start. A wheelchair-accessible picnic area and restrooms are near the trail.

Tranquility Trail
Distance from wooden footbridge at parking area to
  • trailhead (circuit): 0.8 mi., 25 min.

Parker Brook Trail (DCR)

This strenuous blue-blazed trail starts in back of the comfort station at the Parker Brook Campground in Pittsfield State Forest. It is open to multi-use, nonmotorized activities. At 500 ft. a cross-country ski trail exits left over a bridge to the blue-blazed Hawthorne Trail (0.3 mi.). The trail then ascends Parker Brook ravine, roughly paralleling the Berry Pond Circuit Rd. that runs along the opposite bank. Small, sparkling cascades are common in the brook along this stretch. At 1.0 mi. the circuit road swings away from the brook, and the path traces a moderate route up the dirt-and-stone trail bed to Tilden Pond, emerging immediately south of the beaver dam at the junction with the Pine Mtn. Trail. To reach Berry Pond turn right, cross the dam, and continue about 0.3 mi. on the Pine Mtn. Trail through beech forest to reach the circuit road. Turn left and ascend about 0.2 mi. to Berry Pond.

Parker Brook Trail
Distance from Parker Brook Campground comfort station (1,263 ft.) to
  • Tilden Pond (1,982 ft.): 1.3 mi., 1 hr. 10 min.

Lulu Brook Trail (DCR)

This narrow blue-blazed hiking path parallels the north bank of Lulu Brook just a few yards from the Berry Pond Circuit Rd. that follows the south bank. It starts at the Lulu Cascade picnic area on the right of the circuit road just before the stone bridge. The trail clings to the steep side of the brook and ends at the Taconic Skyline Trail.

Lulu Brook Trail
Distances from Lulu Cascade picnic area to
• Taconic Skyline Trail: 1.9 mi., 1 hr. 25 min.

Shaker Trail (DCR, BSA)

This very attractive moderate trail combines history and nature into one exciting experience. The 5.0-mi.-long loop trail begins and ends at Hancock Shaker Village on US 20 in Hancock and includes portions of Hancock Shaker Village and Pittsfield State Forest. The trail is maintained by the Boy Scouts of America (Hancock Shaker Village) and DCR (Pittsfield State Forest).

To reach the trailhead, travel 4.2 mi. west along US 20 from its intersection with US 7 in Pittsfield. Park in the Shaker Village parking area and proceed to the visitor center a few yards away. In the visitor center ask to hike the Shaker Trail; a "hiker" sticker will be provided. Once registered, walk to the brick meetinghouse and cross US 20 on the crosswalk. Pass through the gate and hike down the grassy unblazed cart path to the beginning of the path. The trail markers begin near the ruins of the Shaker dam. The path now turns right past more ruins, then heads left and begins to ascend Shaker Mtn. on a wide cart path. At 1.5 mi. the path reaches the top of Shaker Mtn. (1,845 ft.), an area used for religious activities in the 1840s. The path then continues north and descends to the junction with the CCC Trail at 2.0 mi. (A shorter loop can be made by turning left and following the CCC Trail to the Shaker Trail and back to Hancock Shaker Village.) The path is level as it passes between Doll Mtn. and Holy Mount. At an abandoned orchard in a marshy area (2.8 mi.) the trail turns left and climbs up to the crest of Holy Mount (1,968 ft.), the hilltop used by the Shaker community in New Lebanon, N.Y. The trail crosses the summit (3.0 mi.) and past a stone wall more than a mile long that completely encloses the mountaintop. The Shaker Trail now joins the CCC Trail, following it along a brook. At 4.0 mi. the CCC Trail leaves left and the Shaker Trail continues south, passing the overgrown remains of a marble quarry and reaching the ruins of the stone dam at 4.5 mi. From the dam it is a short walk back to the crosswalk at US 20.

Shaker Trail
Distances from Meeting House, Hancock Shaker Village (1,170 ft.) to
- top of Shaker Mtn. (1,845 ft.): 1.5 mi., 45 min.
- north junction with CCC Trail: 2.0 mi., 1 hr. 5 min.
- old orchard: 2.8 mi., 1 hr. 45 min.
- top of Holy Mount (1,968 ft.): 3.0 mi., 2 hr.
- washed-out dam: 4.5 mi., 2 hr. 45 min.
- Shaker Meeting House (circuit): 5.0 mi., 3 hr.

Housatonic River Greenway Trail (HVA)

The easy Housatonic River Greenway Trail runs along the East Branch of the Housatonic River in Hinsdale and Dalton. The path runs about 0.8 mi. from the trailhead off Old Dalton Rd. in Hinsdale to MA 8 in Dalton. The trail follows the river through fields and hemlock forests to historic ruins of the Plunkett mill, including remains of the old dam and penstock.

To reach the trailhead, travel about 2.8 mi. south on MA 8 from the intersection of MA 8 and 8A in Dalton. Turn left onto Old Dalton Rd., cross the bridge, then turn left into the parking area. The trail is on land owned by the Crane Paper Company and is maintained by the Housatonic Valley Association (HVA).

Housatonic River Greenway Trail
Distance from Old Dalton Rd. trailhead to
- MA 8 in Dalton: 0.8 mi., 25 min.

October Mtn. State Forest

October Mtn. State Forest is the largest state forest in the commonwealth, with more than 16,000 acres of woodlands and lakes. The forest sports five large lakes—Buckley-Dunton Lake, October Mtn. Reservoir, Finerty Pond, Schoolhouse Reservoir, and Felton Lake. Halfway Pond is a wonderful example of a quaking bog, and Washington Mtn. Meadow is a huge fen with many exciting plant and animal communities. Some of the higher points include Walling Mtn. (2,220 ft.), Bald Top (2,040 ft.), and Beckett Mtn. (2,200 ft.). Forty-six campsites are available at the camping area on Woodland St. in Lee; many are universally accessible.

Appalachian Trail (DCR, AMC)

The Appalachian Trail runs through nearly 7 mi. of October Mtn. State Forest from near Greenwater Pond in the south to just east of Sandwash Reservoir in the north. For a complete description see Appalachian Trail, Section 6, US 20 to Pittsfield Rd., on page 12.

Washington Mtn. Meadow Interpretive Trail System

This little-known trail system is one of the pleasant surprises of the Berkshires, incorporating a 0.2-mi.-long universal-access nature trail and nearly 3.4 mi. of hiking through one of the most unique ecosystems in Massachusetts. The Washington Mtn. Meadow Interpretive Trail is a complex of four trails—the Interpretive Loop Trail (1.5 mi.), Knob Loop Trail (0.4 mi.), Outer Loop Trail (1.4 mi.), and Marsh View Accessible Trail (0.2 mi.). The trail complex thoroughly explores Washington Mtn. Meadow, a high elevation (1,800 ft.) boggy fen that is the remnant of failed attempts in the 1980s to build a lake on this site. The timber was removed and the dams constructed, but the huge earth-and-stone creations leaked and the lake never came to be. What did come to be was an immense wet meadow that has become a haven for myriad plants and animals.

The Washington Mtn. Meadow Interpretive Trail is in the heart of October Mtn. State Forest, but situated so as to be easily overlooked. To reach the trailhead from Lee and the junction of US 20 and the Massachusetts Turnpike (Exit 2) follow US 20 east 1.2 mi. and turn left onto Maple St. Continue 2.3 mi. to Mill St. At the stop sign turn right and travel 0.5 mi. to Willow Hill Rd. Turn sharp right onto Willow Hill Rd. (this becomes Woodland Rd.), and drive past the state forest campground on the right, followed by the October Mtn. State Forest Headquarters on the left (maps available). Follow Woodland Rd. to Woods Pond on the left, bear right onto Roaring Brook Rd., and follow the dirt road along the pond's shore for 0.5 mi. to paved but steep Schermerhorn Rd. on the right. Turn right and travel 3.4 mi. over mostly dirt roads to Lenox-Whitney Place Rd. Turn right onto Lenox-Whitney Place Rd. and continue 1.3 mi. to a fourway junction. Turn right onto Meadow Trail and drive 0.5 mi. to a parking area on the left. The trailhead is at the north end of the parking area. Trail maps are available at the trailhead.

Interpretive Loop Trail (DCR)

From the parking area follow the Marsh View Accessible Trail to the overlook at 0.2 mi., where the blue-blazed Interpretive Loop Trail begins. Turn left from the overlook and descend through shrubby growth to the base of the meadow. The trail crosses the fen on a long run of bog bridging, climbs the far shore, and passes two junctions with the Knob Loop Trail on the left. The path crosses a hemlock swamp on more bridging before reaching the Outer Loop junction at 0.8 mi. Turn right to an overlook with a beautiful view of the marsh and a large beaver pond usually teeming with wildlife. The path climbs up the ridge and wanders through woods, rejoining the Marsh View Accessible Trail a few yards south of the accessible overlook. *(Note: The portion of the trail that crosses the meadow between the Outer Loop Trail junctions has been affected by beaver flooding and may be closed or impassable; hikers seeking a circuit can incorporate the longer but easy Outer Loop Trail.)*

Interpretive Loop Trail

Distances from parking area to
- Knob Loop Trail: 0.4 mi., 15 min.
- west junction with Outer Loop Trail: 0.8 mi., 25 min.
- east junction with Outer Loop Trail: 1.1 mi., 40 min.
- junction with Marsh View Accessible Trail: 1.7 mi., 55 min.

Outer Loop Trail (DCR)

This woodland path begins on a bluff at a signed junction with the Interpretive Loop Trail. From the junction the path descends to the marsh and crosses the outlet of a beaver dam on bog bridging. The path then climbs onto high ground and traces the perimeter of the immense north portion of the meadow. At the far north end of the meadow the trail crosses Washington Mtn. Brook before swinging south and ending at the junction with the Interpretive Loop Trail on the eastern end of the meadow.

Outer Loop Trail

Distances from Interpretive Loop Trail (western trailhead) to
- crossing of beaver pond outlet: 0.1 mi., 5 min.
- crossing of Washington Mtn. Brook: 0.8 mi., 20 min.
- junction with Interpretive Loop Trail (eastern trailhead): 1.4 mi., 40 min.

Schermerhorn Gorge Trail (DCR)

To reach the trailhead from Lee and the junction of US 20 and the Massachusetts Turnpike (Exit 2), follow US 20 east 1.2 mi. and turn left onto Maple St. Continue 2.3 mi. to Mill St. At the stop sign turn right and travel 0.5 mi. to Willow Hill Rd., turn sharp right onto Willow Hill Rd. (which becomes Woodland Rd.), and drive past the state forest campground on the right, followed by the October Mtn. State Forest Headquarters on the left (maps available). Follow Woodland Rd. to Woods Pond on the left, bear right onto Roaring Brook Rd., and follow the dirt road along the pond's shore for 0.5 mi. to paved but steep Schermerhorn Rd. on the right. Turn right and travel up the hill 1.0 mi. to the parking area on the left by the state forest gate. From the gate walk down the woods road about 0.1 mi. and cross the stone bridge below Fenton Lake.

The Schermerhorn Gorge Trail is a moderately difficult loop path that runs along both sides of the brook as it passes through the gorge. On descent, the path following the north bank is best. On ascent, use the south route. The steepest portion is near Roaring Brook Rd., with an overall elevation gain of more than 500 ft. in 0.8 mi. It is also possible to park at the base of the circuit at a turnout on Roaring Brook Road, which allows a descent on the return route.

Schermerhorn Gorge Trail

Distances from trailhead at old stone bridge at Fenton Lake (1,578 ft.) to
- Roaring Brook Rd. (800 ft.): 0.8 mi., 30 min.
- old stone bridge (circuit): 1.6 mi., 1 hr. 15 min.

Pleasant Valley Sanctuary

This 1,300-acre wildlife sanctuary, maintained by the Massachusetts Audubon Society, is located on the east slope of Lenox Mtn. in the town of

Lenox. A large trail network explores beaver ponds, marshes, streams, and forests. All 7.0 mi. of trails are blazed with blue and yellow marks: the blue blazes lead away from the sanctuary office (primary trailhead), while the yellow blazes lead toward the office. All trail junctions are clearly signed.

From the intersection of US 7 and 20 drive north 3 mi. to West Dugway Rd. on the left. Follow West Dugway Rd. to the intersection at 0.75 mi. Turn left onto West Mtn. Rd. (dirt) and travel 0.8 mi. to the sanctuary entrance and parking. Trail information is available at the office near the parking area.

Pike's Pond Trail (MAS)

This trail, which offers an easy, relaxing walk around the waters and wetlands of Pike's Pond, begins at the office and heads across the lawn to a long boardwalk that negotiates a shrubby swamp. The path then roughly follows the south shore of the pond before crossing a section of Yokun Brook on a wooden bridge at 0.3 mi. The trail swings around the west shore, passing the Trail of the Ledges (left) and Yokun Trail (left) before running very closely along the north shore. The path then leaves the pond and ends at the Bluebird Trail about 400 ft. north of the office. A wheelchair-accessible trail here, opened in 2008, includes benches and an observation deck.

Pike's Pond Trail

Distances from the sanctuary office to
- bridge over Yokun Brook: 0.3 mi., 15 min.
- junction with Bluebird Trail: 0.5 mi., 25 min.
- office (circuit): 0.6 mi., 30 min.

Trail of the Ledges (MAS, DCR)

This strenuous, sometimes very steep trail leads from the Pike's Pond Trail to the top of Lenox Mtn. (2,126 ft.), an elevation gain of about 800 ft. The summit area is owned by the state of Massachusetts and managed by the Department of Conservation and Recreation (DCR). It offers excellent views to the west and north.

The trail begins from its junction with the Pike's Pond Trail located 0.3 mi. from the office. The trail initially ascends along a stream and past the junctions of the Waycross and Ravine Trails. The trail then leaves the brook and climbs steeply to the Laurel Trail, where a ledge offers an excellent view. It continues past another lookout on the right at 0.75 mi. and reaches the summit at 1.25 mi. *(Note: The Trail of the Ledges is not recommended for descent; use the Overbrook Trail on the return trip!)* ⚠

Trail of the Ledges
Distances from junction with Pike's Pond Trail (1,327 ft.) to
- Laurel Trail: 0.5 mi., 20 min.
- lookout: 0.8 mi., 45 min.
- summit of Lenox Mtn. (2,126 ft.): 1.25 mi., 1 hr.

Overbrook Trail (MAS, DCR)

The recommended route for descent in all weather conditions, this steep and strenuous trail also offers an alternate route to the summit. To reach the trail, follow the Bluebird Trail north from the office to the Ovenbird Trail at 0.3 mi. Turn left onto the Ovenbird Trail, which follows a brook a short distance to the Overbrook Trail. The Overbrook Trail heads northwest up the slope of Lenox Mtn., passing the four-way junction with the Great Hemlock and Laurel Trails at 0.5 mi. The path ascends along a ravine, weaving from bank to bank before leaving the sanctuary and climbing to the summit at 1.3 mi.

Overbrook Trail
Distances from sanctuary office (1,346 ft.) to
- Overbrook Trail: 0.3 mi., 15 min.
- Laurel Trail: 0.5 mi., 25 min.
- summit of Lenox Mtn. (2,126 ft.): 1.3 mi., 1 hr.

Field Farm

Field Farm in Williamstown holds more than 300 acres of pasture, fields, wetlands, and woodlands explored by over 4 mi. of trails. The property includes a guest house accommodating up to fourteen visitors and landscaped gardens dotted with modern art sculptures. Much of the land surrounding the house has been used for agriculture since at least 1750. The property is shaped like an elongated rectangle 1.5 mi. long astride the foot-hills of the northern Taconics, offering grand views of Mt. Greylock across the valley to the east. Trails are blazed in yellow.

To reach Field Farm, from the five-corners junction in South Wil-liamstown (intersection of US 7 and MA 43) turn onto MA 43 west for a few yards, then turn immediately right onto Sloan Rd. Travel 1.1 mi. to the entrance on the right. To hike, follow the right fork of the driveway, which leads to a parking area near the garage. For the guest house continue straight to the parking area on the west side of the house.

South Trail (TTOR)

This trail leaves the Pond Trail at the southeast end of the pond and heads south along a marshy area. It soon crosses Sloan Rd. and continues along the wetland, crossing the outflow at 0.2 mi. The trail then splits. Turning right to begin the loop, the path heads northwest, then west along the bor-der of forest and field, coming to a brook at 0.45 mi. Following the stream for a short distance, the path then wanders downslope, crosses a low ridge, and heads uphill to complete the loop at 1.3 mi., returning to the trailhead at 1.5 mi.

South Trail (map 1: D2)
Distances from pond side trailhead (1,000 ft.) to
- wetland outlet (1,000 ft.): 0.2 mi., 10 min.
- brook (1,000 ft.): 0.45 mi., 20 min.
- close of trail loop: 1.3 mi., 50 ft., 50 min.
- pond trailhead (circuit): 1.5 mi., 50 ft., 1 hr.

North Trail (TTOR)

The North Trail begins west of the guest house at a sign in an open field, then runs directly to the fence line at the west end of a cornfield. Turning north, the path reaches a fenced pasture at 0.3 mi. The trail passes through the stile and continues along the fence line, exiting the pasture at 0.5 mi. The path enters the woods, then turns right, descending, swinging right again, and reentering the pasture. This portion of the trail can be difficult to follow, as the trail posts are sometimes knocked over by cows and the animals make their own trails through the bush. At 1.0 mi. the Oak Loop Trail leaves left, and at 1.1 mi. rejoins at its eastern junction. The North Trail follows the fence line, exits the pasture for the last time, then runs south through a cornfield to the southeast corner of the pond. To return to the guest house follow the Pond Trail northwest through the fields to the north side of the house.

North Trail (map 1: D2)
Distances from the Field Farm guest house (1,000 ft.) to
- first pasture stile (1,000 ft.): 0.3 mi., 15 min.
- second pasture stile (1,000 ft.): 0.5 mi., 25 min.
- Oak Loop Trail junction (1,000 ft.): 1.0 mi., 45 min.
- southeast end of pond (1,000 ft.): 1.5 mi., 1 hr. 5 min.

Oak Loop and Caves Trail (TTOR)

The Oak Loop Trail also includes the Caves Trail, a very interesting path that passes by the McMaster cave system. From the eastern junction with the North Trail, the Oak Loop Trail passes through the fence line and into the woods. It crosses a brook and climbs easily through the forest, coming to a short connector path at 0.25 mi.

The trail continues up the ridge through open woods and over the height-of-land at about 1,090 ft. The path now descends along the ridge line to an intersection in a low, level spot at 0.6 mi. The trail turns left (another dead-end path leaves right) and follows the very level trail bed to underground streams at 0.8 mi. The trail is actually on top of the caves, so it is hard to see them. They are a series of three entrances 2 to 3 ft. wide, at the drainage line of the wetland to the west of the trail. In winter the caves can be clogged with ice, damming the wetland and forming a pond. In spring when everything melts the pond can disappear in minutes as the water floods down the caves. From the caves the path continues easily past the connector trail to a brook, then back into the pasture to meet the North Trail at 1.1 mi.

Oak Loop and Caves Trail (map 1: D2)
Distance from eastern junction with North Trail (1,000 ft.) to
- connector path (1,000 ft.): 0.25 mi., 10 min. ▶

- north end of loop (1,000 ft.): 0.6 mi., 20 min.
- caves (1,000 ft.): 0.8 mi., 30 min.
- western junction with North Trail (1,000 ft.): 1.1 mi., 45 min.

Taconic Crest Trail (THC, DCR)

The white-blazed Taconic Crest Trail (TCT) runs for 35 mi. in a north-south direction along the ridge of the Taconic Range, passing through Massachusetts, New York, and Vermont. The trail runs from Prosser Hollow in Petersburg, N.Y., to US 20 in Hancock, Mass. The trail elevation varies from 1,000 ft. at Prosser Hollow to 2,818 ft. on the summit of Berlin Mtn. The cumulative ascent along the trail in a south-north direction is 6,700 ft. The trail's average elevation exceeds 2,200 ft. The Taconic Range is densely covered by mixed hardwood forests with red spruce and balsam fir in the highest elevations. Open, grassy balds and meadows dot the mountains, offering many places to sit and enjoy the view of the Green Mtns., the Catskills, Greylock and the Hoosac Range, and even the far-off Adirondacks.

The TCT is marked at intersections with blue squares with white-diamond inserts that say Taconic Crest Trail, and within the trail corridor with white diamonds. Access trails are designated by similar blue markers. Because this is a ridge trail, water sources close to the trail are infrequent. The following descriptions run from north to south and are divided into sections, each a day's hike apart. Several side trails and access trails that connect with the Taconic Crest Trail are described later in the book, under North Taconic Trails.

Section 1. Prosser Hollow, N.Y. to Petersburg Pass (NY 2) (7.4 mi.)

Note: This section of the trail is closed to mountain bikes and motorized vehicles. The northern terminus of the TCT is located on Prosser Hollow Rd., which is off NY 22 about 2.4 mi. north of NY 2 in Petersburg. The trail rises steeply to the ridge and turns south, reaching a sharp drop off to the east. Continuing south, at 4.5 mi. a side trail (marked S.H.) enters from the left (east). Following it downhill a short distance leads to the fabled Snow Hole. The side trail approaches the cliff from the crest, then swings around to the narrow mouth of the crevice. The rock is similar to soapstone, and there are initials with dates as far back as the middle 1800s here. In the Snow Hole it's cold all the time, with snow frequently lasting until June.

From the Snow Hole the trail continues south through hardwoods, emerging into a number of clearings—some brushy, some grassy—on the western side of the ridge that look out over the valley. Visible below is NY 2 to Petersburg, N.Y., the old abandoned ski area at Petersburg Pass, and Mt. Greylock to the southeast. About 1.0 mi. after the clearings the red-blazed Birch Brook Trail descends left to Hopkins Memorial Forest. In another 0.75 mi. the blue-blazed Shepherd's Well Trail exits left. The TCT now eventually emerges in a clearing near a sign prohibiting mountain bikes and motorized vehicles from this section of trail, and descends to meet NY 2 at Petersburg Pass at 7.4 mi. Parking is available on the south side of NY 2.

Taconic Crest Trail: Prosser Hollow, N.Y. to Petersburg Pass (NY 2) (map 1: A1–B1)

Distances from Prosser Hollow Rd. to
- top of ridge: 1.8 mi., 1 hr.
- side trail to Snow Hole (2,490 ft.): 4.5 mi., 2 hr. 50 min.
- Birch Brook Trail (2,300 ft.): 5.5 mi., 3 hr. 30 min.
- Shepherd's Well Trail (2,200 ft.): 6.9 mi., 4 hr. 30 min.
- Petersburg Pass (NY 2) (2,100 ft.): 7.4 mi., 4 hr. 50 min.

Section 2. Petersburg Pass (NY 2) to Southeast Hollow and Mills Hollow Trails (5.2 mi.)

Note: This section is heavily used by mountain bikes, all-terrain vehicles, and dirt bikes. The trail from the south side of Mt. Raimer to the top of Berlin Mtn. is a mess of mud holes, erosion, and bootleg bypass trails. The parking lot is located 4.0 mi. west from the intersection of MA 2 and US 7 in Williamstown. The parking area has a kiosk at the south end near bootleg trails that dirt bikes and mountain bikes have created up the north slope of Mt. Raimer. The white-blazed TCT exits the parking area at the southwest corner, past placed boulders and a small view west. It soon reaches a side trail that descends right while the TCT keeps left, briefly dips, then rises steeply on a badly eroded old woods roads with sections of loose rock. The path ascends to a junction with a red-blazed trail that leaves left to climb to the top of Mt. Raimer. Stay to the right, following white markers on a heavily rutted woods road that winds along the wooded ridge. The trail turns right and descends to an open clearing high above Berlin Pass, with extensive views over the back of Berlin Mtn.

Descending to the pass on a path of loose stone and ruts, the trail intersects the old Albany–Boston Post Rd. (also known as the Greene Hollow Access Trail and the Berlin Pass Trail; description under North Taconic Trails). To the west it is 1.4 mi. to Greene Hollow and 4.5 mi. to Berlin, N.Y. To the east it is 0.8 mi. to Berlin Rd., in Williamstown, Mass. There is water down the Berlin Pass Trail to the east. Bottle gentians are common here in late summer.

Crossing Post Rd. and ascending the woods road south, the trail winds up the woods road toward Berlin Mtn. Near the top is a badly eroded section of staircase ledge and a long bootleg bypass on the left used by all-terrain vehicles and mountain bikes. The summit is a grassy meadow dotted with hardwoods and evergreens. The concrete footings of the fire tower mark the summit (2,818 ft.) at 2.8 mi. To the east the Class of '33 Trail descends into the woods toward the old Williams College ski area. From the summit, the highest point on the trail, there are fine views in all directions. Especially prominent is Mt. Greylock to the east.

From Berlin Mtn. the TCT descends southeast through a dense spruce grove then open, predominantly hardwood, forest, crossing the crest of an unnamed peak (2,721 ft.) 0.35 mi. southeast of Berlin Mtn. The trail now makes a long descent along the ridge, reaching a saddle at 3.7 mi. It then climbs steeply for 0.25 mi. and moderates as it crests the next summit (2,542 ft.), overlooking South Williamstown. The trail now descends to a col where the Phelps Trail (Williamstown Rural Lands Foundation) enters left at 4.2 mi. This steep 1.5-mi.-long blue-blazed trail follows the ravine of a brook down to Oblong Rd. in South Williamstown.

From the Phelps Trail the path cruises over a pretty section of ridge, crossing two low peaks before dropping down to the saddle at the head of Southeast Hollow. Here it intersects the Southeast Hollow Trail at 5.2 mi.; this trail leads 1.7 mi. to Southeast Hollow Rd., then on to Berlin, N.Y. To the left is Mills Hollow Trail, which leads to Oblong Rd. in Williamstown, Mass.

Wild ginger is found near the junction with the Southeast Hollow Trail. Water is found about 0.7 mi. down this access trail. A few yards south of the junction is a stone monument marking the New York–Massachusetts border.

Taconic Crest Trail: Petersburg Pass (NY 2) to Southeast Hollow and Mills Hollow Trails (map 1: B1–D1)

Distance from Petersburg Pass (NY 2) (2,100 ft.) to
- Albany-Boston Post Rd. (Berlin Pass Trail) (2,200 ft.): 1.6 mi., 300 ft. (rev. 200 ft.), 1 hr. 15 min.
- summit of Berlin Mtn. (2,818 ft.): 2.8 mi., 900 ft., 1 hr. 50 min.
- Phelps Trail (2,450 ft.): 4.4 mi., 1,250 ft. (rev. 500 ft.), 3 hr.
- Southeast Hollow and Mills Hollow Trails (2,100 ft.): 5.2 mi., 1,250 ft. (rev. 200 ft.), 3 hr. 30 min.

Section 3. Southeast Hollow and Mills Hollow Trails to Mattison Hollow Trail (2.6 mi.)

The TCT proceeds south from the junction with the Southeast Hollow Trail and in a few yards turns sharp left at the stone monument marking the New York–Massachusetts border. After a short distance it climbs steeply to a nearly level terrace, runs its length, and then climbs to an open peak (2,646 ft.) that straddles the state line at 0.7 mi. From the peak the trail makes an easy descent over a really nice stretch to a trail passing over three small knobby summits before bending right (southwest) and dropping to the junction of the Mattison Hollow Trail in a col at 2.6 mi.

Taconic Crest Trail: Southeast Hollow and Mills Hollow Trails to Mattison Hollow Trail (map 1: D1–E1)

Distances from Southeast Hollow and Mills Hollow Trails (1,900 ft.) to
- open peak (2,646 ft.): 0.7 mi., 750 ft., 30 min.
- Mattison Hollow Trail (2,150 ft.): 2.6 mi., 750 ft. (rev. 500 ft.) 1 hr. 15 min.

Section 4. Mattison Hollow Trail to Potter Mtn. Rd. Trailhead (9.8 mi.)

The TCT proceeds south from the junction with the Mattison Hollow Trail, climbing moderately for about 0.4 mi., then leveling out as it crosses the wide shoulder of a peak. At 0.5 mi. is a metal state-line marker; farther on is a stone state-line monument. Water is available in the next low place, where the TCT joins a snowmobile trail.

The trail now wanders over Misery Mtn., a ridge with steep slopes creased with deep ravines on the east and west. The ridge crest is broad and generally level, with undulations typical of mountainous terrain. The wide nature of the ridge and the wooded knolls along the way can make following the path more challenging here than elsewhere on the range. After crossing the main peak (2,611 ft.) of Misery Mtn. at 2.2 mi., the trail veers south through hardwoods and across several knobs. It exits off the jeep trail that was the old TCT (watch for blazes) and comes out on the last summit in an open meadow. From the last summit the trail descends steeply about 0.4 mi. to the crest of Rathburn Hollow at 3.2 mi.

The trail crosses a small stream immediately south of Rathburn Hollow, then easily ascends along the ridge through hardwoods to the top of an open meadow known as Bill's Lunch. Here there is a small grove of evergreens and good views of the Taconic Valley.

For the next 0.75 mi. the trail descends steeply through the meadow, enters the woods, and follows a small stream. It then turns westward downhill through mixed hardwoods and evergreens. After crossing a stream, it crosses a snowmobile trail and begins a long ascent to the open summit of Rounds Mtn. (2,257 ft.) at 2.5 mi.

At Rounds Mtn. the trail turns left for about 100 yd. on a well-used dirt road, then turns sharp left into the woods. The unmarked Rounds Mtn. Trail continues straight ahead. (*Caution: Due to an absence of trees, neither of the two trail junctions with this dirt road is well marked.*) The trail now descends steadily, steeply in spots, finally meeting a well-used woods road at about 3.2 mi. Crossing the road, the trail makes a gradual ascent through a birch grove, turns sharp right, and descends steeply to the village of Hancock, Mass. From here the trail follows roads a short distance through the village to MA 43 and Potter Mtn. Rd., then continues on Potter Mtn. Rd. about 1.2 mi. to a trailhead at 5.9 mi.

Taconic Crest Trail: Mattison Hollow Trail to Potter Mtn. Rd. Trailhead

Distances from Mattison Hollow Trail (2,150 ft.) to
- main peak of Misery Mtn. (2,611 ft.): 2.2 mi., 1 hr. 15 min.
- meadow on last summit: 2.8 mi., 2 hr. 15 min. ▶

- Rathburn Hollow: 3.2 mi., 2 hr. 35 min.
- summit of Rounds Mtn. (2,257 ft.): 6.4 mi., 3 hr. 45 min.
- woods road: 7.1 mi., 4 hr. 10 min.
- Potter Mtn. Rd. trailhead (1,510 ft.): 9.8 mi., 5 hr. 30 min.

Section 5. Hancock (Potter Mtn. Rd.) to US 20 (8.9 mi.)

The TCT was relocated through Pittsfield State Forest so that it no longer intersects the Taconic Skyline Trail at any point between Potter Mtn. Rd. and the trail's southern terminus at US 20 in Hancock. The TCT is open only as a footpath and is closed to all-terrain vehicles (ATVs), off-road vehicles (ORVs), and mountain bikes in the forest. Due to the heavy use of ATVs, ORVs, and mountain bikes, the Taconic Skyline Trail is not recommended for hiking.

From the trailhead on Potter Mtn. Rd. located about 0.25 mi. west for the trailhead of the Taconic Skyline Trail and about 1.2 mi. east of MA 43 in Hancock, the trail heads south, downhill. It then turns left (east) for a short distance, then regains its southerly course. As it nears the Taconic Skyline Trail the TCT begins a long slab of Pease Ridge, hugging the extreme western edge of the mountain. The trail reaches the far northwestern loop of Berry Pond Circuit Rd. (paved) at 2.5 mi., emerging to a great view west amid the azalea fields.

The trail then follows the road for a short distance, passing more azaleas (bloom time is late May to June) and Berry Pond (campground here)—the highest or second highest pond in the state, depending on whom you talk to. The trail now leaves Berry Pond Circuit Rd. for the last time at 3.0 mi. and heads southwest, descends to a low point, and then climbs to the top of Tower Mtn. and the junction with the Pine Mtn. Trail at 3.7 mi. From Tower Mtn. the path descends to Brickhouse Mtn. Rd., crosses this woods road at 4.0 mi. a few yards west of the Taconic Skyline Trail, then very closely parallels the Taconic Skyline Trail to Lebanon Springs Rd. at 5.7 mi. The trail along this section is most often thickly wooded with oak and other hardwoods, with some narrow glimpses of the valley to the west through the trees.

The trail continues to closely parallel the Taconic Skyline Trail, staying just to its west and crossing a woods road at 6.7 mi. The TCT continues south, skirting the Taconic Skyline Trail near the dam of Twin Ponds at 7.3 mi. Twin Ponds were built generations ago by the Shakers of New Lebanon as a water source, and the stonework of the dam is an example of their precise craftsmanship. From Twin Ponds the TCT continues south, coming close to the Taconic Skyline Trail near Cranberry Pond, then tracing a path down the slope to end at the west end of the parking area on the north side of US 20 at 8.9 mi.

Taconic Crest Trail: Hancock (Potter Mtn. Rd.) to US 20

Distances from Potter Mtn. Rd. (1,510 ft.) to
- Berry Pond Circuit Rd. (2,075 ft.): 2.5 mi., 1 hr. 20 min.
- Lebanon Springs Rd.: 5.7 mi., 3 hr.
- woods road: 6.7 mi., 3 hr. 50 min.
- Twin Ponds (1,695 ft.): 7.3 mi., 4 hr. 40 min.
- southern terminus at US 20 (1,500 ft.): 8.9 mi., 5 hr. 35 min.

North Taconic Range

This portion of the Taconic Range is situated at Massachusetts's northwest corner near the Vermont and New York state boundaries, north and west of Mt. Greylock. A number of trails, including the popular route to Pine Cobble's summit, are located here, mostly under the management of the Williams College Outing Club (WOC) and the Williamstown Rural Lands Foundation (WRLF). The trails are easily accessible from the center of Williamstown. From the Massachusetts line the Taconic Range stretches north along Vermont's western border, capped by 3,816-ft. Mt. Equinox near Manchester.

Birch Brook Trail (WOC)

This access trail to the Taconic Crest Trail, which is accessed via the Carriage Rd. and Upper Loop trails, begins in the Hopkins Memorial Forest of Williams College in Williamstown, Mass. To get to the forest, go west on Main St. in Williamstown to US 7 north, turn right, and proceed north for 0.3 mi. Bear left onto Bulkley St., continue 1.0 mi. to Northwest Hill Rd., and turn right. The trailhead is 1.4 mi. along Northwest Hill Rd.

From the road, the Carriage Rd. Trail leads south for 0.4 mi. to the Upper Loop trail. Turn right (west) on the Upper Loop trail and continue 0.6 mi. to the start of the Birch Brook Trail. The Birch Brook Trail continues west through deciduous forest interspersed with beautiful patches of ferns, crossing the New York state line and reaching the junction with the white-blazed Taconic Crest Trail at 1.5 mi. from the Upper Loop.

Birch Brook Trail (map 1: B2–B1)

Distances from Northwest Hill Rd. (1,000 ft.) to
- Birch Brook Trail (1,250 ft.): 1 mi., 250 ft., 35 min.
- Taconic Crest Trail (2,350 ft.): 2.7 mi., 1,350 ft., 1 hr. 50 min.

Berlin Pass Trail (WOC)

To reach this blue-blazed trail, start 3 mi. southwest of Williamstown at the junction of US 7 and MA 2. Take MA 2 uphill (west) for 0.5 mi. and turn left onto Torrey Woods Rd., which meets Berlin Rd.; continue west on Berlin Rd. to the abandoned Williams College ski area parking lot. Park on the right (north) side of the lot and take the path to the dirt road just ahead. (Do not take the trail blocked by a vandalized gate.)

This strenuous trail, once a section of the Boston-Albany Post Rd., leads uphill through a forest that gradually transitions from ash, sugar maple, poplar, and red oak to a beech and paper birch mix with oak, hop hornbeam, and red maple. At 1 mi. the trail reaches the Taconic Ridge at Berlin Pass (2,220 ft.), where it intersects the white-blazed Taconic Crest Trail. Following the TCT to the left (south), it is 1.2 mi. to the summit of Berlin Mtn. (The remains of an old charcoal kiln are located off the trail 100 ft. to the right, 0.5 mi. beyond the pass.) For a loop back to the parking lot climb Berlin Mtn. and then descend via the Class of '33 Trail (4.5 mi.) or the steep and unmaintained paths of the old Williams College ski area (3.0 mi.). The old Post Rd. crosses the pass and descends the west slope of the Taconic Range to Berlin, N.Y. Following the TCT to the right (north) from the junction leads across scenic open meadows to an abandoned ski area and NY 2 in Petersburg Pass.

Berlin Pass Trail (map 1: C1)

Distances from Williams College ski area parking lot (1,500 ft.) to
- Berlin Pass (Taconic Crest Trail) (2,220 ft.): 1 mi., 700 ft., 1 hr.
- summit of Berlin Mtn. (via TCT south) (2,818 ft.): 2.2 mi., 1,300 ft., 1 hr. 30 min.
- NY 2 in Petersburg Pass (via TCT north) (2,100 ft): 2.6 mi., 1,500 ft. (rev. 300 ft.), 2 hr. 15 min.

Class of '33 Trail (WOC)

This blue-blazed trail, once known as the Berlin Mtn. Trail, was originally constructed in 1933 by members of the Williams Outing Club. It was relocated around its original trailhead at Haskin Farm in 1980. To reach the trailhead by car, follow the instructions under the Berlin Pass Trail. The trail begins on Berlin Rd., 1.1 mi. from the junction with Torrey Woods Rd. The parking lot, located on the left side of the road a short distance past the Haskin Farm, can accommodate two to three cars.

From the parking area, the blue-blazed trail enters the woods, quickly turning left along a woods road. Follow blazes through left and right turns to Haley Brook and the first interpretive sign of the WRLF Loop Trail (0.2 mi.). Cross the brook and climb the far bank to a well-signed junction. Bear left (east) to stay on the Class of '33 Trail; the WRLF Loop Trail continues to the right. After crossing the brook, it joins another woods road, turning left along it and then right up a steep gully. The trail levels off and then descends to the site of the old Williams Outing Club Berlin Cabin, marked by the remains of an outhouse, at 0.7 mi. Here the trail turns sharp right, crosses a stream, and turns right again onto another woods road. At 1.0 mi. the trail leaves the woods road and begins a steep ascent to a ridge at 1.2 mi. Logging that occurred in this area during the late 1990s widened old tracks into a potentially confusing network. Large blue blazes mark a boundary line, not the trail that follows the ridge-line logging road. Stay high on the ridge—if you start to head downhill, you are going the wrong way.

At 1.5 mi. is a fantastic view of Broad Brook and the Dome to the northeast. At 1.8 mi. continue straight on the ridge through a confusing nexus of roads toward the summit. One last turn left up the top of the old Williams College ski area leads to the clear summit of Berlin Mtn. at 2.0 mi.

Four small cement piers mark the site of an old fire tower. A panoramic view includes the rolling hills of Southeast Hollow to the southwest, with the Catskills rising in the distance. Albany and Troy are visible to the west, and on a clear day the southern Adirondacks to the northwest may be in view.

There are three options for the return to the parking lot. The Class of '33 Trail can be retraced for a 4.0-mi. round trip. Alternatively, instead of taking the first right onto the '33 Trail, continue straight (northeast) down the abandoned ski slope (3.5 mi. total). This route is unmaintained and extremely steep, so use caution. Finally, you can follow the Taconic Crest Trail (white markers) and off-road vehicle tracks north to the Berlin Pass Trail and back to the lot at 4.3 mi.

Class of '33 Trail (map 1: C1)

Distances from Berlin Rd. trailhead (1,400 ft.) to
- Hemlock Brook (1,300 ft.): 0.3 mi., (rev. 100 ft.) 15 min.
- ridge (2,000 ft.): 1.2 mi., 700 ft., 1 hr.
- summit of Berlin Mtn. (2,818 ft.): 2.0 mi., 1,500 ft., 1 hr. 50 min.

R.R.R. Brooks Trail (WOC)

Paralleling MA 2, this blue-blazed trail is a direct route from Williamstown toward Petersburg Pass through 930-acre Taconic Trail State Forest. One of the highlights is Flora Glen, a beautiful wooded area that is believed to have been the inspiration for William Cullen Bryant's poem "Thanatopsis." From the junction of MA 2 and US 7 at the Williams Inn in Williamstown, go south on US 7 for 0.8 mi. to graveled Bee Hill Rd. on the right. Ascend to a small reservoir and dam.

The moderate trail starts on the left end of the dam, turns right into the woods, clings to the side of Flora Glen, and gradually meets a stream. Vegetation along the valley side above the stream alternates between northern hardwood (mostly maple, beech, and birch) and evergreen (spruce and hemlock). The trail descends to the level of the stream (0.5 mi.), then makes an abrupt left (0.6 mi.) to climb steeply up a series of steps out of the streambed. Just below the remains of an old Boy Scout shelter (0.8 mi.), the Fitch Trail enters from the left.

At 1.4 mi. the trail comes out on the southeast end of a field and continues across the field on a barely noticeable footpath until the narrow field opens up on both sides. The trail is often wet and waist-high with weeds. It goes diagonally left across the field and toward the treeline straight ahead. (When MA 2 becomes visible, keep it in sight but do not hike toward it, heading instead for the opposite treeline.) The trail bears left along a dirt road after entering the treeline and becomes more visible just before the dirt road meets the highway. The trail follows the woods road that parallels the highway for 0.5 mi., reaching the junction with the Shepherd's Well Trail at 2.4 mi. The Shepherd's Well Trail eventually ascends the ridge past a scenic clearing, enters the woods, and soon meets the white-blazed Taconic Crest Trail at 3.7 mi.

R.R.R. Brooks Trail (map 1: C2)

Distances from dam on Bee Hill Rd. (810 ft.) to
- Fitch Trail (1,100 ft.): 0.8 mi., 300 ft., 40 min.
- Shepherd's Well Trail (1,900 ft.): 2.6 mi., 1,100 ft., 2 hr. 10 min.
- Taconic Crest Trail via the Shepherd's Well Trail (2,200 ft.): 3.7 mi., 1,400 ft., 2 hr. 30 min.

Pine Cobble Trail (WOC, WRLF)

Pine Cobble (1,894 ft.), to the northeast of Williamstown, offers one of the finest panoramic views of the Hoosic River Valley. Within easy walking distance of the Williams College campus, this blue-blazed trail is a favorite with Williams College students. The word cobble refers to the exposed outcropping of quartzite bedrock that is the destination of most of those who use the trail. On a clear day, the outcrop is easily visible from the valley floor, several miles away.

To reach the Pine Cobble trailhead by car, take MA 2 east from its intersection with US 7 at the Williams Inn in Williamstown. After 0.6 mi. turn left onto Cole Ave. at the first stoplight. Cross a bridge over the Hoosic River and railroad tracks just before North Hoosac Rd. Turn right onto North Hoosac Rd. (1.4 mi from the Williams Inn), then left onto Pine Cobble Rd. (1.8 mi.). Park in the parking area on the left 0.2 mi. up the hill. The trailhead is across the road.

To reach the trailhead on foot from the Williams College campus, walk down Stetson Rd. past the tennis courts to Cole Field. Follow the road around Eph's Pond, east through a gate to Cole Ave. Turn left and cross the Hoosic River to the intersection with North Hoosac Rd. Head diagonally right across North Hoosac Rd. to Cole's Grove Rd., around a gate, and into the Pine Cobble Development. At the mailboxes, turn right. The trailhead is 300 yd. down the road on the left.

From the Pine Cobble Trail sign hike parallel to the road for 200 yd. before turning left and ascending gradually into the woods. At 0.5 mi. the trail levels out on a plateau that was once the shore of glacial Lake Bascom, which once filled the entire Hoosic Valley to a depth of about 500 ft.

At 0.8 mi. a side trail to the right marks the halfway point. It leads 350 ft. downhill to Bear Spring, a slight upwelling at the base of a steep cliff topped with hemlocks. Since the spring is the only open water on the south side of Pine Cobble, it attracts many species of wildlife, including chipmunks, rabbits, and deer. About 200 ft. above the Bear Spring Trail, the blue-diamond-blazed Class of '98 Trail diverges to the left. Currently, there is no sign announcing the beginning of the '98 Trail, but there is a sign at this intersection labeling the Pine Cobble Trail.

Continue at a moderately steep grade to a more level area at 1.0 mi., where the trail turns to the southeast. Yellow diamond-shaped blazes mark the entrance to the Williamstown Rural Lands Foundation Pine Cobble Summit Natural Area of Clarksburg State Forest. Cross two small jumbled rock outcroppings and follow a sharp left turn at the intersection with an old trail at 1.1 mi.

Watch for an unusual triplet oak tree with a water-filled basin at its center at 1.4 mi. After the original tree was cut down, three shoots sprouted around the edges of the old stump while the center rotted away. This flat section of the trail is also an excellent place to see trailing arbutus, the Massachusetts state flower, which usually blooms in early April.

A steep stretch completes the climb (1.5 mi.). From the trail sign at the crest of the hill, several short paths to the right lead out onto the quartzite outcrops of Pine Cobble, with its excellent view of Mt. Greylock across the valley to the south, its summit clearly distinguished by the War Memorial and communications towers. The Taconic Range forms the western horizon, while the top of the Dome is visible to the north. Looking down into the Hoosic River Valley, North Adams is to the east and Williamstown is to the south.

North of the trail sign, pass an anchor point for an old fire tower and emerge onto a boulder field. A short climb leads to the summit of East Mtn., where the Pine Cobble Trail joins the white-blazed Appalachian Trail at 1.9 mi. The site of an old forest fire, now covered with blueberry bushes, it provides additional views of the Taconic and Greylock Ranges.

Pine Cobble Trail (map 1: B3)
Distances from Pine Cobble Rd. trailhead (707 ft.) to
- Class of '98 Trail (1,250 ft.): 0.9 mi., 550 ft., 30 min.
- Pine Cobble summit (1,894 ft.): 1.5 mi., 1,200 ft., 1 hr.
- AT (2,100 ft.): 1.9 mi., 1,400 ft., 1 hr. 20 min.

Class of '98 Trail (WOC)

The Class of '98 Trail was conceived by Chris Elkinton (Williams College class of 1998) as a gift from his class to the Williams College and Williamstown communities. Following the tradition of the Class of '33 Trail, the Class of '98 Trail was constructed by members of the Williams Outing Club between 1998 and 2000. Together with the Pine Cobble Trail and the AT, the Class of '98 Trail forms a pleasant 5.0-mi. lollipop-shaped loop on the side of Pine Cobble. A similar loop can be formed by substituting the Chestnut Hill Trail for the lower section of the Pine Cobble Trail. The '98 Trail can only be reached via the Pine Cobble, Chestnut Hill, or Appalachian Trails.

The '98 Trail begins on the northwest side of the blue-blazed Pine Cobble Trail approximately halfway between the trailhead and the Pine Cobble summit. Currently there is no sign announcing the beginning of the '98 Trail, but there is a sign at this intersection labeling the Pine Cobble Trail. At first the blue-diamond-blazed trail meanders through forest at easy grades. After 0.3 mi. sheer granite cliffs become visible through the trees on the right and a significant logging road diverges to the left. At this point the trail becomes noticeably wider. Granite cliffs and boulders of varying size continue to be visible on the right side of the trail. At 0.6 mi.

the blue-blazed Chestnut Trail, which is marked by a sign about 30 ft. below the '98 Trail, enters from the left. The '98 Trail makes a slight right at this intersection.

After the Chestnut Trail the '98 Trail narrows and the forest surrounding it gradually becomes denser. At 0.7 mi. the trail makes a sharp right, marked by a double blaze, then begins to climb somewhat steeply over progressively larger rocks. After 100 yd. a sign warns hikers to watch their step because of loose rock. At 0.9 mi. the trail emerges from the rocky ascent and reenters a relatively dense forest. After several gradual ascents the trail begins a steeper climb at 1.5 mi. At the top of this final ascent the trail winds through dense underbrush until it terminates at the white-blazed AT at 1.6 mi. The upper terminus of the Pine Cobble Trail is 0.2 mi. to the right.

Class of '98 Trail (map 1: B3)

Distances from Pine Cobble Trail junction (1,250 ft.) to
- Chestnut Trail (1,290 ft.): 0.6 mi., 50 ft., 20 min.
- AT (2,100 ft.): 1.6 mi., 850 ft., 1 hr.

Chestnut Trail (WRLF)

To reach the Chestnut trailhead by car, take MA 2 east from its intersection with US 7 at the Williams Inn in Williamstown. After 0.6 mi. turn left onto Cole Ave. at the first stoplight. Cross a bridge over the Hoosic River and railroad tracks just before North Hoosac Rd. Turn left onto North Hoosac Rd. (1.4 mi from the Williams Inn), then right onto Chestnut St. Follow Chestnut St. up a hill and around a sharp left turn. The Chestnut Trail begins as a gated logging road on the right side of Chestnut St. 0.25 mi. from North Hoosac Rd. A sign to the left of the logging road labels the trail, and a sign on the gate prohibits vehicles.

The trail climbs moderately through the oak forest on a wide logging road. Follow the blue blazes carefully—streambeds and other logging roads branch off from the trail at various locations. The trail is likely to be wet in places. At 0.2 mi. the trail makes a slight right at a double blaze and a streambed continues straight ahead. At 0.6 mi. the trail makes a sharp right, marked by double blazes, while other logging roads continue straight and left. The trail levels off shortly after the right turn, then terminates at the Class of '98 Trail at 0.7 mi.

Chestnut Trail

Distance from Chestnut St. trailhead (780 ft.) to
• Class of '98 Trail (1,290 ft.): 0.7 mi., 500 ft., 25 min.

Hopkins Memorial Forest Loop (Williams College Center for Environmental Studies)

Hopkins Memorial Forest is a 2,425-acre research site operated by the Williams College Center for Environmental Studies (CES). There is a wide variety of forest types, ranging from recently overgrown farmland to old woodlot stands from the 19th century. Old farm roads, stone walls, and partially visible cellar holes reflect the complex human history of the property. Much of this information is recorded in *Farms to Forest*, a naturalist's guide published by the Center for Environmental Studies and available in local bookstores. This book also features a "guided" tour of the ecology of the lower loop trail. Research projects are in progress throughout the forest. To avoid disturbing them, please stay on trails and do not remove stakes or other markers.

The Hopkins Memorial Forest Loop Trail is actually a figure-eight composed of a 1.5-mi. Lower Loop and a 2.6-mi. Upper Loop. Information at the Rosenburg Center describes more trails within the forest. To reach the trailhead, follow US 7 north from its intersection with MA 2 at the Williams Inn in Williamstown. After 0.3 mi. turn left onto Bulkley St., cross a bridge over Hemlock Brook (0.4 mi.), and ascend a long, gradual rise. At the T-junction with Northwest Hill Rd. at 1.1 mi., turn right. The entrance to Hopkins Memorial Forest is on the left. Please park in the first parking area to the left. A few hundred feet beyond is the Rosenburg Center, which contains a small historical museum; and the Moon Barn, a historic structure that once stood on the farm belonging to Albert Moon.

The Lower Loop starts at the Moon Barn along a carriage road improved by the Civilian Conservation Corps during the 1930s. Walk to the right past the Williams Outing Club Cabin (0.1 mi.) and an experimental weather station in a vestigial field. The trail winds through forest of various composition and age before reaching a four-way intersection at 0.8 mi.

To return to the Moon Barn via the Lower Loop, turn left, away from the Upper Loop. This section of the trail may be a little swampy in spring, but please resist the temptation to trample the vegetation to either side. After a level section the trail descends steeply back to the Rosenburg Center, which it reaches at 1.5 mi.

For a longer hike, venture on to the Upper Loop Trail. If in search of the Birch Brook Trail, follow the north (right) leg of the Upper Loop for a more direct approach. Otherwise, choose either at whim. The wide path was once a carriage road from which Amos Lawrence Hopkins would view his estate. The trail crosses the middle and north branches of Birch Brook while passing through beautiful forest. This route is an excellent ski or snowshoe jaunt with enough snow. Upon returning to the four-way intersection, return along the Lower Loop for a 4.0-mi. total trip.

Hopkins Forest Loop (map 1: B1–B2)

Distances from Moon Barn (850 ft.) to
- Moon Barn via Lower Loop (circuit): 1.5 mi., 150 ft., 45 min.
- Moon Barn via Lower and Upper Loops (circuit): 4.0 mi., 450 ft. (rev. 300 ft.), 2 hr.

Fitch Trail (WRLF)

For a short hike ascend Bee Hill through the Edward H. Fitch Memorial Woodlands, protected by the Williamstown Rural Lands Foundation. For a pleasant loop link up with the R.R.R. Brooks Trail and return to Bee Hill Rd. To reach the trailhead by car, follow US 7 south from its intersection with MA 2 at the Williams Inn in Williamstown. Turn right onto Bee Hill Rd. at 0.6 mi. and drive up the hill, over a bridge, and up a steeper hill. At 1.3 mi. a wooden sign on the right marks the Fitch Trail. Several small pull-outs along the left side of the road provide space for two to three cars here. Within 0.1 mi. are three more, larger pull-outs for additional parking, and another parking area is 0.3 mi. south.

From Bee Hill Rd. follow the well-marked path on gentle grades through young forest. At 0.7 mi. reach the rounded top of Bee Hill, where only a few decades ago a clear view of the Greylock Range and valley below was visible.

For a 2.4-mi. loop, continue over the west side of the hill to meet up with the blue-blazed R.R.R. Brooks Trail at 1.1 mi. near an old Boy Scout shelter. Turn right to reach Bee Hill Rd. at 1.9 mi. through Flora Glen. To return to your car, turn right and walk 0.5 mi. uphill to the Fitch Trail parking.

Fitch Trail (map 1: C2)

Distances from Bee Hill Rd. (1,000 ft.) to
- Bee Hill (1,428 ft.): 0.7 mi., 425 ft., 30 min.
- R.R.R. Brooks Trail (1,100 ft.): 1.1 mi., 425 ft. (rev. 350 ft.), 45 min.

Shepherd's Well Trail (WOC)

The Shepherd's Well Trail can be reached either from the R.R.R. Brooks Trail (see page 85) or the Taconic Crest Trail (see page 76). From the R.R.R. Brooks Trail junction, the Shepherd's Well Trail branches to the right and climbs gently through a forest of maple, beech, and oak trees.

At 0.4 mi. a white sign indicates the boundary of Hopkins Memorial Forest. Notice the red and yellow bands painted on the trees. These are part of a permanent grid system for vegetation surveys established by the USFS in 1936 and still maintained by Williams College professors and students.

Just beyond a double blaze signaling an abrupt left turn, the trail enters an open area filled with huckleberries and blueberries. The spectacular view encompasses the Greylock Range to the east and the Taconic Range, the old Williams ski area, and Petersburg Pass to the south.

Across the clearing, the trail levels off, passing through a stand of birch and reentering the hardwood forest at 0.6 mi. Descend gradually and turn right at 0.9 mi. to skirt the ridge. To the right was once a well belonging to a farmer named Shepherd, but all traces of it have now disappeared. Follow the contours around the rise in the ridge to meet the Taconic Crest Trail at a trail sign at 1.0 mi.

Shepherd's Well Trail (map 1: B1)

Distance from R.R.R. Brooks Trail (1,900 ft.) to
- Taconic Crest Trail (2,300 ft.): 1.0 mi., 400 ft., 40 min.

WRLF Loop Trail (WRLF)

During the summer of 1998 the Williamstown Rural Lands Foundation designed and installed this short interpretive loop trail, which is part of the Berlin Rd. trail system. Small signs along the loop trail offer natural history information to hikers. The trail begins at the same parking area as the Class of '33 Trail (see page 84).

From the parking area you can begin directly on the Haley Brook Cut-Off Trail for a shorter loop; or walk 400 ft. down the entrance road to the trailhead for the Loop Trail and the blue-blazed Class of '33 Trail. Both trails are well blazed and cross Haley Brook to reach a relatively level logging grade. On the road, walk west, passing four old pits on the left that were once used to make charcoal from trees on this land. The trail ends at the old Williams College ski area. Retrace the hike or return via Berlin Rd.

WRLF Loop Trail
Distance from Berlin Rd. (1,400 ft.) to
• Berlin Rd. (circuit): 1.4 mi., 100 ft., 1 hr.

Stone Hill

Early settlers of the Williamstown area named Stone Hill for the outcroppings of white, garnet, and amethyst quartzite that were visible along the ridge when all trees had been cleared from the hill in the 18th century. Geologists speculate that these rocks, now obscured by vegetation, are the solidified and metamorphosed remains of submarine landslides that occurred 550 to 600 million years ago, when the majority of this region was underwater and in the tropical latitudes. Settlers often used the intensely fractured rock for building.

Stone Hill is one of the most popular places to walk and hike in the Williamstown area. A number of trails may be combined to form loops of various lengths and difficulty. Described here are the Pasture Loop, Stone Bench Loop, Stone Hill Loop, Stone Hill Rd., and Gale Rd. Cut-Off, in that order. The town of Williamstown, the Clark Art Institute, and several private landholders own and manage the land here. While Stone Hill has long been open to public wandering, please respect postings and private property.

Pasture Loop (WOC and Clark Art Institute)

This is a wonderful walk to and through the pasture above the Clark Art Institute. Students and townspeople alike return again and again to enjoy the spectacular view of Williamstown, Pine Cobble, and the Dome to the north.

From the intersection of MA 2 and US 7 at the Williams Inn in Williamstown, go south on South St. (opposite US 7 north). After 0.5 mi. turn right into the Clark Art Institute. Those on foot may continue around the building through the grassy area on the left. In a car, go under the overhead walkway, turn left, and park in the rear of the parking lot. A sign and two small gravestones mark the trailhead.

The two small gravestones mark the burial place of dogs that belonged to an earlier property owner, Dr. Vanderpool Adriance. The lower portion of this trail, and the footbridge that leads to it, were constructed in 1985 to help celebrate the thirtieth anniversary of the Clark Art Institute.

Crossing the footbridge at 0.1 mi., the trail winds uphill past birch, beech, and maple, as well as some hemlock and pine. At 0.3 mi. a signed trail junction marks the turnoff for the pasture loop to the right. Straight ahead the trail leads to the Stone Bench Loop, Stone Hill Loop, Stone Hill Rd., and Gale Rd. Cut-Off.

To continue the Pasture Loop, turn right and continue to a gate. Pass through the gate, being sure to close it behind you. A worn path leads west across the pasture to a grove of trees with excellent views. Grazing cows may glance at you, but pose no threat to your safety. To return to the Clark Art Institute below, follow a worn grassy double-track downhill on the far side of the field, through a hedgerow, and either right or straight to gates in the fence (0.7 mi.). Again, please close the gates behind you.

Pasture Loop (map 1: C2)
Distance from Clark Art Institute parking lot (705 ft.) to
• Clark Art Institute parking lot (circuit): 0.7 mi., 200 ft., 30 min.

Stone Bench Loop (WOC and Clark Art Institute)

For a slightly longer walk than the Pasture Loop, try a trip to the Stone Bench, which is dedicated to George Moritz Wahl, a former professor of German at Williams College who climbed to this spot every evening to watch the sunset. During World War I he was subjected to substantial abuse because of his German heritage, but when he died shortly after the war his students and fellow townspeople erected the bench as a memorial and symbol of their regret. Although trees now obscure the view, the bench is a pleasant place for a quiet moment of reflection.

To reach the trailhead, refer to directions for the Pasture Loop. Begin at the trail sign and gravestones as for the Pasture Loop. At the first junction (0.3 mi.) continue straight to a gravel road that services Williamstown's buried water tank (0.4 mi.). The road links up to Stone Hill Rd. and the Stone Bench. For a more pleasant walk, cross the road and reenter the woods on a wide trail that ascends more steeply.

During fall and early winter a thick carpet of leaves covers the trail and adds wonderful crinkle to your steps (but also slippery footing, so beware). At 0.6 mi. the trail forks with a double orange blaze. Straight ahead is the Stone Hill Loop; bear right to find the Stone Bench over a small rise at 0.7 mi., a bit tilted after 80 years.

Return by crossing a small clearing to the west and then following a path north to a gate. Alternatively, turn right (north) along Stone Hill Rd. to the gravel road and clearing. Ahead and to the left is another gate to enter the pasture. Either way, please close the gate behind you. Walk across the pasture to the grove of trees and follow the directions in the Pasture Loop section to return to the Clark Art Institute below.

Stone Bench Loop (map 1: C2)
Distance from Clark Art Institute parking lot (1,000 ft.) to
  • Clark Art Institute parking lot (circuit): 1.5 mi., 200 ft., 1 hr.

Stone Hill Loop (WOC)

As its name suggests, this trail winds up and around Stone Hill before looping back to its starting point. It shares trails with the Pasture Loop and Stone Bench Loop. To reach the trailhead, refer to directions for the Pasture Loop.

Start at the sign and gravestones, continue past the Pasture Loop turnoff to the right (0.3 mi.), across the gravel road (0.4 mi.), and uphill to a junction at 0.6 mi., marked with a double orange blaze. Approximately 100 yd. to the right is the Stone Bench; the Stone Hill Loop continues straight ahead.

This is perhaps the most pleasant path on Stone Hill: wide, smooth, and rolling, with hemlock groves and intermittent phyllite outcrops. In fall the bare trees afford a fantastic view east and south of the Taconic Range. At 0.9 mi. a lone hemlock marks a spot to sit, reflect, and enjoy the view.

At 1.0 mi. a stone wall marks the former boundary between two fields, and a junction offers a spur trail right to the Gale Rd. Cut-Off. Bear left instead and follow the wide track down a couple of switchbacks, ignoring the logging roads that cross the trail. At 1.7 mi. small yellow diamonds on trees to the left mark Williamstown land; a hedgerow of large red oak and sugar maple dominates the boundary. At a small creek follow the sign straight ahead across a footbridge, avoiding the roped-off road to the right. The trail continues on town land to the gravel water tank road at 2.0 mi.

To return to the Clark Art Institute, turn right and descend to Gale Rd. Proceed straight and enter the delivery or main entrance on the left at 2.3 mi.

Stone Hill Loop (map 1: C2)

Distance from Clark Art Institute parking lot (705 ft.) to
• Clark Art Institute parking lot (circuit): 2.3 mi., 400 ft., 1 hr. 30 min.

Stone Hill Rd. (WOC)

"This, after all, was the prime North–South road in New England. Over this road went soldiers to Bennington in 1777; President Washington, riding over the hill in 1790, paused at this spot to take in what was then an open view of the fledgling town, with its new Free School; and every day townsfolk trafficked the road between North and South villages. To the struggling college this was the slender umbilicus of an indifferent world."—Arthur Latham Perry, professor of history and political economy, Williams College, 1853–1891

To reach the trailhead, refer to directions for the Pasture Loop. From the Clark Art Institute there are a number of ways to join Stone Hill Rd. If on foot, follow the first 0.7 mi. of the Stone Bench Loop.

Another option takes a wider road grade the entire way. From the trailhead return to South St. using the main or delivery entrance. Turn right and follow the gated gravel road that ascends steeply as South St. bears left and becomes Gale Rd. At the top of the steep rise the Stone Hill Loop returns from the left; continue uphill. The Stone Bench Loop crosses the road before reaching a field under which the Williamstown water tank lies buried.

Gravel gives way to mulch and dirt as the road leads to the Stone Bench on the left. The Stone Bench Loop joins at this point. From here Stone Hill Rd. continues to the south, just below and to the west of Stone Hill, and passes a number of quartzite outcrops on the left. At approximately 1.3 mi. the Gale Rd. Cut-Off heads east while Stone Hill Rd. continues south. A number of fields border the road and offer fine views east and west.

At about 2.0 mi. Stone Hill Rd. becomes a maintained town road and continues to Scott Hill Rd. at 2.6 mi. Return along the same route or be picked up; the alternative is a long return trip on US 7 or MA 43.

Stone Hill Rd. (map 1: C2–D2)
Distance from South St. just south of Clark Art Institute (705 ft.) to
 • Scott Hill Rd.: 2.6 mi., 300 ft., 1 hr. 15 min.

Gale Rd. Cut-Off (WOC)

In 1994 the Williams Outing Club and townspeople cut this trail to connect Stone Hill Rd. to the Pine Cobble School and Gale Rd. A spur trail also connects it to the main Stone Hill Loop Trail.

To reach the trailhead follow the description for Stone Hill Rd. This trail begins on the east side of Stone Hill Rd., 0.5 mi. beyond the Stone Bench. A white sign stating Trail West to Gale Rd. marks the turnoff. Alternatively, hike the Stone Hill Loop to the spur trail at 1.0 mi. and turn right (south). Walk 0.2 mi. to reach the yellow blazes of the Gale Rd. Cut-Off.

From Stone Hill Rd. the trail ascends gently into the woods, passing through the remains of an old stone wall. At 0.1 mi., after covering some rolling terrain, reach the orange-blazed spur trail that connects to the Stone Hill Loop Trail. From here the Gale Rd. Cut-Off makes a gradual descent through a mixed deciduous forest.

At 0.3 mi., just beyond a small clearing, watch for a sharp right turn down the hill, while an old woods road continues straight ahead. Be aware of unstable footing and several crisscrossing skidder trails. Cross a stream on a small log bridge at 0.5 mi. and ascend to a level open wood. Notice the old rusted gate left open one last time by a farmer years ago. Across another small stream the trail empties into a wide-open cornfield at 0.7 mi. To reach Gale Rd. follow the treeline left (north) to the foot of the hill at 1.0 mi. Please respect the lands of the Pine Cobble School. Turn left (northwest) on Gale Rd. to return to the Clark Art Institute.

Gale Rd. Cut-Off (map 1: C2)

Distance from Stone Hill Rd. (1,000 ft.) to
  • Gale Rd. (800 ft.): 1.0 mi., 40 min.

Mountain Meadow Preserve

Mountain Meadow Preserve is a 176-acre reservation that protects a wet meadow hillside at the northern edge of Williamstown in the north Berkshires. The property has two main trails. To reach the reservation, from the north junction of US 7 and MA 2 in Williamstown, travel north on US 7 for 1.7 mi. to Mason St. on the right. Follow Mason St. about 0.1 mi. to a parking area and kiosk.

Meadow Trail (TTOR)

The scenic Meadow Trail traces a path around the edge of an impressive open field with eye-popping views of the Taconic and Greylock Ranges. The trail (1.2 mi. long) is unmarked, but the mowed path is easy to follow and walk.

Meadow Trail (map 1: B2)

Distance from parking area trailhead (660 ft.) to
  • parking area (circuit): 1.2 mi., 100 ft., 35 min.

Woodland Loop (TTOR)

The woodland path leaves from the meadow trail and loops over a wooded hill to a narrow view before returning down to the meadow. The woodland loop trail (0.8 mi. long) is blazed in yellow and is moderately steep.

> **Woodland Loop Trail (map 1: B2)**
> Distance from junction with meadow trail (starting elev. 660 ft.) to:
> • meadow trail (circuit): 0.8 mi., 200 ft., 35 min.

Monroe State Forest

Monroe State Forest in the towns of Florida and Monroe covers some 4,321 acres in the northern part of the Hoosac Range, including several blocks of old-growth forest. A 9-mi. trail system explores the ravines and overlooks throughout the forest. The trails are blue-blazed, and elevations range from almost 1,000 ft. to 2,730 ft. on Spruce Mtn. Trail information is available at the Bear Swamp Visitor Center on River Rd.

To reach the visitor center and eastern trailhead from MA 2, turn north at the Mohawk Bridge (1.7 mi. west of Charlemont) onto Zoar-Rowe Rd. Continue 2.4 mi. to a T-intersection. Turn left onto River Rd., crossing the Florida Bridge 1.0 mi. from the junction, and continue on River Rd. through the village of Hoosac Tunnel. Pass the railroad tunnel on the left at 4.5 mi. The Bear Swamp Visitor Center is on the right at 7.6 mi. The trail parking area is on the left at 8.5 mi., just before the Monroe–Florida line.

Raycroft Lookout Trail (DCR)

To reach the Raycroft Lookout Trail from MA 2 and Monroe Rd. (about 0.5 mi. south of the Whitcomb Summit lookout on MA 2), turn north on Whitcomb Hill Rd., then bear left along Monroe Rd. At 2.3 miles from MA 2, look for a marked short dirt road on the left that leads 0.2 mi. along Hunt Hill to where transmission lines cross overhead. Parking, and partial views of Mts. Greylock and Monadnock, are available here. From the transmission lines the Lookout Trail follows the ridge downhill 0.3 mi. to Raycroft Lookout (1,826 ft.), a stone "balcony" built by the CCC that stands 1,000 ft. above the Deerfield River and dam, affording an outstanding view of the Deerfield River Gorge.

Raycroft Lookout Trail

Distance from parking area (2,048 ft.) to
- lookout on Hunt Hill (1,826 ft.): 0.3 mi., 15 min.

Dunbar Brook Trail (DCR)

This trail follows cascading Dunbar Brook through a rocky, rugged landscape of mossy boulders and giant old-growth trees. From the parking area on River Rd. just north of the Bear Swamp Visitor Center the trail races a route along the south bank of Dunbar Brook. At 0.7 mi. the path turns right (north), crosses the stream on a bridge, then goes up the north bank about 0.1 mi., passing three small camping areas. The trail then climbs moderately northwest, crossing two brooks on bridges and reaching the Dunbar Shelter at 1.2 mi. at the confluence of Haley and Dunbar Brooks. The trail continues to trace the stream bank, passing under transmission lines at 1.5 mi. and crossing Parsonage Brook at 1.8 mi.

A short distance past the brook the path turns right, climbing uphill steeply, and zigzags among large boulders. After passing almost under one of the largest, it turns sharp left (an obscure turn on the descent) and soon reaches the top of the hill, continuing nearly level on an old woods road. About 0.3 mi. from the boulder field the trail branches left and continues downhill. (The right fork leads shortly to paved Main Rd. 100 ft. east of its junction with Raycroft Rd.) After descending some worn wooden steps, the trail bears right, paralleling the brook, crosses a small stream, passes an old foundation on the right, and ends just north of the bridge on Raycroft Rd.

To reach the blue-blazed Spruce Mtn. Trail, turn left onto Raycroft Rd. and continue 0.2 mi. across a bridge and past a small parking area on the left. The Spruce Mtn. Trail is on the right.

Dunbar Brook Trail

Distances from parking area on River Rd. to
- Dunbar Shelter: 1.2 mi., 30 min.
- transmission lines: 1.5 mi., 45 min.
- Raycroft Rd.: 2.8 mi., 1 hr. 30 min.

Spruce Mtn. Trail (DCR)

Spruce Mtn. (2,730 ft.), the highest point in Monroe State Forest, is reached by a clearly defined, blue-blazed trail that begins and ends on Raycroft Rd. 0.2 mi. south of the intersection of Raycroft and Main Rds. From the trailhead the trail climbs moderately southwest, reaching a ledge outcrop with views east at 0.5 mi. The path continues climbing, becoming relatively level as it swings more westerly. Turning south at 1.0 mi., the path continues gradually uphill, reaching the summit in 1.3 mi. The summit itself is wooded, but a rocky clearing reached by a short path on the right offers good views to the west and south.

From the summit the path heads east, reaching Spruce Mtn.'s second summit (2,592 ft.) at 1.6 mi. with a nice view to the south. The trail then descends southeast along the crest of the ridge through open hardwoods. At 2.5 mi. the trail passes under transmission lines, then ends on Raycroft Rd. at 3.1 mi.

Spruce Mtn. Trail

Distances from Raycroft Rd. (northern trailhead) (1,797 ft.) to
- overlook: 0.5 mi., 20 min.
- summit of Spruce Mtn. (2,730 ft.): 1.3 mi., 50 min.
- second summit, Spruce Mtn. (2,592 ft.): 1.6 mi., 1 hr. 5 min.
- transmission lines: 2.5 mi., 1 hr. 30 min.
- Raycroft Rd. (southern terminus): 3.1 mi., 1 hr. 50 min.

Savoy Mtn. State Forest

This 11,118-acre state forest is located in the Hoosac Range, a highland region that is an extension of the Green Mtns. in Vermont. Savoy Mtn. State Forest is known for its population of bears that like to loiter around campgrounds; listen to the advice of the rangers and follow it exactly. Most of the forest roads are passable by car, but some are not, and advice from the rangers is often better than the current maps. There are 45 camping sites available, as well as four rustic log cabins on the edge of South Pond. There are about 60 mi. of multiuse trails and roads but few hiking trails.

The forest headquarters can be reached from North Adams by traveling east 5.3 mi. from the intersection of MA 2 and 8 to Central Shaft Rd. on the right. Follow the signs to the headquarters.

Busby Trail (DCR)

This blue-blazed trail provides access to Spruce Hill (2,566 ft.) and Hawk Lookout, a rocky crag atop the mountain. Spruce Hill is on the western edge of the Hoosac Range, with a splendid view across the Hoosic River Valley to Mt. Greylock and the southern end of the Green Mtns. In fall the mountaintop perch is used by hawk watchers to view the annual raptor migrations.

The trail begins at the parking area on Old Florida Rd. about 0.2 mi. southwest of the forest headquarters on Central Shaft Rd. The trail ascends easily, crossing beneath two transmission lines (0.1 and 0.4 mi.). It then traces a path along a small brook, passing spruce plantations planted by the CCC in the 1930s. At 1.0 mi. the ruins of the Sherman farm, built in the 1830s, are reached. The trail becomes briefly steep as it climbs toward the top of the mountain. Beneath the summit the path splits into a loop trail; both paths climb to the top at 1.3 mi. The north route (right) passes through a picturesque area with good views.

Busby Trail

Distances from trailhead on Old Florida Rd. (1,878 ft.) to
- second transmission line: 0.4 mi., 15 min.
- Sherman farm ruins: 1.0 mi., 40 min.
- summit of Spruce Hill (Hawk Lookout) (2,566 ft.): 1.3 mi., 1 hr.

Tyler Swamp Loop Trail (DCR)

To reach the trailhead from the forest headquarters travel south 1.7 mi. along paved Central Shaft Rd. and then unpaved Florida Rd. to a small pull-off on the right. From the pull-off the trail splits into the swamp loop. Turning left, the path follows the edge of a marsh, though the treadway stays in the woods. The trail then becomes a wide cart path that leads to rocky talus slopes. The trail swings north through beds of ferns before coming to a swamp of tall standing driftwood-gray trees where great blue herons nest. The path continues north to the junction with the South Pond Loop, which leads (0.3 mi.) to the campground on South Pond. The trail now swings south through open woods to return to the trailhead at 2.0 mi.

Tyler Swamp Loop Trail
Distances from trailhead on Florida Rd. to
  • junction with South Pond Loop Trail: 1.3 mi., 45 min.
  • trailhead (circuit): 2.0 mi., 1 hr. 30 min.

Notchview Reservation

Notchview consists of 3,108 acres of forests, hills, and open fields traversed by 23 mi. of trails. The reservation is astride the Hoosac Range, with much of the property above 2,000 ft. in elevation. The highest point is Judges Hill at 2,297 ft. Some of the fields are still used for agriculture, but the majority of the property is cloaked in hardwood-red spruce forest interspersed with spruce plantations. Notchview is famous for its cross-country ski trails, which double as comfortable hiking paths in the warmer months.

Information (and year-round restrooms) can be obtained at the Arthur D. Budd Visitor Center located near the parking lot (30 cars) off MA 9 in Windsor. Notchview is located on MA 9 about 1 mi. east of the junction of MA 9 and 8A in Windsor or 8.4 mi. west of the intersection of MA 112 and 9 in Cummington. The extensive trail system has wide trails well-marked at the trailheads. A map is available on site. Most trails range in difficulty from easy to moderate.

Judges Hill Trail (TTOR)

This 1.1-mi.-long path to the crest of wooded Judges Hill begins on the north portion of the Circuit Trail. To reach the Judges Hill Trail from the parking area follow the Circuit Trail north to the Ant Hill Trail, which begins soon after entering the woods. Follow the Ant Hill Trail to its end, where it rejoins the Circuit Trail near the Judges Hill trailhead. The path now heads north through wet woods, reaching and crossing Shaw Rd. Pass some cellar holes and descend to cross Shaw Brook on a bridge. The path then climbs up the slopes of Judges Hill, where the woods are a sea of trout lily in spring, and passes the Windsor Trail on the right. The summit hosts Judges Fort, a stonework "patio" where a social group, some of whom were judges, used to meet to cook lunch in the fireplace and eat at the stone table. From the summit the trail descends steeply through open hardwoods to end at Bates Rd.

Judges Hill Trail

Distances from Budd Visitor Center (2,020 ft.) to
- Judges Hill trailhead: 0.4 mi., 20 min.
- Shaw Brook: 0.8 mi., 40 min.
- Judges Fort and summit of Judges Hill (2,297 ft.): 1.1 mi., 1 hr.
- Bates Rd.: 1.5 mi., 1 hr. 15 min.

Circuit Trail (TTOR)

The Circuit Trail is an easy 1.8-mi.-long loop path that passes through a wide array of forests and fields. From the Budd Visitor Center follow the mowed path southeast through a field and between two farm buildings. The trail then comes to an overgrown landscape of rhododendrons and conifers at 0.3 mi. In a grove of red spruce the Spruce Hill Trail leaves left just before passing a maintenance garage on the right. The Circuit Trail then passes the Quill Tree Trail, crosses over a small brook, and then passes junctions for the Mixed Woods Trail, Elbow Tucker Trail, and Mushroom Trail in quick succession.

At a sharp left (0.7 mi.) the trail heads north on a wide woods road, then shortly turns left as the Minor Trail continues straight (there is a weatherproof map on a post here). The trail now heads northwest through a spruce plantation, passing a slew of trail junctions and a glacial boulder at 1.3 mi. The Ant Hill and Judges Hill Trails are passed before the path begins a comfortable stretch ending at a bench under a beech tree at 1.6 mi. The path now makes an easy descent back to the visitor center.

Circuit Trail

Distances from Budd Visitor Center to
- weatherproof map at Minor Trail: 0.8 mi., 30 min.
- glacial boulder: 1.3 mi., 50 min.
- bench under beech tree: 1.6 mi., 1 hr. 15 min.
- Budd Visitor Center (circuit): 1.8 mi., 1 hr. 30 min.

SUGGESTED HIKES

Easy Hikes

Hurlburt's Hill via the Tractor Path [rt: 1.8 mi., 1:00], page 58. A pleasant walk through woods and wide fields to the grand views atop Hurlburt's Hill.

Ledges Interpretive Trail [lp: 0.5 mi., 0:30], page 58. A winding interpretive path that skirts the Housatonic River and weaves through limestone cobbles.

Meadow Trail [rt: 1.2 mi., 0:35], page 89. A wide mowed path around a high meadow with stunning views of the northern Taconics and Mt. Greylock.

Rounds Rock Trail [lp: 0.9 mi., 0:40], page 49. An easy walk through forest and blueberry barrens, punctuated with long southerly views.

Moderate Hikes

Tyringham Cobble Loop Trail [lp: 1.9 mi., 1:10], page 63. A climb to the top of Tyringham Cobble that follows the Appalachian Trail and affords fine views of the pastoral village below.

Circuit Trail, Ant Hill Trail, and Judges Hill Trail [rt: 2.2 mi., 1: 20], pages 103–104. A hike through the cool Berkshire woodlands to stone ruins atop Judges Hill.

Pine Cobble Trail [rt: 3.2 mi., 1:45], page 86. This attractive hike travels along a wooded path to reach the summit of Pine Cobble and its views of the Hoosic River Valley.

Hickey Trail, Squaw Peak Trail, and Indian Monument Trail [lp: 2.4 mi., 2:30], pages 61–62. One of the most popular hikes in the Berkshires, this loop crosses the spine of the mountain and visits overlooks with great views and gliding raptors.

Strenuous Hikes

Race Brook Trail [rt: 7.2 mi., 6:00], page 223. This sometimes demanding route ascends past a number of waterfalls and cascades before climbing the south flank of Mt. Everett, with excellent views scattered throughout.

Jones Nose Trail [rt: 5.1 mi., 4:00], page 49. This route scales Jones Nose and then runs along the balsam ridge of Saddleball Mtn. to reach the summit of Mt. Greylock.

PART TWO
Pioneer Valley and Vicinity

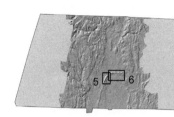

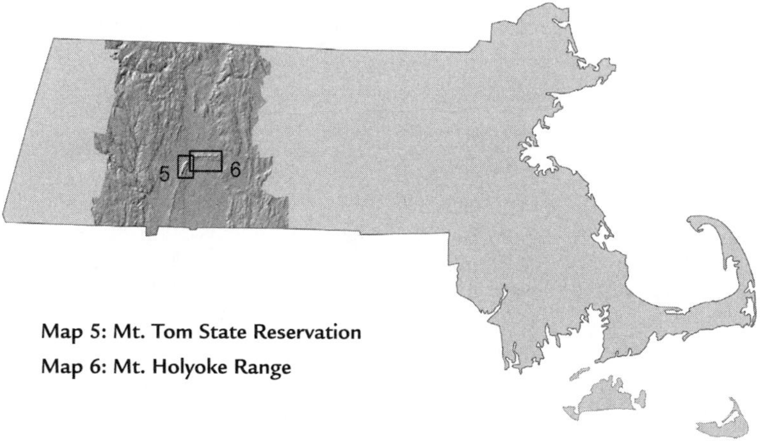

Map 5: Mt. Tom State Reservation
Map 6: Mt. Holyoke Range

The Pioneer Valley and Vicinity includes the part of the state between Worcester County on the east and Berkshire County on the west. It is composed of Hampden, Hampshire, and Franklin Counties, generally forming the Massachusetts watershed of the Connecticut River and its principal tributaries, the Millers, Deerfield, Chicopee, and Westfield Rivers. This is an area of natural beauty and historic interest. From the fertile valley of the Connecticut River rise sturdy hills, mostly wooded but many with rocky summits or open ledges, the sources of clear, tumbling brooks. Heavily traveled Native American trails once crisscrossed the region, and some of the bloodiest battles of the Indian wars were fought here. At one time or another elegant summit houses or hotels, accessible by carriage roads or inclined railways, graced the tops of Mt. Tom, Mt. Nonotuck, Mt. Holyoke, Mt. Toby, and Mt. Sugarloaf.

Metacomet–Monadnock Trail (BCAMC)

The Metacomet–Monadnock (M–M) Trail is a 114-mi. continuation of the Metacomet Trail in Connecticut that begins in the Hanging Hills of Meriden, Conn. Commencing at the Connecticut–Massachusetts state line near the Southwick-Agawam town line, it runs north 114 mi. along the Traprock Ridges that border the Connecticut River Valley on the west, over Provin Mtn., East Mtn., and the Mt. Tom Range in the towns of Agawam, Southwick, West Springfield, Westfield, and Holyoke. Leaping the Connecticut River at Mt. Tom Junction in Easthampton, the trail proceeds east over the ridgeline of the Mt. Holyoke Range in Hadley and South Hadley, continuing east to Amherst and Granby, including Mt. Norwottuck and Long Mtn., then north along the hills that line the eastern edge of the Connecticut River Valley. Turning east in the Upper Bald Hills of Northfield to the summit of Mt. Grace in the town of Warwick, it continues to the Massachusetts–New Hampshire state line. An additional 20 mi. section of trail in southern New Hampshire brings the hiker to the summit of Mt. Monadnock, where the M–M trail joins the 51-mi. Monadnock–Sunapee Greenway Trail to the summit of Mt. Sunapee.

The trail has four shelters and other established campsites along its route. At suitable intervals it crosses paved highways and other roads passable by car and may be traversed easily in successive one-day or half-day trips. The descriptions below are divided into short segments of varying lengths that connect trailheads on town roads and highways. White blazes mark the route; double blazes (one above the other) indicate abrupt changes in direction or turns in the trail. White plastic triangles are often used at road crossings and trail junctions.

The M–M Trail was originally conceived and laid out by Professor Walter M. Banfield of the University of Massachusetts during the 1950s. It is maintained by the AMC's Berkshire Chapter (BCAMC), with the aid of local groups and individuals belonging to the Metacomet–Monadnock Trail Conference. The Trail's existence is a tribute to the cooperation of numerous state forest and park agencies, town conservation and water departments, nonprofit land trusts, wildlife sanctuaries, and the many private landowners whose generosity and foresight allows hikers to use of this special resource. At press time, Congress was considering a bill which would designate the Metacomet–Monadnock–Mattabesett trail system a National Scenic Trail. The New England National Scenic Trail Designation Act would provide opportunities for technical and financial assistance to manage and protect the trail. Land protection would continue to be accomplished through state and local entities on a willing seller basis only.

As this edition went to press, a significant change in the portion of the trail from Mt. Lincoln to the Wendell State Forest was pending approval and funding. This proposed route would lead from Mt. Lincoln's summit east to Rte. 202 and Quabbin Reservoir watershed lands at Gate 9, then follow Davis Rd. at Quabbin north to Gate 15. The trail would then leave Quabbin Reservation and continue to Lake Wyola in Shutesbury, rejoining the existing route in the Wendell State Forest. Beginning as early as spring 2009, hikers should watch for signs marking any changes in this area.

A published guidebook for the trail with maps is available. For more information, see www.amcberkshire.org/mm-trail.

Section 1. Massachusetts–Connecticut Line (Rising Corner, Conn.) to MA 57 (2.3 mi.)

From the intersection of Stone St. and Barry St. at Rising Corner, Conn., the trail runs left up South Longyard Rd. After 0.3 mi., the trail leaves the road sharply to the right, and enters an open field, following a fence. After crossing the field, the trail drops down left to a wet, swampy area crossed with bog bridges. After crossing the bridges over the swamp, a side trail leaves left. The trail then proceeds steeply up the side of the Provin Mtn. ridge.

At 0.8 mi., the trail reaches the ridge top, bears left into the woods, and continues north to cross a gas pipeline at 1.0 mi. There are limited views here to the west. The trail continues north on an old logging road, turns east, crosses a small brook, and after some sharp turns reaches a crossroad at 1.4 mi. The trail turns left, passing land owned by the Agawam Bowman Archery Club, and eventually comes out in front of a private residence just before reaching MA 57. At 2.1 mi. turn left (west) onto a paved access road which meets MA 57 at 2.3 mi. There is parking available on this access road. *(Note: The crossing of MA 57 may change if an extension into Southwick is funded; watch for potential construction and changes in this area.)*

Metacomet–Monadnock Trail: Massachusetts–Connecticut Line (Rising Corner CT) to MA 57

Distance from intersection of Stone St. and Barry St. (Rising Corner) (268 ft.) to
- MA 57 (319 ft.): 2.3 mi., 1 hr. 35 min.

Section 2. MA 57 to US 20 (Westfield River) (6.7 mi.)

This section of the trail follows the ridge of Provin Mtn., mostly along the western rim. The trail begins on MA 57, entering a wide driveway on the right leading to a locked iron gate. The Lane Quarry sign reads, No Trespassing, but permission has been granted to use this right-of-way. Do not block the gate or private driveway nearby on the right with cars. The trail goes straight ahead on a gravel road to the first blaze on a tree 200 ft. down the roadway visible from the gate. The trail goes straight along a gravel surface, and then bears left with an old quarry excavation on the right. (*Caution: The excavation area is dangerous due to loose stone.)* The trail now enters woods, turns sharp right, and climbs moderately along the bottom of a talus slope to reach the top of the ridge at 0.5 mi.

Turning left at an intersection, the trail passes the old route of the M–M Trail to the right. A short side hike on this unmarked path leads to the lip of the quarry, with excellent views south. Continuing north along the ridge, the trail passes a stone town-line marker at 1.4 mi. At 1.6 mi., it follows the rim of some cliffs, with extensive views west. Soon after the vista, the trail passes an observation tower and the old WWLP-TV station. From the parking area behind the building, follow the paved driveway to the left of the TV station. Just beyond the TV station at 1.8 mi., the trail turns left, away from the paved access road into the woods downhill. It bears right (north), and descends along the ridge.

With little ups and downs, the trail continues along this ridge, passing near and just above the hairpin turn on the access road for the Springfield's underground reservoir. The trail now descends the western slope of the ridge side and crosses a large open field on a grassy trail at 2.7 mi. Follow along the right edge of the open field at the base of the rock slope on the right for about 300 yd. Enter the woods, proceed to a chain link fence at 3.0 mi., following it steeply uphill through a stand of hemlocks to the ridge. From the ridge the trail descends on a wide path to a town-line boundary marker. It then turns left and descends steeply to a power line at 3.2 mi. and crosses directly under the lines and into the woods of Robinson State Park. The trail soon joins MA 187 near a utility shed just above the Westfield River at 4.3 mi. *(Note: Because the river cannot be forded safely, thru-hikers must make a long detour to the left (west) on MA 187 to the US 20 bridge that is reached at 5.0 mi.)* From the bridge follow US 20 back east to the traffic light across from the Big Y Shopping Center (6.7 mi.), where the trail resumes.

Metacomet–Monadnock Trail: MA 57 to US 20

Distances from MA 57 (319 ft.) to
- observation tower and WWLP-TV: 1.8 mi., 1 hr. 0 min.
- Westfield River: 4.3 mi., 1 hr. 50 min.
- bridge on US 20: 5 mi., 3 hr. 15 min.
- resumption of trail on US 20 (120 ft.): 6.7 mi. 4 hr.

Section 3. US 20 to Bush Notch (3.9 mi.)

This section of the trail has been relocated away from what used to be East Mtn. (now a quarry). It meanders below a sandy plateau and passes below the Pioneer Valley Sportsman's Club before gaining higher ground. The trail heads north on West Springfield water supply land towards the Massachusetts Turnpike (I-90), with the Lane Quarry periodically visible to the west. The section along Paucatuck Brook was relocated in 2003 off of the quarry access road.

From the traffic light at the shopping center on US 20, turn left at the light beneath a railroad overpass, and left again onto Sykes Ave. Proceed about 0.2 mi. to a gravel road with a Pioneer Valley Sportsman's Club sign on the left. Here the trail turns sharp left, past a large rock barrier onto an off-road vehicle trail leading uphill. After passing a sand and gravel pit on the left, turn sharp right at an intersection and proceed on level footing through a reclamation stand of red pines. An abandoned and overgrown sand pit is visible on the right at 0.6 mi. Proceeding along the rim of this sandy plateau and bearing left, the trail shortly reaches a gravel quarry access road at 0.8 mi. The trail crosses this road and descends to a small ravine on a recently relocated section to a stream crossing at 0.9 mi. The trail skirts above the swampy bank of Paucatuck Brook, then crosses several small brooks before emerging at a power line at 1.4 mi. At 1.7 mi. it crosses a wider stream bed and begins a short climb, re-crossing the power line and meeting an all-terrain vehicle trail.

The trail turns left off the ATV trail, then ascends to the top of the ridge. It soon enters a hemlock grove with the Lane Quarry to the west. *(Caution: this is a blasting area; trespassing is prohibited.)* The trail passes a recently logged area and descends to a brook at 2.3 mi. It continues north, ascending the ridge once again, then descends the slope past another timber harvest. The fallen chestnut trees are relics of the chestnut blight that swept across New England during the early 1900s.

The trail now turns northeast under a power line at 2.7 mi. and slowly descends, passing through a long stretch of hemlock-hardwood forest. It crosses an east-west tote road diagonally, a small brook, and another east-west woods road. The trail now bears left uphill, continues along a ridge, and descends. After turning left it continues up a shallow gully, climbing steeply. It then bears right to the top of the ridge's shoulder, and winds along, always on about the same contour.

After turning left, the trail continues up and over the main ridge and descends toward the Massachusetts Turnpike (I-90). Turn left near the turnpike fence, and proceed along it to its end. Scramble down below the bank and, now, with the turnpike on the right continue west through a gravelly open area (no blazes). At 3.8 mi. turn right on a quarry access road to an underpass beneath the Massachusetts Turnpike, then climb over a locked gate. The trail crosses the railroad tracks to a small clearing, then turns right onto Old Holyoke Rd. at Bush Notch.

Metacomet–Monadnock Trail: US 20 to Bush Notch

Distances from Riverbend Shopping Center (US 20) (120 ft.) to
- quarry access road crossing: 0.8 mi., 25 min.
- Bush Notch (330 ft.): 3.9 mi., 2 hr.

Section 4. Bush Notch to US 202 at Hugh McLean Reservoir (4.0 mi.)

Note: Portions of the trails in this section are heavily used by ATVs. From Bush Notch northward, the trail climbs to the crest of East Mountain and follows its ridge. It proceeds in the solitude of seemingly remote woodlands and passes a spectacular viewpoint from the west edge of the escarpment. An alternate route to the main trail meanders along old, mossy woods roads near the lovely shores of the Hugh McLean Reservoir, joining the main route south of US 202.

The trail goes right and down on Old Holyoke Rd. in Bush Notch for about 25 yd. and exits left opposite a small swampy pond. It climbs very steeply up the end of the ridge and bears right uphill, with the ridge crest above to the left. It passes a fine outlook to the right on the edge of the traprock cliff, then descends on a well-worn path before ascending sharply to the ridge top just beyond an iron pipe town-line post. The trail now descends gradually to the left. At 0.4 mi. it crosses a tote road and climbs to the west side of the East Mtn. ridge. The trail turns right near the top and follows several jeep roads north, continuing past an abandoned beacon tower at 0.8 mi. and another tower at 1.0 mi. There are excellent views south and west. Soon the trail turns left, briefly follows the ledges on the western end of the ridge, and turns right to proceed down the center of the descending north slope.

At 2.2 mi. the trail ascends the southern end of Snake Pond Mtn., reaches its bare ledge crest with views west, continues along the narrow, rocky ridge, and descends to join an old woods road at 2.8 mi. Proceed left (west) down the well-worn road, passing the blue-blazed loop trail to the right (this was the former M–M Trail route along McLean Reservoir's service road to US 202). The new route descends left for 100 yd. and leaves the woods road, turns sharply right on steep, loose footing, and ascends to a summit with some views. Descending from the summit, the trail comes out at a woods road at 3.2 mi., crosses the woods road to the right, and leaves it abruptly to the left. The trail now follows a footpath on the ridge north, crossing a buried telephone cable and descending gradually to a woods road. Follow the road and soon bear right and descend to US 202 at 4.0 mi., where limited parking is available.

Metacomet–Monadnock Trail: Bush Notch to US 202 (Hugh McLean Reservoir)

Distances from Bush Notch (330 ft.) to
- Snake Pond Mtn.: 2.2 mi., 1 hr. 40 min.
- US 202 (450 ft.): 4.0 mi., 3 hr.

Section 5. US 202 to MA 141 (Easthampton Rd.) (5.7 mi.)

This very scenic section of the trail runs along the wooded crest of the northern spur of East Mtn., from whose abrupt traprock ledges a succession of fine views of the valley unfolds. It follows old logging roads up the south slope of the mountain, and similar woods roads and footpaths north of East Mtn. to Mt. Tom. The section north of Cherry St. to MA 141 was significantly relocated in 2004 onto land owned by the Massachusetts Division of Fisheries and Wildlife.

From US 202 the trail enters the woods to the right of a water line and fence and turns right, paralleling the highway to a shallow draw. At the old reservoir access road turn left, noticing an interesting rock wall on the right that separates the trail from the isolated northern tip of the McLean Reservoir. Proceed to paved Apremont Way and cross it directly into the woods. Soon, veer right, uphill and away from a wetland on the left. The trail follows this narrow, flat ridge north with occasional views west.

At 0.8 mi. cross a steep, eroded off-road vehicle trail that goes left. Continue up a knob on the ridge; at 1.0 mi. watch for a sudden turn left and descend steeply on a talus slope with uncertain footing. The trail swings south for a short distance before finally veering west to cross the old Westfield–Holyoke street car route at 1.2 mi. The trail then ascends a talus slope. Turning right and picking up the old route, it continues north along the ridge about 100 yd., then turns abruptly west away from the steep eastern face. It crosses the top of the ridge, and at 1.8 mi. crosses a bare, rocky ledge on the southern end of the ridge with views of the Hugh McLean Reservoir and Hampden Ponds.

The trail now runs north along the western rim of this ridge through hardwoods and some hemlock. The trail crosses a little steep-sided hillock, turns away from the western rim of this ridge, and crosses a narrow rock ledge with views south, west, and north. From here the top of the abandoned East Mtn. radio beacon appears above the treetops to the north. After crossing this ledge and descending into the woods, the trail winds around north and then east to a junction at 2.1 mi. with a service road descending the mountain from the abandoned beacon. The trail passes under the tower of the beacon at 2.2 mi., continues north, and passes a huge rock.

The trail continues southwest down a draw with many fallen trees, including chestnut poles scattered around. At the end of the descent, the trail turns right and climbs to the top of a rock escarpment. There are splendid views westward all along the rim of these cliffs to 3.1 mi., at which point the trail leaves the ridge to the right. It enters a shallow wooded draw and climbs easily to a minor summit. Descend to Cherry St. Extension at 3.4 mi., a dirt secondary town road that the trail crosses directly.

The trail exits left off Cherry St. near the edge of a small swamp on the boundary of the Holyoke Revolver Club. Please stay to the right of the stone wall in this area. The trail crosses a stone wall and a normally dry streambed at 3.5 mi. and climbs steeply to the crest of a small ridge, which it follows along the rim of cliffs overlooking the western countryside. Following the ridge, it crosses a buried pipeline and passes several vernal pools. The trail continues north through mixed hardwood forest, then descends easily on a footpath along the narrow ridge to a woods road junction at 5.2 mi. Turn right onto this woods road and climb easily to the height-of land at 5.3 mi., where the trail now turns abruptly left, leaving this woods road. Proceed north along this low, forested ridge on a narrow trail and descend to a quiet side street. MA 141 is just ahead at 5.7 mi. There is plenty of parking here and across MA 141 at the entrance to the abandoned Whiting St. Reservoir.

Metacomet–Monadnock Trail: US 202 to MA 141 (Easthampton Rd.)

Distances from US 202 (450 ft.) to
- Cherry St. extension: 3.4 mi., 1 hr. 50 min.
- MA 141 (535 ft.): 5.7 mi., 4 hr. 15 min.

Section 6. MA 141 to MA 47 (5.8 mi.)

This is one of the more spectacular sections of the Metacomet–Monadnock trail, cruising the skyline near the rim of the steep talus slides and cliffs of Mt. Tom (1,202 ft.) and Whiting Peak (1,014 ft.). It then passes through the hemlock glens of the Mt. Tom Reservation on its way over Goat Peak and Mt. Nonotuck. From there the path descends on an old carriage road that leads to the Eyrie House, the remains of which can be seen via a short spur trail from the parking area. The final segment, from the boat ramp US 5 to MA 47, requires a crossing of the Connecticut River.

Leaving MA 141 (Easthampton Rd.), the trail turns east on a mossy woods road that skirts the edge of a swamp. At 0.3 mi. it bears right and climbs to a narrow ridge, then passes a glacial boulder and swings left around the northern tip of the swamp, then leaves the tote road abruptly to the right at 0.8 mi. It climbs into a ravine with cliffs on the right, passes under power lines, and after numerous switchbacks reaches the top of Mt. Tom and the site of old Mt. Tom Hotel, now occupied by a radio and TV transmission station, at 1.2 mi. The trail continues north along the top of the cliffs to the west, offering a succession of panoramic views of the countryside to the south, west and north.

At about 1.9 mi., the trail meets and coincides for a few feet with the red-blazed DOC trail. (The upper branch of this trail leads right 0.2 mi. to the tote road of the former Mt. Tom Ski Area; the lower branch bears left 1.1 mi. to the Quarry Trail). At 2.5 mi., after a steep descent from Whiting Peak, partly on stone steps, the trail passes near the woodsheds and shop area of the Mt. Tom State Reservation. The northern terminus of the Quarry Trail (yellow blazes) is at this point. (It leads to the old Mt. Tom Ski Area at 1.1 mi.) The Metacomet–Monadnock trail continues north through hemlock groves and a picnic area, reaching paved Smith's Ferry Rd. at 2.7 mi. It exits right onto the road for 70 yd., then turns left into the woods opposite the Mt. Tom Reservation's water supply pump house driveway. There is a water sprinkler and pavilion about 100 ft. to the left.

The trail proceeds north, soon leading up a low ridge clad with hemlocks. At 3.0 mi., the trail turns right and goes steeply uphill, then bears left, following the northern edge of the escarpment.

Widening views herald the summit clearing of Goat Peak (830 ft.) at 3.2 mi. The trail crosses the clearing, with the summit observation tower on the right, then renters the woods, following a zigzag course downhill through mountain laurel and mixed hardwoods. It crosses paved Goat Peak Rd. and continues through the woods to the blue-blazed Beau Bridge Trail at 3.5 mi., which exits right and leads to Hampden Field in 0.7 mi. Within a few yards the red-blazed Tea Bag trail also branches right and leads to lower Lake Bray and Smith's Ferry Rd. in 1 mi. The Metacomet–Monadnock trail continues north, reaching Dry Knoll at 3.9 mi., which overlooks the oxbow and floodplain of the Connecticut River.

Descending and proceeding northeast, the trail meets with a paved road at 4.1 mi. To reach the summit of Mt. Nonotuck (827 ft.), whose northern ledges provide wide views of the countryside, turn right on the paved road and continue to a parking lot. From there follow a well-worn path to the ledges and ruins of the old Eyrie House hotel. The Metacomet–Monadnock trail turns left onto the paved road, then right in about 50 yd. down the bank onto the old carriage road that also leads to the summit of Mt. Nonotuck.

The trail descends on the carriage road under a continuous arch of majestic giant hemlocks, past a woods road entering at the left at 4.6 mi. On a sweeping curve at 4.7 mi., the trail, still descending, turns left into another carriage road, which descends the mountain on a long gentle grade. The trail follows the carriage road past two side roads coming down from the hill on the left at each of two side roads coming down off the hill on the left, and turns right a fork in the carriage road, reaching a clearing and a power line at 4.8 mi. It turns right on a path under the power line and continues to Underwood St. The trail turns left on Underwood St., and follows it a short distance to East St. It turns right on East St. and soon passes under the I-91 overpass to reach US 5 at the Mt. Tom Junction at 5.1 mi. The trail follows blazed telephone poles left on a grassy section next to an electric transformer yard and the entrance to the Manhan Railtrail a short distance adjacent to US 5. The trail leads to the state boat ramp parking area on the Connecticut River Oxbow at 5.3 mi.

(Note: There is no public service by which thru-hikers can cross the river here. However, a free boat ride from this heavily used ramp can usually be obtained in season. Hikers should ask to be let off on the sandy beach between the two power-line crossings just upstream from a private camping area referred to as "tent city.")

From the opposite bank, the white blazes lead a short distance to a large open field, where the trail follows the blazed power line right-of-way to MA 47 on the Hadley–South Hadley line next to an old cemetery. The old Hockanum Cemetery is located at the intersection of MA 47 and the dirt entrance road into Skinner State Park.

Metacomet–Monadnock Trail: MA 141 to MA 47 (map 5: E1–A3)

Distances from MA 141 (535 ft.) to
- summit of Mt. Tom (1,202 ft.): 0.8 mi., 700 ft., 1 hr.
- DOC Trail (950 ft.): est. 1.9 mi., 1,100 ft. (rev. 750 ft.), 1 hr. 40 min.
- Mt. Tom Reservation woodsheds and Quarry Trail (600 ft.): 2.5 mi., 1,100 ft. (rev. 350 ft.), 2 hr. 10 min.
- Smiths Ferry Rd. (575 ft.): 2.7 mi., 1,100 ft., 2 hr. 25 min.
- Goat Peak (822 ft.): 3.2 mi., 1,350 ft., 2 hr 40 min.
- Beau Bridge Trail and Teabag Trail (625 ft.): 3.5 mi., 1,350 ft. (rev. 200 ft.), 2 hr. 55 min.
- paved road to Eyrie House (700 ft.): 4.1 mi., 1,550 ft. (rev. 100 ft.), 3 hr. 25 min.
- US 5 (128 ft.): 5.1 mi., 1,550 ft. (rev. 550 ft.), 4 hr. 10 min.
- MA 47 (Hockanum Cemetery) across Connecticut River (102 ft.): 5.8 mi., 1,550 ft., 4 hr. 45 min.

Section 7. MA 47 (Hockanum Cemetery) to MA 116 (6.6 mi.)

The first 2.0-mi. portion of this trail (from Hockanum Cemetery to Taylor Notch) contains some of the nicest views along the Metacomet–Monadnock Trail, with a succession of views of the Connecticut River and patchwork farm fields. At the center of this section in the western Mt. Holyoke Range is the restored Mt. Holyoke Summit House (accessible by car) with its beautiful picnic grounds. East of the Summit House is Taylor Notch; from here to Granby Notch (MA 116) there are fewer overlooks. This section of the range is comprised of a series of minor hills that result in what seems like an endless succession of ascents and descents. This area is forested, wild, and quite unspoiled.

From MA 47 the trail turns left onto the entrance to Skinner State Park across from the Hockanum Cemetery. It proceeds about 200 yd., then turns right up a steep footpath (no parking). The trail bears left and ascends the ridge over rock ledges, passing right of a private cabin (no trespassing). It turns left at 0.9 mi. near the west bank of a small swamp on the right, then left again at the junction of the red-blazed Dry Brook Trail. The trail turns left (north) uphill through hemlocks, and passes under high-tension lines. It proceeds briefly along the ledges, then turns northeast into the woods.

After descending into a hemlock dell, the trail turns turn right (east) and then south through a narrow defile. It turns east again and goes uphill, reaching a bare ledge with good views of the Connecticut River to the south. The trail continues north up a bare rock slope, descends into another hemlock dell, bears north up a grade on rock ledges, and reaches the top of a narrow rock ridge at 1.7 mi. It then descends a talus slope to the western rim of traprock cliffs overlooking the river and valley.

Turning east and then north, the trail climbs a ledge farther back in the woods, reaching a junction with a green-blazed side trail coming from the west at 1.1 mi. (This trail leads to an overlook that is popular with hang gliders.) The merged trails climb higher on the rising ridge, heading east and then north. The trail crosses a rock wall and bears left, descending on an old road northward. At 2.2 mi. it intersects the blue-blazed Halfway House Trail, which descends left to the Halfway House parking lot. The Metacomet–Monadnock Trail follows this broad trail right, ascending to the Mt. Holyoke Summit House at 2.3 mi.

The Summit House affords superb views across the Pioneer Valley. The trail follows wooden steps to the Summit House porch, then continues east through the picnic area. Water and restrooms are available when the house is open to the public from May to October. At 2.5 mi., it descends abruptly east from the end of the open picnic areas along broad switchbacks and reaches Taylor Notch Rd. at 2.7 mi. (This road leads back 1.5 mi. to Hockanum Cemetery at the southern entrance to the park.)

After crossing the road to the Summit House, the trail now climbs steeply east to a rocky ledge along the eastern rim of Taylor Notch. It continues to the top of one hill (858 ft.), with limited views north, and at 4.2 mi. the top of a second hill (919 ft.). At 5.2 mi. the trail passes the crest of Mt. Hitchcock (1,005 ft.). At 6.0 mi. it reaches the crest of Bare Mtn. (1,002 ft.), with superb views of the countryside in all directions. The trail bears right and descends by steep gradients and stone steps on a switchback route to MA 116 opposite the Mt. Holyoke Range State Park's Notch Visitor Center at 6.6 mi.

Metacomet–Monadnock Trail: MA 47 (Hockanum Cemetery) to MA 116

Distances from MA 47 (Hockanum Cemetery) (102 ft.) to
- Halfway House Trail (900 ft.): 2.2 mi., 1 hr. 15 min.
- Mt. Holyoke Summit House (940 ft.): 2.3 mi., 1 hr. 20 min.
- Taylor Notch Rd. (700 ft.): 2.7 mi., 1 hr. 45 min.
- Mt. Hitchcock (1,005 ft.): 5.2 mi., 3 hr. 40 min.
- Bare Mtn. (1,002 ft.): 6 mi., 4 hr. 30 min.
- MA 116 (520 ft.): 6.6 mi., 5 hr.

Section 8. MA 116 to Harris Mtn. Rd. (5.0 mi.)

The commanding views from Mt. Norwottuck (1,106 ft.) and Long Mtn. (920 ft.) and the historic overhanging ledges of Mt. Norwottuck (the so-called "horse-caves" of Revolutionary War days) make this a very popular section of the trail. It runs along the ridge-top through a naturalist's delight of unbroken hardwood forests and hemlock coves.

From MA 116, the trail proceeds across the Holyoke Range State Park Notch Visitor Center parking lot and up the driveway to the right of the building. It enters woods, turns right, and descends to an old streetcar right of way. The trail turns onto the right-of-way for a short distance, then follows a gravel road, skirting the quarry on the right. The trail soon crosses a high-tension line, and bears right (south) at 0.6 mi. to ascend the ridge. (The orange-blazed Robert Frost Trail leaves straight from this intersection.) At 1.3 mi. it reaches the summit of Mt. Norwottuck, with excellent views. The trail continues southeast above the high cliff on the eastern edge of the ridge, then descends steeply on a rocky section. At 1.5 mi. it reaches the horse caves, a series of overhanging ledges, then climbs through a crevice descending to the bottom of the ledge (caves on the right) and proceeds gradually downhill on a wide path to the saddle of Mt. Norwottuck and Rattlesnake Knob, where the Robert Frost Trail reenters from the left and the red-blazed Swamp Trail leaves to the right. (From here to Harris Mtn. Rd. in Amherst, the Robert Frost and M–M Trails coincide). The trail continues east along the ridge, passing the yellow-blazed Ken Cuddeback Trail on the left, then turns sharp right (just before a scenic viewpoint) onto a steep descent on an old woods road. A short distance left is a view of Long Mountain from Rattlesnake Knob. At 2.3 mi. the road goes right and the trail merges with another woods road, bears left, and enters a hemlock stand.

At 2.6 mi. the trail turns right, leaving the woods road at the Amherst–Granby town line. It reaches a ridge crest (775 ft.) with a good view of Mt. Norwottuck. The trail continues east-northeast along the ridge and descends into a little dell. It continues uphill, swinging to the right and reaching a ledge top at 3.2 mi., with a good view southeast. The trail proceeds east, then north, on this ridge, reaching a steep descent into a small flat. It meets a woods road and follows it southeast, ascending. It leaves the road at 3.7 mi., bearing left, and ascends a steep, narrow ridge up Long Mtn. (920 ft.). to reach cliff ledges with superb 180-degree views west.

The trail turns left at an abandoned beacon at 4.1 mi., descending briefly, then continues along the ridge to reach another open ledge. It now bears right, descending into a hardwood forest and then east on an old tote road. At 4.5 mi. the trail turns abruptly left (northeast) off the tote road, ascends a gentle slope through hardwood cover, crosses over the top of a knob, then drops steeply. It turns abruptly right (east), continuing through more hardwood forest to paved Harris Mtn. Rd. at 5.0 mi.

Metacomet–Monadnock Trail: MA 116 to Harris Mtn. Rd.

Distances from MA 116 (520 ft.) to
- summit of Mt. Norwottuck (1,106 ft.): 1.3 mi., 1 hr.
- horse caves (800 ft.): 1.5 mi., 1 hr. 20 min.
- Robert Frost Trail (second junction): 1.9 mi., 1 hr. 40 min.
- Harris Mtn. Rd. (388 ft.): 5.0 mi., 3 hr. 55 min.

Section 9. Harris Mtn. Rd. to MA 9 (Holland Glen) (4.0 mi.)

This is a very pleasant walk over a succession of low, forested hills with occasional glimpses of the Mt. Holyoke Range to the west and the Belchertown ponds to the east, offering the hiker plenty of solitude. Extensive logging has occurred in the section between Bay Rd. and Orchard St.; watch carefully for the trail blazes.

From Harris Mtn. Rd. the trail continues east on a sandy woods road. At 0.2 mi. the trail leaves the road to the right (while the Robert Frost Trail continues straight) and ascends a gentle slope through hardwood forest, briefly following an old tote road northeast. At 0.3 mi., turn abruptly southeast, ascend a steep hillside, and continue along the hilltops through a hardwood forest on rolling ground. At 0.5 mi., ascend a short, steep slope to the crest of the ridge, then abruptly left (northeast) and continue along the ridge, crossing a power line. A loop trail on the right just before the power line descends to a town conservation area. At the eastern end of the ridge, the trail bears right down a steep bank, crosses a little flat, and climbs again eastward to a knoll close by a house, with a limited view of Mt. Toby to the north. It then descends steeply to Bay Rd. at 1 mile and turns right along the road.

At 1.2 mi., the trail continues on Bay Rd. past its intersection with Wright Rd., then turns sharply left turn onto an old woods road, ascending into a hemlock mixed forest, part of a conservation area managed by the Kestrel Trust and other groups. At 1.4 mi. the trail reaches the top of a hill (517 ft.), then bears right, descending steeply. It merges with a sandy lane at 1.6 mi., follows the lane briefly north, and bears right at a fork.

The trail ascends, traverses a low hill, and descends into a tall pine stand on a flat, crossing a stone wall and then a ditch at 1.9 mi. Soon ascending, it traverses a second low hill covered with mixed forest, descends through tall pines to a tote road that crosses a tiny stream at 2.2 mi. The trail follows the tote road east through a hardwood stand with clumps of hemlocks, crosses the plateau at 2.6 mi. and abruptly turns south through a mature hardwood forest. At 2.8 mi. it abruptly turns left at the south edge of this plateau overlooking Lake Metacomet.

The trail turns sharp left at right angles to and away from the top edge of the plateau and continues north to a junction with a woods road coming up from Federal St. just north of Arcadia Lake in Belchertown. After bearing right at the top of the ridge, the trail reaches a side trail to a ledge overlooking Holland Lake. It then turns left downhill through hardwoods. At 3.2 mi. it bears right on a skid road, then turns left onto a path and descends about 100 ft. to Federal St. Turn left before a private home, and proceed on a level contour through a brushy area, and descend steeply to Orchard St. Care should be taken here.

Turn right just before the road. Cross it, then Federal St., and then follow Cheryl Circle for about 200 yd., making a left just after the steep-banked stream bed. The trail continues over a brushy knoll and descends to the Central Vermont railroad tracks at 3.7 mi. It crosses the tracks, continues east briefly on the shoulder of the railroad bed, then turns left (north) into the woods. After crossing the brook, it ascends the bank of MA 9 across from the entrance to Holland Glen at 4.0 mi.

Metacomet–Monadnock Trail: Harris Mtn. Rd. to MA 9 (Holland Glen)

Distances from Harris Mtn. Rd. (388 ft.) to
- Bay Rd. (350 ft.): 1.0 mi., 55 min.
- MA 9 at Holland Glen (346 ft.): 4.0 mi., 3 hr.

Section 10. MA 9 (Holland Glen) to Enfield Rd. (1.5 mi.)

An interesting walk over ridges and along streams on footpaths and old town roads, this section of the trail is bordered on the west by sturdy stone walls and old cellar holes that mark the site of an old agrarian community, now covered with mixed forest. Holland Glen is a steep-sided ravine with a clear stream shaded by a mature hemlock stand, which has been preserved by the Belchertown Historical Society.

From MA 9 the trail continues east through the woods into Holland Glen. At 0.2 mi., it crosses the brook and follows its right bank into the ravine. The trail climbs the steep side of the ravine, exiting right from the stream, continuing amid mature hemlocks, and passing a waterfall at 0.4 mi. at the top of the glen. The trail continues upstream on the right bank, crossing a tributary stream. At this point, the trail has been discontinued at the request of the private landowner. It starts again at Gulf Rd.

After 0.3 mi. on Gulf Rd., turn right. Follow the blazing for another 0.4 mi., where the trail passes near an open field on the right with abandoned cars on the left. This route is followed west along the woods line, bearing left in another 0.4 mi. Turning right, the trail passes through a scrub oak woodland. Be sure to follow the blazes and keep to the left of the septic system. The trail crosses Enfield Rd. and proceeds north through the Cadwell Memorial Forest (University of Massachusetts).

Metacomet–Monadnock Trail: MA 9 (Holland Glen) to Enfield Rd.

Distance from Holland Glen (346 ft.) to
  • Tributary Stream: 0.5 mi., 30 min.
Distance from from Gulf Rd. to
  • Enfield Road. (1,010 ft.): 1.5 mi., 1 hr. 30 min.

Section 11. Enfield Rd. to North Valley Rd. (3.7 mi.)

The portion of the trail between Mt. Lincoln and the Wendell State Forest is subject to a proposed potential reroute that would lead from Mt. Lincoln's summit east to Rte. 202 and Quabbin Reservoir watershed lands at Gate 9, then follow Davis Rd. to Gate 15. The trail would then leave Quabbin Reservation and continue to Lake Wyola in Shutesbury, rejoining the existing route in the Wendell State Forest. Though this change is pending approval and the route is tentative, beginning as early as spring 2009 hikers should watch for signs marking any changes.

A delightful walk in any season, the section of the trail crosses Mt. Lincoln with its sweeping views, then descends the northwest slope beside a small, fast-falling brook in a narrow hemlock glen. It passes through beautiful pine and hemlock mixed forests to Amherst's Hill Reservoir, and continues downstream beside Harris Brook. From the confluence of Harris and Amethyst Brooks the trail continues upstream under a canopy of pines and hemlocks beside a succession of waterfalls to a footbridge over Buffam Brook beside North Valley Rd. in Pelham.

The trail leaves the road at 0.3 mi. and bears right uphill through a scrub oak stand. At 0.6 mi., it passes the fire tower atop 1,240-ft. Mt. Lincoln (360-degree view), passing left of a maintenance shed. From the summit, the trail continues west down the service road, and at 0.7 mi., exits right into the woods and descends across a gravel road at 0.9 mi. It continues downhill to the north, crossing a wet area on bog bridges, and at 1.4 mi., turns right onto another gravel road and crosses over a brook. The trail turns left onto a woods road, then almost at once turns left again, descending and crossing the brook twice. The trail continues past the site of an old mill, and at 2.0 mi. turns right on another woods road, which crosses the brook. The trail then emerges into a brushy open area on Amherst Rd. at 2.1 mi.

After crossing Amherst Rd. the trail bears left up a steep, sand bank into pines on a plateau. It continues through a dense pine grove, then slowly descends to the west through beautiful pines to an intersection with an old, grassy road at 2.3 mi. The trail turns right on the grassy road and then quickly left onto a trail leading west through mixed woods and then hemlocks. It descends gradually, then steeply, to a gravel road at 2.7 mi. and turns right. The trail proceeds north for 300 yd., crossing Amethyst Brook on a road bridge before turning left on a narrow trail into Pelham Conservation land at a white pine stand at 2.9 mi. Turn left and descend to just below the Amherst Central Reservoir dam and the bank of Amethyst Brook at 3.1 mi. and turn right (west).

The trail through here follows Amethyst and Buffam Brooks. After bearing right, and ascending, it continues left at a junction above the brook under tall pines and hemlocks, then soon descends again to the water and continues to the base of Buffam Falls at 3.5 mi. Here the trail turns right (north), ascending beside a series of cascades along Buffam Brook. After crossing a bridge on the left, it emerges on North Valley Rd. at 3.7 mi. Parking is available on a paved road shoulder under the power lines to the left at 3.9 mi.

Metacomet–Monadnock Trail: Enfield Rd. to North Valley Rd.

Distances from Enfield Rd. (1,010 ft.) to
- Mt. Lincoln summit (1,240 ft.): 0.6 mi., 30 min.
- Pelham–Amherst Rd.: 2.1 mi., 1 hr. 40 min.
- Amherst Reservoir spillway: 3.1 mi., 2 hr. 25 min.
- Buffum Falls: 3.5 mi., 2 hr. 50 min.
- North Valley Rd. (460 ft.): 3.7 mi., 3 hr.

Section 12. North Valley Rd. to Pratt Corner–Cushman Rd., Atkins Reservoir (4.5 mi.)

This section of the trail has been designated the Walter Banfield Memorial portion of the M–M Trail in honor of the trail's founder. The trail ascends the bare ledges of Mt. Orient, then runs the length of this ridge through oak and white birch woods, eventually descending to a gravel road to Heatherstone Brook. The path then swings west over the shoulder of Poverty Mtn., and follows a pleasant old woods road down the western slope through cool evergreen woods. The trail reaches the old Adams Homestead, the former home of the late Walter Banfield, on Pratt Corner Rd.

Because of a request from the private landowner the trail has been discontinued for 2.7 mi. from North Valley Rd. until it continues on a woods road that ascends up and over a shoulder of Poverty Mtn. Follow this road steeply downhill through tall pines and a hardwood forest to a woods road, descend more steeply, then bear right (north) onto another tote road.

From here the trail turns left, descending through a mature mixed forest. It then turns right, descending through hemlock woods. After crossing a streamlet, the trail turns right on dirt Pratt Corner Rd. at 1 mi. The orange-blazed Robert Frost Trail crosses the road directly into the woods on its way to Atkins Reservoir. The trail follows Pratt Corner Rd. (light traffic) to a left turn at 1.3 mi. Bear left again onto Cushman Rd. at 1.4 mi. A small trailhead parking area is on the right at 1.5 mi. on town of Amherst watershed land.

Metacomet–Monadnock Trail: North Valley Rd. to Pratt Corner–Cushman Rd., Atkins Reservoir

Distance from woods road to
• Pratt Corner/Cushman Rd., Atkins Reservoir (445 ft.): 4.5 mi., 1 hr. 30 min.

Section 13. Atkins Reservoir to Shutesbury–Leverett Rd. (1.0 mi.)

In forested country, mostly on narrow footpaths, the trail here climbs over the January Hills through groves of oak, white birch, and white pine, ultimately reaching the Roaring Brook Conservation Area on the Shutesbury–Leverett Rd.

The trail crosses a bridge over Dean and Nurse Brooks, and after less than 100 yd., bears left into the woods on a narrow trail. The trail then follows closely the red-blazed watershed boundary inside Amherst watershed land for the next 0.4 mi. At 0.5 mi. it crosses an old cable, but the 1.2-mi. portion after this has been discontinued at the request of a private landowner.

The trail picks up at a tote road at 1.7 mi. from Atkins Reservoir, crosses the road, then passes through a boggy area on foot bridges at 0.2 mi. It descends easily along the wider path, then turns abruptly right off of it at 0.3 mi., arriving at Leverett Conservation land. Cross a bog bridge and footbridge and turn left, continuing downstream along the bank of Roaring Brook. At 0.4 mi. the trails crosses the Banfield Bridge, then turns right and left up a short, steep bank to Shutesbury Rd. A blue-blazed side trail turns right a short distance to a small parking area just before the M–M road crossing at 0.5 mi.

Metacomet–Monadnock Trail: Atkins Reservoir to Shutesbury–Leverett Rd.

Distance from Atkins Reservoir to
- old cable: 0.5 mi., 30 min.

Distance from tote road to
- Shutesbury–Leverett Rd.: 1.0 mi., 30 min.

Section 14. Shutesbury–Leverett Rd. to North Leverett Rd. (1.0 mi.)

Cross to the right for 30 yd. on paved Shutesbury Rd. to a woods road on the left. Proceed left for some 300 yd. ascending. Pass through a clearing to the left of a power line and make a left on an old town road, descending. At 0.7 mi. turn abruptly right, leaving this road, and follow a level contour on narrow trail. Come to a blue-blazed trail to the right leading to the Mosher Shelter (built in 2005) at 1.0 mi. From this point until Rattlesnake Gutter Rd., the trail has been discontinued at the request of the landowner and is not blazed. You can pick up the trail again at the Leverett co-op at the junction of Rattlesnake Gutter Rd. and North Leverett Rd.

Metacomet–Monadnock Trail: Shutesbury–Leverett Rd. to North Leverett–Lake Wyola Rd.

Distance from Shutesbury–Leverett Rd. (550 ft.) to
- Mosher Shelter: 1.0 mi., 1 hr.

Section 15. North Leverett Rd. to Farley (11.6 mi.)

This lengthy, remote section is almost entirely over backcountry gravel roads, woods roads, and forest service access roads with colorful wildflower blooms in the summer. From North Leverett Rd. the trail ascends the north slope of the Sawmill River Valley along Diamond Match Ridge on narrow foot trails, gradually descends via Ruggles Pond, Lyons Brook, and

Mormon Hollow Brook to the village of Farley in the Millers River Valley. Much of this section is inside Wendell State Forest on the south slope of the Millers River Valley.

From the Village Co-op store, the trail continues left (west) along North Leverett Rd. At 0.4 mi., it turns right off of the road onto the power line right-of-way, and follows the power line, ascending to the height-of-land and at 1.1 mi. turning right into the woods. The trail continues easily uphill to a left at a swampy, level area onto a narrow footpath that leads to the top of Diamond Match Ridge. At 2.1 mi. it reaches the wooded summit of Hill 1123 and continues along the ridge to a stone town boundary marker at 2.6 mi. The trail bears right (east) after the marker, and then left on a low ridge to an open area thick with low bush blueberries at 2.9 mi., then descends to a bridge crossing of Red Brook at 3.7 mi. It soon turns left (north) and enters Wendell State Forest via Hemmenway Rd. The trail continues north, crosses Montague Rd. at 5.1 mi., and reaches Carlton Rd. at 5.4 mi. Turn left on this road, then immediately right, and descend to the junction with the blue-blazed Ruggles Pond Trail, which follows the scenic west side of the boggy pond to a large open field and picnic pavilion area at 6.0 mi.

The foundation and clearing at 6.2 mi. mark the site of an old CCC camp, now maintained by DCR with picnic tables, fireplaces, and a swimming beach. (A parking fee is charged in season.) The trail crosses the parking lot, then proceeds about 200 yd. downhill to an Adirondack shelter suitable for six people. A fire pit, wood, and outhouse are available. The trail continues downhill on an old tote road along the east bank of Lyons Brook, passing through an area of forest blown down by a tornado in July 2006, before reaching the crossing of a smaller brook at its confluence with Lyons Brook near Lynne's Falls in the area called Hidden Valley at 6.9 mi. It soon bears right, leaving the brook up a steep bank through laurel scrub, before crossing the brook at 7.1 mi. The trail then heads north along the base of a ridge, before turning right and ascending south on a woods road to unpaved Jerusalem Rd.

From the junction, the trail takes a sharp right turn, going uphill on Jerusalem Rd. to a junction with a side trail next to a small parking area. The trail turns left up this side trail to the ridge and then bears right (north) to follow the ridge line, where there are excellent views to the west from two rocky overlooks. The narrow track trail continues over several wooded hills to the junction of two woods roads.

Following woods roads, the trail drops down at the end of the ridge to unpaved Damon Camp Rd. and turns left. Follow the road a short distance to Davis Rd., then descend steeply to the right on Davis Rd. toward Mormon Hollow Brook.

The trail continues right and downhill on a washed-out section of Davis Rd. and crosses Mormon Hollow Brook on a sturdy bridge at 9.5 mi. After crossing the bridge, take a sharp left and follow the scenic brook. The trail passes some old dam structures and cellar holes to emerge on Mormon Hollow Rd. at 9.8 mi. Go left on the road, then sharp right under the power lines down to a meadow used for parking by local anglers. The trail leaves Wendell State Forest near Mormon Hollow Rd. and continues along Mormon Hollow Brook with its attractive cascades, pools and glades of mature hemlock. Crossing the brook two times (use caution here; a steep blue-blazed trail on the left is used by hikers during high water to avoid the crossings) it finally picks up an old skid road on the north side and proceeds to the Millers River, passing just below the railroad bridge. Climb the steep railroad bank, cross the bridge, and descend to the river. *(Note: During low water, it may be possible to ford the river on a gravel bar under the bridge.)*

At the river the trail heads east along the densely vegetated floodplain. At the end of the floodplain the trail rises up on to the railroad embankment and follows the tracks for several hundred yards before going again into the woods. *(Caution: The railroad tracks are active.)* The trail continues through woods parallel to the river before passing the foundations of a nineteenth century knitting factory and piano works. The trail emerges on Farley Rd. next to the Farley Bridge at 11.4 mi. There is limited parking here. Cross the bridge and follow the paved road to MA 2 at 11.6 mi.

Metacomet–Monadnock Trail: North Leverett–Lake Wyola Rd. to Farley

Distances from North Leverett–Lake Wyola Rd. (640 ft.) to

- recreation area and Adirondack shelter at Ruggles Pond: 6.2 mi., 3 hr. 30 min.
- Lyons Brook crossing: 6.9 mi., 3 hr. 55 min.
- MA 2 at Farley (430 ft.): 11.6 mi., 6 hr. 15 min.

Section 16. MA 2 (Farley) to Gulf Rd. (6.7 mi.)

This section of the trail climbs steeply from Farley in the shadow of the high cliffs of Rattlesnake Mtn., then continues along the hemlock-shaded ravine of Briggs Brook. From here it proceeds northeast on the ridge and ledges of Hermit Mtn., passing the blue-blazed trail that leads to Hermit Castle. After passing several good viewpoints from high above the Millers River Valley, the trail turns north through Erving State Forest toward the bare ledges of Crag Mtn. in Northfield.

Cross MA 2 next to a log cabin style building (parking available at Farley Rd. across the bridge on the right) and continue to Holmes St. Turn left on Wells St., following it uphill to its end. Pass Cross St. (limited parking here) and enter the woods at a private driveway. At 0.4 mi. the trail crosses Briggs Brook a short distance above the lip of a waterfall on a footbridge and turns left, ascending the right bank of the brook on a steep path. At the top of the waterfall, a side trail goes left to the cliffs of Rattlesnake Mtn. The trail crosses the brook twice, then passes a side trail to Rose Ledge at 0.8 mi. (This trail runs upstream along Briggs Brook, then west and south to the southern rim of Northfield Mtn., known as Rose Ledge. There are fine views of the Connecticut River Valley from the ledge. This trail is part of the extensive trail system of the Northfield Mtn. Recreational Area. For maps and information, write to: Northfield Mtn. Recreational and Environmental Center, 99 Millers Falls Rd., Northfield, MA 01360.)

At this junction the M–M Trail turns right (northeast) and crosses the brook. In a few yards it turns right again and climbs to a rocky ledge. The trail crosses a woods road, continuing north while staying close to the rim of the ridge, which falls away steeply to the valley. The Northfield Mtn. pumped-storage reservoir is on the left. At 1.4 mi. the trail turns right away from the reservoir and crosses Packard Brook on a footbridge. At 1.8 mi. it reaches the junction with the blue-blazed side trail on the right that leads 0.4 mi. to the Hermit's Castle site. Twenty yards past this side trail, the M–M trail bears right next to an intersection with a woods road that goes left. From this junction it ascends to the ridge. At 2.2 mi. the trail traverses ledges overlooking the Millers River Valley and continues eastward from ledge to ledge. It passes the second junction with the Hermit Castle trail and descends to a dry brook bed.

The trail now turns sharp left (north) and continues ascending moderately for 0.3 mi. on a north-northwest bearing through hardwood forest. The terrain levels off, and hemlocks soon become the principal forest component. At 3.1 mi. the trail turns right (east) onto a tote road, then, as this road changes its bearing from east to southeast, turns left (north). At 3.5 mi., it turns left again onto a much broader tote road but soon jogs south from this broad road onto a narrower road and within 100 ft. leaves the road, turning east. It climbs slightly, reaching a high ledge at 3.6 mi, and shortly descends the ledges, bearing north to more level terrain. It proceeds northeast through hardwoods with some pines to the junction with Mtn. Rd. at 3.8 mi., just south of the padlocked gate on the west side of the road (1,108 ft.). This gate leads to Northfield Mtn. Reservoir, which is off-limits to hikers.

The trail continues north on Mtn. Rd. to the Northfield-Erving line at 4.1 mi., where it turns right (east) onto an abandoned town road. After crossing a tiny streamlet it continues east. The trail turns left (north) into a gray birch-pine forest and soon crosses a small swampy area at 4.3 mi. It continues north through stands of birch, maple, and pine, then begins climbing gently. It jogs left through pines, turns north, descending slightly and crosses a little dell, turning west as it skirts the base of a rock outcrop. It soon turns north again through a break in the ledge and within 150 ft. turns right onto South Mtn. Rd. At the road's height-of-land at 4.9 mi., the trail turns left (north) onto a long gravel private driveway. Turn right before reaching the house and begin a short, steep climb to the summit of Crag Mtn., which offers views east to Mt. Grace, east-northeast to Mt. Monadnock in New Hampshire, and south to the Northfield Mtn. reservoir. The trail descends to the north along the ridge, makes a right and then a left jog, and continues on a woods road to a rocky gully at 5.8 mi. The trail then leaves the woods road, bearing straight into the woods. It crosses a low ridgeline and continues north along the base of the low ledge. After crossing a small stream and passing a wetland with old black gum trees, the trail passes through an open, rocky area with partial views of Mt. Grace and Mt. Monadnock. It then reenters the woods and descends on a woods road that runs parallel to a power line, reaching Gulf Rd. in Northfield at 6.7 mi. A short, blue-blazed side trail passes the historic Swan home site en route to the parking area on Gulf Rd.

Metacomet–Monadnock Trail: MA 2 (Farley) to Gulf Rd.

Distances from MA 2 at Farley (430 ft.) to
- Rose Ledge side trail: 0.8 mi., 30 min.
- ledges overlooking Millers River: 2.2 mi., 1 hr. 15 min.
- Mtn. Rd. (1,108 ft.): 3.8 mi., 2 hr. 5 min.
- South Mtn. Rd. below Crag Mtn.: 4.9 mi., 2 hr. 50 min.
- Gulf Rd. (1,204 ft.): 6.7 mi., 3 hr. 50 min.

Section 17. Gulf Rd., Northfield to MA 78, Warwick (8.3 mi.)

Passing across the tops of Northfield's Bald Hills, the trail descends the ridge via the historic Fifth Massachusetts Turnpike, then continues eastward on a remote route away from and north of Warwick's White Road to the southern tip of Mt. Grace State Forest. Thence it climbs on the old Snowshoe Trail to the fire tower on the summit of Mt. Grace (1,617 ft.), before descending to MA 78.

At 0.2 mi. the trail turns right off Gulf Rd. under a power line, then left onto a service road before reaching the first pylon, proceeding northeast. At 0.5 mi. it turns left from the woods road onto an old tote road, proceeding on the same contour north to a brook at 0.8 mi. The trail crosses the brook, proceeds on its north bank upstream for 100 ft., then turns left and follows the trail another 100 yd. northeast. It bears left, climbing hills, and soon reaches some rock outcrops. At 1.1 mi. it turns right from the ledge and continues through an open pine forest, soon ascending sharply through hardwoods to cross a power line near the top of the Bald Hills. There are views under the power line at the height-of-land. The trail continues east on bare rock, following several cairns to the eastern rim of the hill (1,345 ft.). Mt. Grace looms ahead through the trees.

Here the trail turns left, descending through pine forests, then ascending. At 1.8 mi. it emerges on the east rim of a hardwood-covered ridge and proceeds north, soon descending. It crosses a boulder-strewn, fast-falling streamlet (mostly dry in summer) at 2.1 mi., then ascends through a hemlock-hardwood forest. Skirting the east slope of the hill (1,285 ft.), the trail drops rapidly to a junction with the woods road extension of Warwick's White Rd. at 2.4 mi. It turns left, ascending to the height-of-land just before the power lines, then turns right (north) on a recent relocation of the trail. This new route follows the ridgeline of the hill north along its wooded crest before descending to join a snowmobile trail at 2.5 mi. The trail proceeds right on this road (the historic Fifth Massachusetts Turnpike, dating from 1775), crossing a junction with unpaved White Rd. at 3.4 mi., and continues east to a small clearing.

The trail crosses a brook on a culvert, then narrows to a woods road, ascending and crossing another woods road at 4.3 mi. after detouring around a house. It continues east on snowmobile trails to connect with paved Northfield Rd. The trail parallels the highway and emerges near the junction of White Rd. and Northfield Rd. The trail crosses the road, passes over a brook on a rustic bridge, and then climbs up to join the Round-the-Mountain Trail in Mt. Grace State Reservation at 5.1 mi.

Continue on the Round-the-Mountain Trail left for a short distance, then turn right off the trail, ascending steeply to the old Snowshoe Trail. The trail continues to an intersection of trails, turns sharp left and descends, then soon begins a steady ascent of a knife-edge ridge. Beneath the hemlocks at the crest of the ridge are lookouts to the west.

The trail descends through the forest to a draw in a tall pine grove at 6.1 mi., then climbs again amid pines and hemlocks past more westward lookouts and a northward glimpse of the Mt. Grace summit and fire tower. With a gradual descent the trail joins the fire tower service road from Warwick village at 6.4 mi. and follows this steep road for 0.2 mi., where it leaves the road to follow a telephone line. It soon rejoins the road and follows it to the summit of Mt. Grace at 6.8 mi.

The trail runs along the summit of Mt. Grace, past the fire tower on the left, and a boulder a plaque on the right, to begin its northerly descent via an old ski trail. It bears left onto the trail away from the service road, and at 7.0 mi. turns abruptly left off of the ski trail to descend steeply past a spring (right) at 7.2 mi. Then it winds down more gently, through old woods to a junction with a tote road. This road descends through hemlocks to a level stretch at 7.8 mi., where it crosses a brook and passes an Adirondack shelter built by DCR in 1970.

The trail continues down the tote road to a beautiful pool, then descends along the edge of the ravine. It bears left around a small opening and crosses Mountain Brook below a broken dam to reach MA 78 at 8.3

mi. (Turning right on MA 78 south leads to the Mt. Grace State Forest picnic area in 1.0 mi.)

Metacomet–Monadnock Trail: Gulf Rd. to Mt. Grace

Distances from base of Crag Mtn. on Gulf Rd. (1,204 ft.) to
- White Rd.: 2.4 mi., 1 hr. 35 min.
- Northfield Rd.: 5 mi., 3 hr. 30 min.
- summit of Mt. Grace (1,625 ft.): 6.8 mi., 4 hr. 50 min.
- MA 78 (575 ft.): 8.3 mi., 5 hr., 30 min.

Section 18. MA 78, Warwick to MA 32 (7.4 mi.)

From MA 78 eastward the trail enters a stretch of unbroken woodland and, after traversing the wilderness solitude of Richards Reservoir inside Warwick State Forest, it proceeds roughly parallel to the Massachusetts–New Hampshire state line to the end of this section. The trail follows narrow footpaths and old roads through once settled farmland, across rolling hills, and a steep, narrow valley with Grand Monadnock beckoning in the distance. This section was substantially relocated onto public land along the north shoreline of Richards Reservoir in 2004 by BCAMC volunteers. A connection is made with the 18-mi. Tully Trail on Bliss Rd.

The trail crosses MA 78, climbs a steep bank, and at the top of a knoll, turns right through a corridor of thick pines. Emerging onto a faint path, it turns abruptly left at 0.1 mi., angles down to cross a brook, and 40 ft. east of the brook meets a woods road. The trail turns left onto the road, proceeds north 0.1 mi., bears right, and travels continuously through a recently logged white pine forest, gradually ascending on an easterly bearing. The trail enters a stand of Scotch pine, skirts an orchard, and emerges on Old Winchester Rd. (gravel) at 0.6 mi. It follows the road right, ascending, and at 0.9 mi. turns left off the road into the woods onto a lane lined with rock walls. The trail descends this washed-out dirt road, and after a small stream crossing, reaches Robbins Rd. at 1.4 mi. It turns right (east) onto the road and climbs easily to its level height-of-land, then turns abruptly left off of it at 1.9 mi.

The trail, now a narrow footpath (recently relocated), reaches the top of a low, forested ridge that overlooks Richards Reservoir. Heading due north, it crosses a power line with views east and west at 2.3 mi. The trail then descends the ridge steeply to the shore of the reservoir, now a boggy beaver wetland. The trail from here heads north along the west shoreline of the bog, and at its northern edge, swings west through a dry, flat area at 2.7 mi., meeting a blue-blazed loop trail that encircles a beaver wetland at the reservoir's north tip. The trail soon bears right (south) at the base of some cliffs along the east side of the reservoir, then turns abruptly left up a steep draw at 2.9 mi., ascending to higher ground and a forest of old pines and hemlocks. The trail meanders along on easy footing, swinging southerly over some minor cliffs before descending to a brook crossing. After a few minor ups and downs it reaches Richmond Rd. at 3.3 mi.

The trail turns left (north), ascending along Richmond Rd., then turns right at 3.8 mi. onto a maintained gravel road. The maintenance ceases at the entrance to the last house. As the road and trail wind steeply down, there are winter views of Mayo and Ball Hills ahead. The trail crosses the headwaters of Tully Brook at 4.2 mi. and continues past a cellar hole, then turns left onto another abandoned road at 4.4 mi. The trail goes up and over the shoulder of Mayo Hill through hemlock woods and then descends past another cellar hole to a road entering right at 5.0 mi. Shortly, the road turns sharp left onto Parker Rd. and the trail goes straight up, down, and up again to reach the south end of a rocky ridge at 5.2 mi. Ball Hill is visible to the south and White Hill is visible to the east across the valley. After climbing and then following the ridge to its north end (where a glimpse of Mt. Monadnock is possible), the path descends in steep zigzags.

At 5.5 mi. the trail proceeds to a brook, goes downstream briefly, then crosses and proceeds right along a logging road. Near a small open area at 5.7 mi., the trail turns left and proceeds up a steep slope on a logging road, which soon narrows to a footpath and then to a tote road. The trail turns right onto the road and follows it up and over the summit of White Hill (1,361 ft.). The trail goes left into an old timber cut, descends steeply, passes a slight rise at the foot of the hill, then follows a private driveway to join gravel Bliss Rd. at 6.4 mi. At this point it meets the yellow-blazed 18-mi. Tully Trail, which it joins from here to Falls Brook.

The trail crosses Bliss Rd. and its stone wall fence and proceeds generally east through interesting forest terrain. It soon crosses another stone wall, and then another at 6.7 mi., at a blue-stake boundary of a former pasture. (Watch carefully for the trail blazes as white property markers can be confusing here.) With another stone wall on the left and descending slightly through hemlock and hardwoods, the trail soon enters a red-pine plantation, bearing left over the needle carpet. It leaves the plantation at 6.9 mi., crosses a small hill, continues over a flat area, then ascends a hardwood slope with a tiny streamlet on the right (south) side. At 7.2 mi., now on a plateau, the trail enters a forest stand of large hemlocks with great boulders scattered over the undulating terrain. At 7.3 mi. it crosses an east-west stone wall about 80 ft. west of MA 32. Turn right and follow MA 32 for 50 ft. to the Royalston Falls Reservation (The Trustees of Reservations) parking area. Those not wishing to end the hike at MA 32 can take a side trip to Falls Brook and Royalston Falls, which are less than 1 mi. farther along the trail.

Metacomet–Monadnock Trail: MA 78 to MA 32

Distances from MA 78 (575 ft.) to
- Old Winchester Rd.: 0.6 mi., 25 min.
- Richmond Rd.: 3.3 mi., 1 hr. 55 min.
- Tully Brook: 4.2 mi., 2 hr. 35 min.
- Bliss Rd.: 6.4 mi., 3 hr. 40 min.
- MA 32 (1,192 ft.): 7.4 mi., 4 hr.10 min.

Section 19. MA 32 to NH 119 (4.8 mi.)

From MA 32 the trail follows Falls Brook upstream and enters New Hampshire south of Greenswoods Rd. The trail then runs east of Wheeler Pond for about 1 mi. before connecting with an abandoned town road. The old road leads to a maintained road that in turn reaches NH 119 in 0.5 mi. Turn right onto NH 119 and hike back to a dirt road that leaves diagonally to the left. The blazes can be picked up along the road.

From the TTOR sign kiosk, the M–M Trail (still coinciding with the Tully Trail) continues east through a small wet area at the head of a draw, then bears left, descending to and crossing a small stream. It briefly ascends to a small ravine, then bears right and descends steeply to the flood-plain of Falls Brook. At 0.5 mi., the trail crosses the brook on a wood bridge. Just before the bridge crossing is a first-come, first-served wooden shelter built in 2003 by the Pioneer Valley Hiking Club. After the crossing, the M–M Trail and Tully Trails split; the M–M Trail turns left upstream, passing interesting rock formations and a tiny natural bridge (the Tully Trail turns right here and goes south downstream, reaching Royalston Falls in 0.3 mi.). At 0.8 mi., the trail enters New Hampshire and continues to a logging road. It crosses Greenwoods Rd. at 1.7 mi., briefly follows a woods road before continuing over a series of ridges and ledges, then joins an abandoned road which ultimately leads to NH 119 at 4.8 mi. Hikers should watch for blazes marking potential relocations planned for this section to NH 119.

Metacomet–Monadnock Trail: MA 32 to NH 119

Distances from MA 32 (1,192 ft.) to

- Falls Brook crossing: 0.5 mi., 20 min.
- New Hampshire line: 0.8 mi., 35 min.
- NH 119 (1,197 ft.): 4.8 mi., 2 hr. 45 min.

Section 20. NH 119 to NH 12 (7.5 mi.)

From NH 119 the trail enters a fairly remote, forested section that passes over undulating terrain. Initially heading north, the path swings east to cross the shallow slopes and marshy floor of the Tully Brook valley. From Tully Brook the trail again gains high ground and long views, including an excellent perspective of Mt. Monadnock, from open ledges below the wooded 1,883-ft. summit of Little Monadnock Mtn.

Section 21. NH 12 to NH 124 (4.7 mi.)

From the village of Troy the trail follows NH 12 before turning onto Quarry Rd. The path ascends Fern Hill, then descends, crossing a tributary of Quarry Brook. From the brook it climbs over the twin summits of 1,826-ft. Gap Mtn., which offers striking views of Mt. Monadnock, the Wapack range, and the distant Green Mtns. The section ends at NH 124, which passes between Gap Mtn. and Mt. Monadnock.

Section 22. NH 124 to Grand Monadnock (2.3 mi.)

From NH 124 the climb up Grand Monadnock follows the Royce and White Arrow Trails southeast of Fassett Brook to an old picnic area. From here the route follows the White Arrow Trail to reach the 3,165-ft. summit of Grand Monadnock, one of the world's most-climbed peaks, and the northern end of the Metacomet–Monadnock Trail.

Robert Frost Trail (Amherst Trails Committee, Kestrel Trust)

The Robert Frost Trail (RFT) was begun in 1982 as a way to link Amherst conservation properties, but has since grown into a major hiking trail that travels some of the most attractive areas of the Connecticut River Valley. The trail covers more than 40 mi., beginning at Mt. Holyoke Range State Park in Granby and ending at Wendell State Forest in Wendell. It traverses a number of attractive ridges and hills with views across the Connecticut River Valley, passes through 1,000-acre Lawrence Swamp, and visits assorted other interesting and scenic places including Mt. Toby and the cascades of Cushman Brook. The Kestrel Trust and the Amherst Trails Committee (413-256-4045) produce detailed, up-to-date maps as well as the very detailed *Guide to the Robert Frost Trail.* Maps and guides are available from the Amherst Conservation Committee's website and local outlets, including stores in downtown Amherst and outfitter shops. Maps of Mt. Holyoke Range State Park and Mt. Toby State Reservation are available at their headquarters.

Motorized vehicles, open fires, and camping are prohibited on the trail. Equestrians and mountain bikers should only use the trail when the trail bed is dry and firm, which helps reduce the erosion and soil compaction that can damage the trail and nearby plant communities. Much of the trail is on private property; please stay on the trail and respect property rights.

The RFT is marked with rectangular orange blazes. It coincides with numerous other trails along its route, especially the white-blazed Metacomet–Monadnock Trail (M–M Trail). The following description traces the trail from south to north, the direction of frequent blazes.

Section 1. Notch Visitor Center (Mt. Holyoke Range West) to Harris Mtn. Rd. (5.1 mi.)

Parking is available at the Notch Visitor Center on MA 116. The well-blazed trail leaves from behind the visitor center, in concert with the M–M Trail. At 0.6 mi. the M–M Trail leaves to the right while the RFT continues east along the wooded slopes of the Holyoke Range. At 1.7 mi. the RFT turns right to rejoin the M–M Trail in the Mt. Norwottuck–Rattlesnake Knob col. A short steep section of the joined trails reaches Rattlesnake Knob (787 ft.), which provides views. The trails continue together for the next 4 mi., crossing the wooded summit of Long Mtn. (no tower) and descending to Harris Mtn. Rd. Parking is available on Harris Mtn. Rd.

Robert Frost Trail: Notch Visitor Center (Mt. Holyoke Range West) to Harris Mtn. Rd.

Distances from Notch Visitor Center (520 ft.) to
- M–M Trail: 1.7 mi., 1 hr. 10 min.
- summit of Long Mtn. (920 ft.): 3.9 mi., 2 hr. 5 min.
- Harris Mtn. Rd. (388 ft.): 5.1 mi., 3 hr.

Section 2. Harris Mtn. Rd. to Goodell St. (1.5 mi.)

Starting from the eastern side of Harris Mtn. Rd. (parking) the RFT and M–M Trail, continue together briefly through the woods of the eastern Mt. Holyoke Range until the M–M Trail branches right and the RFT turns north (left) then northeast. The RFT reaches the power lines at 0.5 mi. and swings left (north) following the power lines right-of-way to Bay Rd. at 0.6 mi. The trail then crosses Bay Rd. and continues under the power lines north to Hulst Rd. (Orchard St. on some maps) at 0.9 mi. The RFT now turns right (east) on Hulst Rd. to the intersection with Warren Wright Rd. at 1.2 mi. The trail turns left (north) following Warren Wright Rd. through a swamp reaching Goodell St. at 1.5 mi.

Robert Frost Trail: Harris Mtn. Rd. to Goodell St.

Distances from Harris Mtn. Rd. (388 ft.) to
- Bay Rd.: 1.0 mi., 30 min.
- Goodell St. (210 ft.): 1.9 mi., 1 hr.

Section 3. Goodell St. to Station Rd. (3.7 mi.)

The RFT turns left (west) off Wright Rd. and follows the edge of a field. Reaching a second field, it turns north, crosses a small stream, and makes a left turn into the woods. The RFT follows a series of woods roads through Lawrence Swamp, heading generally northwest past Town Well No. 4, a cinder-block building approx. 1.5 mi. from Goodell St. From the building the trail follows a gravel road west that merges with the Baby Carriage Brook Trail at 2.4 mi. Just before the gravel road leaves the woods, the RFT turns sharp right (north) while the Baby Carriage Brook Trail continues west to S. East St. The RFT now passes the east end of farm fields, turns left into the woods, and emerges onto Station Rd., where there is a white sign for Lawrence Swamp and parking to the east on the roadside.

Robert Frost Trail: Goodell St. to Station Rd.

Distances from Goodell St. (210 ft.) to
- Town Well No. 4: 1.4 mi., 40 min.
- Baby Carriage Trail: 2.4 mi., 1hr. 10 min.
- Station Rd. (160 ft.): 3.7 mi., 2 hr.

Section 4. Station Rd. to Pelham Rd. (4.2 mi.)

The trail turns right (east) onto Station Rd. (parking) and continues across the Norwottuck Rail-Trail at Norwottuck Depot, then turns left (north) onto an old road at 0.5 mi. The trail turns right (east) to follow the southern edge of the last small field, then picks up a woods road and turns left into the Amherst Woods subdivision. Zigzag north through the development, following easements and short sections of road to Wildflower Dr. Turn left onto Wildflower Dr. and in 0.1 mi. reenter the woods on the right. The trail continues north to Old Belchertown Rd. at 1.8 mi., where it turns left for 0.2 mi. to reach MA 9, 0.5 mi. west of the Amherst–Belchertown line.

Following MA 9 west for 200 ft., the trail then turns right (northeast) near a chain-link fence and continues north past the Amherst landfill and into the Harkness Brook Conservation Area. At 2.7 mi. the trail turns left (east) onto Stony Hill Rd., continues past Gatehouse Rd., and turns left onto a woods path. At 4.2 mi. it reaches Ward St., heads north 200 yd., and crosses Pelham Rd. to the Amethyst Brook Conservation Area parking lot.

Robert Frost Trail: Station Rd. to Pelham Rd.

Distances from Station Rd. (160 ft.) to
- Old Belchertown Rd.: 1.8 mi., 45 min.
- Stony Hill Rd.: 2.7 mi., 1 hr. 15 min.
- Pelham Rd. and Amethyst Brook Conservation Area (194 ft.): 4.2 mi., 2 hr.

Section 5. Pelham Rd. to Pratts Corner Rd. (4.4 mi.)

The RFT heads north from the parking lot, then east along garden plots and into the woods. It crosses a bridge over Amethyst Brook, then turns left across a second bridge to the north side of the brook. The trail now follows Amethyst Brook to a third bridge. After crossing, the path turns left (northeast) away from the brook and toward Mt. Orient. The trail ascends a woods road (passing a very old car) and rejoins the M–M Trail. There is a short steep section, but the route is generally moderate to the wooded summit of Mt. Orient (957 ft.) at 1.9 mi. There are excellent views from the ledges, with vistas to the west and south. From the summit the RFT continues around the side of Poverty Mtn. through some wooded tracts with active logging operations, journeys through the remainder of the Pelham woods, and reaches Pratts Corner Rd. at 4.4 mi.

Robert Frost Trail: Pelham Rd. to Pratts Corner Rd.

Distances from Pelham Rd. and Amethyst Brook Conservation Area (194 ft.) to
- Mt. Orient (957 ft.): 1.9 mi., 1 hr. 10 min.
- Pratts Corner Rd. (410 ft.): 4.4 mi., 2 hr. 20 min.

Section 6. Pratts Corner Rd. to Juggler Meadow Rd. (4.9 mi.)

The RFT continues from Pratts Corner Rd. (a.k.a. Shutesbury Rd.) generally northward through the woods to Market Hill Rd. and Atkins Reservoir, a good place to view waterfowl, especially in fall. There the trail turns left (west) along the reservoir before turning left (southwest) away from the water and into the woods. It ascends wooded Mt. Boreas at 1.6 mi. before reaching Flat Hills Rd. (parking). The trail then descends, following Cushman Brook's southern bank in deep woods. Crossing Market Hill Rd., it then stays left of the power lines and ascends a steep bank.

The trail continues north to Bridge St., crosses the brook south of the bridge, passes numerous cascades and pools, and eventually reaches the railroad tracks at the south end of the Cushman Brook trestle. Crossing the tracks, the path descends to the Kevin R. Flood Universal Access Trail on the left. The RFT continues to the Robert Francis footbridge, crossing the 70-ft.-long steel span over Cushman Brook and reaching State St. at 2.8 mi. It crosses State St. and goes to the right of Puffer's Pond at 3.2 mi. What looks like an asphalt spillway is all that is left of a gravel road of the Ruxton Gravel Co. The RFT turns right up this "road," then turns left onto a dirt trail and continues to Pulpit Hill Rd. 0.6 mi. east of MA 63. After passing Pulpit Hill Rd., the path proceeds generally north through maple woods and enters the fields of the Eastman Brook Conservation Area. It proceeds west for a short distance, then turns north again, staying on the left side of the fields until it reaches a junction with a loop trail (marked with a white sign) going into the woods. The RFT turns right (east) and heads toward the railroad tracks, tracing a course along the side of a field. At the railroad tracks (white signs and a brown conservation sign) the trail turns north parallel to the tracks, reaching Juggler Meadow Rd. at 4.9 mi.

Robert Frost Trail: Pratts Corner Rd. to Juggler Meadow Rd.

Distance from Pratts Corner Rd. (410 ft.) to

- Mt. Boreas: 1.6 mi., 40 min.
- State St.: 2.8 mi., 1 hr.
- Puffer's Pond: 3.2 mi., 1 hr. 25 min.
- Juggler Meadow Rd. parking (301 ft.): 4.9 mi., 2 hr. 10 min.

Section 7. Juggler Meadow Rd. to Reservation Rd. (9.4 mi.)

The trail continues north through wooded country west of the tracks, turns east and crosses the tracks, and follows a series of rocky knolls to Depot Rd. at 0.9 mi. It turns left (west) onto Depot Rd. and follows it to MA 63. The trail turns left onto MA 63 and then right onto Bull Hill Rd. Just past the bridge over Long Plain Brook (2.5 mi.), a short distance before reaching the Leverett–Sunderland line, the trail turns right into the woods along the west bank of the brook.

There are maps specifically for Mt. Toby and its numerous interwoven trails. The well-blazed RFT leaves from the Bull Hill parking lot to ascend on a woods road, then bears right at a saddle. It continues east, and ascends a steep ridge, which it follows northwest to the wooded summit of Bull Hill at 3.0 mi. The trail continues on the ridge to blue-blazed South Mtn. Rd., an abandoned woods road. It turns right (east) onto the road and descends, crossing a stream and a north-south woods road. Continuing northeast, the trail crosses several more streams before ascending steeply to a power-line crossing and a left turn onto yet another woods road. As the ascent becomes steeper, the Frost Bypass Trail leaves on the left. The main trail continues to a saddle, where it turns left (north) to cross a broad plateau and descend to an old cabin. A side trail leading east from the cabin ascends Roaring Mtn.

The RFT descends northwest to Roaring Brook, then turns left and follows a well-hiked old road south. Finally winding back around to the north and passing the other end of the Frost Bypass Trail, the trail reaches the Mt. Toby fire tower (1,269 ft.) at 7.4 mi. The descent follows a cleared power line that strikes off to the northeast. A left at a saddle and another left off the power line leads to a woods road near Cranberry Pond. The trail turns left here and continues to a gate on Reservation Rd. in Sunderland at 9.4 mi.

Robert Frost Trail: Juggler Meadow Rd. to Reservation Rd.

Distance from Juggler Meadow Rd. (301 ft.) to
- Bull Hill: 3.0 mi., 1 hr. 10 min.
- Mt. Toby fire tower (1,269 ft.): 7.4 mi., 2 hr. 45 min.
- Reservation Rd. (420 ft.): 9.4 mi., 3 hr. 30 min.

Section 8. Reservation Rd. to Ruggles Pond (Wendell State Forest) (7.0 mi.)

From the gate on Reservation Rd. (parking), the RFT turns right, follows Reservation Rd. downhill and then turns left into the woods, passing over Stoddard Hill. The trail reaches MA 63 at 0.6 mi., and North Leverett Rd. at the Sawmill River at 2.1 mi. Weaving through the Montague Wildlife Management Area, the trail then follows Chestnut Hill Rd. roughly northeast to the intersection with Montague Rd. (white sign) opposite the

Wendell State Forest headquarters. The trail continues a short distance into the state forest and ends near the day-use area of Ruggles Pond (parking) and the junction with the M–M Trail.

> **Robert Frost Trail: Reservation Rd. to Ruggles Pond (Wendell State Forest)**
>
> Distance from Reservation Rd. (420 ft.) to
> - MA 63: 0.6 mi., 25 min.
> - North Leverett Rd.: 2.1 mi., 1 hr.
> - Ruggles Pond at Wendell State Forest (970 ft.): 7.0 mi., 3 hr. 15 min.

Pocumtuck Ridge Trail (BCAMC)

The Pocumtuck Ridge Trail (PRT) is a 15-mi. hiking path that runs from South Sugarloaf Mtn. in the Mt. Sugarloaf State Reservation, South Deerfield, Mass., north to the Poet's Seat tower in the town of Greenfield. Completed by the BCAMC in 2001 with the assistance of AmeriCorps and trail crews from nearby Deerfield Academy, it traces a ridge-top route high above the Connecticut and Deerfield River Valleys connecting public and quasi-public lands managed by DCR tracts, town conservation, land trust, and Deerfield Academy properties. To date, approximately 70 percent of the trail corridor lies on these protected lands. The trail is marked with blue paint blazes and supplemental blue metal diamonds at road crossings and trail intersections.

Section 1. Base of Mt. Sugarloaf Reservation to Pine Nook Rd. (7.9 mi.)

Trailhead parking is available on Sugarloaf Ave. at its junction with MA 116 in South Deerfield. The PRT enters the reservation on a sandy lane and quickly turns right to cross the paved summit access road leading to the summit of South Sugarloaf Mtn. From here, the trail climbs steeply on a switchback route to the summit (652 ft.) at 0.5 mi. An observation platform offers extensive panoramic views of the Pioneer Valley and beyond. Water and restrooms are available May to October. Descend a paved walkway to a parking area and follow alongside a chain-link fence a short distance to another, larger parking area.

The PRT enters the woods and descends easily along the forested eastern edge of the mountain's steep escarpment. Turning left, descend steeply on a narrow switchback route to a hairpin turn on the paved summit access road. Descend on wooden stairs and follow a wide footpath to the col separating the summits of South and North Sugarloaf Mtns. at 0.8 mi. Bear right, then left, and finally right again, ascending below the cliffs of North Sugarloaf Mtn. The route descends an old all-terrain vehicle trail and leaves it to the left after 100 yd. Follow this narrow footpath along the steep eastern base of the mountain, passing an abandoned field visible through the trees on the right.

The trail now ascends steadily along the base of a talus slope and swings left to gain the forested eastern ridge of the mountain. Turn left at a trail intersection for a pleasant, gradual climb on a narrow foot trail. Along the way are limited views of South Sugarloaf Mtn. to the south. Continue along to a viewpoint on the summit of North Sugarloaf Mtn. (791 ft.). at 1.5 mi., which offers extensive views west of the Deerfield River Valley, the Berkshire Hills, and the southern Green Mtns.

From the view, proceed downhill on a wider trail passing a yellow-blazed side trail on the right. Continue downhill on the western ridge of North Sugarloaf, passing over a narrow drainage stream of a red maple swamp visible on the right. At 2.0 mi., come to an intersection with the red-blazed Hillside Trail and turn right onto it. The PRT and Hillside Trails run together from this point to Hillside Rd.—follow the dual red and blue blazes. The trail swings around the north side of the red maple swamp and then begins descending moderately, crossing a small stream. Descend along the north bank of the stream to an intersection with a yellow-blazed trail that goes off to the right. Go left at this intersection on level footing northbound. Come to a brief switchback and descend to the gated parking area on Hillside Rd. at 3.1 mi. There is parking here for four vehicles. Turn left onto paved Hillside Rd. for 30 yd. and enter the woods to the right on University of Massachusetts property, following a fence line downhill to a footbridge over a brook. Climb steeply 50 ft. to the top of a rise above a second brook and descend to cross it over another footbridge.

The trail climbs to the left of a small hill, then levels out, passing through a shaded hemlock forest following close to and above a stream. Heading due north come to an old wire fence and turn left, descending to cross the brook (no bridge). After the crossing, bear right onto Deerfield conservation land and climb briefly to the remains of an old cinder-block slaughterhouse. From here the trail follows a wider, forested track on a trail easement close to and behind a private residence. Come out to paved Pocumtuck Ave. and turn right, following the road for 300 yd. to a small parking area on the left at 4.0 mi. Enter the woods through a small grassy clearing onto protected land trust property. Come to a trail intersection in 100 yd. and bear left, climbing easily to the top of the Pocumtuck Range at 4.3 mi. From here to Pine Nook Rd., the PRT utilizes the ridge line of this mountain range. *(Note: This section is not yet well blazed but is easy to follow, as the trail never leaves the ridge.)*

Proceeding due north along the ridge on gentle terrain, pass under power lines at 5.3 mi. Scenic views west and east are available here. Continuing north over several minor ups and downs, the PRT comes out to the summit area of Pocumtuck Rock at 6.1 mi., marked with a communication tower and utility shed. Turn left from the tower onto a narrow trail to a scenic viewpoint overlooking the Deerfield River Valley, Berkshire Hills, and the southern Green Mtns. From here the trail follows a wide, gravel service road. Swing to the right on this road, descending to the first switchback turn. The PRT leaves the service road directly into the woods. Descend moderately to a woods road, crossing it directly and passing over some exposed bedrock to the base of a talus slope and small, abandoned, concrete service building on the left. Climb briefly on steep footing to the top of some cliffs. Follow along the top of the cliffs for 50 yd. and leave the ledge to the right into a small dell. Climb briefly again to the summit area of the abandoned Deerfield Academy Ski Area at 6.9 mi., following a grassy ski trail past the remains of some tow-rope equipment near the summit. Limited views are available just off the trail to the left at the top of some cliffs.

From the summit, enter a thick hemlock grove, descending to a narrow woods road and turn left onto it. After 200 yd., turn abruptly right and follow a narrower trail as it swings around joining the gravel summit access road. Turn right onto this road and descend to the gated entrance off of unpaved Pine Nook Rd at 7.9 mi. There is parking on the road shoulder for a few vehicles.

Pocumtuck Ridge Trail: Base of Mt. Sugarloaf Reservation to Pine Nook Rd.

Distances from base of Mt. Sugarloaf (185 ft.) to
- South Sugarloaf summit (652 ft.): 0.5 mi., 30 min.
- North Sugarloaf summit (791 ft.): 1.5 mi., 1 hr. 15 min.
- Pocumtuck Rock: 6.1 mi., 2 hr. 55 min.
- Pine Nook Rd. (530 ft.): 7.9 mi., 3 hr. 45 min.

Section 2. Pine Nook Rd. to Canada Hill via Poet's Seat Tower (6.9 mi.)

Turn left onto Pine Nook Rd., following it for 300 yd. The PRT leaves the road, turning right to follow a level contour to dirt Rices Ferry Rd., an abandoned town road, at 0.8 mi. Turn right following this road descending past a small swamp on the right. After the swamp, turn left on narrow trail, heading north onto land owned by the Woolman Hill Conference Center. Turn left, uphill through a red pine plantation onto traprock ledges.

The PRT goes along the top of this small ridge, passing two separate viewpoints looking west. After the second viewpoint begin a steeper descent over several narrow switchbacks, coming out onto paved Keets Rd. at 1.8 mi. Turn left onto this road and, at the bottom of its sharp turn, go right onto a power line service road. Follow this a short distance and re-enter the forest. The trail parallels the power lines out of sight inside the woods. Approach the railroad tracks *(Caution: these are in use)* and cross them directly into a narrow draw, descending a paved road above the Deerfield River. Turn left, then right onto MA 5, crossing the river safely on the bridge's sidewalk at 2.8 mi. Turn right onto Cheapside St., following it a short distance to Hope St. on the left. Pass under a small railroad bridge and immediately leave Hope St., to enter the woods on the right. This section of trail from Hope St. to Poet's Seat tower lies entirely on conservation land owned by the Town of Greenfield.

The PRT first follows an old railroad grade, then leaves it left to join the trail system of Rocky Mtn. Park. Turn right, then left and come to a five-way intersection of trails. The PRT swings left briefly, then turns right and climbs a small, unnamed rocky summit. Passing under a power line, it descends to gravel Bears Den Rd. The Bears Den, an open fissure in the cliff face, is 50 yd. to the left on this road. The PRT turns right a short distance, then goes left up a short, steep track to the summit of Sachem Head with the remains of an old wooden viewing platform. Caution is needed here, as a steep cliff is close by. Continue north along this ridgeline on a narrow footpath to paved Mtn. Rd. at 4.2 mi. Use caution crossing this busy road. The PRT follows close to the paved access road that leads to Poet's Seat Tower, and then follows the road for 200 yd. to the tower at 4.5 mi. The tower offers commanding views of Greenfield and the surrounding countryside.

Proceed north from the tower over a bare rock ledge with more views and enter the woods descending along the ridge top. Come to an intersection with a red-blazed trail, part of the extensive trail system of Greenfield's Rocky Mt. Park/Temple Woods Conservation Area, and turn right, following dual blue and red blazes. The PRT soon turns left, descending steeply from the ridge to the banks of the Connecticut River. Proceed left following the river upstream to an ascending left turn. Climb from here to paved Turners Falls Rd. at 5.5 mi. Use caution crossing this busy road. Enter the woods, pass under a power line with views east, and continue along the ridge of Canada Hill. The PRT ends at a small residential neighborhood at 6.9 mi. A trail extension is planned that will end the PRT on MA 2A.

Pocumtuck Ridge Trail: Pine Nook Rd. to Canada Hill via Poet's Seat Tower

Distances from Pine Nook Rd. (530 ft.) to
- Keet's Rd.: 1.8 mi., 45 min.
- Poet's Seat Tower (494 ft.): 4.5 mi., 2 hr. 5 min.
- Turners Falls Rd.: 5.5 mi., 2 hr. 35 min.
- end of PRT (300 ft.): 6.9 mi., 3 hr. 20 min.

Mt. Tom State Reservation

Mt. Tom State Reservation preserves an area of 1,800 acres, including a section of tall traprock cliffs that lie between Easthampton and Holyoke just west of the Connecticut River commonly known as the Mt. Tom Range. It sports some of the best views in all the Connecticut River Valley, from the Berkshires in the west to the Pelham Hills to the east and long vistas north and south. In fall Mt. Tom is one of the premier raptor-watching sites in the valley, with thousands of hawks and other birds of prey soaring past the mountain. Mt. Tom's summit is 1,202 ft.; other peaks of the ridge include Mt. Nonotuck (827 ft.), Goat Peak (822 ft.), Whiting Peak (1,014 ft.), and Dry Knoll (835 ft.). The Mt. Tom Range hosts one of the largest tracts of unbroken forest in the Connecticut River Valley and is an oasis of biodiversity in the area.

Picnic areas, two observation towers, five scenic vistas, canoeing and fishing on Lake Bray, and ice skating (in season) are some of the additional attractions. Mt. Tom Reservation also offers a universal-access (UA) fishing pier on Lake Bray, a UA hiking trail on the shores of the lake, and nearby UA restrooms. The Mt. Tom Reservation trail system consists of 20 mi. of blazed and maintained trails. Trail signs at road heads are usually posted a short distance in from the road. (*Note: On trail signs the Metacomet–Monadnock Trail and Smiths Ferry Rd. are identified as M–M Tr. and Bray Rd., respectively.*) About half the trails are suitable for cross-country skiing, of easy-to-moderate difficulty. Mountain bikes and motorized vehicles are not permitted on the trails.

Recently some important changes have taken place on the mountain. The former Mt. Tom ski area was purchased for conservation, recreation, and environmental education by a group of partners that includes the United States Fish and Wildlife Service (USFWS), the Massachusetts Department of Conservation and Recreation (DCR), The Trustees of Reservations (TTOR), and the Holyoke Boys and Girls Club (HBGC). DCR owns the northern portion of the area, adjacent to the existing Mt. Tom reservation. USFWS owns the southern part of the property, including the former ski trails and a small pond; it is managed as part of the Silvio O. Conte National Fish and Wildlife Refuge. TTOR owns the northern portion of Little Tom Mtn., and HBGC owns the former base lodge and surrounding area.

The partners are cooperating in inventorying and planning for passive recreation. As activities are allowed, information will be available on signs and kiosks at the property, or by contacting any of the partners. The road accessing the base lodge is currently gated; only authorized vehicles are allowed beyond it. Caution should be used in this area since there is an active quarry on site and large, heavy trucks frequently use the roads.

To reach the Easthampton/MA 141 entrance from the south, take I-91 Exit 17-B to MA 141 west. Travel west about 4 mi. on MA 141 to the entrance on the right. From the north, take I-91 Exit 18 to US 5. Travel US 5 south about 1.5 mi. and turn right onto East St. Follow this road for

3 mi., turn left onto MA 141, and continue to the entrance on the left. To reach the main Holyoke entrance from the south, take Exit 17-A off I-91 to US 5 north. Follow US 5 north for 4 mi. to the entrance on the left. From the north, take Exit 18 off I-91 to US 5 south. Follow US 5 about 4 mi. to the entrance on the right. Information on trails and regulations can be obtained at the visitor center near the junction of Christopher Clark Rd. and Smiths Ferry Rd., and at park headquarters near Lake Bray at the south end of Smiths Ferry Rd. See maps 5 and 6 included with this book.

Metacomet–Monadnock Trail (DCR, BCAMC)

This is perhaps the most scenic section of this long-distance hiking trail. For a complete description of this section, see Metacomet–Monadnock Trail, Section 6, MA 141 to MA 47 on page 116.

Beau Bridge Trail (DCR)

This blue-blazed trail begins on a short dead-end road off Smiths Ferry Rd. From the visitor center follow Smiths Ferry Rd. about 0.4 mi. northwest to the dead-end road on the left. There is a parking area a short distance down the road; the trailhead is on the western bank of Cascade Brook. The trail proceeds northwest for about 100 yd. through open woods, then turns sharp right (the obvious path straight ahead is an unmarked route that leads to Goat Peak in 0.3 mi.) and descends to Cascade Creek. For the next 0.3 mi. the trail follows the creek downstream, repeatedly crossing it on the bridges for which the trail was named. After the ninth bridge the trail leaves the stream and heads north. The path makes a beeline up the hill, merging with and following an old woods road for 0.3 mi. to its junction with the white-blazed Metacomet–Monadnock Trail. To reach the observation tower on Goat Peak turn left onto the M–M Trail and proceed along the top of the ridge for about 0.4 mi.

Beau Bridge Trail (map 5: B2)

Distances from trailhead on Cascade Brook (524 ft.) to

- final crossing of Cascade Creek (450 ft.): 0.3 mi. (rev. 100 ft.), 20 min.
- Metacomet-Monadnock Trail (600 ft.): 0.6 mi., 150 ft., 35 min.
- Goat Peak observation tower via M-M Trail (830 ft.): 1.0 mi., 350 ft., 50 min.

Lake Bray Universal Access Trail (DCR)

This 0.5-mi.-long trail begins near the north shore of Lake Bray near restrooms and a picnic area. From the trailhead the path follows the shore of Lake Bray, passing a universal-access fishing pier along the way. At the junction with the Bray Loop Trail (which continues straight) the UA trail turns right, cruises gently uphill, and reaches the Kay Bee trailhead. The UA trail turns right and proceeds on a slight downhill grade back to the starting point.

Lake Bray Universal Access Trail (map 5: C3)
Distance from trailhead near picnic area (160 ft.) to
- trailhead (circuit): 0.5 mi., 0 ft., 25 min.

Link, Bee Line, and Lost Boulder Trails (DCR)

These trails serve as a link between Smiths Ferry Rd. and some of the major interior trails of the reservation, including the Keystone Trail, Kay Bee Trail, and Bray Loop Trail. Marked with white blazes, the trail begins at a bar way on the south side of Smiths Ferry Rd., a short distance above the bridge over Cascade Brook. The path ascends the moderately steep hillside to reach the Kay Bee Trail at 0.2 mi. The grade moderates and at 0.3 mi. crosses the Keystone Trail. The path crosses a small stream, then steeply climbs a loose rock embankment before proceeding through hemlock, then open hardwoods, reaching a large glacial erratic (the Lost Boulder) at 0.7 mi. From the boulder the trail descends, steeply at times, on a straight southeasterly course to end at the junction with the Bray Loop Trail.

Link, Bee Line, and Lost Boulder Trails (map 5: C2)
Distances from Smiths Ferry Rd. (343 ft.) to
- Kay Bee Trail (425 ft.): 0.2 mi., 100 ft., 10 min.
- Keystone Trail (375 ft.): 0.3 mi., 100 ft. (rev. 50 ft.), 15 min.
- Lost Boulder (550 ft.): 0.7 mi., 200 ft., 30 min.
- Bray Loop Trail (300 ft.): 1.0 mi., 50 min.

Bray Inner Loop Trail (DCR)

The Bray Inner Loop Trail is a short, easy walk around much of the shore of Lake Bray. At the north shore the blue-blazed path joins the universal-access path for the short walk back to the trailhead at the northern end of Bray Lake. The loop ends on Smiths Ferry Rd. near the picnic area about 0.3 mi. north of the trailhead.

Bray Inner Loop Trail (map 5: C3)

Distances from Smiths Ferry Rd. (169 ft.) to
- upper loop of Bray Loop Trail (200 ft.): 0.3 mi., 50 ft., 15 min.
- Smiths Ferry Rd. via UA trail (180 ft.): 0.8 mi., 50 ft., 35 min.

Bray Loop Trail (DCR)

This occasionally steep trail begins at the western end of Lake Bray at the junction of the Keystone Trail and the Bray Inner Loop Trail. It can be combined with the UA trail and Inner Loop Trail to provide a moderate-to-strenuous woodland hike through the Bray Brook ravine that encircles much of Lake Bray. From the junction of the Keystone and Bray Inner Loop Trails the Bray Loop Trail swings northwest and ascends, sometimes steeply, before turning southwest. The grade moderates as the path crosses several seasonal streams, and, shortly before it reaches its highest point, the white-blazed Lost Boulder Trail branches right.

The trail now descends at a moderate rate and crosses Bray Brook on a ridge at 0.9 mi. The Bray Valley Trail is passed on the right as the path begins to cross a level, frequently wet area, passing the Knox Trail at 0.9 mi. The trail then makes an easy descent to the junction with the Inner Loop Trail at 1.2 mi., and then gradually descends toward the lake. It reaches the Inner Bridge Link at 1.4 mi. and continues almost at water level along the southeastern shore of the lake. This section is frequently very muddy. The trail ends on Smiths Ferry Rd., about 0.2 mi. below the Lake Bray parking area.

Bray Loop Trail (map 5: C3)

Distances from Keystone and Bray Inner Loop Trail junction (175 ft.) to
- Lost Boulder Trail (300 ft.): 0.4 mi., 100 ft., 15 min.
- Bray Valley Trail (200 ft.): 0.7 mi., 100 ft. (rev. 100 ft.), 30 min.   ▶

- Knox Trail (300 ft.): 0.9 mi., 200 ft., 45 min.
- lower end of Inner Loop Trail (200 ft.): 1.2 mi., 200 ft. (rev. 100 ft.), 1 hr.
- Smiths Ferry Rd. via Inner Loop Trail (200 ft.): 1.6 mi., 200 ft., 1 hr. 15 min.

Kay Bee Trail (DCR)

This blue-blazed woods road connects the Lake Bray area with the central part of the reservation and is an alternative to the longer and somewhat steeper Keystone Trail. It begins at the west end of the loop on the UA trail about 0.1 mi. from the Lake Bray parking area. The trail immediately begins a steady climb westward, away from the lake. At 0.4 mi., just before a small rocky knoll on the right, the junction of the white-blazed Bee Line/Link Trail is reached and the grade soon eases. The final 0.3 mi. is almost level, and the trail ends at Keystone Junction, where it meets the Keystone Trail and the Keystone Extension.

Kay Bee Trail (map 5: C2)
Distances from Lake Bray parking area (160 ft.) to
- Bee Line/Link Trail (425 ft.): 0.4 mi., 250 ft., 15 min.
- Keystone Junction (575 ft.): 0.7 mi., 400 ft., 25 min.

Keystone Trail (DCR)

This was one of the original ski trails cleared in the reservation long before the advent of private ski areas. The trail follows a woods road for much of its length; it is unblazed but sparsely marked with red wooden Keystone signs. It begins as a path on the south side of Smiths Ferry Rd., opposite the second of the two upper parking areas, about 0.3 mi. from the visitor center and a short distance before the dead-end road to Hamden Field. At 0.1 mi. a blue-blazed trail linking the Nature Trails is reached. The Keystone Trail veers southeast, ascending slightly and reaching Keystone Junction in a clearing at 0.3 mi. Here the Kay Bee Trail branches left, the Keystone Extension branches right, and the Keystone Trail continues along a woods road straight ahead, descending in wide-sweeping curves through hemlock and hardwood forests. It crosses the Bee Line/Link Trail at 0.6 mi., and descends, steeply at times, to the foot of the hill where the trail reaches its lowest point. It then ascends easily and ends at the junction of the Bray Loop Trail and Bray Inner Loop Trail. The Lake Bray parking areas are about 0.2 mi. to the left.

Keystone Trail (map 5: C2)
Distances from Smiths Ferry Rd. (553 ft.) to
- Keystone Junction (575 ft.): 0.3 mi., 15 min.
- Bee Line/Link Trail (425 ft.): 0.6 mi., 50 ft., 20 min.
- Bray Loop Trail (200 ft.): 0.9 mi., 50 ft. (rev. 200 ft.), 30 min.

Keystone Extension (DCR)

The red-blazed Keystone Extension links the Keystone Trail with the Quarry Trail and can then be used to access the M–M Trail by following either the orange-blazed DOC Trail west or the Quarry Trail northwest. The path begins at Keystone Junction, 0.3 mi. from the Keystone Trail trailhead on Smiths Ferry Rd. Proceeding west, the trail crosses several ledged areas and at 0.3 mi. descends from a rise to cross a swampy section on a series of bog bridges. At 0.6 mi., near the top of a second rise, a blue-blazed link trail branches right and leads in 0.1 mi. to the Nature Trails. Just over the rise, the trail makes a sharp left and circles a swamp. The trail now descends and reaches the valley floor at 0.5 mi. The path swings left as it runs over level ground, crossing a stream on a bridge before ending at the Quarry Trail, opposite the junction with the DOC Trail.

Keystone Extension (map 5: C2)
Distance from Keystone Junction (Keystone Trail, 553 ft.) to
- Quarry Trail (775 ft.): 0.6 mi., 200 ft., 30 min.

Quarry Trail (DCR)

This yellow-blazed woods road is the shortest and most convenient route across the range from the visitor center and provides access to several other trails, thus permitting circuits of varying length and difficulty. From the visitor center on Smiths Ferry Rd., go southwest 0.1 mi. along Christopher Clark Rd., then turn left uphill onto a paved road, passing the maintenance buildings and a small parking area. Continue through a metal gate and follow an old road about 100 yd. to the beginning of the Quarry Trail, where it crosses the Metacomet–Monadnock Trail.

Initially almost level, the trail soon circles a small pond on the left, gradually bears south, and begins a gentle climb. At 0.2 mi. the orange-blazed DOC Trail and the red-blazed Keystone Extension diverge right and left, respectively. At 0.5 mi., shortly before reaching the height-of-land, the Middle Loop Trail branches right. The descent to the south is noticeably rougher and steeper. At 1.0 mi. the trail crosses a stream and, just beyond the Knox Extension, branches left. Presently the trail ends, but it may be extended into recently acquired lands or be connected to other trails in the system shortly.

Quarry Trail (map 5: C1–D2)

Distances from Metacomet–Monadnock Trail (572 ft.) to
- DOC Trail and Keystone Extension (625 ft.): 0.2 mi., 50 ft., 20 min.
- Middle Loop Trail (700 ft.): 0.5 mi., 150 ft., 30 min.
- Knox Extension (375 ft.): 1 mi., 150 ft. (rev. 400 ft.), 40 min.

Knox Extension (DCR)

The Knox Extension swings south from the Quarry Trail near the reservation's western boundary, roughly following that boundary for about 0.3 mi. to its end near the Knox and Bray Valley Trails.

Knox Extension (map 5: D2)

Distance from Quarry Trail (375 ft.) to
- Knox Trail (300 ft.): 0.2 mi. (rev. 50 ft.), 20 min.

Bray Valley Trail (DCR)

The Bray Valley Trail runs from the southwestern end of the Bray Loop Trail generally west to near the southern end of the Knox Extension. The trail begins along the south bank of Bray Brook and follows the stream southwest for less than 0.2 mi. It then begins to climb and ends at about 0.3 mi., near the Knox Extension and Knox Trail at the end of the DCR reservation property.

Bray Valley Trail (map 5: C2)

Distance from Bray Loop Trail (200 ft.) to
- trail's end (300 ft.): 0.3 mi., 100 ft., 20 min.

Teabag Trail (DCR)

The Teabag Trail links the southern portion of Smiths Ferry Rd. and the M–M Trail on the ridge line about 0.2 mi. east of Goat Peak. The trailhead is on the north side of the road, about 0.25 mi. north of the Smiths Ferry Rd. gate near Lake Bray. The red-blazed strenuous path climbs, very steeply at times, gaining about 500 ft. of elevation over its 1.0-mi. length. It proceeds at an easy grade through mature hemlock woods, then crosses and descends a rocky outcrop at 0.5 mi. The trail now resumes its climb, with numerous changes of direction, and soon enters a more open hardwood forest with luxuriant mountain laurel thickets. Crossing a small divide at 0.9 mi., it bears slightly west and follows another woods road to the trail's end at the M–M Trail, a few yards east of the Beau Bridge Trail.

Teabag Trail (map 5: B3–B2)

Distance from Smiths Ferry Rd. (250 ft.) to
- Metacomet–Monadnock Trail (625 ft.): 1 mi., 400 ft., 50 min.

Knox Trail (DCR)

The Knox Trail begins on the southern portion of the Bray Loop Trail about 0.5 mi. from the western end of Lake Bray. The trail begins on a fairly flat portion of the Bray Loop Trail and heads south, climbing easily. The path levels out and veers more southwest for nearly 0.3 mi. Beginning an easy-to-moderate climb, the trail now turns west and ends near the point that the Knox Extension and Bray Valley Trail end near the reservation's boundary with The Trustees of Reservations property.

Knox Trail (map 5: D2)

Distance from Bray Loop Trail (300 ft.) to
- trail's end near TTOR boundary (300 ft.): 0.8 mi., 100 ft. (rev. 100 ft.), 35 min.

Mt. Holyoke Range: West

Named for Elizur Holyoke, one of three men appointed by the General Court of the Massachusetts Bay Colony in 1653 to divide lands in this region into plantations for the first settlers, this traprock range extends from the Connecticut River east about 7 mi. in the towns of Hadley, South Hadley, Granby, and Amherst. It includes Mt. Holyoke (940 ft.); Mt. Hitchcock (1,002 ft.), named in honor of Edward Hitchcock, a president of Amherst College who did much geological research in the area; Bare Mtn. (1,014 ft.); Mt. Norwottuck (1,106 ft.), which takes its name from the Norwottuck native who lived in the area; and Long Mtn. (920 ft.). The range contains two passes, or notches: Taylor Notch east of Mt. Holyoke, through which runs the automobile road to the summit of Mt. Holyoke (closed in winter), and Amherst Notch (or simply "the Notch") between Bare Mtn. and Mt. Norwottuck, through which runs MA 116. The Notch Visitor Center, operated by DCR, is located here.

With its open ledges providing extensive views, its lush deciduous, hemlock, and pine forests, and the Metacomet–Monadnock Trail along its entire length, the Holyoke Range is attractive to hikers, skiers, geologists, and naturalists. Much of the land is protected as part of the Skinner and Holyoke Range State Parks, and adjoining town conservation lands. Refer to maps 5 and 6 included with this book, and also the USGS Mt. Holyoke and Belchertown quadrangles.

The western part of the range, between MA 47 and MA 116, has three principal summits: Mt. Holyoke, Mt. Hitchcock, and Bare Mtn. Mt. Holyoke is the farthest west and provides impressive views of the Connecticut River Valley and of the Mt. Tom Range extending southwest on the opposite side of the river. An automobile road (closed in winter) leads to the summit, where the Summit House is a popular picnic spot.

J. A. Skinner State Park (390 acres) off MA 47 in Hadley includes the summit area of Mt. Holyoke. It offers universally accessible restrooms, 20 picnic sites (many with great views), and the Summit House atop the mountain.

Tramway Trail (DCR)

This yellow-blazed trail begins on MA 47 about 0.3 mi. north of the main entrance. The trail heads directly and strenuously up the western side of the mountain, jogging back and forth on switchbacks as it gains elevation. The trail crosses the summit road below the Summit House, then makes a final steep climb to the Summit House at the mountaintop.

Tramway Trail

Distance from MA 47 trailhead (111 ft.) to
 • Summit House (940 ft.): 0.8 mi., 40 min.

Dry Brook Trail (DCR)

This red-blazed trail on the south side of Mt. Holyoke makes a good snow-shoe and ski route in winter and a pleasant hiking route in spring because of the profusion of wildflowers. The trail leaves the summit road (not open to cars in winter) at Taylor Notch, where the Metacomet–Monadnock Trail crosses the road heading east and west. Leaving the south side of the summit road, the trail descends gradually along the western edge (right) of a broad, wooded hollow. Bearing more right at the head of a ravine with a small brook, the trail soon becomes a cleared path on the hillside and continues down the ridge line to join a well-defined woods road. The yellow-blazed Lithia Springs Trail exits left (south) here.

The Dry Brook Trail turns right (southwest) down the road and continues through a splendid forested glen. Beyond a power-line crossing, the trail bears right onto a road just above a deep, rocky ravine and follows it to a small pond on the left. The trail soon turns right onto the cleared strip of an underground telephone line (marked with posts). It continues several yards to its junction with the Metacomet–Monadnock Trail. Continuing straight, the trail ends at a gravel one-way road that connects MA 47 to the summit road.

Dry Brook Trail

Distances from summit road (202 ft.) to
 • Lithia Springs Trail: 0.4 mi., 20 min.
 • Metacomet–Monadnock Trail (750 ft.): 1.7 mi., 1 hr. 15 min.

Taylors Notch Trail (DCR)

Starting from the dirt parking area on MA 47 in Hadley, this yellow-blazed trail follows the same route as the blue-blazed Halfway House Trail for 0.2 mi., where the Halfway House Trail turns right. The Taylors Notch Trail goes left a short distance, then turns right and begins a gradual ascent. Soon the trail follows a gully and begins a steeper ascent, terminating at the elbow of the paved summit road. The white-blazed Metacomet–Monadnock Trail crosses the summit road just ahead, and the red-blazed Dry Brook Trail descends from Taylors Notch on the south side of the road.

Taylors Notch Trail

Distance from MA 47 parking area trailhead (205 ft.) to
* summit road (750 ft.): 0.9 mi., 40 min.

Metacomet–Monadnock Trail (DCR, BCAMC)

This white-blazed long-distance hiking trail passes through the Mt. Holyoke Range and Skinner State Parks for about 9 mi. of its total length. It is a scenic hike that never leaves the ridge of the Mt. Holyoke Range. For a complete description, see Metacomet–Monadnock Trail, Section 7, MA 47 to MA 116 on page 118.

Halfway House Trail (DCR)

This blue-blazed trail starts from the same parking area as the Taylors Notch Trail. It follows the yellow-blazed Taylors Notch Trail for 0.2 mi., then turns right (west) where the two trails split. It immediately crosses a wooden footbridge and follows a well-worn woods road across another stream, where the trail begins to climb after turning left. After a series of gentle switchbacks and moderate climbing, the trail terminates at the paved summit road. (Parking is available here.)

Halfway House Trail

Distance from MA 47 parking area (205 ft.) to
* summit road (600 ft.): 0.8 mi., 35 min

Mt. Holyoke Range: East

The eastern portion of the Mt. Holyoke Range is roughly bounded by MA 116 on the west and Harris Mtn. Rd. to the east, a distance of about 3 mi. In between are the two principal peaks of the range, Mt. Norwottuck (1,106 ft.) and Long Mtn. (920 ft.), the summits connected by a broad traprock ridge covered with hardwoods, hemlock stands, and laurel. The overhanging ledges on Mt. Norwottuck are the so-called horse caves of the late eighteenth century, supposed to have been used to shelter the horses of Daniel Shays and his men at the time of Shays' Rebellion. There are several cliffs and open ledges accessed by trails that afford excellent views. The eastern Mt. Holyoke Range is traversed by both the Metacomet–Monadnock and Robert Frost Trails. Information and maps are available in the state park's Notch Visitor Center on MA 116 in Amherst.

Brookbank Trail (DCR)

To reach the trailhead follow Laurel Loop Trail to the Trolley Bed Trail, turn left (north) onto the Trolley Bed Trail, and travel to the trail junction where the Brookbank Trail leaves right. The trail is marked with yellow blazes and descends along the ravine of Sweet Alice Brook. It follows the brook for a while, roughly parallel to the Trolley Bed Trail to the west. At the junction with the combined Northside Trail and Sweet Alice Trail on the right, the Brookbank Trail swings left (west) and meets the Trolley Bed Trail about 0.25 mi. south of Bay Rd. To return to the visitor center, turn left (south) onto the Trolley Bed Trail.

Brookbank Trail

Distances from Trolley Bed Trail (via Laurel Loop, starting elev. 520 ft.) to
- Sweet Alice Brook (300 ft.): 0.4 mi., 20 min.
- Notch Visitor Center via Laurel Loop Trail and Trolley Bed Trail: 2.4 mi., 1 hr. 20 min.

Northside Trail (DCR)

The Northside Trail is marked by blue triangles and is used primarily as a cross-country ski trail. It connects with the Brookbank Trail near Sweet Alice Brook and winds eastward along a series of old logging roads. The trail exits right (east) from the Brookbank Trail and in 0.1 mi. turns sharp left, then sharp right. After crossing a small brook it immediately goes left and ascends across a side slope to a large white pine stand. It turns left onto a logging road and in 100 yd. comes to the corner of an orchard, where it turns right, ascending gradually to a power-line right of way. The trail bears right, following the power line a short distance, then bears left under the line and into the woods. After crossing a brook, the trail turns right onto a logging road and ascends, eventually turning right onto another logging road. It follows this road north for 0.3 mi., then turns sharp left into a hemlock grove. After descending a hill, the trail bears right and then turns sharp right onto a logging road. In 25 yd. it exits left, ascending a steep hill and then turning left onto yet another logging road. The trail leaves this road on the right and continues through the woods until it ends at a yellow-blazed trail in the town of Amherst's Holyoke Range Conservation Area.

Northside Trail

Distance from Brookbank Trail (via Laurel Loop, starting elev. 520 ft.) to
* Holyoke Range Conservation Area: 1.6 mi., 1 hr. 10 min.

Metacomet–Monadnock Trail and Robert Frost Trail (DCR, BCAMC, Amherst Trails Committee)

These two long-distance trails coincide for much of the traverse of the range except near Mt. Norwottuck, where the M–M Trail goes over the mountain, passing near the horse caves, and the Robert Frost Trail (RFT) circles the base of the mountain. See Metacomet–Monadnock Trail, Section 8, MA 116 to Harris Rd. on page 120, or Robert Frost Trail, Section 1, Notch Visitor Center to Harris Rd on page 139.

Amherst Conservation Commission Trails

A significant portion of the land in this part of the range belongs to the town of Amherst's Conservation Commission, acquired by purchase or gift. Amherst Conservation Land and Trails, the Conservation Commission's guide to the properties, is available in local bookstores. Conservation area trailheads and access points can be found as follows (all areas have trails unless otherwise noted):

Eastman Brook: Entrance at a gate on the west side of Leverett Rd. in North Amherst, 0.1 mi. south of the Leverett–Amherst line.

Podick Sanctuary and Katharine Cole Sanctuary: Entrance and parking area on the west side of MA 116, 0.4 mi. south of the Amherst–Sunderland line.

Mill River: Entrance from Pine St., State St., Mill St., or MA 63 in North Amherst; universally-accessible trail parking is on the south side of State St., 100 yd. east of the main gate and entrance to Puffer's (Factory Hollow) Pond.

Wildwood: Entrance from the back (east) end of the Village Park Apartments off E. Pleasant St., 1.3 mi. north of Amherst center.

Amethyst Brook: Entrance and parking on the north side of Pelham Rd., 0.5 mi. west of the Amherst–Pelham line.

Skillings Path: Trailhead just south of the junior high school on the corner of Chestnut St. and High St.

Larch Hill: Parking and environmental education headquarters building (Hitchcock Center for the Environment) on the west side of MA 116 (S. Pleasant St.), 1.1 mi. south of Amherst center.

Larch Hill North: Entrance from Larch Hill (see previous entry) or from the end of Hillcrest Place (west off S. Pleasant St., 1 mi. south of Amherst center).

Upper Fort River: Entrance and parking on S. East St., just north of the bridge over the Fort River, 1.1 mi. south of MA 9.

Lower Fort River: Trailhead on the west side of MA 116, across from the entrance to Crocker Farm School, 2 mi. south of MA 9.

Harkness Brook: Entrance on the west side of Harkness Rd. on the Amherst–Pelham line, 0.6 mi. north of MA 9.

Mt. Castor: Entrance at the end of Valley View Dr., off S. East St., 1.6 mi. south of MA 9.

Hop Brook: Entrance on the east side of S. East St., 2.1 mi. south of MA 9.

Plum Brook: Entrance on the south side of Potwine Lane, 0.5 mi. east of MA 116 in South Amherst and on the north and south sides of Pomeroy La., 0.5 mi. east of MA 116.

Mt. Pollux: Entrance at 1403 S. East St. (Take the gravel road uphill through the gate to the parking area.) There is no trail, but it's possible to walk through the orchard to the summit, which affords fine 360-degree views.

Lawrence Swamp: Entrance and parking on Station Rd. at the Central Vermont Railroad crossing, 0.9 mi. east of the South Amherst common; other entrances at 1290 S. East St. (Baby Carriage Trail) and Station Rd., just west of the Hop Brook road crossing.

Elf Meadow: Entrances on Hulst Rd., off Bay Rd., in South Amherst.

Mt. Holyoke Range: Take Bay Rd. from MA 116. Entrance and parking via a paved drive off the south side of Bay Rd., just west of the junction of Chapel Rd. and Bay Rd.

Kenneth Cuddebank Trail: Entrance is 7 mi. from Rattlesnake Knob on the Holyoke Range north to MA 9 via the Plum Springs, Plum Brook, and Mt. Castor Trails.

Hop Brook Conservation Areas: Access points on Chapel Rd., 200 ft. north of Bay Rd.; Middle St., 0.25 mi. north of Bay Rd.; Shays St., 0.6 mi. east of MA 116; S. East St., 1.5 mi. south of MA 9; and Old Belchertown Rd., 0.1 mi. south of MA 9.

Arcadia Nature Center and Wildlife Sanctuary

Managed by the Massachusetts Audubon Society, this 766-acre sanctuary is located in Easthampton and Northampton. Its diverse habitats include floodplain forest, marsh, meadow, and upland forest on an ancient oxbow of the Connecticut River that borders the present famous oxbow. The sanctuary offers 5 mi. of trails and a nature center with a solar greenhouse. It is noted for its exhibitions of food and cover plantings for wildlife and the observation tower that overlooks Arcadia Marsh. A modest admission fee is charged.

To reach the sanctuary, take I-91 to Exit 18 (US 5, Northampton). Turn right onto US 5 south and travel 1.4 mi. Turn right onto East St. at the sign for Easthampton Center (Oxbow Sports is on the corner); follow East St. for 1.2 mi. and turn right onto Fort Hill Rd. at the Massachusetts

Audubon sign. Travel 0.9 mi. and bear right at the next Massachusetts Audubon sign, then turn left into the sanctuary entrance.

Old Coach Rd.–River Trail Loop (MAS)

For a pleasant circuit that follows the river and marsh, from the nature center follow the Old Coach Rd. for approximately 0.5 mi. to where it bears right to the River Trail. Turn right and follow the River Trail southeast along Wood Duck Pond and the Mill River. After crossing the Trolley Line, the River Trail becomes the Fern Trail, which continues along the wetlands, passing the observation tower and its sweeping view of the marsh; watch for a variety of waterfowl and wildlife such as muskrats and beavers. Turn right on the Cedar Trail, then shortly bear right on the Tulip Tree Trail to return to the nature center and parking area.

Old Coach Road–River Trail Loop

Distances from start of Old Coach Rd. at nature center to
- River Trail: 0.5 mi., 20 min.
- nature center (circuit): 1.2 mi., 50 min.

Mt. Lincoln

Mt. Lincoln (1,240 ft.), located in the town of Pelham, has a flat summit and offers extensive views in all directions from the fire tower. The University of Massachusetts Department of Forestry and Wildlife Management owns and manages 1,195 acres as Cadwell Memorial Forest. Several miles of unmarked woods roads are open to the public. There is presently a debate whether the area should support hiking and mountain biking—an issue that is still unresolved. A section of the white-blazed Metacomet–Monadnock Trail passes through the forest and over the summit. The summit also has transmission facilities for the five-college radio station. Refer to the USGS Belchertown and Shutesbury quadrangles.

Metacomet–Monadnock Trail (BCAMC)

Several miles of the 98-mi. Metacomet–Monadnock Trail pass through Cadwell Memorial Forest and over the summit of Mt. Lincoln. For a complete description, see Metacomet–Monadnock Trail, Section 10, MA 9 (Holland Glen) to Enfield Rd. on page 123.

Northfield Mtn.

Northfield Mtn. (1,100 ft.), which rises out of the upper Connecticut River Valley, is home to a huge electrical generating station and a summit reservoir that stores water for hydroelectric power. Best known as a center for winter sports, including cross-country skiing and snowshoeing, the Northfield Mtn. Recreation Center maintains 26 mi. of mountaintop trails that offer excellent hiking in the warmer months (hiking is not allowed once the ski season begins, or during mud season). Most of the trails are wide woods roads; some have been set aside just for hikers. As of mid-2008, the recreation center was owned and operated by First Light Power, but this is subject to change with a sale pending.

In addition to hiking, the Northfield Mtn. Recreation Center offers diverse educational programs, including fly-fishing, bird watching, studying old-growth forests, snowshoe hikes, and carving your own canoe paddle.

The visitor center is located off MA 63 about 2.1 mi. north of the junction of MA 2 and MA 63 in Millers Falls.

Rose Ledge Trail (NMRC)

The Rose Ledge Trail begins at the edge of the field behind the pond near the nature center. Here the Rose Ledge and Hidden Quarry Trails, marked with red and blue blazes, lead into the woods. After crossing a power line clearing, the trails split and the Rose Ledge Trail turns right. After a few minutes, the Lower Ledge Trail (also red-blazed) branches off to the right, then the West Slope Trail leads left. The Rose Ledge Trail continues straight at a moderate to steep grade, crossing the Yellow Jacket Pass multi use trail at junction 8. At about 0.9 mi., the trail passes a series of rocky ledges to the right that provide views south across the wooded hills of the Connecticut Valley, including North and South Sugarloaf Mtns. and the Pocumtuck Ridge.

Beyond the ledges, the Rose Ledge Trail levels off and curves left, crossing another multi-use trail at junction 29. After this junction, the trail ends at the junction with the Summit Trail, which comes in from the left. From the junction, it's an easy, 10-min. walk to the top of Northfield Mtn. via the Summit Trail; continue to follow the red blazes.

Rose Ledge Trail

Distances from trailhead near visitor center (283 ft.) to
- rock ledges: 0.9 mi., 40 min.
- junction with Summit Trail: 1.5 mi., 1 hr.
- summit via Summit Trail (1,100 ft.): 1.8 mi., 1 hr. 10 min.

Summit Trail (NMRC)

The narrow Summit Trail serves as a connecting route between the West Slope and Rose Ledge foot trails, and leads to Northfield Mtn.'s summit from its junction with the Rose Ledge Trail. From the trailhead on the West Slope Trail, the Summit Trail climbs steeply through hemlock-hardwood forest, reaching the Rose Ledge Trail at 0.4 mi. From here the Summit Trail turns left and continues at an easy grade to the summit. At the trail's end, walk across paved Reservoir Rd. to the wooden observation deck, which provides views across the summit reservoir to nearby Crag and Hermit Mtns., as well as the distant southern Green Mtns. of Vermont, including Stratton Mtn. and Mt. Snow.

Summit Trail

Distances from West Side Trail to
- Rose Ledge Trail junction: 0.4 mi., 25 min.
- Northfield Mtn. summit observation deck: 0.7 mi., 35 min.

West Slope Trail (NMRC)

The West Slope Trail traces a mostly east-west course across Northfield Mtn., crossing a number of the multi use and hiking trails. It can be used as part of a circuit that combines the Rose Ledge and Summit Trails. From its junction with the Rose Ledge Trail, the West Slope Trail climbs to the northwest through hemlock-hardwood forest, reaching the Summit Trail at 0.4 mi. From this junction, the trail continues west, crossing the Hemlock Hill multi use trail near the Chocolate Pot shelter, then crossing Reservoir Rd. shortly before ending at the Tooleybush Turnpike at 1.2 mi.

West Slope Trail
Distance from Rose Ledge Trail junction to
- Summit Trail: 0.4 mi., 15 min.
- Tooleybush Turnpike: 1.2 mi., 45 min.

Mt. Grace State Forest

Mt. Grace (1,625 ft.) is the third highest peak in Massachusetts east of the Connecticut River. During King Philip's War in 1676 warriors of the Wampanoag Nation captured Mary Rowlandson and her infant daughter Grace. As they were being taken west, the baby died and was buried by her mother at the mountain that has since borne her child's name. Situated in the town of Warwick, this 1,458-acre state forest features a steel fire tower that rises above Mt. Grace's wooded summit, providing a 360-degree view that includes Mt. Monadnock in New Hampshire, the southern Green Mtns. and Mt. Ascutney in Vermont, and the Quabbin Reservoir in Massachusetts. The summit is reached via the white-blazed Metacomet–Monadnock Trail (M–M Trail) or by Fire Tower Rd. For a description of the trail, see Metacomet–Monadnock Trail, Sections 17 and 18, Gulf Rd. to Mt. Grace, and Mt. Grace to MA 32, on pages 132 and 134, respectively. A blue-blazed trail at the back of Ohlson Field also provides a connecting route to the tower road. To reach Mt. Grace, take MA 2 to MA 2A, travel east to MA 78, then continue north to Warwick. The park entrance at Ohlson Field is on the left, just north of the village center.

Fire Tower Rd. (DCR)

The trail begins on MA 78 opposite the fountain on the common of Warwick village. The trail follows a road that is one house north of the village store (a sign reads, Northfield 8). It turns right in 100 yd. onto a dead-end lane beside a barn (where parking is available in summer), passes through a gate leaving a new house on the right, continues past a barn on the left, and goes through a second gate into the woods. Water is available on the right, just inside this gate. The trail ascends along the road, with a telephone line close by. The M–M Trail enters on the left at the foot of the final steep climb to the summit.

Fire Tower Rd.

Distances from Warwick village (MA 78) (940 ft.) to
- Metacomet-Monadnock Trail: 0.9 mi., 30 min.
- summit of Mt. Grace (1,625 ft.): 1.3 mi., 40 min.

Mt. Toby State Demonstration Forest

Mt. Toby (1,269 ft.) lies partly in Sunderland and partly in Leverett on the east bank of the Connecticut River roughly across the river from Mt. Sugarloaf. Its rugged sides are well forested, including some of the last remaining old-growth in the Pioneer Valley, and have numerous brooks. There is a fire tower on the summit affording excellent views. Mt. Toby State Demonstration Forest, operated by the University of Massachusetts, comprises 755 acres. The trails described here are the usual routes used to climb the mountain, but numerous woods roads also invite exploration. The kiosk at the Reservation Rd. parking area includes a large map of the various trails; also refer to the USGS Mt. Toby quadrangle.

Woodbury Trail/Middle Mtn. Rd. (University of Massachusetts)

This trail is for the most part a logging or jeep road. To reach the trailhead follow MA 116 for 1.0 mi. south of Sunderland (6.0 mi. north of Amherst) to N. Silver La. Turn left (north) onto N. Silver La., continue 0.4 mi., then turn right onto Reservoir Rd. Follow this 0.2 mi. to Nebo Rd., turn left, and continue for a short distance to a place where cars can be parked on the left.

The trail enters the woods and climbs gradually in a generally northeast direction, following white blazes at each of several junctions. It passes a deep, forested brook ravine on the right and at 1.5 mi. passes the blue-blazed Link Trail on the left. At about 1.8 mi. the trail passes under a power line, where a side path leads left to a view from the height-of-land, and becomes less traveled. A short distance beyond, after a moderate climb, the trail emerges in a clearing. In the 1800s this area was farmed by Irish immigrants and was referred to as the Paddy Farms area. The trail leads right onto a level grade, following the white blazes over an eroded streambed. In a short distance the trail joins the orange-blazed Robert Frost Trail, which eventually leads over the summits of Roaring Mtn. and Mt. Toby.

Woodbury Trail (Middle Mtn. Rd.)

Distances from Nebo Rd. to
- Link Trail: 1.5 mi., 35 min.
- clearing: 2 mi., 50 min.
- Robert Frost Trail: 2.2 mi., 1 hr.

North Mtn. Rd. (University of Massachusetts)

This red-blazed trail follows a jeep road from MA 116 to near the summit and from there follows a cleared and blazed path. To reach the trailhead, follow MA 47 north from the center of Sunderland (at the junction of MA 116 and MA 47) for 0.5 mi. to N. Silver La. Turn right onto N. Silver La. and continue 0.2 mi. to Park St. Turn left onto Park St. and continue to the end. Parking is available near the entrance to Sunderland Town Park or at the small pond a short distance down gravel North Mtn. Rd. on the right. The trail continues straight ahead on the gravel road, which goes uphill past a house on the left and bears left into the woods. The trail passes puddingstone ledges on the right and soon a small clearing on the left. (Avoid the gravel road that comes in on the left. This road leads to Sunderland–Montague Rd. 1.0 mi. north of Sunderland.)

The trail follows the red blazes through a red-pine plantation and gradually ascends to blue-blazed Gunn Mtn. Rd. on the left. Eventually the trail crosses under power lines and bears left. The blue-blazed Link Trail bears right here to cross a small stream and eventually connect with the white-blazed Middle Mtn. Rd. After passing under the power lines, North Mtn. Rd. soon passes the blue-blazed Sugar Farms Trail on the left. It continues uphill past an abandoned sugar shack on the left (last water) and soon leaves the woods road on the right. The trail ascends steeply 0.3 mi. to the summit of Mt. Toby and its junction with the orange-blazed Robert Frost Trail.

North Mtn. Rd.

Distances from Park St. trailhead (225 ft.) to
- Gunn Mtn. Rd.: 1 mi., 35 min.
- Link Trail: 1.3 mi., 50 min.
- Sugar Farms Trail: 1.4 mi., 55 min.
- summit of Mt. Toby (1,269 ft.): 2.1 mi., 1 hr. 25 min.

Summit Rd. (University of Massachusetts)

This white-blazed service road is closed to all motorized traffic except for university research and maintenance vehicles. It provides an easy descent after dark, and unless it is icy, it is suitable for travel on snowshoes and skis in winter. The road was used to reach the summit with mountain wagons in the late 1800s. At that time there was a passenger stop and picnic area at a railroad station at the foot of the mountain in Leverett. To reach the trail, follow Reservation Rd. to the gate into Mt. Toby State Demonstration Forest, where parking is available. (Reservation Rd. runs south of the Sunderland–Montague line between MA 47 and MA 63.) The gate is just west of the white forest headquarters building and shed. The Central Vermont Railroad tracks are a short distance east at Cranberry Pond, and both the tracks and the pond are just off MA 63.

The road, which is well maintained, leads south through conifer plantations, leaving the orange-blazed Robert Frost Trail, which it follows for a short distance in the beginning on the right. At 0.2 mi. leave the Robert Frost Trail and follow the white blazes. Soon after the road passes a clearing on the left, the red-blazed Telephone Line Trail exits right from the road. The road continues straight ahead and ascends into the glen of Roaring Brook, passes the blue-blazed Roaring Brook Trail on the left, and swings right and close to the brook. After several brook crossings, the road climbs gently, joins again with the Robert Frost Trail, and continues straight ahead. (Do not turn left onto the Robert Frost Trail, which climbs past the Metawampe Cabin.) The road soon passes the red-blazed Upper Link Trail on the right, then bears left to reach the junction with the yellow-blazed Robert Frost Bypass Trail. Summit Rd. turns sharp right at the junction with the Robert Frost Bypass Trail and follows the Robert Frost Trail to the summit.

Summit Rd.

Distances from gate to Mt. Toby State Demonstration Forest (403 ft.) to
- Telephone Line Trail: 0.5 mi., 20 min.
- Roaring Brook Trail: 0.8 mi., 30 min.
- Robert Frost Trail: 1 mi., 40 min.
- Upper Link Trail: 1.2 mi., 50 min.
- Robert Frost Bypass Trail: 1.6 mi., 1 hr. 15 min.
- summit of Mt. Toby (1,269 ft.): 3 mi., 1 hr. 45 min.

Telephone Line Trail (University of Massachusetts)

Many hikers use this trail to descend the mountain because it is somewhat steep just below the summit. Combined with Summit Rd., it provides an alternate route on the eastern side of the mountain. Follow the white-blazed Summit Rd. 0.8 mi. south to the red-blazed Telephone Line Trail, which exits right. The trail soon merges with the orange-blazed Robert Frost Trail, but stays left under the lines as the Robert Frost Trail exits right. The trail continues uphill past the red-blazed Hemlock Hill Loop Trail on the right. At a notch well up on the mountain, it turns right at the junction with the red-blazed Upper Link Trail, which goes left. The trail continues under the telephone lines as it steeply ascends to the summit. (*Note: When descending, it is important to turn left at the foot of the steep section below the summit and again left at the junction with white-blazed Summit Rd.*) Most of this trail is part of the long-distance Robert Frost Trail and is marked with its orange blazes.

Telephone Line Trail

Distances from Summit Rd. (403 ft.) to
- Hemlock Hill Loop Trail: 0.5 mi., 25 min.
- Upper Link Trail: 0.9 mi., 45 min.
- summit of Mt. Toby (1,269 ft.): 1.7 mi., 1 hr. 10 min.

Mt. Sugarloaf Reservation

Mt. Sugarloaf Reservation (532 acres) includes South Sugarloaf Mtn. (652 ft.) and North Sugarloaf Mtn. (791 ft.). South Sugarloaf, commonly called Mt. Sugarloaf, offers an unsurpassed view of the Connecticut River and its fertile valley. A narrow, paved automobile road (not open in winter, small fee for parking at the summit) winds up to the summit, where it terminates at an ample paved parking area. The original summit house, built in 1864, burned years ago, but a modern pavilion has been built and a caretaker is on the premises during summer. The steep Pocumtuck Ridge Trail at the southern end of the mountain ascends via many switchbacks to the summit directly from the parking area off Sugarloaf St. near the junction of MA 116 and the summit road. Several picnic tables and restrooms are located on the summit. The summit road leaves MA 116 about 1 mi. west of its intersection with MA 47 in Sunderland and 1 mi. east of South Deerfield and US 5. Refer to the USGS Mt. Toby quadrangle.

West Side Trail (DCR)

This trail begins at the dirt parking area at the junction of MA 116 and the paved summit road. The trail skirts a ball field on the left and follows along a telephone line a short distance into the woods. From here it follows a level grade, then ascends gently to its junction with the blue-blazed Pocumtuck Ridge Trail in the saddle between South Sugarloaf Mtn. and North Sugarloaf Mtn. The Pocumtuck Ridge Trail leads to the summit of South Sugarloaf Mtn.

West Side Trail

Distances from parking area at beginning of summit road (185 ft.) to
- Pocumtuck Ridge Trail: 0.6 mi., 35 min.
- summit of South Sugarloaf Mtn. via Pocumtuck Ridge Trail (652 ft.): 1.1 mi., 1 hr. 15 min.

Hillside Trail (DCR)

This trail is a good access path to the summit on the northern side of North Sugarloaf Mtn. from the gate on paved Hillside Rd. in Deerfield. To reach the trailhead, take River Rd. north from its junction with MA 116 next to the Sunderland Bridge over the Connecticut River. Follow River Rd. several miles, past the open fields of the University of Massachusetts experimental farm, to its junction with Hillside Rd. on the left. Proceed up Hillside Rd. a short distance to the gated trail entrance on the left. The trail goes south on a level grade, then turns right to follow a small stream gully, rather steeply at times, to a lovely swamp on the left. There it joins the blue-blazed Pocumtuck Ridge Trail, which continues to the summit of North Sugarloaf Mtn.

Hillside Trail

Distances from Hillside Rd. to
- Pocumtuck Ridge Trail: 1.1 mi., 1 hr.
- summit of North Sugarloaf Mtn. via Pocumtuck Ridge Trail (791 ft.): 1.3 mi., 1 hr. 15 min.

DAR State Forest

The fire tower on Moore's Hill (1,697 ft.) in the Daughters of the American Revolution (DAR) State Forest affords a panoramic view across the hills of western Massachusetts. This 1,517-acre state forest has two lakes (Upper and Lower Highland Lakes), more than 15 mi. of hiking, skiing, and snowmobile trails, two camping areas with 50 campsites, and a swimming beach. DAR State Forest has been a leader in providing universally accessible (UA) facilities; it now offers UA restrooms, swimming, fishing, nature trails, boating, camping, and picnicking. Hiking trails are marked with blue triangles, and multiuse trails have orange markers. Bridle paths are marked with red triangles and are suitable for hiking, skiing, and snowmobile use. Refer to the USGS Goshen quadrangle.

To reach the DAR State Forest Headquarters and campground, take Route 112 (Goshen–Ashfield Rd.) north from MA 9 in Goshen. Turn right on the marked entrance road that leads to the headquarters and campground. Parking is available here.

Universal Access Nature Trail (DCR)

This short trail—about 0.4 mi. long—runs along the south shore of Upper Highland Lake. Starting from the south boat launch area just east of the grassy earthen dam, it leads to the parking area on the east bay just south of the camping area and the Long Trail trailhead. An information kiosk by the south boat launch has maps as well as additional information in braille. There is a UA fishing area and UA gazebo perched on a promontory along the way. The trail, wooded and cool, passes through hardwoods and hemlocks. There are many relaxing views of the lake and a scattering of benches as well.

Universal Access Nature Trail
Distance from south boat launch to
 • parking area near camping area: 0.4 mi., 20 min.

Long Trail (DCR)

The trail starts just north of the southeastern boat launch on Upper Highland Lake and just south of the campground. The trail closely follows the upper shore of the lake, starting out as a narrow footpath and gradually widening. At about 0.5 mi. the blue-marked Darling–Fisher Trail enters on the right. The Long Trail, not to be confused with Vermont's Long Trail, continues cruising along the lakeshore, reaching the northern end of the lake at 0.75 mi. The trail now briefly follows a feeder brook northeast before swinging southeast to a trail junction at 1.0 mi. From the junction a connector path leads south about 0.25 mi. to the northern end of the main forest campground. The Long Trail continues northeast, climbing steadily. At 1.5 mi. the Twinning Brook Trail (left) leads in 0.3 mi. to the campground near Twinning Pond. The Long Trail continues the short way to Moore Hill Rd.

Long Trail
Distances from trailhead to
 • north end of lake: 0.75 mi., 25 min.
 • Moore Hill Rd.: 1.6 mi., 45 min.

Darling–Fisher Trail (DCR)

Marked with blue triangles, this trail climbs east from its junction with the Long Trail on the eastern shore of Upper Highland Lake. It passes through the campground, then climbs steadily through the forest, crossing power lines twice along the way. It reaches Moore Hill Rd. at 0.75 mi., with the fire tower about 0.1 mi. farther on.

Darling–Fisher Trail
Distance from Long Trail (1,458 ft.) to
 • summit of Moore's Hill (1,697 ft.): 0.8 mi., 30 min.

Sunset Trail (DCR)

Marked with blue blazes (other colors may also be evident), the trail leaves from near the boat launch on Lower Highland Lake. The one-lane access road is nearly opposite the information booth at the MA 112 forest entrance on the right upon entering. It climbs gradually to the fire tower on Moore Hill.

Sunset Trail
Distance from boat launch (1,405 ft.) to
 • summit of Moore Hill (1,697 ft.): 2.3 mi., 1 hr. 15 min.

Dubuque Memorial State Forest

This 7,822-acre forest, situated principally in the town of Hawley but also extending south into the town of Plainfield, is adjacent to Savoy State Forest and Mohawk Trail State Forest. It comprises rugged terrain, much of it above 1,500 ft. with some points as high as 1,800 ft., and includes several ponds and brooks. Many grassy woods roads and old town roads bordered by stone walls crisscross the forest. To follow these roads, refer the USGS Plainfield quadrangle.

The DCR has constructed a trail system in the central part of the forest and has erected four large Adirondack shelters, three of which are accessible by Forest Service roads and hiking trails, and the fourth by trail only. The shelters are available on a first-come, first-served basis. Each shelter site has a stone fireplace, a picnic table, a good source of drinking water, and an outhouse. The trails are not uniformly blazed (although there are some paint blazes), but the footway is clear except when obscured by forest litter. There are signs at some intersections.

The trail system is accessible from the south via Central St., which exits north from MA 116 about 9 mi. west of Ashfield center. The Shaw-Hudson House is located on the northwest corner of MA 116 and Central St. At the junction of Central St. and Union St. (0.5 mi.), continue northeast on Union St. until it makes an abrupt right (east) turn and becomes North St. at 1.3 mi. Proceed straight ahead, approx. north, on gravel Middle Rd. (not plowed in winter) to the Hawley–Plainfield line at 2.3 mi. Continue past a path on the right (east) of the road at 3.6 mi. (The path leads into a grove and to a small pond.) At 3.8 mi. turn left (west) onto Moody Spring Rd. (there might not be a sign). (*Note: When traveling in the reverse direction, be sure to turn right at this intersection. The corner is somewhat confusing because the roads form a small triangle.*) Continue on Moody Spring Rd. past a small cemetery on the right at 4.3 mi. At 4.5 mi. look for a parking area on the right (north). This is Gould Meadow (no sign) and probably the best place to begin a circuit walk on the trails.

Gould Meadow also is accessible from the west via a Forest Service road (Hallockville Rd.) that exits east from MA 8A (Hawley Rd.) at a point about 1 mi. north of its intersection with MA 116 in Plainfield. Going northeast on the Forest Service road, avoid a road on the left at 0.9 mi. (King Corner Rd.) and a road on the right at 1.3 mi. Pass the Basin Brook Trail on the left at 1.4 mi., the Gould Meadow Trail on the right at 1.5 mi., and Moody Spring Rd. on the left at 1.8 mi. At 1.9 mi. note a parking area on the left (north) and the beginning of the Basin Brook Trail on the right (south). This is Gould Meadow (no sign).

A 5.1-mi. continuous walk that begins and ends at Gould Meadow can be made via the Moody Spring Trail, the Hitchcock Meadow Trail, and the Basin Brook Trail (with or without the Ridge Trail as an alternative for part of the Hitchcock Meadow Trail). See the following trail descriptions.

Moody Spring Rd. (DCR)

This Forest Service road begins near the junction of Middle Rd. and Hunt Rd. and runs west-northwest to Gould Meadow, then southwest to a corner where it turns sharp right (northwest). (The road that goes straight ahead at the corner is the Forest Service road to MA 8A.) Moody Spring Rd. continues to Moody Spring and the Moody Spring Shelter, built of stone with a dirt floor. Beyond Moody Spring, the road continues northwest to Hitchcock Meadow.

Moody Spring Rd.
Distance from junction of Middle Rd. and Hunt Rd. to
• Hitchcock Meadow: 1.4 mi., 55 min.

Moody Spring Trail (DCR)

This trail begins at a sign at the northwest corner of the Gould Meadow parking area and runs north. Gould Meadow Shelter, facing an open field with good views east and north, is on the right of the trail a short distance from the parking area. Drinking water is available at a spring about 100 yd. down a little grade to the left (west) of the trail and shelter. The trail runs northwest, bearing left (west), and continuing past a good view south at 0.5 mi. It then starts steeply downhill, crosses a lovely brook at 0.6 mi., and climbs, bearing right and then left, to Moody Spring and Moody Spring Shelter. Here it joins the Hitchcock Meadow Trail and Moody Spring Rd.

Moody Spring Trail
Distances from Gould Meadow (1,562 ft.) to
• brook: 0.6 mi., 25 min.
• Moody Spring (1,565 ft.): 0.9 mi., 35 min.

Hitchcock Meadow Trail (DCR)

This trail begins at the dead end of Moody Springs Rd. about 0.25 mi. northwest of Moody Spring. It heads northwest over level ground, then climbs to the southern shoulder of a low ridge at 0.5 mi. The trail then follows the contour of the hill, swinging south before tracing a course along the ridge, heading again northwest. When the trail reaches a second shoulder, this one reaching west, it descends the slope in a generally westerly direction, reaching Basin Brook and the junction with the Basin Brook Trail at 1.2 mi. The trail then continues west to reach MA 8A at 1.5 mi.

Hitchcock Meadow Trail
Distances from trailhead (0.25 mi. from Moody Spring) (1,535 ft.) to
• south shoulder of hill: 0.5 mi., 20 min.
• Basin Brook Trail: 1.2 mi., 50 min.
• MA 8A (1,070 ft.): 1.5 mi., 1 hr. 5 min

Basin Brook Trail (DCR)

This trail begins on Hallockville Rd., an unpaved Forest Service road that bisects the forest from west to east. To reach the trailhead from the parking area at the northeast end of Hallockville Pond (just off MA 8A) travel 1.4 mi. east along Hallockville Rd. The trail begins on the left and heads north. At a trail junction the path turns left (west) and descends the short distance to Basin Brook, which it follows for the remainder of the trek. At 1.25 mi. a tributary enters left at the junction of the Hawley Pass Trail. The Basin Brook Trail continues to descend the ravine, reaching the Hitchcock Meadow Trail at 1.6 mi. and MA 8A at 2.0 mi.

Basin Brook Trail

Distances from trailhead on Hallockville Rd. (1,538 ft.) to

- Hawley Pass Trail: 1.25 mi., 45 min.
- Hitchcock Meadow Trail: 1.6 mi., 1 hr.
- MA 8A (1,070 ft.): 2.0 mi., 1 hr., 20 min.

Pond Trail (DCR)

This attractive trail loops around the shore of Hallockville Pond on the west side of MA 8A about 1 mi. north of its junction with MA 116. The parking area and trailhead are at the north end of the pond, north of the stone dam. Some of the buildings here are now used as a camp for AmeriCorps volunteers. From the trailhead on the northwest shore the trail passes a picnic area (with tables) and a primitive camping area (with a stone fireplace) on the left, then continues amid large white pines and evidence of former beaver activity. It crosses two brooks at the southwestern end of the pond, one on a rock causeway. Nearby on the higher land are the stone foundations of an old dam, spillway, and mill.

After crossing another brook on a plank bridge laid close to the water, the trail turns left and continues northeast on the eastern side of the pond. There are several huge boulders in this area and considerable evidence of former beaver activity. Side trails on the right lead to pump houses and a dwelling. Shortly beyond on the right is a spring with water flowing from a pipe. MA 8A appears through the trees on the right, and a short trail leads to the highway. The Pond Trail continues close to the water until it ends at the eastern side of the concrete dam on the northern end of the pond. A short trail leads right (east) to MA 8A. To the left (west) of the dam are the buildings and parking area where the trail begins.

Pond Trail
Distance from sign at Hallockville Pond to
• eastern side of dam (circuit): 1.0 mi., 40 min.

Hawley Pass Trail (DCR)

The Hawley Pass Trail has two trailheads, but the one near Hallockville Pond is close to parking. From the parking area at Hallockville Pond head up Kingholt Rd. (dirt) the few yards to the trailhead on the right. The trail heads north and soon crosses King Brook and MA 8A. The trail then slowly swings from north to east, reaching a fork at 0.2 mi. The path heads north, reaching King Corner Rd. at 0.7 mi. Crossing the road, the trail jogs east and descends to the brook, following the ravine, to reach the junction with the Basin Brook Trail at 1.5 mi. To reach MA 8A follow the Basin Brook Trail west for 0.7 mi.

Hawley Pass Trail
Distances from trailhead at Hallockville Pond (1,605 ft.) to
• King Corner Rd.: 0.7 mi., 25 min.
• Basin Brook Trail: 1.5 mi., 45 min.
• MA 8A via Basin Brook Trail (1,070 ft.): 2.2 mi., 1 hr. 5 min.

High Ledges Wildlife Sanctuary (MAS)

Named for its open ledges that provide a commanding view south and west across the Deerfield River Valley to Mt. Greylock and the Berkshire Hills, this 570-acre sanctuary is also known for its abundant wildflower blooms in spring, which include hundreds of pink lady's slippers along the hillside, as well as much rarer yellow lady's slippers.

To reach the unstaffed sanctuary, follow MA 2 6 mi. west from Greenfield. Turn north on Little Mohawk Rd. (look for a sign for the Davenport maple farm) and continue for 1.3 miles, then bear left on Patten Rd. Follow Patten Rd., bearing left, then right at successive junctions, following signs for High Ledges. The parking area on Sanctuary Rd. is 0.5 mi. after the second junction. The entrance gate and parking area were originally farther down the road and closer to the ledges, but have been relocated in recent years due to deteriorating road conditions.

From the parking area, it's an easy walk of roughly 1.0 mi. along Sanctuary Rd. to the ledges. A well-marked trail network offers a number of options for exploring the sanctuary's diverse habitats, which include woodlands, old fields, swamps, and streams. The Lady's Slipper and Waterthrush Trails offer good wildflower viewing (come in late May and June for orchids). The outer Wolve's Den and North Trails are more rugged, steep, and lead to a number of features, including an interesting series of rocky outcroppings.

Mohawk Trail State Forest

This forest lies in the towns of Charlemont, Florida, Savoy, and Hawley and is accessible from MA 2. It includes 6,457 acres of mountain ridges, deep gorges, and 18 mi. of cold rivers and streams with excellent trout fishing. Champion trees are scattered throughout the forest, including a 130-ft.-tall red oak that is the tallest in New England. The forest has 56 campsites and four cabins that can be reserved year-round. There is also a swimming area and day-use picnic area. The trails within Mohawk Trail State Forest explore some of the most beautiful wilderness left in Massachusetts, with old-growth stands towering 100 ft. tall. Some of the hiking trails, including the Mahican–Mohawk Trail, were originally paths used by American Indians centuries ago. Good views are available from Clark Mtn. (1,920 ft.) and Todd Mtn. (1,697 ft.).

Mahican–Mohawk Trail (DCR)

A 1.5-mi.-long segment of this historic trail traces a path over Clark and Todd Mtns. It is blazed with round golden markers with a green maple leaf in the center. The trailhead is located off MA 2. From the main entrance on MA 2 cross over the Cold River, reaching the forest headquarters at 0.1 mi. Continue on the road, bear right, and follow it to the gate. Just beyond the gate is the trailhead for a short loop path called the Nature Trail. Head north on the Nature Trail about 0.25 mi. to the junction with the Mahican–Mohawk Trail.

The Mahican–Mohawk Trail continues north (the Nature Trail loops south to follow along the Deerfield River) along the edge of the Deerfield River floodplain and just to the east of Todd Mtn. The trail then follows the contour of the mountain and swings roughly west around the north buttress. It slabs the north slope, reaching the saddle between Todd Mtn. and Clark Mtn. at 1.3 mi. and the junction with the Indian Trail. The Mahican–Mohawk Trail continues west, climbing the narrow ridge in a nearly straight line to the summit of Clark Mtn. (1,919 ft.) and excellent views at 2.1 mi.

Mahican–Mohawk Trail

Distances from the north end of the Nature Trail loop (campground elev. 806 ft.) to
- saddle between Todd and Clark Mtns.: 1.3 mi., 50 min.
- summit of Clark Mtn. (1,919 ft.): 2.1 mi., 1 hr. 40 min.

Indian Trail (DCR)

The Indian Trail begins at the north end of the campground about 0.7 mi. from the forest entrance. The trail heads northwest and strikes a steep, strenuous course up the flank of the Cold River ravine. It reaches the saddle between Todd and Clark Mtns. and the junction with the Mahican–Mohawk Trail at 0.3 mi. after gaining about 700 ft. in elevation. From the junction the Indian Trail heads east and ascends the double peaks of Todd Mtn. The climb begins moderately, then becomes steep as it crests the first summit (1,580 ft.). The path now descends before scrambling up to the true summit (1,697 ft.) at 0.75 mi.

Indian Trail

Distances from Mohawk Trail State Forest camping area (806 ft) to
- saddle: 0.3 mi., 35 min.
- summit of Clark Mtn. (1,919 ft.): 0.75 mi., 1 hr. 10 min.

Totem Lookout Trail (DCR)

This trail leaves the south side of MA 2 opposite the state forest picnic area, about 1 mi. west of the main entrance. (A sign that says Leaving Pioneer Valley is located a short distance west on MA 2.) The trail enters the woods near a brook, follows a short woods road leading to a small forest service building, and almost immediately turns left (east). It then starts to ascend the side of the hill, climbing southeast through the woods. The grade moderates near the crest of the hill, then the trail turns a sharp left (east) and emerges on a rocky ledge (1,627 ft.), which affords views of the steep valley to the north and northeast.

Totem Lookout Trail

Distance from Mohawk Trail Highway (MA 2) (820 ft.) to
  • lookout on ledge (1,627 ft.): 1.1 mi., 50 min.

Fannie Stebbins Memorial Wildlife Refuge

This 338-acre wildlife refuge is maintained by The Fannie Stebbins Memorial Wildlife Refuge, Inc., whose officers and trustees are members of the Allen Bird Club of Springfield, the founding organization. The refuge is located in Longmeadow, just above the Connecticut state border on the floodplain of the Connecticut River known as the Longmeadow Flats. The tract is set between the Connecticut River and I-91.

To reach the refuge, follow US 5 (Longmeadow St.) 2.4 mi. south of the Springfield–Longmeadow line to Bark Haul Rd. Turn right (west) onto Bark Haul Rd., continue 0.4 mi. to the intersection of Pondside Rd., and park there. A large map of the refuge and adjacent town conservation lands, including the main walking roads and trails, is at the parking area. The Stebbins Refuge is very popular with birders. The trails are concentrated at the southern end of the property, where the Fern Trail, Knoll Trail, Perimeter Trail, Elm Trail, and Meadow Trail go through the swamps and floodplain forest; portions of these routes can be wet or flooded at times. An interesting path is the Peninsula Trail, which explores a narrow spit of land extending south into the river. A small map of the area is available by writing to the refuge in care of the Allen Bird Club, P.O. Box 1084, Springfield, MA 01101.

Laughing Brook Wildlife Sanctuary

This property of the Massachusetts Audubon Society is located at 789 Main St. in Hampden. The sanctuary has 356 acres of woodland, fields, and streams, and offers miles of well-maintained and blazed trails. The area includes pleasant woods with wildflowers in season, Laughing Brook, the Scantic River, and the home of the writer Thornton Burgess. The sanctuary reopened in April 2008 after being closed following a fire that destroyed the headquarters building and nature center in 2004, and subsequent extensive flooding of the trails in 2005.

The many trails that course through the property can be divided into short, high-interest walks and longer hikes. Short walks include Smiling Pond Path that wraps around the pond, and Big River Loop that explores the Scantic River. Longer trails include the Storyteller's Trail, Green Forest Trail, and Neff Trail.

To reach the sanctuary from I-91 in Springfield, take either Exit 2 (northbound) or Exit 4 (southbound) to MA 83. Follow MA 83 (which becomes Summer Ave., then Allen St.) for 8.1 mi.; it swings right near a McDonald's restaurant. At the end of Allen St. (by the Mobil station) take a left onto Main St. The sanctuary entrance is 2 mi. down Main St. on the left. From Boston and Worcester, take the Massachussetts Turnpike (I-90) to Exit 8 in Palmer. Take a right to reach Palmer Center and US 20. Proceed west on US 20 for 5.3 mi., and turn left on to Main St. (opposite the Wilbraham Fire Department). Travel 6.6 mi. on Main St. (which turns into Wilbraham Rd. in Hampden) to a stop sign and turn left onto Allen St. After 0.2 mi. on Allen St. take a left onto Main St. The sanctuary entrance is 2 mi. down Main St. on the left.

Ridge Trail (Boy Scout Troops 171 and 172)

This pleasant forest trail, also known as the Boy Scout Trail, extends roughly north and south along a ridge forming the eastern boundary of the Connecticut River Valley, including Minnichaug Mtn. The trail, which involves some mild climbing, runs through the towns of Hampden and Wilbraham and is marked by orange and red blazes. It is maintained by Boy Scout Troops 171 and 172. The southern terminus of the trail is located on Main St. in Hampden, opposite the VFW building, which is about 0.4

mi. east of Wilbraham and about 0.8 mi. west of the Hampden Post Office. The northern terminus lies at the eastern end of the American Foreign Legion building parking lot, located on US 20 just west of the railroad overpass in North Wilbraham. The intention is eventually to connect this trail with the Shenipsit Trail in Connecticut. Efforts to upgrade and blaze the trails are ongoing.

Beginning at the VFW in Hampden, the trail is marked by an orange blaze on a tree high on the hillside above the paved road. It heads north along the edge of the woods and through a clearing atop the first rise, then turns uphill onto a logging road. In 0.1 mi. Goat Rock is located on the left, with fine views to the south and east. The trail follows the logging road on and off for 0.4 mi. and bears right uphill after a grove of hemlocks. It then levels off for 0.2 mi. before it turns sharp left at a spot overlooking Hampden center.

The trail soon rejoins the logging road and heads downhill to the northeast. (*Note: Watch carefully for blazes, as other trails intersect.*) In 0.2 mi. the trail turns left (north) at an intersection, and in 0.4 mi. it comes out in an extensively logged area. It continues north and then east on the logging road, crosses a small brook, and bears right off the road at the next rise. It soon passes a small pond on the left and in 0.1 mi. turns north onto another logging road. In 100 ft. it bears right into a wet, logged-over area. It continues 0.1 mi., then turns west to parallel some power lines.

At 2.1 mi. the trail turns left onto Mtn. Rd. and then turns right, following the power lines uphill. At the top of the hill the trail heads north through a young forest. After crossing a stone wall and a small brook, the trail begins to ascend forested Mt. Vision. It bears right and shortly reaches the summit. In 0.2 mi. the trail joins a private drive to Burleigh Rd. It turns right onto Burleigh Rd., passes the Hampden–Wilbraham townline marker, and shortly turns northeast onto a logging road. In 0.6 mi. the trail passes a small hill on the right with fine views west. In another 0.6 mi. the logging road becomes paved and intersects Monson Rd. at 4.6 mi. From here to the American Foreign Legion in North Wilbraham (at 9.0 mi.) the trail is in the process of being blazed and relocated; it may be hard to follow in places during this time.

Ridge Trail

Distances from VFW in Hampden to
- Goat Rock: 0.1 mi., 5 min.
- Mtn. Rd.: 2.1 mi., 1 hr. 20 min.
- summit of Mt. Vision: 2.6 mi., 1 hr. 45 min.
- Burleigh Rd.: 3.3 mi., 2 hr. 10 min.
- Monson Rd.: 4.6 mi., 3 hr. 30 min.
- American Foreign Legion: 9.0 mi., 6 hr. 10 min.

Chester–Blandford State Forest

Chester–Blandford State Forest has several outstanding natural attractions and one signature feature—Sanderson Brook Falls, one of the most striking waterfalls in the region. Like many other state forests, Chester–Blandford is a mix of gravel forest roads and narrow hiking trails. The roads are closed to motor vehicles, making them good walking routes. The trails explore the steep hills and brooks, often passing by holes dug into the mountain years ago by miners of mica, emery, and corundum. The forest headquarters are off US 20. About 0.5 mi. east of the headquarters is the parking area for the Boulder Park Accessible Trail.

To reach the forest from the Massachusetts Turnpike (I-90), take Exit 3. Turn onto MA 10/US 202 south and continue to US 20. Proceed on US 20 west of Huntington and follow signs.

Sanderson Brook Falls Trail (DCR)

To reach the falls from the parking area off US 20 (4 mi. west of Huntington near a concrete bridge over Sanderson Brook) hike south on the gravel road along the brook. The grade is easy, and the footing is good. Over the next mile the road crosses over three bridges before coming to the side trail on the right (west) side of Sanderson Brook Rd. The unmarked but easy-to-follow path descends from the road and reaches the foot of the falls in about 5 min.

Sanderson Brook Falls Trail

Distances from parking area on US 20 to
- falls: 0.8 mi., 35 min.

Boulder Park Accessible Trail (DCR)

The Boulder Park Accessible Trail is a short, universally accessible path off US 20 about 0.5 mi. east of the forest headquarters, where parking is available.. The trail runs roughly parallel to the highway along the Westfield River valley. The trail, named for the numerous glacial erratics in this area, passes several viewpoints, a pavilion, and interpretive signs that detail the geology and history of the area.

Boulder Park Accessible Trail

Distance from US 20 parking area to
  • trail's end: 0.3 mi., 15 min.

Mica Mine Trail (DCR)

This steep 1.5-mi.-long trail begins at the forest headquarters on US 20 in Chester. From the trailhead the path ascends straight up the slope for about 0.1 mi. before slabbing to the side of Gold Mine Brook. The trail now hugs the stream, reaching the junction of the Bad Weather Bypass at about 0.6 mi. The bypass takes a route over higher ground with better footing and is used mostly in winter and during periods of high water in Gold Mine Brook. The main trail continues along the stream, reaching the junction with the Bad Weather Bypass and Mica Mine Rd. at 0.9 mi. Mica Mine Rd. and the Mica Mine Trail both lead to Observation Hill and the H. Newman Marsh Memorial Trail. From Mica Mine Rd. the trail crosses undulating, mostly level ground fairly close to the ridge overlooking the Westfield River valley. At about 1.2 mi. the path swings northwest and climbs to the junction with the H. Newman Marsh Memorial Trail at 1.5 mi. Turn right onto the H. Newman Marsh Memorial Trail and proceed 0.1 mi. to a scenic vista on the right.

Mica Mine Trail

Distances from Chester–Blandford State Forest Headquarters to
  • first Bad Weather Bypass junction: 0.6 mi., 35 min.
  • Mica Mine Rd. and second Bad Weather Bypass junction: 0.9 mi., 55 min.
  • H. Newman Marsh Memorial Trail: 1.5 mi., 1 hr. 15 min.
  • scenic vista via H. Newman Marsh Memorial Trail: 1.6 mi., 1 hr. 25 min.

Dynamite Box Trail (DCR)

This 1.1-mi.-long path begins and ends at different points along Beulah Land Rd. From a parking area near a wetland at about 1,400 ft. elevation the trail ends just 0.1 mi. from the junction of Beulah Land Rd. and Sanderson Brook Rd. The path leaves the road at the trailhead and descends the slope fairly steeply for nearly 0.5 mi. It then jogs right and begins to run nearly due north, roughly parallel to Sanderson Brook about 100 ft. below. At 0.75 mi. the path crosses a tributary stream of Sanderson Brook to end at Beulah Land Rd. at 1.1 mi.

Dynamite Box Trail

Distances from parking area on Beulah Land Rd. (1,412 ft.) to
- tributary stream: 0.75 mi., 40 min.
- lower trailhead on Beulah Land Rd. (975 ft.): 1.1 mi., 1 hr.

H. Newman Marsh Memorial Trail (DCR)

The H. Newman Marsh Memorial Trail begins on Sanderson Brook Rd. and aggressively climbs up the hillside. The path reaches a ravine and follows the valley upslope, cresting the plateau at about 0.5 mi. The trail splits into a loop path. Continuing straight, the trail jogs along the base of Observation Hill, reaching a fork in the path at 0.7 mi. Mica Mine Rd. is a short walk to the right, while the loop trail continues left. The trail turns left (north) and passes the Mica Mine Trail on the right at 0.8 mi., then quickly reaches an overlook of the valley at 0.9 mi. The trail continues to wander along the edge of the long shoulder of Observation Hill to an overlook at the tip of the shoulder. The trail then turns south and closes the loop at 1.2 mi. Retracing its path down the slope, the path reaches Sanderson Brook Rd. at 1.7 mi.

H. Newman Marsh Memorial Trail

Distances from trailhead on Sanderson Brook Rd. to
- loop junction: 0.5 mi., 35 min.
- Mica Mine Rd. link: 0.7 mi., 50 min.
- Mica Mine Trail junction: 0.8 mi., 55 min.
- first observation area: 0.9 mi., 1 hr.
- end of loop: 1.2 mi., 1 hr. 15 min.
- Sanderson Brook Rd. trailhead: 1.7 mi., 1 hr. 35 min.

Bear Swamp

Bear Swamp is a 285-acre preserve owned and managed by The Trustees of Reservations in Ashfield. The property has about 3 mi. of trails that explore the forests, beaver pond, and ridges; its rich soils provide excellent wildflower viewing in spring. Pastoral views over orchards to the Green Mtns. are found at the Apple Valley Overlook and the vista on the Lookout Trail. The path to Apple Valley Overlook (1,544 ft.) begins opposite the entrance on Hawley Rd. The Beaver Brook Trail traces a path along an old beaver dam that sits astride a long-abandoned stone mill dam. To reach Bear Swamp from the junction of MA 116, MA 112, and Hawley Rd. in Ashfield, turn onto Hawley Rd. and proceed west for 1.7 mi. The entrance and parking are on the left.

Apple Valley Overlook Trail
Distances from Hawley Rd. (1495 ft.) to
• overlook (1,544 ft.): 0.5 mi., 15 min.

William Cullen Bryant Homestead

William Cullen Bryant was a famous nineteenth-century poet, editor, and proponent of the outdoors. His family home in Cummington is now part of a 195-acre reservation owned and managed by The Trustees of Reservations. Near the house and other buildings is a loop path called the Rivulet Trail that explores the banks and environs of this feisty stream, which inspired a number of Bryant's writings. The trail also passes through acres of old-growth forest that was ancient when Bryant tramped the woods.

To reach the William Cullen Bryant Homestead from the MA 9 and MA 112 junction in Cummington, turn onto MA 112 south and travel 1.5 mi. to a five-way junction (Bryant five-corners). Continue straight through the intersection onto Bryant Rd. and proceed 0.2 mi. to the parking area behind the red barn on the right.

Rivulet Trail (TTOR)

Near the parking area behind the big red barn is a kiosk with information and a large map. Follow the mowed path down the field, which will lead to the entrance of the Rivulet trail across Cummington Rd.

The yellow-blazed path goes easily downhill, gradually entering an area of old-growth forest along the banks of the brook. The trail splits at the beginning of the loop. Follow the brook to where the path veers away from the stream. Here a plaque etched with some verses of Bryant's poem "Rivulet" adds a nice touch to the hike. The trail continues through the woods, crosses a brook on a bridge, and comes to a fork. The left trail is a short connector path to the main loop, while the trail straight ahead curves through tall pines before rejoining the connector trail. The path swings right and soon closes the loop at Rivulet Brook. Turn right and follow the path to the trailhead by the road.

Rivulet Trail
Distance from parking area to
• parking area (circuit): 1.8 mi., 1 hr.

SUGGESTED HIKES

Easy Hikes

Rivulet Trail [lp: 1.8 mi., 1:00], page 189. A relaxing walk through woods and rare old-growth forest. The poet William Cullen Bryant played here as a child.

Universal Access Nature Trail [rt: 0.8 mi., 0:30], page 173. An easy walk that meanders along the shore of attractive Upper Highland Lake.

Pond Trail [lp: 1.0 mi., 0:40], page 187. This trail traces a path around elliptic Hallockville Pond. It can be wet in spots and caution is advised when crossing the brooks.

Moderate Hikes

Beau Bridge Trail [rt: 2.0 mi., 1:40], page 150. A hike to the observation tower and wide views atop Goat Peak.

West Side Trail, Pocumtuck Ridge Trail [rt: 2.2 miles, 2:30], page 172. This periodically steep hike leads to the top of South Sugarloaf Mtn. and its extensive views of the Connecticut River Valley.

Totem Lookout Trail [rt: 2.2 miles, 1:40], page 182. Leaving from the Mohawk Trail (MA 2) this hike climbs to ledges and rocky outcrops with beautiful views.

Strenuous Hikes

Metacomet–Monadnock Trail, Section 16: Farley to Gulf Rd. [ow: 6.7 mi., 3:50 min.] page 130. From the Miller's River in Erving, the M-M trail climbs to ledges with fine views across the valley, then continues on a mostly easy grade to the summit of Crag Mtn., which offers a sweeping perspective of the region from Mt. Monadnock to the Berkshire Hills.

Pocumtuck Ridge Trail, Section 2: Pine Nook Rd. to Canada Hill: [rt: 9.0 mi., 4:10], page 147. This long hike along the northern portion of the ridge passes many viewpoints, including the Poet's Seat Tower, which offers long views of Greenfield and the surrounding Connecticut River Valley.

PART THREE
CENTRAL MASSACHUSETTS

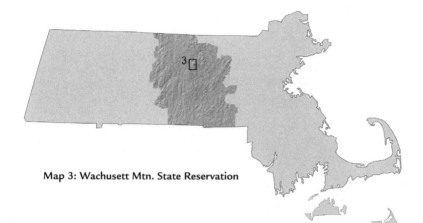

Map 3: Wachusett Mtn. State Reservation

The uplands of central Massachusetts, which include all of Worcester County and far eastern portions of adjacent Franklin, Hampshire, and Hampden Counties, are an area of low, rolling hills dominated by woodlands and the watershed of the Quabbin Reservoir, the state's largest conservation area. Reaching from Connecticut to New Hampshire, this area of Massachusetts averages about 800 ft. above sea level, with its highest point at the summit of Wachusett Mtn. (2,006 ft.) in the town of Princeton. The region is home to the 92-mi.-long Midstate Trail, which bisects the heart of the state, and the 18-mi. Tully Trail, which loops along the Tully River Valley. A small portion of the Bay Circuit Trail crosses through Southborough, the easternmost town of Worcester County. This section of the Bay Circuit Trail is covered in parts 4 and 6 of this book.

Tully Trail (TTOR)

The Tully Trail is an 18-mi. loop trail maintained by The Trustees of Reservations. Completed in 2001, it connects TTOR's Jacob's Hill and Royalston Falls Reservations, as well as Tully Lake Campground and a portion of the lake itself. It travels through both the Tully Mtn. and the Fish Brook Wildlife Management Areas, managed by MassWildlife, and through three state forests—Orange, Royalston, and Warwick. The high point is Tully Mtn. (1,163 ft.) with its extensive views from open ledges. Much of the eastern section passes through the Tully Lake Flood Control Area. Some of this section can be flooded in wet weather; call the Tully Lake Park Office (978-249-9150) for current conditions.

The trail is well marked with yellow rectangular blazes, as well as an occasional white-and-purple Tully Trail sign. In some areas, the trail is lightly traveled and the path is indistinct; please pay careful attention to the blazes, which are highly visible. Maps can be downloaded from www. thetrustees.org. and are available at the Tully Lake Campground and Royalston Falls trailheads.

To reach the trailhead at Tully Lake Campground in Royalston from MA 2, take Exit 18, then turn left onto MA 2A toward Athol. From Main St. (MA 2A) in Athol follow MA 32 north about 4 mi., crossing Tully Dam and passing the Tully Recreation Area on the right. Continue for another 0.5 mi., then turn right onto Doane Hill Rd. Proceed 1.0 mi to the Tully Lake Campground entrance on the right.

Section 1. Tully Lake Campground to Athol–Richmond Rd. (6.5 mi.)

This section begins at the entrance to the Tully Lake Campground. From the campground head right (east) on Doane Hill Rd., crossing the east branch of the Tully River on a bridge. Just beyond the bridge the trail turns left (north) and follows a wide, flat woods road that borders the Tully Lake Flood Control Area. At 0.7 mi. the trail turns right (east) and begins a steep ascent of the escarpment using switchbacks. At the top of the ridge the trail levels off and bears left (north) to run the edge of the ridge. At 1.0 mi. the scenic overlook called the Ledges is reached, with a view across the Tully Valley.

The trail continues on easy grades along the forested ridge, enters Jacob's Hill Reservation (TTOR), then descends and crosses the brook on the rocks above Spirit Falls at 1.5 mi. (use caution on crossing, especially at high water). At the north bank of the brook the trail crosses the Jacobs Hill Reservation main trail; turning right leads to the reservation parking area while the rocky path on the left descends steeply along the falls to the woods road at the base of the valley.

At 2.0 mi. the trail reaches a rocky overlook providing extensive views of Long Pond below as well as Tully Mtn., Mt. Grace, and the Berkshire Hills. From here the trail descends slightly to a woods road and follows it north out to a large power line. At 2.2 mi. it crosses the power line and turns left (yellow arrow on tree), descending the power line on a rough, indistinct footpath.

Near the bottom of the hill it merges with the orange-blazed trail coming from the left (south), and turns right into the woods. From there it continues north, skirting along the east side of a beaver wetland for 0.3 mi., then crossing the stream on a footbridge (Caution: This area can be wet or flooded during high water periods). The Tully and orange-blazed trails continue west for 0.3 mi., turn north toward the clearing near a house, then turn left (northwest) down a grassy right of way, crossing the Tully River on a footbridge at 3.5 mi. At 3.7 mi. the Tully Trail reenters the woods; the orange-blazed path leaves left (south) as it heads to Tully Lake Campground.

The Tully Trail continues straight ahead with the steep slope of Davis Hill on the left, crossing through a yellow gate onto Warwick Rd. (MA 68) at 4.0 mi. The trail turns left (northwest) uphill on Warwick Rd., then bears right into the woods and enters Royalston State Forest at 4.2 mi. on a wide woods road. The trail follows this road northwest through pine and mixed forest on an almost level grade. At 5.4 mi. the trail crosses Falls Brook and enters Royalston Falls Reservation (TTOR). On a rough pathway it ascends partway up the steep hillside on the northeast side of the brook, then continues along the hillside with many small ups and downs, finally climbing to the top of Royalston Falls at 5.8 mi. A cable railing allows safe views of the 50-ft. falls from several perspectives atop the dramatic gorge.

Above the falls, the trail continues along the brook. At 6.0 mi., it crosses Falls Brook on a wood bridge and joins the white-blazed Metacomet–Monadnock trail. A wood shelter at the crossing offers first-come, first-served accommodations for campers. The trail climbs the hillside on moderate grades, reaching Athol–Richmond Rd. and the parking area for Royalston Falls adjacent the Newton Cemetery at 6.5 mi.

Tully Trail: Tully Lake Campground to Athol–Richmond Rd.

Distances from Tully Lake Campground (650 ft.) to
- the Ledges: 1.0 mi., 45 min.
- Spirit Falls Brook: 1.5 mi., 1 hr.
- Royalston Falls: 5.8 mi., 3 hr.
- Royalston Falls parking area on MA 32 (1,192 ft.): 6.5 mi., 3 hr. 50 min.

Section 2. Athol–Richmond Rd. to Tully–Warwick Rd. (6.7 mi.)

This portion of the trail begins at the parking area for the Royalston Falls property. To reach the trailhead, from the intersection of MA 68 and 32 in West Royalston, proceed on Rt. 32 N about 1.7 mi. to the parking area for Royalston Falls, marked with a Trustees of Reservations sign. There is a small information board where maps for the Tully Trail can sometimes be obtained. The beginning of the section also coincides with the white-blazed Metacomet–Monadnock Trail.

From the parking lot cross Athol–Richmond Rd. (MA 32), heading west across the broad crest of Wyman Hill and descending through a red pine grove at 0.4 mi. to gravel Bliss Hill Rd. at 0.8 mi. Here the M–M Trail crosses Bliss Hill Rd. and the yellow-blazed Tully Trail turns left (south), following the road for 0.4 mi. At 1.2 mi., the trail turns right (west) into a private driveway. *Note: For the next 2 mi. the trail exists through the courtesy of private landowners. Please stay on the trail.*

At 1.6 mi. the path runs straight ahead, heading slightly uphill at a fork. The road climbs slightly, curves left, and then descends gently downhill, crossing a power line at 2.2 mi. At 2.4 mi. the trail joins a private drive coming from Warwick Rd., turning left (southwest) downhill on this road. At 2.5 mi. the trail turns abruptly left on a woods road, ascending in pleasant grades up the slope of Bliss Hill. The trail narrows to a footpath, coming to an outlook at ledges at 3.3 mi. with views to the west across the valley to Mt. Grace. The trail turns left (east) away from the outlook, ascending to the wooded summit of Bliss Hill at 3.5 mi. Steeply descend the south slope of Bliss Hill on a rough path; watch blazes with care here.

The grade soon becomes easier, and the trail descends gradually through mixed woods to (paved) Bliss Hill Rd. at 4.2 mi. The trail crosses the road and ascends to the top of a low ridge at 4.5 mi. It then descends steadily to Fish Brook, entering the Fish Brook Wildlife Management Area. The trail curves left (north), following this lively brook, then bears slightly away from it on an abandoned cart road.

At 4.9 mi. the trail crosses Fish Brook on a bridge and bears sharp right (southeast), ascending Butterworth Ridge on easy grades. It crosses the wooded ridge, enters Orange State Forest, then descends on moderate grades through hemlock mixed forest to unpaved Butterworth Rd. at 6.2 mi. The trail turns right (southwest) onto Butterworth Rd., following it on mostly level grades to its intersection with Tully–Warwick Rd. at 6.7 mi.

Tully Trail: Athol–Richmond Rd. to Tully–Warwick Rd.

Distances from Athol–Richmond Rd. (MA 32) (1,192 ft.) to
- Bliss Hill Rd.: 0.8 mi., 25 min.
- summit of Bliss Hill: 3.5 mi., 1 hr. 40 min.
- Fish Brook Bridge: 4.9 mi., 2 hr. 35 min.
- Tully–Warwick Rd. (583 ft): 6.7 mi., 3 hr. 25 min.

Section 3. Tully–Warwick Rd. to Tully Lake Campground (5.2 mi.)

This section begins at the intersection of Tully–Warwick Rd. and Butterworth Rd, about 2 mi. northwest of the village of North Orange. The trail begins with a road walk generally southeast on Tully–Warwick Rd., passing between Gale Farm and the Tully Meadow Wildlife Management Area (WMA). *Caution: The road has narrow shoulders.*

At 1.5 mi. cross a road bridge over the Tully River, then turn abruptly left onto a wide logging road. The trail proceeds north through pine forest on flat grades, passing a clearing at 1.7 mi. At 1.8 mi., in a logged area, the trail turns right (east), ascending the fairly steep west side of Tully Mtn. on moderate grades through forest that is being actively logged. Pay close attention to the yellow blazes here, ignoring other blazes and flagging. At 2.1 mi., just north of the Tully Mtn. summit, the path comes to a T-intersection. The Tully Trail now forks into a loop path at 2.5 mi. The right (south) fork passes over the summit of Tully Mtn. (1,163 ft.) at 0.1 mi. from the T-junction before making a steep descent of the mountain's south flank. Just downslope of the summit is a long rock ledge providing extensive views, including Tully Lake to the east, Mt. Monadnock to the north (left), and Wachusett Mtn. and the Wapack Range in the distance. At 0.5 mi. from the junction the loop trail turns left (north) while the access trail continues to the Mountain Rd. parking area (0.6 mi.). The left fork heads north on easy grades down a woods road through mixed forest. The trail makes a long curve right eventually turning south, meeting the south loop trail at about 0.3 mi. from the T-junction (the parking area on Mountain Rd. is about 0.5 mi. down the south loop).

From the loop junction the Tully Trail heads east, descending easily into a pine forest, crossing a brook on logs and reaching a grassy driveway at 3.1 mi. The trail continues straight ahead (east) through the Tully Mtn. WMA, following the edge of a bouldery hillside through hemlock woods. Crossing a wet area, the trail reaches an old woods road and turns right (south). It follows the road gently downhill, passing through a marshy area and reaching unpaved Royalston Rd. at 3.7 mi. It turns left (east) onto Royalston Rd., climbing slightly, then descends a short hill to paved Athol–Richmond Rd. (MA 32) at 3.9 mi.

The trail turns right (south) onto MA 32, crosses the road, and turns left into the parking lot for the Tully Lake Recreation Area at 4.0 mi. Continue straight (east) toward the lake at a sign for the Tully Trail. Turn left at the lakeshore, to pass through beautiful pine forest on easy grades. The interpretive Storey Trail leaves left, then rejoins the trail at 4.3 mi. At the northern end of Tully Lake the trail approaches Doane Hill Rd. and turns right, briefly parallel to the road. At 4.7 mi. turn abruptly right (southwest) away from the road to travel on a lovely point of land extending along one arm of the lake. The trail soon heads left (east) along the lake, finally leaving the lakeshore and passing through thick woods, portions of which bear evidence of damage from a 2006 microburst, to reach the Tully Lake Campground at 5.2 mi. Popular Doane's Falls, a long series of cascades and falls, lies just east of the campground, with parking areas on Doane Hill Rd.

Tully Trail: Tully–Warwick Rd. to Tully Lake Campground

Distances from Tully–Warwick Rd. (583 ft.) to
- Tully River Bridge: 1.5 mi., 40 min.
- trail junction on Tully Mtn. (1,164 ft.): 2.5 mi., 1 hr. 20 min.
- parking area for Tully Lake Recreation Area: 4.0 mi., 2 hr. 35 min.
- Tully Lake Campground (650 ft.): 5.2 mi., 3 hr. 20 min.

Midstate Trail (WCAMC)

The yellow-triangle-blazed Midstate Trail runs north-south through Worcester County from the Rhode Island to the New Hampshire border. It provides hikers with access to most of the significant summits and many of the scenic areas of central Massachusetts. Its 92-mi. length provides numerous opportunities for overnight treks, and its connection in the north with the Wapack Trail extending into New Hampshire makes it part of one of the longest trail networks in the region.

The Midstate Trail was originally developed in the 1920s, when it ran from Mt. Watatic to Wachusett Mtn. In 1972 plans for the trail's extension to the Rhode Island line were formulated, and the complete trail was dedicated on September 7, 1985. The AMC Worcester Chapter's Midstate Trail Committee produces the 55-page *Massachusetts Midstate Trail Guide* containing topographical maps, trail descriptions, and community highlights covering the entire length of the trail. For more information call 508-797-9744 or visit www.midstatetrail.org for trail updates.

Section 1. New Hampshire State Line to MA 12 (7.7 mi.)

The Midstate Trail begins east of the state boundary marker on the Massachusetts–New Hampshire line. Heading south on the combined Midstate and Wapack Trails (blazed with yellow triangles), the path follows old cart roads, climbs Nutting Hill (1,615 ft.), and descends to a saddle before ascending Mt. Watatic (1,813 ft.) via switchbacks. From the summit the trail proceeds west at a steep grade down the mountain and reaches the state parking area on MA 119 at about 1.1 mi. This parking area is 1.6 mi. west of the intersection with MA 101, and is the closest car access to the northern end of the trail. From the parking area the Midstate Trail crosses MA 119 and goes south on paved Pierce Rd., turning left off the road at 1.7 mi. to ascend Fisher Hill (1,548 ft.) at 2.4 mi. From here the trail descends to a saddle then climbs to the crest of Blueberry Hill (1,473 ft.) before skirting a timber harvest and descending to the Camp Winnekeag parking lot on MA 101 at 3.8 mi.

From the junction of MA 101 and Holt Rd. (look for a sign on a tree) the trail briefly follows Holt Rd., then turns right off it onto a woods trail at 4.1 mi. It is temporarily rerouted here around a subdivision construction project; watch for obvious markers along the edge of the site. The trail now climbs steeply up the ridge, passing an excellent view of Stodge Pond and Mt. Watatic, en route to the flat crest of Mt. Hunger (1,450 ft.) at 5.5 mi. The trail descends and crosses Russell Hill Rd. (6.3 mi.). From the road the trail has been relocated and is marked with yellow tape flags to MA 12, which it reaches at 7.7 mi.

Midstate Trail: New Hampshire State Line to MA 12

Distances from New Hampshire state line (1,562 ft.) to
- Camp Winnekeag parking lot: 3.8 mi., 1 hr. 45 min.
- Mt. Hunger (1,450 ft.): 5.5 mi., 3 hr.
- MA 12 (869 ft.): 7.7 mi., 3 hr. 35 min.

Section 2. MA 12 to Wyman Brook (10.6 mi.)

The trail crosses Route 12 near Jewell Hill Rd. It crosses Phillips Brook and Whitney Hill Rd., continues along a low ridge, and enters an isolated section of state forest where a blue-blazed connector trail leaves right to a parking area in less than 0.2 mi. The path reaches Muddy Pond Shelter (Westminster Conservation Commission) at 2.3 mi. on the shore of Muddy Pond.

After following a circuitous route around Muddy Pond on an old road-way, the trail turns right into the woods, continues about 1 mi., and comes to a junction with Bragg Hill Rd. and S. Ashburnham Rd. Cross S. Ash-burnham Rd. and follow Whitmanville Rd. (paved) to its end and continue under the railroad trestle known as the Graffiti Bridge into the woods. The trail heads in a generally south-southeast direction, passing many trail in-tersections. It turns to follow the back edge of farm fields, then crosses Bathrick Rd., MA 2A, and then MA 2. After crossing MA 2 on the Wy-man Rd. overpass, the trail heads back through woods briefly, then skirts the rear parking lot of the Wachusett Village Inn. The trail continues up a cart road, then onto a footpath which crosses Wyman Brook before reach-ing the junction of Narrows Rd. and Stone Hill Rd. at 10.6 mi.

Midstate Trail: MA 12 to Wyman Brook

Distances from MA 12 (809 ft.) to
- Muddy Pond Shelter (1,041 ft.): 2.3 mi., 55 min.
- Wyman Brook: 10.1 mi., 4 hr. 50 min.
- Stone Hill Rd. (805 ft.): 10.6 mi., 5 hr. 10 min.

Section 3. Wyman Brook to Redemption Rock (MA 140) (3.4 mi.)

From Wyman Brook at the junction of Narrows Rd. and Stone Hill Rd. (cumulative mile mark 18.3) the trail follows Stone Hill Rd. about 400 ft., then turns left into the woods. After 600 ft. it descends along a stone wall, then turns right. After passing through a boulder-strewn area, the trail turns right at an unmarked trail junction. Continuing south in the Leom-inster State Forest, it reaches a stone stairway built by the CCC in the 1930s that leads to a fine view at Crow Hills, from which Boston is visible in the distance *(caution: rock climbers use the cliffs here)*. The trail descends very steeply as it reaches a rocky outlook with a view of Wachusett Mtn., passes a large glacial boulder, then crosses MA 140 about 200 ft. from Re-demption Rock, a historic site, at 3.4 mi.

Midstate Trail: Wyman Brook to Redemption Rock (MA 140)

Distance from Stone Hill Rd. (805 ft.) to

- junction and overlook at Crow Hill: 1.8 mi., 50 min.
- view of Wachusett Mtn.: 3 mi., 1 hr. 25 min.
- MA 140 (Redemption Rock) (910 ft.): 3.4 mi., 1 hr. 50 min.

Section 4. Redemption Rock (MA 140) to Wachusett Meadows (5.2 mi.)

The trail leaves Redemption Rock (cumulative mile mark 21.8) in a south-westerly direction and soon crosses a brook. For the next 1.0 mi. the trail traverses city of Fitchburg water supply lands. After 0.75 mi. the trail crosses Mountain Rd. (paved) and proceeds into the Wachusett Mtn. Ski Area and Wachusett Mtn. State Reservation parking area. Information, water, and toilet facilities are available at the state park visitor center, about 1.0 mi. south on Mountain Rd. The trail continues uphill behind the buildings on a woods road, bearing right, and passes the glacial boulder called Balance Rock at 1.6 mi. It proceeds up the slope to a junction with the Old Indian Trail and Semuhenna Trail. At 2.2 mi. the trail crosses paved Up Summit Rd. then proceeds steeply through old-growth forest as it ascends Wachusett Mtn., reaching the top (2,006 ft.) with its stone lookouts at 2.3 mi.

Descend the mountain on a number of trails, including Moutain House and Link Trails, to a bridge where the Midstate Trail follows the Harrington Trail west past the Princeton Wind Electric Generator Farm and enters the Massachusetts Audubon Society's Wachusett Meadows Wildlife Sanctuary at 5.2 mi. The trail follows well-marked trails (yellow Midstate blazes) on relatively level ground through the sanctuary to Goodnough Rd., where the sanctuary's offices and a parking area are located.

Midstate Trail: Redemption Rock (MA 140) to Wachusett Meadows (map 3: A3–E1)

Distances from MA 140 (Redemption Rock) (910 ft.) to

- Balance Rock (1,200 ft.): 1.7 mi., 300 ft., 40 min.
- Wachusett Mtn. (2,006 ft.): 2.7 mi., 1,100 ft., 2 hr.
- Wachusett Meadows Wildlife Sanctuary (1,030 ft.): 5.2 mi., 1,200 ft. (rev. 150 ft.) 3 hr. 50 min.

Section 5. Wachusett Meadows to Barre Falls Dam (10.8 mi.)

From Goodnough Rd. the Midstate Trail continues atop a low ridge through woodlands and open fields with wetlands below to the east to its intersection with MA 62 in Princeton opposite Ball Hill Rd. at 2.25 mi. (cumulative mile mark 29.25). The trail here follows several paved roads (Ball Hill Rd., Wheeler Rd., and Bigelow Rd.), the last of which turns into unpaved Bushy La. The trail follows Bushy La. across MA 68 at 5.5 mi., and less than 0.25 mi. farther on crosses MA 56. (*Caution: both highways are busy.*) After crossing MA 56 the trail briefly follows a cart road before joining Davis St. heading into North Rutland. Davis St. ends at MA 68. Cross the Ware River on a highway bridge (6.4 mi.). On the far side of the river the Midstate Trail picks up a woods path on the west bank.

The path follows the river, then turns away from it and crosses Intervale Rd. at 7.0 mi. Follow woods paths and roads around a small hill, reaching an old foundation at 9.6 mi. Cross the west branch of the Ware River on a plank bridge (use caution, the bridge is in poor condition) at Brigham Rd. (9.8 mi.), then enter land managed by Massachusetts Division of Fish and Wildlife and cross the Barre Falls flood-control dam, operated by the Corps of Engineers, at 10.8 mi.

Midstate Trail: Wachusett Meadows to Barre Falls Dam

Distances from Wachusett Meadows Sanctuary (1,030 ft.) to
- MA 62 (961 ft.): 2.25 mi., 1 hr. 10 min.
- Ware River: 6.4 mi., 2 hr. 25 min.
- Intervale Rd.: 7.0 mi., 2 hr. 50 min.
- Barre Falls Dam (830 ft): 10.8 mi., 4 hr. 10 min.

Section 6. Barre Falls Dam to MA 122 (5.7 mi.)

The Midstate Trail at Barre Falls Dam is accessible from the junction of MA 62 and MA 68 by following MA 62 west about 2.2 mi. The road to the dam and recreation area exits left (marked by a sign). Continue down the road 1.5 mi. to a parking area. *This portion of the trail passes through a wildlife management area that is actively hunted in fall.* From the parking area the trail follows the road east 0.1 mi. There it turns left into the woods and continues to Harding Hill (1,031 ft.), where there is no view. After descending 0.5 mi., the trail crosses dirt Ruben Walker Rd. near a small pond. It traverses a small field, continues through pines, and skirts Stevens Brook before following alongside Blood Swamp for a considerable distance. Just before coming to a dike, the trail turns left onto an old road and continues as far as the Rutland–Oakham town-line marker, where it turns left toward another dike. After ascending the dike, it goes straight ahead (south) on a ramp road, then at 3.5 mi. passes under a power line onto a gravel road (closed to vehicles). It continues on this road 1.6 mi. to a junction of roads, where it enters the woods. After 0.6 mi. it comes out on MA 122 (busy) in Rutland at 5.7 mi.

Midstate Trail: Barre Falls Dam to MA 122

Distances from Barre Falls Dam (830 ft.) to
- gravel road: 3.5 mi., 1 hr. 15 min.
- MA 122 (862 ft.): 5.7 mi., 1 hr. 55 min.

Section 7. MA 122 to MA 31 (6.9 mi.)

From MA 122 the Midstate Trail climbs around a hill, first southeast and then south through several stone walls, and continues to Crawford St. at 0.6 mi. It crosses Crawford St. and a small brook, then climbs gradually to a woods road and enters Rutland State Park. A pipe spring is passed at 1.9 mi., just 0.1 mi. from the shore of Long Pond. The trail turns left (south) onto this road and continues through open woods to an access trail on the right. A shelter that can house four to five persons (no water) is located here. The trail proceeds downhill (south) on the woods road past the Midstate Trail halfway marker to reach the Treasure Valley Boy Scout Reservation. After passing under high-tension lines, it crosses diagonally to the right and continues through a deciduous forest. After crossing a stream, it passes an old cottage on the right. In 0.5 mi. the trail crosses a cutover area 50 yd. south of East Hill Rd.

The trail continues south through mixed woods to a large glacial erratic called Samson's Pebble at 4.7 mi. (cumulative mile mark 48.1; watch blazes carefully as there are a number of other trails here). After descending southeast and skirting the edge of a swamp on the left, the trail passes over several stone walls. After a long downgrade it reaches the southern shore of Browning Pond. Browning Pond Rd. is just 100 yd. south. The trail turns left onto Browning Pond Rd. and passes several houses, then turns left onto Boy Scout land. After continuing 0.7 mi. through the woods, the trail again intersects Browning Pond Rd. It turns left onto the road and in 0.2 mi. reaches MA 31 (paved) in North Spencer, across from a sign for Camp Marshall 4-H camp at 6.9 mi.

Midstate Trail: MA 122 to MA 31

Distances from MA 122 (862 ft.) to
- spring: 1.9 mi., 45 min.
- MA 31 (878 ft.): 6.9 mi., 2 hr. 50 min.

Section 8. MA 31 to MA 9 (7.2 mi.)

Reach the parking area for this section from MA 9 by traveling north on Paxton Rd. for 1.4 mi., turning left onto Gold Nugget Rd., and traveling 0.6 mi. to McCormack Rd. Take a right onto McCormack Rd. and continue north 1.9 mi. to the 4-H Club and parking area on the left.

From MA 31 the trail enters Spencer State Forest and follows a path marked Wildflower Trail. At the end of this nature walk the Midstate Trail ascends Buck Hill (1,014 ft.), where there are no views. It then descends steeply southeast past Buck Hill Shelter on the right. The trail reaches Paxton Rd. at 3.3 mi., turns right onto Paxton Rd., proceeds 100 ft., then turns left through open woods bordering the Spencer Airport.

After passing a small pond and shelter, the trail ascends to the open top of Moose Hill (1,099 ft.), with excellent views at 5.1 mi. Sugden Reservoir can be seen just below the hill. At the bottom of the hill parking is available off Cross Rd. at the gate to the dam (5.6 mi.). From here the trail proceeds south through Spencer on paths and roads, finally reaching its intersection with MA 9 at 7.2 mi.

Midstate Trail: MA 31 to MA 9

Distances from MA 31 (878 ft.) to
- Paxton Rd. (997 ft.): 3.3 mi., 1 hr. 25 min.
- Moose Hill (1,099 ft.): 5.1 mi., 2 hr. 40 min.
- MA 9 (1,010 ft.): 7.2 mi., 3 hr. 40 min.

Section 9. MA 9 to Railroad Bridge (Charlton) (8.4 mi.)

Parking for this section is in the lot of the abandoned courthouse on MA 9 across from the Spencer Country Inn and about 100 yd. east of the trail crossing.

From MA 9 the trail enters a driveway and continues along the town line. When the driveway bends right the trail goes straight along the edge of a field for 0.4 mi. to reach the Sibley memorial stone at 0.8 mi. Sibley Audubon Reservation is entered at 1.5 mi. The trail turns left onto the road and in 0.1 mi. comes to Greenville St. (paved). It follows a stone wall for about 500 ft., passes by a woodland for the same distance, then cruises atop a stone wall and beneath a power line, soon reaching Jones Rd. at 3.5 mi. It turns right onto Jones Rd., then continues 0.8 mi. to Wilson Rd. (paved), turns right onto Wilson Rd., then turns left onto Charlton Rd. It follows Charlton Rd. 0.8 mi., then turns left onto Clark Rd.

In 0.1 mi. the trail turns onto Borkum Rd., follows Borkum Rd. across the Four Chimneys Wildlife Management Area (parking available). At 7.5 mi. the trail takes a cart road over the pipeline and reaches the intersection of the pipeline and Gould Rd. at 7.9 mi. The trail turns right onto Gould Rd. and arrives at the railroad bridge at Charlton at 8.4 mi.

Midstate Trail: MA 9 to Railroad Bridge (Charlton)

Distances from MA 9 (1,010 ft.) to
- Sibley Audubon Reservation: 1.5 mi., 40 min.
- Jones Rd.: 3.5 mi., 1 hr. 20 min.
- Gould Rd.: 7.9 mi., 3 hr. 45 min.
- railroad bridge (Charlton) (860 ft.): 8.4 mi., 4 hr. 5 min.

Section 10. Railroad Bridge (Charlton) to Cascade Brook (6.1 mi.)

After crossing the railroad bridge onto a blacktop road, the trail continues south, passing a campground on the left (east) and Wee Laddie Pond on the right (west). At a road junction the path continues on Cemetery Rd. to Fay Mtn. Orchard—a white colonial homestead that was the home of Dr. William T. Morton, the first doctor to use ether as an anesthetic. (See the historical marker there.) The trail turns left onto a paved road, then right onto Northside Rd. to the historic Ryder Tavern on the corner. The trail follows.

Northside Rd. over a bridge spanning the Massachusetts Turnpike (I-90) at 1.4 mi., then turns left over wire fences into the woods. In 0.4 mi. it turns right onto a gas pipeline and follows this 0.3 mi. to a dirt road. The trail turns left onto the road toward some abandoned buildings and continues 0.3 mi. to paved Carroll Hill Rd., where it turns right and passes beneath US 20 using a cow tunnel at 3.1 mi.

Bearing left at the crossing, the trail enters the woods, turns right onto a blacktop road, then turns left onto a woods road. At a horse pasture it crosses a barbed-wire fence on a stile, then crosses a dam and passes a small pond on the right to emerge from the woods at a power line at 4.1 mi. The trail follows the power line 0.3 mi. to paved Putnam Hill Rd. It turns right onto Putnam Hill Rd., left onto paved Turner Rd., and reaches Cascade Brook as it is piped beneath Old Charlton Rd. at 6.1 mi.

Midstate Trail: Railroad Bridge (Charlton) to Cascade Brook

Distances from railroad bridge (860 ft.) to

- Massachusetts Turnpike: 1.4 mi., 35 min.
- cow tunnel (US 20): 3.1 mi., 1 hr. 20 min.
- power lines: 4.1 mi., 1 hr. 55 min.
- Old Charlton Rd. (487 ft.): 6.1 mi., 2 hr. 50 min.

Section 11. Cascade Brook to MA 16 (Douglas) (14.9 mi.)

The trail leaves Old Charlton Rd. in Oxford at the Cascade Brook crossing, bearing right. It follows the left side of this attractive brook, which might be dry in fall. The trail passes a large pile of rocks along the brook and in less than 0.5 mi. crosses the French River on a pedestrian bridge, coming to a dirt road that ends on paved Rocky Hill Rd. at 2.8 mi. The trail turns right (east) and continues through a residential area to MA 12 at a traffic light, then proceeds past the Oxford Police Station to reach paved Dana Rd. and heads beneath I-395 through the underpass. From Dana Rd. the trail travels on Brown Rd. for about 1.25 mi., then turns left onto Lovett Rd. The trail heads east to the end of Lovett Rd. and a cable gate with views of Sacarrappa Pond. From the gate the road becomes rutted and steep at 6.9 mi., then evens out and crosses a brook on a plank bridge before turning right onto Town Farm Rd. at 7.8 mi. The path runs up Whittier Hill (849 ft.), with long pastoral views including Wachusett

Mtn. to the north. At Central Turnpike in West Sutton the trail turns left and proceeds 1 block, then bears right to continue south on Douglas Rd. (paved) past the Whittier dairy farm. The path crosses the town line, where the road changes its name to Northwest Main St. and after another 0.3 mi. turns right onto an old woods road at 10.6 mi.

The trail now follows paths and old woods roads on a winding, 4.2-mi. route through Douglas State Forest, generally skirting rather than climbing the hills. It emerges from the forest just north of its intersection with MA 16 at 14.9 mi.

Midstate Trail: Cascade Brook to MA 16 (Douglas)

Distances from Cascade Brook (487 ft.) to
- Rocky Hill Rd. (520 ft.): 2.8 mi., 1 hr. 10 min.
- Town Farm Rd.: 7.8 mi., 2 hr. 35 min.
- MA 16 (705 ft.): 14.9 mi., 5 hr. 10 min.

Section 12. MA 16 (Douglas) to Rhode Island Line (5.5 mi.)

To reach the parking area for the Midstate Trail from Exit 2 off I-395, drive east on MA 16 for 4.3 mi. to the trailhead and small parking area located just east of the trail. The final section of the Midstate Trail is in many respects the most remote. The trail meanders for slightly more than 5 mi. through the southern section of Douglas State Forest, following paths and woods roads and crossing several old railroad grades and jeep roads. At 2.0 mi. it crosses Southwest Main St. An open shelter with a table and fireplace near an old cellar hole is reached at 5.0 mi. The trail ends 0.5 mi. beyond, at the Rhode Island state line at 5.5 mi.

Midstate Trail: MA 16 (Douglas) to Rhode Island Line

Distances from MA 16 (705 ft.) to
- Southwest Main St.: 2.0 mi., 50 min.
- southern terminus of Midstate Trail (680 ft.): 5.5 mi., 2 hr. 35 min

Mt. Watatic

Home to the second-highest summit in Massachusetts east of the Berkshires, 1,832-ft. Mt. Watatic offers outstanding views from its rocky upper and lower summits that include Wachusett Mtn., the city of Boston, Mt. Monadnock, and, on clear days, the Berkshire Hills. Mt. Watatic is the southern terminus of the Wapack Range, a chain of low mountains that extends for more than 20 mi. into southern New Hampshire. The summit was once home to a ski area and fire tower, both of which have been removed. The mountain was protected in 2001 thanks to collaborative efforts of the Mount Grace Land Conservation Trust and the Ashburnham and Ashby Land Trusts. Adjacent Nutting Hill, a shoulder of Mt. Watatic, offers additional views from its partially open top. Thousands of raptors may be seen on optimal days during autumn migrations here.

Wapack and Midstate Trails (FOW, WCAMC)

The Massachusetts portion of the Wapack Trail coincides with the northernmost section of the Midstate Trail. From the parking lot on MA 119, 1.4 mi. west of MA 101, the combined routes lead over the summit of Mt. Watatic and Nutting Hill to the New Hampshire state line, where the Midstate Trail ends and the Wapack Trail continues north over the mountains of the Wapack Range to its northern terminus on North Pack Monadnock Mtn. near Greenfield, N.H.

From the parking area, the trail leads north past a small pond to reach a marked junction at 0.3 mi. Here the State Line Trail (blue blazes) now follows the old route of the Midstate Trail and continues north about 1 mi. to the New Hampshire border. The combined Midstate and Wapack Trails turn right and ascend the south face of Mt. Watatic, with moderate grades alternating with steep pitches. After passing through a rocky section under hemlocks and passing an overlook, the trail reaches the summit at 1.2 mi.

From the summit the Wapack and Midstate Trails head northwest past the site of the recently removed fire tower, following a grassy path downhill about 30 ft. to the trees (look for a sign and/or directions painted on the ledges). A ski area once operated on the north slope, though the lifts have been removed and the old ski slopes and grassy areas are now largely grown in. The trail descends moderately through woods and stone walls before ascending to the partially open ledges of Nutting Hill at 1.9 mi., with views of Mt. Watatic's west side and Wachusett Mtn. Descending from Nutting Hill, the trail widens into an old cart track, passes a junction at 2.1 mi. (those making a loop hike via the State Line Trail should follow signs for the MA 119 parking area), and at 2.4 mi. reaches a stone wall marking the New Hampshire state line.

Wapack and Midstate Trails

Distances from MA 119 parking area (1,242 ft.) to
- summit of Mt. Watatic (1,832 ft.): 1.2 mi., 1 hr.
- Massachusetts–New Hampshire line: 2.4 mi., 1 hr. 35 min

State Line Trail (FOW, WCAMC)

This blue-blazed trail runs generally north-south from near MA 119 in Ashburnham to the original terminus of the Midstate Trail on the New Hampshire border. The lower portion is often combined with the Midstate Trail as a circuit over Mt. Watatic and Nutting Hill. From the Wapack Trail parking area follow the Wapack-Midstate Trail (yellow triangles) north 0.3 mi. to the start of the State Line Trail. Here the Wapack-Midstate Trail turns right (east), while the State Line Trail makes a rocky climb north along the old route of the Midstate Trail. At a marked junction, the path bears left off the wide trail (continue straight here to the nearby junction with the Wapack and Midstate Trails if doing the Nutting Hill–Watatic circuit) and winds on a narrow track to a marker at the Massachusetts–New Hampshire state line at 1.1 mi.

State Line Trail

Distance from MA 119 parking area to
- New Hampshire state line: 1.1 mi., 40 min.

Wachusett Mtn. State Reservation

The summit of Wachusett Mtn. (2,006 ft.) is the highest point east of the Connecticut River and south of New Hampshire. The Wachusett Mtn. State Reservation encompasses the mountain and protects 2,250 acres in the towns of Princeton and Westminster. Though its height is modest by the standards of other New England peaks, Wachusett Mtn. rises alone above the surrounding landscape, and panoramic views from the summit stretch the length of Massachusetts from the Boston skyline to the Berkshire Hills on clear days.

The reservation offers 17 mi. of hiking trails, including 3.9 mi. of the Midstate Trail, and is home to the largest tract of old-growth forest east of the Connecticut River, with trees up to 350 years old. The park headquarters and visitor center is located on Mountain Rd. in Princeton, which is also the starting point for several of the hiking trails; trail maps are available here. A paved automobile road to the summit is open to vehicular traffic from late spring to early fall. Other roads on the reservation are closed to cars at all times. A popular ski area operates on the north slope of the mountain during winter. Hikers are not permitted on the alpine ski slopes and trails except at crossings. Universal-access restrooms and picnic areas are available.

Hiking trails are generally marked with blue triangles. Those trails that are part of the Midstate Trail system also have yellow blazes. To reach the Wachusett Mtn. State Reservation headquarters and visitor center from MA 2, take MA 140 south 2 mi. and turn right onto to Mile Hill Rd. Follow Mile Hill Rd. for 0.5 mi., passing the ski area on the right, and continue uphill to the reservation entrance and visitor center on the right-hand side of Mountain Rd. Approaching from the south, take Mountain Rd. about 3.0 mi. north of the MA 31 and MA 62 junction in Princeton center.

Midstate Trail

The long-distance Midstate Trail, marked by yellow triangular blazes, traverses Wachusett Mtn. See Midstate Trail, Section 4, Redemption Rock (MA 140) to Wachusett Meadows, on page 200.

Jack Frost Trail (DCR)

This trail was named for the late Dr. Harold P. Frost, who scouted and cleared most of its length. Located on the south side of the mountain, it climbs the peak's southern shoulder. To reach the trailhead, take Mtn. Rd. 1.2 mi. north from Princeton center. Turn left (uphill) at a Y-intersection onto Westminster Rd. Parking is available at the intersection with Administration Rd., which is closed to motor vehicles. Machias Pool is the small pond adjacent the parking area; the water is not potable, and swimming is prohibited. Proceed on foot up Administration Rd. for 0.4 mi., where the trail begins on a woods road on the right.

The trail crosses a brook and an intersection with the Lower Link Trail, then turns right and continues east until it crosses a power line at 0.3 mi. Here it begins to ascend more steeply through old hemlocks, gaining the lower ridge and passing High Meadow Trail on the right. The trail then turns north along the brow of the ridge before climbing to the Mountain House Trail about 0.2 mi. below the summit.

Jack Frost Trail (map 3: C2)
Distances from Administration Rd. trailhead (1,275 ft.) to
- Mountain House Trail (1,800 ft.): 0.8 mi., 500 ft., 40 min.
- summit of Wachusett Mtn. via Mountain House Trail (2,006 ft.): 1.0 mi., 700 ft., 50 min.

Pine Hill Trail (DCR)

The shortest route to the top of Wachusett Mtn. is via this very steep old ski trail on the eastern side of the mountain. From the visitor center parking take Bicentennial Trail south to the Pine Hill Trail junction. Turn right onto Pine Hill Trail, which strenuously scales the buttress to emerge at the top at a break in the stone wall about 200 ft. from the end of the "up" road.

Pine Hill Trail (map 3: B2)
Distance from visitor center on Mtn. Rd. (1,390 ft.) to
- summit of Wachusett Mtn. (2,006 ft.): 0.6 mi., 600 ft., 40 min.

Mountain House Trail (DCR)

This trail ascends Wachusett Mtn. from the south. Parking is available at the trailhead near the junction of Gregory Rd. and Mtn. Rd., 2.4 mi. north of Princeton center. The trail takes its name from the famous Mountain House, which was formerly located nearby. (The stone walls and cellar holes are still visible.) The trail is broad and easy to follow.

The trail climbs rather steeply up an eroded path through hardwood forest, passing junctions with the Bicentennial Trail, the Loop Trail, the Jack Frost Trail, and the Link Trail. It then turns more to the north, crossing a stone wall and the summit road. From here the trail levels off and parallels the summit road, reaching the summit at 1.0 mi.

Mountain House Trail (map 3: C2)
Distance from Mountain Rd. trailhead (1,190 ft.) to
  • summit of Wachusett Mtn. (2,006 ft.): 1.0 mi., 800 ft., 45 min.

Harrington Trail (DCR)

This trail begins on Westminster Rd., 0.5 mi. west of its junction with Administration Rd. It leaves on the north side of the road opposite the Dickens Trail. Limited parking is available at the trailhead.

The trail begins by heading uphill through a field, switching to the northeast, and following a stone wall on the left as it enters the woods. Shortly the trail turns left onto a woods road and continues until it meets the Stage Coach Trail at 0.4 mi. The Harrington Trail soon crosses a stone wall, then passes through a stand of large hemlocks. Shortly the trail bears left (north) and crosses a streambed. It then bears right (northeast) to cross West Rd.

As the trail starts climbing again, painted white blazes are visible, and at 0.9 mi. the trail crosses Administration Rd. (This point is about 0.8 mi. north of the lower end of Administration Rd.) After passing the Lower Link Trail and crossing three streams (dry in summer), the trail climbs more steeply, levels off, and resumes climbing among rocks. The Semuhenna Trail enters left; the path slabs to the right and climbs onto ledges, then turns sharp left, paralleling the ledges for a short distance, then turns right and climbs steeply over rocks. The Link Trail enters on the right, and the Harrington Trail continues climbing steeply over rocks.

Shortly the trail goes over a stone wall along the side of the summit road, crosses the road, then climbs northeast over less difficult rocks and ledges. The open summit is soon visible, and the trail terminates on the flat rocks southwest of the fire tower.

Harrington Trail (map 3: C1–B2)
Distances from Westminster Rd. (1,254 ft.) to
  • Administration Rd. (1,500 ft.): 0.9 mi., 250 ft., 40 min.
  • summit of Wachusett Mtn. (2,006 ft): 1.4 mi., 750 ft., 1 hr. 15 min.

West Side Trail (DCR)

This trail ascends Wachusett Mtn. from its western side and begins on W. Princeton Rd. (gravel) in Westminster, 1 mi. north of its junction with Westminster Rd. and 200 yd. north of the intersection of West Rd. A parking area is near the trailhead. The trail terminates at the Old Indian Trail, about 0.3 mi. below the summit. The trail enters the woods on the eastern side of W. Princeton Rd., passing through a fairly large hemlock stand and over rocks, then swings south to slab up a hillside. The trail crosses more rocks and climbs steeply straight ahead over a cliff.

Above the cliff the trail levels off into hardwoods, mostly small beeches, and then climbs gradually. It swings left and right and climbs steeply before leveling off again. A short distance along, the trail crosses the Up Summit Rd. and continues southeast to an open spot with large, flat rocks surrounded by scrub oak. Nearby, a cairn marks the Princeton–Westminster line.

The trail veers northeast and briefly runs parallel to the road. Here the trail crosses the Semuhenna Trail and passes near a picnic table within sight of the road, then heads back into the woods. It climbs gradually to the junction with the Old Indian Trail.

West Side Trail (map 3: B1–B2)

Distances from W. Princeton Rd. (1,317 ft.) to

- Old Indian Trail (1,700 ft.): 0.9 mi., 400 ft., 50 min.
- summit of Wachusett Mtn. via Old Indian Trail (2,006 ft.): 1.2 mi., 700 ft. 1 hr. 30 min.

Semuhenna Trail (DCR)

This trail, constructed in 1971 and named for longtime trail volunteer Anne Humes (her name spelled backward), proceeds essentially north from the ledges on the Harrington Trail southwest of the summit to the Old Indian Trail near Balance Rock on the north slope. It crosses the West Side Trail once and Up Summit Rd. twice. Through the Link Trail, it also has access to the Jack Frost Trail and the Mtn. House Trail, providing opportunities for a variety of loops.

The upper end of this trail starts at the Harrington Trail 0.2 mi. east of Administration Rd., just below the ledges, and about 40 yd. below the western end of the Link Trail. Descending from the Harrington Trail, it follows a low ridge, crosses a small intermittent stream, rises slightly over two open ledges, and crosses Up Summit Rd. at a picnic site. Almost immediately it crosses the West Side Trail and enters a stand of large hemlocks. It passes the top of the west ski lift (right) and continues gently descending through the hemlocks to the second crossing of Up Summit Rd., 60 yd. east of its intersection with North Rd. Beyond this crossing the trail passes through another old hemlock grove, swings gently left to cross another intermittent stream, then ascends slightly on approach to a stone wall. Beyond the wall the trail soon intersects the Old Indian Trail 0.2 mi. from Balance Rock.

Semuhenna Trail (map 3: B2)
Distance from Harrington Trail (1,625 ft.) to
• Old Indian Trail (1,400 ft.): 1.1 mi (rev. 200 ft.), 45 min.

Old Indian Trail (DCR)

This steep, rocky trail ascends the north slope of Wachusett Mtn. It begins on Balance Rock Rd. (closed to vehicular traffic), opposite the end of the Balance Rock Trail. To reach the trailhead begin at the parking area for the Balance Rock Trail, located to the north of the ski lodge off Mile Hill Rd. Alternatively, park on Bolton Rd. and climb to the trailhead on the Bolton Pond Trail. The Old Indian Trail leaves the road on the south side and proceeds through mixed hardwoods and pines. The Semuhenna Trail enters right at 0.2 mi. At 0.4 mi. the trail diagonally crosses a ski trail, reenters the woods, and passes under the ski lift at pole 12. The trail crosses Up Summit Rd. and then begins to climb gradually. After crossing an intermittent stream the trail climbs steeply to a junction with the West Side Trail. It continues steeply upward over stone steps and zigzags over rocks, crossing a ledge where there where there is a view of Mt. Monadnock and Mt. Greylock on a clear day. A few hundred feet above this point the trail levels off and climbs gradually to the summit. It ends at the beacon tower on the north side of the summit.

Old Indian Trail (map 3: A2–B2)

Distances from trailhead on Balance Rock Rd. (1,210 ft.) to
- West Side Trail (1,700 ft.): 0.6 mi., 500 ft., 30 min.
- summit of Wachusett Mtn. (2,006 ft.): 1.1 mi., 800 ft., 50 min.

Balance Rock Trail (DCR)

This trail begins at the far end of the ski area parking lot on Mtn. Rd., about 1.2 mi. north of the park visitor center. Follow the jeep path for about 0.3 mi. before turning onto a woods path, which soon reaches Balance Rock, a glacial erratic. The path continues a few hundred feet farther to Balance Rock Rd. (closed to vehicles). Across the road, the Old Indian Trail continues toward the summit.

Balance Rock Trail (map 3: A2)

Distances from ski area parking lot (1,030 ft.) to
- Balance Rock near Balance Rock Rd. (1,200 ft.): 0.4 mi., 150 ft., 20 min.

Dickens Trail (DCR)

This trail, an extension of the Wachusett Meadows Wildlife Sanctuary's Chapman Trail, connects the sanctuary with the Wachusett Mtn. State Reservation trail system. It starts at the sanctuary boundary north of Thompson Rd. and continues north to Westminster Rd. opposite the Harrington Trail. The trail joins a woods road and continues, crossing the right of way for the AT&T continental underground lines just before it terminates on Westminster Rd.

Dickens Trail (map 3: D1)

Distance from sanctuary boundary (1,250 ft.) to
- Westminster Rd. (1,250 ft.): 0.4 mi., 20 min.

Connecting Trails

The following trails, although relatively short, provide useful connections among the major trails described above, permitting a number of interesting loops and circuits.

Lower Link Trail (DCR). This 0.3-mi. trail parallels Administration Rd. and a brook. It serves as a short connecting route between the lower end of the Jack Frost Trail and the Harrington Trail.

Loop Trail (DCR). The 0.4-mi. Loop Trail provides a cutoff route that connects the Bicentennial Trail and the middle part of the Mountain House Trail. The trailhead on the Bicentennial Trail is just south of the Pine Hill Trail.

Bicentennial Trail (DCR). The rocky Bicentennial Trail serves as a connecting route for several of the popular summit trails. It begins at the visitor center and runs south parallel to Mountain Rd., passing junctions with the Pine Hill Trail, the Loop Trail, and the Mountain House Trail before turning steeply upward to end at the High Meadow Trail at 0.7 mi.

Stage Coach Trail (DCR). Originally called Old County Rd., this 0.5-mi. trail explores the quiet southwest corner of the reservation. It connects the Harrington Trail to the parking area on Westminster Rd. next to Machias Pool, just below the Administration Rd. gate.

Wachusett Meadow Wildlife Sanctuary

This 1,024-acre wildlife sanctuary is located 1.5 mi. west of Princeton center, and is owned and maintained by the Massachusetts Audubon Society. An 11-mi. trail network explores the sanctuary, including an 85-acre beaver pond. Located near Wachusett Mtn., one of the best hawk-watching sites in New England, the sanctuary often treats visitors in fall to the sight of many raptors soaring overhead.

To reach the sanctuary, follow MA 62 west from Princeton center for 0.5 mi., then turn right onto Goodnow Rd. (blacktop) at a Wachusett Meadow Sanctuary sign. In 1.1 mi. there is a parking area on the left at the road's end, across from the sanctuary headquarters. Three suggested walks are described below. (The long-distance Midstate Trail also passes through the Wachusett Meadows; see Midstate Trail, Section 5, Wachusett Meadows to Barre Falls Dam, on page 201.)

Beaver Bend–Pasture Trail Circuit (MAS)

The Beaver Bend trail, which begins on the right-hand side of the parking lot, is a pleasant walk that leads to several wildlife viewing areas along the edge of the large wetland across the meadow south of the headquarters. At 0.5 mi., it joins the Pasture Trail, a woodland-and-field walk that passes through a series of old fields and a small pond. At the west junction with Fern Forest Trail the Pasture Trail turns right (northwest) and continues to the second junction with the Fern Forest Trail on the left (following the entire Fern Forest trail adds 0.7 mi. to the loop). Pasture Trail soon bends right, crosses a rock wall, then turns left (west) as the Hemlock Seep Trail leaves straight (north). The Pasture Trail meanders through the woods to Goodnow Rd., which it follows back to the junction with Beaver Bend Trail.

Beaver Bend–Pasture Trail Circuit (map 3: E1)

Distance from Goodnow Rd. (1,023 ft.) via Beaver Bend Trail to
• Goodnow Rd. (circuit): 2.2 mi., 50 ft., 1 hr.

Chapman Trail (MAS)

The Chapman Trail, named for the late Lawrence B. Chapman, a former MIT professor, ornithologist, and chairman of the Wachusett Meadows Advisory Committee, begins at Goodnow Rd., west of the sanctuary headquarters. The trail leads north through mature forest that provides habitat for a variety of migratory songbirds. After passing the junction with the Glacial Boulder Trail. It passes a walled spring hole (dry in summer), then crosses a pair of small seasonal brooks.

Shortly after the second brook the trail swings gently right through a brushy area, then turns left again to join the West Border Trail. Beyond this junction the trail turns 90 degrees left, and crosses a stone wall to follow another stone wall, which marks the sanctuary boundary. About 30 yd. from this turn the trail veers slightly right and drops gently down to Thompson Rd. The trail leaves the north side of Thompson Rd. at the western end of a small pond. It starts uphill and continues to a logging road, where it turns left onto a road for a short distance and then turns right, leaving the road. It passes a communications tower on the right and then crosses the sanctuary boundary line at a break in a stone wall. From this point on it becomes the Dickens Trail, which serves as a connector to the Harrington Trail at Wachusett Mtn. State Reservation.

Chapman Trail (map 3: D1)
Distance from Goodnough Rd. (via entrance, starting elevation 1,023 ft.) to
- Thompson Rd. (1,150 ft.): 0.9 mi., 150 ft., 25 min.
- sanctuary boundary (1,200 ft.): 1.8 mi., 200 ft., 55 min.

Leominster State Forest

This forest of 4,300 acres is known for its scenic ponds, beautiful stands of mountain laurel, and outstanding views from Crow Hill. It is easily reached from Worcester and Boston, with several parking areas located off MA 31. Wooden signs in the parking areas show most of the marked trails. The Midstate Trail traverses the property, and there are many miles of hiking and multi use trails. The hiking trails are closed to cyclists. There is a swimming beach at Crow Hill Pond with lifeguards on duty in season; restrooms are available.

To reach the state forest, from MA 2 take Exit 28 and follow MA 31 south past the park headquarters on the right. The Crow Hills dirt parking lot is on the right (west) side of MA 31 2.5 miles from the junction with MA 2; the main entrance (open in summer months for beach access) is 2.0 mi. from the MA 2 junction on the left. Other parking areas are spread along MA 31.

Midstate Trail (WCAMC, DCR)

The Midstate Trail enters the northwest corner of the reservation from Stone Hill Rd. and continues over the top of the Crow Hill Ledges. See Section 3, Wyman Brook to Redemption Rock, on page 196

Crow Hill (DCR)

Crow Hill (1,234 ft.) rises high above the west side of MA 31, and offers spectacular views across the ponds and woodlands of the state forest to

Wachusett Mtn. and Boston. A short hike to the ridge of Crow Hill—also the usual approach to the cliff by rock climbers—is from the parking area on the west side of MA 31, just south of the tip of Crow Hill Pond (the named Crow Hill Trail begins at the Crow Hill Pond parking lot farther north on MA 31, but this lot is closed during summer months).

From Gate 6 at the parking area, the trail follows a gravel road that is used for emergency access to the ledges. Though it's marked as a straight road on the park map, the road curves as it rises uphill to a small clearing. Follow the path on a quick climb over rocks to a junction where bearing left (straight) leads to the top of the ledges, while going right leads along the base of the cliffs before looping over the top. Both routes make short, rocky climbs to the Midstate Trail, which passes over the ridge with a pair of outstanding views from open ledges. *Use caution around the edge of the cliffs and wherever rock climbers are present.*

Crow Hill

Distance from MA 31 parking area to
* top of ridge via Midstate Trail: 0.7 mi., 35 min.

Wolf Rock Trail (DCR)

The Wolf Rock Trail follows the eastern edge of Crow Hill Pond, with nice views across the pond of Crow Hill. From its northern trailhead near the main entrance (it can also be accessed via the Crow Hill Pond causeway off of MA 31), it leads south, ending near the junction of Rocky Pond Rd. and Wolf Rock Rd., which lead to the central and southern portions of the forest, respectively.

Wolf Rock Trail

Distance from main entrance to
* Rocky Pond Rd.: 1.1 mi., 35 min.

Rocky Pond Trail (DCR)

The Rocky Pond Trail branches left off Rocky Pond Rd., a wide woods road, just north of the Wolf Rock Trail junction. The trail climbs at an easy-to-moderate grade through mixed woodlands. Bear right at two successive junctions, following occasional yellow blazes and signs for the Rocky Pond Trail. After the second junction (where the Ball Hill Trail leads left), the trail narrows and passes through a tunnel of laurel and maple saplings. Befitting its name, the trail gets increasingly rocky as it approaches, then follows the shore of Rocky Pond before ending at dirt Fenton Rd. Turn right and walk a short distance to a nice view of the top of Wachusett Mtn. rising across the pond.

Rocky Pond Trail
Distance from Rocky Pond Rd. parking area (818 ft.) to
- start of Rocky Pond Trail: 0.75 mi., 10 min.
- T-junctions: 1.4 mi., 35 min.
- Fenton Rd. at Rocky Pond (940 ft.): 2.1 mi., 1 hr.

Purgatory Chasm

Located west of MA 146 in Sutton, Purgatory Chasm State Reservation includes 900 acres of scenic land and unique rock formations. The reservation has picnic facilities that include fireplaces, tables, and spring water. Universal access restrooms are available. The chasm is a great fissure in solid granite approximately 0.5 mi. long with sheer walls rising 70 ft. The origin of the gorge is believed to trace back to the massive erosion caused by the immense floods at the end of the last ice age. While the exact origin of the reservation's colorful name remains unknown, one account credits the Quakers for the label; they reputedly viewed the rocky chasm as a place "halfway between earth and hell."

Chasm Loop Trail (DCR)

The well-marked 0.5-mi. Chasm Loop Trail courses through the gorge, then offers a different perspective from atop the cliffs. Beginning at the chasm entrance near the pavilion on Purgatory Rd., the trail heads southwest through the length of the chasm. It turns left and gains the top of the cliffs, skirts a long rock ledge, then passes by side trails that lead to some of the colorfully named rock formations for which the chasm is famous. *(Use caution near the edge of the cliffs.)* The Chasm Loop Trail then ends at the ⚠ starting point near the parking area.

Chasm Loop Trail
Distance from start of chasm to
  • trailhead (circuit): 0.5 mi., 35 min.

Blackstone River and Canal State Park

This state park occupies slightly more than 1,000 acres in the towns of Northbridge and Uxbridge. Included within the park are 6 mi. of the Blackstone River and some of the best-preserved sections of the historic Blackstone Canal, built between 1826 and 1828.

Parking is available at both ends of the route: in the north at Plummer's Landing on Church St. in Northbridge, just east of MA 122; in the south at the Stanley Woolen Mill on Cross St., just off MA 16 in Uxbridge. Parking is also available at the Stone Arch Bridge off Hartford Ave. in Uxbridge, which bisects the trail about 2.4 mi. from its northern end.

Blackstone Valley Trail (DCR)

This route follows a 3.75-mi. patchwork of trails that runs roughly north-south through the valley with gentle grades. Portions of the trail follow the original canal towpath. Along its route the trail passes locks, dams, bridge abutments, and other remnants of the early industrial era, as well as scenic outlooks over Rice City Pond and the Blackstone River valley.

From the north the route begins on Church St. at Plummer's Landing. The Plummer's Trail (a.k.a. the Tow Path Trail) heads south from here following the river, but continues straight as the river bends left. It reaches the river again in a wetland area roughly opposite Lookout Rock. At 1.7 mi. the Goat Hill lock is reached and the Goat Hill Loop branches into two paths, one that runs the high ground to Goat Hill, and another loop that continues south along the river. There are fine views from the top of Goat Hill in fall, winter, and spring. The southern end of the Goat Hill Trail Loop ends at Stone Arch Bridge opposite Rice City Pond. From the Hartford Ave. bridge the Tow Path Trail crosses the river and follows the eastern bank to the Cross St. parking area near the Stanley Woolen Mill. The distance for the hike (one way) is about 3.5 mi.

Blackstone Valley Trail
Distance from Plummer's Landing to
- Goat Hill Lock and Goat Hill loop trail: 1.7 mi., 55 min.
- Cross St. entrance: 3.5 mi., 2 hr.

King Philip's Rock Trail (DCR)

This easy 1.5-mi. (one-way) trail leads to the King Philip's Rock overlook, which offers an excellent overview of the Blackstone River as it snakes through the valley below. The trailhead is located at the Rice City Pond parking area on Hartford Ave., next to the stone bridge.

The trail begins near the southeast corner of Rice City Pond, an impoundment of the river. It passes through an open field, then bears right past a picnic area in a pine grove. After crossing a small stream on a wood bridge, follow the main path left, passing an unmarked trail that forks right. The trail, marked with intermittent blue blazes, follows the edge of the pond and its associated wetlands, then passes a field of glacial boulders on a rocky hillside to the right. After forking left, it crosses another small stream and gradually rises above the wetland. Continue to a T-junction and go left; King Philip's Rock comes into view on the right. The trail soon leads to the base of the rock, then makes a quick climb to the 365-ft. overlook.

King Philip's Rock Trail
Distance from Rice City Pond trailhead to
- King Philip's Rock: 1.5 mi., 45 min.

Upton State Forest

The 2,600-acre Upton State Forest lies in Worcester County's southeast corner, just beyond the reach of the city of Worcester's suburbs. Like many areas in New England, the landscape has seen a variety of uses over time. During the late eighteenth and early nineteenth centuries, several mills and a stone cutter operated along the preserve's waterways.

To reach the entrance, from Interstate 495 just south of the Massachusetts Turnpike, take Exit 21B, turn west (right if coming from the north) on Hopkinton Rd. and continue 3.5 mi. into Upton. Make a sharp right on Westboro Rd., and continue 2.0 mi. to the state forest entrance on the right.

Whistling Caves–Loop Rd. Circuit (DCR)

Several of the forest's roads and trails can be combined for an easy 3.3-mi. loop, including the unique Whistling Caves Trail, which leads to a cluster of large boulders, a forest stream, and Dean Pond. From the gate at the parking area, follow the woods road east to the nearby junction with Park Rd. Turn right on Park Rd., which climbs easily past the link to the Middle Trail on the left to the junction with the Whistling Caves Trail, also on the left, 0.7 mi. from the parking area.

The blue-blazed Whistling Caves trail drops steeply into the ravine (ignore a side path at the top of the descent that forks to the right). The path then continues on a more level grade to a wet area and stream crossing, then passes through an extensive field of large glacial boulders for which the trail is named. Most of these boulders are covered with rock tripe, a dark brown and black lichen.

Just beyond the boulders, the trail arrives at the three-way junction with Middle and Loop Rd. near the edge of Dean Pond on the right. There are several views from the woods along the shore of the pond, which was created by the CCC during the 1930s. Return to the three-way junction, and follow Middle Rd. for 0.25 mi. to the junction with the blue-blazed Hawk Trail. Bear right and follow the Hawk Trail for another 0.25 mi. to Loop Rd.

Turn left on Loop Rd., and continue for an easy half-mile, passing the Grouse and Mammoth Rock trails on the right. At an old foundation, turn right on the Swamp Trail, which makes a short loop as it passes under a grove of tall pines before paralleling the east edge of the wetland adjacent the parking area. When the trail rejoins Loop Rd., go right to the nearby junction with Park Rd., then continue straight and make the short walk to the gate and parking area.

Upton State Forest: Whistling Caves–Loop Rd. Circuit

Distances from entrance gate to
- Whistling Caves Trail: 0.7 mi., 20 min.
- three-way junction at Dean Pond: 1.4 mi., 45 min.
- parking area (circuit): 3.3 mi., 2 hr.

Bearsden Forest

Bearsden Forest is an area totaling about 3,000 acres under the supervision of the Athol Conservation Commission, and is located off Bearsden Rd., an old stagecoach road that formerly connected Athol with South Royalston. The bridge over the Millers River was swept away by the floods of 1938 and was never replaced. The farms along the northern end of the road have long been abandoned, and the fields and pastures have been replaced by woodlands which are classified by the Massachusetts Natural Heritage and Endangered Species program as one of the state's best examples of interior forest habitat. About 20 mi. of trails traverse the hills, brooks, ponds, and scenic vistas. A descriptive map flier is available on request from the Athol Conservation Commission, Town Hall, Athol, MA 01331. Also refer to the USGS Athol quadrangle.

To reach Bearsden Forest, take MA 2A (Main St.) in Athol east to Athol Memorial Hospital. The turn for Bearsden Rd. is located opposite the hospital on the north side of MA 2A and is marked by an Athol Conservation Area sign. Follow Bearsden Rd. to the end of the tar surface, then continue straight ahead on a rough road for 0.4 mi. to its end at the large parking area, where a posted map shows the trails and roads in the forest.

Bearsden Circuit (ACC)

This moderately difficult circuit combines several of the reservation's trails and footpaths and leads to a number of interesting features and overlooks. There is a steep climb from Duck Pond to Sheep Rock, and a steep descent from Round Top Hill to the trailhead.

The loop begins on Bearsden Rd. at the yellow gate at the parking area. After 0.3 mi., at the sign for Fire Road–Thompson's Corner, follow the old road to the left, passing a picnic site and a yellow gate. This grassy road slopes downhill, curves sharply right at Thompson's Corner, then follows rolling terrain, crossing a small wood bridge and becoming increasingly sandy and rocky as it descends the valley gradually to Duck Pond near the river's edge at 1.5 mi. Trains can often be seen or heard on the tracks along the base of the valley.

At Duck Pond, turn right on the narrow, yellow-blazed trail that climbs steeply to a 12-ft. wooden observation platform at Sheep Rock at

1.9 mi., where there's a fine panoramic view across the hilly valley. From the platform, continue straight down the dirt road to a T-junction with Bearsden Rd. at 2.2 mi. Turn right here, and follow the road through an interesting small gorge lined with hemlocks. Stay straight as the road passes a yellow gate at a road leading to Bemis Hill, and look for a clearing on the left, opposite another picnic area.

From the back of this clearing, follow the logging road uphill toward the ridge of Round Top Hill. Turn right at a marked junction and continue toward Sunday Wall/Warren Vista/Round Top. The yellow-blazed trail continues on an easy climb before leveling off, passing several stone walls and the Warren Vista, a small clearing on the right that offers a view to the west. The trail arrives at the partially open 1,282-ft. summit of Round Top Hill at 3.2 mi., which offers views to Mt. Monadnock, and Wachusett Mtn. The summit is also a good hawk-watching site during spring and fall migrations.

From Round Top, the trail descends steeply through a grove of tall pines, curving right at a junction, before leveling off for an easy walk to the parking area, 0.4 mi. from the summit.

Bearsden Forest Circuit

Distances from parking area to
- Duck Pond: 1.5 mi., 45 min.
- Sheep Rock observation platform: 1.9 mi., 1 hr. 5 min.
- Round Top Hill summit: 3.2 mi., 1 hr. 45 min.
- parking area (circuit): 3.6 mi., 2 hr.

Tully Lake and Doane's Falls

A flood control lake completed in 1949 in response to devastating floods in 1936 and 1938, Tully Lake has saved the Millers River communities of Athol and Orange millions of dollars by mitigating floodwaters. The lake, which is part of a popular recreation area that includes adjacent Long Pond, is situated at the confluence of the east branch of the Tully River and Lawrence Brook, both major tributaries of the Millers River. At Doane's Falls near the lake's northeast corner, Lawrence Brook drops 200 ft. in a dramatic series of cascades.

To reach Tully Lake, from MA 2, take Exit 17 and follow MA 32 north to the junction with MA 2A in Athol. Turn left on MA 32 and 2A, then right on MA 32 north. Continue on MA 32 north for 3.2 mi. to the dam and recreation area near the Athol-Royalston town line.

Loop Trail (USACE, TTOR)

From the parking area at the boat launch, walk back up to MA 32, then turn left (south) and follow the road (light traffic) for 0.3 mi. to the dam, which offers an excellent overview of the lake. The yellow-blazed loop trail continues to the right of the dam at an information sign and map at the start of the disc golf course. The trail slopes down the hill, passing portions of the disc golf course and an area clear-cut in 2007 for a wildlife meadow (watch for minor potential reroutes in this area). The trail crosses an abandoned road, then winds and rolls to a nice overlook at the south end of the lake and a rocky crossing of an outlet stream. It then continues northerly along the lake's east shore.

At the lake's northeast corner, the trail bends away from the water and enters the Doane's Falls Reservation (TTOR), climbing moderately through the forest. At the crest of the climb, the trail turns left on Chestnut Hill Rd. (light traffic), crosses Lawrence Brook above the main falls, then immediately reenters the woods on the left. The trail then descends through hemlocks along the falls and cascades at a moderate grade, passing several overlooks. After the final drop, the trail levels and bears right to Doane Hill Rd. (light traffic). Turn left here, and follow the road across the Tully River to the Tully Lake Campground (parking, restrooms) on the left.

At the back of the campground parking area in front of the ranger station, the loop trail joins the Tully Trail, and leads back into the woods. The lake soon comes back into view, including a view of the dam in the distance. The trail winds along the lake's northwest corner, passing a large blowdown area from a 2006 microburst, several nice vistas, and abundant blueberry bushes.

After briefly paralleling Doane Hill Rd., the trail turns southwest and follows the west shore, passing two junctions with an interpretive trail on the right. A short side path on the left at a Y-junction leads to another nice view of the lake. The loop trail soon returns to the parking area; stay straight at a sign for the picnic area where the Tully Trail branches off to the right.

Tully Lake Loop Trail

Distances from parking area at boat launch to
- Doane's Falls: 2.3 mi., 1 hr 10 min.
- parking area (circuit): 4.5 mi., 2 hr. 10 min.

Brooks Woodland Preserve

This 558-acre tract in Petersham was once the home of the Nipmucks, and was subsequently cleared for agriculture by colonists, as evidenced by miles of stone walls, in the eighteenth century. Today the hillsides are once again covered with forests and accented with scenic views. An extensive network of more than 13 mi. of footpaths and woods roads course through the woods, which are drained by the East Branch of the Swift River, and Roaring and Mocassin Brooks; some of these paths provide connecting routes with the adjacent Rutland Brook, Swift River, and Harvard Forest reservations. Swamps and ponds have formed behind the beaver dams that cross the streams, and bedrock ledges provide habitat for many animals, including porcupines. The numerous trail junctions are numbered but not labeled; a map (available online, at the Petersham Country Store, or at the information signs) is strongly recommended.

The reservation is divided into three tracts—Roaring Brook, Swift River, and Connor's Pond. To reach the Roaring Brook tract from Petersham center, follow East St. for 0.8 mi. to the entrance on the left. To reach the Swift River and Connor's Pond tracts, from the junction of MA 122 and MA 32 south of Petersham, drive south on combined MA 122/32 for 1.5 mi. Turn left onto Quaker Dr., cross the bridge over the East Branch of the Swift River, and continue for 0.5 mi. to a small grass parking area and information sign on the left-hand side of the road.

Rutland Brook Wildlife Sanctuary

This wildlife sanctuary in Petersham and Barre, which abuts the Brooks Woodland Preserve, consists of 1,500 acres of rolling terrain along the valley of the East Branch of the Swift River, where cascading streams, rocky outcroppings, upland wetlands, and large old hemlocks and white pines can be found.

To reach this unstaffed Massachusetts Audubon Society sanctuary, take MA 122 to the Petersham-Barre town line. At the bridge and dam at the south end of Connor's Pond, turn north on Pat Connor Rd., and continue on the dirt road that runs parallel to the pond for 0.2 mi. to the Audubon Society parking area on the left.

Rutland Brook–Connor's Pond Loop (MAS)

From the parking area, follow the sign marking the trails, and continue on the Connor's Pond Trail along the shore of the pond. Enter the woods and proceed to the far entrance of the Rutland Brook loop trail. The trail climbs easily along the cascading brook, passing under giant white pine and hemlock trees. At the wet meadow at the top of the hill, bear right, walk past a large glacial boulder, and follow the signs to the Connors Pond trail and the parking area.

For those seeking a longer outing, the Sherman Hill Trail, which begins at the junction just above the marsh, makes a steep ascent of Sherman Hill to a series of large rocky outcroppings, where there are no views, but interesting rock ledges that provide wildlife habitat. A trail map of this area is available from the Massachusetts Audubon Society.

Rutland Brook Loop Trail
Distance from parking area at Connor's Pond to
• trailhead (circuit): 1.0 mi., 35 min.

Harvard Forest

Harvard Forest is a 3,000-acre research and experimental forest in Petersham maintained by Harvard University and open to the public, with many miles of trails and roads available for hiking. The headquarters and museum are on the east side of MA 32, approximately 3.0 mi. north of Petersham center, and 2.5 mi. south of the junction of MA 2 and MA 32 in Athol. The museum is well-known for a series of famous, intricately crafted dioramas that depict the history of central New England forests. Trail maps and guides are available at the information kiosk at the museum.

Black Gum Trail (HF)

This 1.5-mi.-long interpretive trail begins at the museum on the right-hand side of the cow pasture and heads east on Locust Opening Rd., a wide woods road. It passes a stone wall and red pine plantations to another old road that leaves right. Just beyond the junction, the path turns sharp left at an arrow (north), passing through a hemlock grove with a wetland to the left. The trail now swings left (west) at another junction, and passes along the edge of a swamp. At a junction, the main trail continues straight (west), and the Black Gum Swamp side trail leaves left, following a boardwalk that leads through the swamp, passing trees that are more than 400 years old, before rejoining the grassy main trail. At a junction at a green gate, the trail turns left (south) on Prospect Hill Rd., another wide woods road lined on both sides by stone walls. Prospect Hill Rd. continues towards the headquarters, passing the cow pasture and private residences en route to the museum parking lot.

Black Gum Trail

Distance from Locust Opening Rd. to
- left turn off Locust Opening Rd.: 0.6 mi., 15 min.
- boardwalk through swamp: 1 mi., 30 min.
- museum via Prospect Hill Rd. (circuit): 1.5 mi, 45 min.

Swift River Loop (HF, TTOR)

This easy, pleasant walk loops along the hemlock-lined east branch of the Swift River, then briefly follows Moccasin Brook before returning to the parking area on Quaker Drive. The route alternates between land owned by Harvard Forest and the adjacent Brooks Woodland Preserve (Trustees of Reservations). To reach the trailhead, from the center of Petersham, follow MA 122/32 south for 1.3 mi. to a left on Quaker Dr., and turn left into the parking area just before the bridge over the Swift River.

The trail begins as a wide woods road at the green gate and soon leads to the west bank of the river, which it follows past several nice viewpoints and a beaver wetland. After the junction with a woods road that leads to MA 122, it narrows to a footpath near The Trustees of Reservations boundary, then joins another woods road at 1.0 mi.

Turn right and cross the river on a wood bridge, then immediately bear right again on a woods road that follows the opposite bank. After passing a short side trail to a huge, spreading 'wolf' pine, the trail turns sharply left at the convergence of the Swift River and Moccasin Brook. It rises easily above Moccasin Brook, then turns right opposite a large wetland and crosses the brook on another wood bridge. Continue briefly uphill, then turn right and follow the path through an open meadow to Quaker Dr. Turn right, and follow the road on a short walk to the Swift River bridge and the parking area.

Swift River Loop

Distances from Quaker Drive parking area to
- wood bridge crossing Swift River: 1.0 mi., 30 min.
- confluence of Swift and Moccasin Brook: 1.9 mi., 1 hr.
- Swift River bridge (circuit): 2.6 mi., 1 hr. 20 min.

Swift River Reservation

This 438-acre preserve is a combination of three separate properties—the Nichewaug tract, the Slab City tract, and the Davis tract. Each tract has its own unique character and hiking opportunities. The east branch of the Swift River runs through each tract en route to its confluence with Quabbin Reservoir.

Nichewaug Trail (TTOR)

The Nichewaug tract is known for a number of attractions, including rocky ledges offering a view across the valley, beaver wetlands, open sunny fields, riverside habitat, and, in spring, vernal pools sought out by salamanders and frogs. To reach the Nichewaug tract from the intersection of MA 122 and

MA 32 south of Petersham center, follow South St. 0.9 mi. to Nichewaug Rd. Turn right onto Nichewaug Rd. and continue 0.6 mi. to the entrance and parking area on the left.

From the cable gate next to the welcome sign, follow the grassy path along the edge of the open field atop the valley. The yellow-blazed trail curves left and enters the woods, passing through a rocky area beneath hardwood-hemlock forest. Bear left at a fork (post 87) and continue to an overlook at 0.6 mi. with an open view east across the narrow, forested valley.

The trail continues along the rocky ridge, climbing down slightly before a sharp right upslope at junction 90. Watch carefully for yellow markings and the faint footpath here; the markings are not prominent in this area and the trail may be difficult to follow (the more prominent path to the left slopes down to junction 92). Just before reaching a field at the edge of the reservation boundary, the trail bears left at junction 91. Continue along the path, which soon becomes much more obvious and easy to follow as it gradually winds down to the river. The trail turns left on the path that parallels the river and follows it on a pleasant walk to a junction with a grassy woods road on the left at 1.5 mi. To the right here is an old bridge site, with the stone supports still visible.

From this junction, continue to follow the yellow blazes straight (east) along the river, passing a wetland (if the trail is flooded here, take the grassy woods road mentioned above to post 85, which bypasses this area and makes for a quicker hike). The trail bends slightly left (north), and continues with more good views of the water. Just before the reservation boundary sign, the trail climbs uphill at post 94 into the woods on the left. Continue past old white pines growing amidst the network of stone walls, then go right on the woods road at junction 88, then turn left off the woods road onto a footpath at post 85. Follow this trail gradually uphill past a timber harvest site back to the field and parking area.

Swift River Reservation: Nichewaug Loop

Distances from Nichewaug Rd. parking area to
- overlook: 0.6 mi., 20 min.
- junction with woods road along river: 1.5 mi., 50 min.
- parking area (circuit): 3.1 mi., 1 hr. 40 min.

Quabbin Reservoir

At 40 sq. mi., the Quabbin Reservoir, the source of drinking water for more than 2.5 million residents in the greater Boston area, is the largest conservation area in southern New England. The construction of the reservoir was a controversial project in which four towns and numerous villages were abandoned and inundated during the 1930s. Today its waters and surrounding forest buffer provide habitat for a wide variety of wildlife, including moose, common loons, and bald eagles.

The reservation is accessible to the public via more than 50 marked gates, mostly old roads, spread around the perimeter of the reservoir. Hiking is the main recreational use permitted at most gates, though on-road bicycle riding is permitted in some areas. Swimming is not permitted in any area. The southernmost portion of the reservation, known as Quabbin Park, is the most visited area, as it is home to a number of attractions and a public auto road. The visitor center at the park includes historic artifacts and recent wildlife sightings.

Quabbin Hill–Webster Rd. Loop (DCR)

This circuit connects several of Quabbin Park's most interesting areas, including the summit of Quabbin Hill and the spectacular Enfield Lookout, before finishing with a pleasant walk along the reservoir's shore. Deer and wild turkeys are abundant and frequently seen in this area. To reach the trailhead, from MA 9 near the Ware/Belchertown town line, turn north on either the middle or east entrance roads and continue to the large open fields known as Hank's Picnic Area. The trailhead is at the west edge of the field, at gate WR15 (opposite the road that leads toward the water).

The trail begins on a wide woods road that rises gently, passing an interesting stone foundation on the left just beyond the gate. At 0.6 mi., turn right off the road onto a narrow footpath, well-marked with yellow blazes. The trail climbs at an easy to moderate grade through mixed woods before leveling off along the ridge, then climbing briefly to the edge of the parking area at the summit of Quabbin Park (1,026 ft.) at 1.0 mi. The large observation tower across the lot offers sweeping views in all directions.

The trail briefly follows the edge of the parking lot, then reenters the woods, descending easily through dense shrubby vegetation and open woods. After crossing a grassy field, it widens into a woods road. Turn right at a junction just beyond the edge of the field, leaving the yellow-blazed trail. The trail quickly descends to the auto road opposite gate WR18 at the left edge of the Enfield Lookout, which offers an outstanding view north across the valley to Mt. Monadnock in New Hampshire.

From gate WR18, the trail curves right beneath the lookout, then slopes downhill for 0.4 mi. to the reservoir's edge, with fine views across the water to Little Quabbin Hill. The trail, now again marked with yellow blazes, continues to the right and follows the woods along the shore. Shortly after crossing a small brook, it reaches the fields near the picnic area. Follow the wide grass path across the edge of the fields, then turn right on the picnic area road and make the short walk to the trailhead at gate WR15.

Quabbin Hill–Webster Rd. Loop

Distances from trailhead at Hank's Picnic Area (623 ft.) to
- junction with yellow trail: 0.5 mi., 15 min.
- Quabbin Hill summit (1,026 ft.): 1.0 mi., 30 min.
- auto road crossing at Enfield Lookout: 2.1 mi., 1 hr.
- picnic area fields (circuit): 3.5 mi., 1 hr. 45 min.

Dana Common Rd. (DCR)

One of the state's most unique and interesting walks, this trail follows the old Petersham–Dana Rd. to the former town common of Dana, which was abandoned because of its proximity to the reservoir. Though the buildings are gone, the common and surrounding old farm fields along the road are mowed and maintained as open areas, and the old cellar holes and foundations are evident. To reach the trailhead at Gate 40, from the junction of MA 122 and MA 32A near Petersham center, follow MA 32A 3.0 mi. south to the parking area in a depression on the west side of the road. On-road bicycling is permitted at this gate.

The wide, level road continues from the gate, passing a pine plantation and a number of open fields that offer wildlife viewing opportunities. Potapaug Pond soon is visible to the left through the trees; at 1.5 mi. from the gate a side road at a large spreading oak leads 0.2 mi. to the shore. At

1.8 mi., the main road reaches a stone monument at the edge of the common, where an old hotel, store, and other town buildings once stood.

Many walkers return from here for a 3.6-mi. round-trip, but for those with more time, a handful of roads branch out from the common, offering additional exploring opportunities. The first road on the right as viewed from the monument is Tamplin Rd., which winds into the woods toward gates 37 to 39. The next is Skinner Hill Rd., which makes a long climb up Skinner Hill before rapidly descending to the shoreline at Graves Landing, 2 mi. from the common. Greenwich Rd., which continues straight from the opposite side of the common, continues for 2.5 mi. over rolling terrain to a series of scenic shoreline views.

Dana Common Rd.

Distance from Quabbin gate 40 to
- large open field on right: 0.5 mi., 15 min.
- side road to Potapaug Pond: 1.5 mi., 40 min.
- Dana Common historic site: 1.8 mi., 50 min..

Soapstone Hill–Federated Women's State Forest

The open ledges of 870-ft. Soapstone Hill offer a spectacular panoramic view of the northern portion of Quabbin Reservoir and its surrounding forests and hills. The hemlock-lined west branch of Fever Brook, one of the reservoir's main sources, feeds beaver ponds that are visited by a variety of wildlife, including bald eagles and one of the state's largest moose populations.

To reach the trailhead, from the junction of MA 122 and MA 202 in New Salem, follow MA 122 south for 3.6 mi. Turn right (south) at a small green state forest sign, and follow the paved entrance road to the parking area on the right just before a T-junction with a dirt forest road. This circuit begins in the Federated Women's State Forest, then enters Quabbin Reservation; both are managed by DCR.

Gorge Loop Trail (DCR)

This 3.3-mi. loop passes a small gorge and beaver pond before climbing steeply to the overlook, then follows the ridge of the hill back to the campground. Aside from the climb to the ledges, the grade is mostly easy.

Begin at the red gate to the right of the parking area and follow the dirt road uphill under power lines towards the small state forest campground (unstaffed, contact the Otter River State Forest in Templeton for information). Watch for a sign for sites 2 and 3, and turn left on the narrow path (the trailhead is not marked as of this writing). The trail follows the edge of a rocky ravine, passing an overlook and sloping easily downhill to the right. The trail is partially overgrown in places and sporadically blazed with blue markers, but easy to follow. It levels off and widens into a grassy road as it approaches, then follows the edge of a large beaver wetland at the base of Soapstone Hill.

Watch carefully for a blue marker on the right where the loop trail turns off the road (going straight leads to a view of the reservoir at the outlet of Fever Brook in 5 min.) near a recent timber harvest. After passing a grove of pines and an old quarry, the trail makes a direct, steep climb to the rocky ledges, with outstanding views south and east; Mt. Monadnock can also be seen to the north on clear days.

From the ledges, the path continues on an easy grade along the ridge before sloping downhill and curving left and passing through a right-of-way clearing. It then meets the grassy road near Quabbin gate 36 just above the campground. Turn right here, walk downhill through the campground, then complete the loop by following the entrance road back to the red gate.

Gorge Loop Trail

Distances from red entrance gate (587 ft.) to
- trailhead at campsites 2 and 3: 0.4 mi., 10 min.
- right turn off road at beaver pond at base of Soapstone Hill: 1.4 mi., 30 min.
- Soapstone Hill ledges and vista (870 ft.): 1.7 mi., 50 min.
- junction with Quabbin gate 36 road: 2.5 mi., 1 hr. 15 min.
- red gate (circuit): 3.3 mi., 1 hr. 35 min.

Rock House Reservation

This 193-acre reservation in West Brookfield was named for the ledge and boulder cave aptly called the Rock House. The shelter includes a large overhanging ledge, with the entrance protected by large blocky boulders. Native American once used this spot as a meeting place and winter camp, and the cave is located near two trails frequented by Native Americans centuries ago. Some of the other features reached by the 3 mi. of trails include Balance Rock, Carter Pond, and a butterfly garden in a power line clearing. There are also plantations of spruce and pine planted in the 1930s and a partial hillside overlook taking in the fields and woods.

To reach Rock House Reservation from the Massachusetts Turnpike, take Exit 8 and pick up MA 32 north toward Ware. MA 32 joins MA 9 in Ware. Stay on combined MA 32/9 and, when the routes separate, follow MA 9 east for 1.1 mi. to a parking area (12 cars) and entrance on the left.

Inner Loop Trail (TTOR)

This easy circuit, an excellent walk for children, passes several of the reservation's features along scenic Carter Pond. From the parking area and information kiosk, follow the path uphill for 500 ft. to the edge of the pond. To make a counterclockwise circuit, turn right and follow the path into the adjacent woods. Bear left at the junction with the Outer Loop and continue north to the junction with Fire Rd. near Balance Rock. Turn left on Fire Rd., then take the short path on the left to the nature center, which offers a fine view from ledges above the pond. The trail briefly continues on Fire Rd., then turns south and leads through the rock caves. The path to the parking area is just south of the caves.

Inner Loop Trail
Distance from parking area to
• rock caves (circuit): 0.5 mi., 35 min.

Outer Loop Trail (TTOR)

The Outer Loop Trail, which branches off the Inner Loop east of Carter Pond, offers the option of a longer walk around the pond. It winds east, then north through oak woodlands interspersed with old conifer plantations. The trail ends at Fire Rd. at a butterfly garden in a power line clearing.

Outer Loop Trail
Distance from Inner Loop Trail junction to
• Fire Rd.: 0.4 mi., 25 min.

Norcross Wildlife Sanctuary

Located in Monson, this approximately 4,000-acre preserve protects woods, hill, lakes, and streams as well as the varied flora and fauna that live here. The mission of the sanctuary is the conservation of biodiversity through the collection and propagation of plants and preservation of bird and other animal species.

Approximately 3 mi. of short marked trails explore a variety of habitats as well as tended gardens, where a variety of native woodland and field wildflowers may be viewed in season. There are two natural history museums and a picnic area. Some of the areas visited by the trails include a woodland stream, cedar swamp, postglacial kettle pond, pine barrens, limestone cobble, and hickory grove. The Cedar Swamp, Meadow Garden, Lime Fern Cobble, and kettle pond are south of the visitor center and can be directly reached via the Lower Trail. The habitat variety makes this an excellent bird-watching destination.

To reach the sanctuary from the west, take the Massachusetts Turnpike (I-90) to Exit 8 (Palmer). Follow MA 32 south through Monson Center and turn left onto Wales Rd. Continue on Wales Rd., bearing right at the fork, for about 3 mi. to Wales. Once in Wales continue about 0.5 mi. to Peck Rd. Turn right onto Peck Rd. and drive the short way to the entrance on the left.

From the east take Massachusetts Turnpike (I-90) west to Exit 9 (Sturbridge). Take US 20 west to Brimfield, then turn left onto MA 19. Travel south on MA 19 to Wales and turn right onto Monson Rd. Drive about 2 mi. (bearing left at the fork) to Peck Rd. Take a left onto Peck Rd.; the entrance is a short distance down this road.

SUGGESTED HIKES

Easy Hikes

Beaver Bend–Pasture Trail [lp: 2.2 mi., 1:00], page 216. This relaxing walk passes through a large wetland through forest and old fields that provide habitat for a variety of wildlife and wildflowers.

Black Gum Trail [lp: 1.5 mi., 0:45], page 228. This hike wanders through pine plantations, a hemlock grove, and a black gum swamp with trees that are more than 400 years old.

Dana Common Rd. [rt: 3.6 mi., 1:20], page 232. This easy walk is rich in history and wildlife and follows a wide, level road to the abandoned town common of Dana.

Moderate Hikes

Wapack and Midstate Trails [rt: 2.4 mi., 2:00], page 207. This energizing hike alternates between steep areas and moderate stretches as it ascends the south side of the mountain to its outstanding views of the region.

Mountain House Trail [rt: 1.8 mi., 1:35], page 210. One of the shorter paths up the mountain, this trail is steep in spots with rough footing, but leads to sweeping views from the Berkshires to Boston from the 2,006-ft. summit.

Gorge Loop Trail [rt: 3.3 mi., 1:35], page 234. This hike passes a rocky gorge and beaver pond before climbing to a fine view of Quabbin Reservoir from Soapstone Hill.

Strenuous Hikes

Midstate Trail, Section 4 [rt: 5.4 mi., 4:00], page 200. Beginning and ending at Redemption Rock, this hike leads to the long views atop Wachusett Mtn.

Tully Trail, Section 1 [rt: 6.5 mi., 3:50], page 193. This exciting hike passes Spirit Falls on its way to ledge views across the Tully River Valley.

PART FOUR
NORTH AND WEST OF BOSTON

This chapter covers most of Essex and Middlesex Counties in Massachusetts, stretching from the Atlantic coast north of Boston to the gently rolling terrain northwest and west of the metropolitan area, including the Merrimack and Charles River watersheds. (Part V, Boston and Vicinity, includes those parts of Middlesex County closest to Boston.) There are no summits of any significance in this area, but a handful of low rolling hills provide surprisingly sweeping vistas. Much of the region is still covered with woodlands or farmland, but development pressures have been intense as suburbanization extends outward from the greater Boston area.

Bay Circuit Trail (Bay Circuit Alliance)

The Bay Circuit Trail (BCT) is a 200-mi. arc that links parks, open spaces, and greenways in a grand arc around the Boston metropolitan area from Plum Island in the north to Kingston Bay in the south. More than 180 mi. of the route in 24 communities are presently open, and the remainder is approaching completion. In addition to hiking, many sections are appropriate for mountain biking, cross-country skiing, and equestrian use, and several sections will incorporate multiple-use paved bike trails.

The original concept was proposed by Henry M. Channing and urban planner Charles Eliot II, both of The Trustees of Reservations, in 1929 as an outer "emerald necklace" to complement Boston's ring of urban parks and open spaces. The Massachusetts legislature first enacted legislation creating the Bay Circuit Program in 1956. In 1985 the Massachusetts Department of Environmental Management (now the Department of Conservation and Recreation) began the planning and acquisition process throughout 50 communities in the Bay Circuit corridor, including the purchase of Bay Farm in Kingston and Duxbury, the southern terminus of the Bay Circuit Trail.

The Bay Circuit Alliance (BCA) was founded in 1990 with the assistance of the National Park Service Conservation Assistance Program, with the goal of establishing a trail connecting green space within the BCT corridor. The BCA is a partnership of public and private organizations and individuals. BCA's membership consists of local, regional, and statewide member organizations and individuals. The BCA helps local communities establish their portions of the Bay Circuit Trail through planning and technical assistance on route identification, land-protection issues, and trail management and construction. The first section of the route opened in 1992, and since that time more than 4,000 acres of additional protected open space have been acquired.

Because of the scope of the BCT project, which includes final completion of the route as well as maintenance of existing sections, volunteers are needed in all of the Bay Circuit communities. Volunteer activities include trail mapping and description (including history and natural history), trail location, trail clearing, cleanup and maintenance, bridge building, contacting landowners for permission, identifying and aiding in the protection of green space, leading walks, and more. A BCA Trail Maintenance Advisory Committee (TMAC) coordinates maintenance and signage. The standard trail marking adopted for the Bay Circuit is a white, vertical blaze the size of a dollar bill; offset double-stacked blazes indicate turns. Four-inch-square Bay Circuit emblems are placed at road crossings and trailheads.

The BCA Website—baycircuit.org—is the best source for both general and specific trail information: detailed map and trail descriptions, volunteer opportunities, suggested hikes, and links to conservation organizations. The TMAC page is a must for those seeking or wishing to provide information on current BCT trail conditions.

Two detailed trail guides have been published that cover a 35-mi. stretch of the Bay Circuit from the Ipswich River in Willowdale State Forest, through Boxford, North Andover, and Andover, to the Merrimack River. These are *The Bay Circuit and AVIS Guide to Walks in Andover*, published by the Andover Trails Committee and the Andover Village Improvement Society; and *The Bay Circuit Guide to Walks In and Around Boxford*, published by the Boxford Bay Circuit Program Committee.

Section 1. Plum Island (Newburyport) to MA 1A (Rowley) (9.6 mi.)

The northern trailhead of the Bay Circuit Trail is located in Newburyport at the large parking lot at the end of the Plum Island Turnpike at the island's north end. From the lot, walk east along the Merrimack River to the unsigned beginning of the Merrimack River Trail (blazed in white). Continue south along the beach to the start of the BCT.

The trail now leads away from the beach and follows the Plum Island Turnpike across the bridge over the Plum Island River, reaching the Joppa Flats Refuge headquarters at 2.1 mi. Continue past the Plum Island Airport, where there is a kiosk with information on the Newbury section of the BCT, following the Eliza Little Trail. The path skirts the end of the airport runway before traversing the fields of the Spencer-Pierce-Little Farm (Society for the Preservation of New England Antiquities). At 2.6 mi. the trail passes the Spencer-Pierce-Little House before wandering down Little's Lane to High Rd.

At High Rd. (MA 1A) turn left (southeast) and follow the road past Tendercrop Farm, then turn right onto Hay St. at 3.5 mi. After 0.5 mi. take a right (north) onto Green St., continue 0.2 mi., then turn left (southwest) onto Boston Rd. The road leads past the Fuller Dome House and enters Old Town Reservation at a gate. The BCT quickly bears left from the path and follows cart paths over boardwalks to Hay Rd. Cross the Little River at 5.3 mi. and turn left (south) onto Newman Rd. Causeway. There are excellent views of the salt marshes here.

From the end of the marsh continue about 0.2 mi. to a trail on the left that ascends knobby Old Town Hill. The crest is about 100 ft. above sea level and offers long views. From the hilltop the trail descends and again reaches Newman Rd. at 6.5 mi. Turn left onto Newman Rd. and hike to historic Newbury Lower Green. Follow a dirt road past the west side of the green before crossing MA 1A (High Rd., use caution crossing), then follow a sidewalk over the Parker River at 6.9 mi. Once over the river bear left onto Newbury Neck Rd. Follow the road as it swings over high ground, crosses MA 1A again, and then follow Old Rowley Rd. to the Newbury–Rowley town line about 0.75 mi. from MA 1A. Head left (west) on Redgate Rd., but do not cross the railroad tracks. Follow along MA 1A for 0.75 mi. and cross over the railroad tracks on the MA 1A bridge at 9.6 mi. *Note: The BCT does not presently continue through Rowley.* To reach the next section of trail follow MA 1A about 1.8 mi. to Summer St. Turn right onto Summer St. and go 0.4 mi. to its end. Turn left onto Bradford, travel 0.2 mi., and turn right onto MA 133. The trailhead parking area is about 0.2 mi. farther, on the left (south) side of the road.

Bay Circuit Trail: Plum Island (Newburyport) to MA 1A (Rowley)
Distances from Plum Island to
- Hay St.: 3.5 mi., 1 hr. 10 min.
- Parker River: 6.9 mi., 2 hr. 30 min.
- MA 1A bridge: 9.6 mi., 3 hr. 50 min.

Section 2. Prospect Hill (Rowley) to Middleton Rd. (Boxford) (19.5 mi.)

From the parking area off MA 133 follow the dirt road past the summit road on the right. Continue straight through a field and ascend Prospect Hill (267 ft.) along a white-blazed trail, reaching the summit at 0.3 mi. Descend Prospect Hill and cross Dow Brook on a bridge at 1.0 mi. Pass beneath power lines, then turn right and continue on the trail to Conservation Commission land. The trail crosses three bridges, then continues through fields to Linebrook Rd.

The trail now enters the Willowdale State Forest at a gate. Trail junctions are numbered in the state forest, with junctions 1–12 following the BCT route. At a T-junction (3.6 mi.) turn left, followed in 0.2 mi. by a sharp right at junction 3. At junction 4 turn left; at junction 5 pass a woods road on the left. Junction 6 is reached at 5.0 mi. and can be confusing, as white blazes of the Discover Hamilton Trail enter from the left. Many side trails enter over the next 0.7 mi.; follow blazes carefully. At junctions 48, 47, 7, 8, and 9 continue straight. At 5.7 mi. turn left at junction 10, then right at junction 11, leaving the woods road and crossing a wetland area. At 6.2 mi. reach a bridge that spans Howlett Brook (Note: As of May 2005 this section was flooded by beaver activity. If the trail is impassable, turn left at junction 12, then at junction 29 go right to reach East St. Turn right on East-West St. and continue to Rte. 1.)

⚠ Follow West St. to its crossing of US 1. (*Caution: Heavy traffic.*) At 7.6 mi. cross Old Right Rd., then turn right onto a side trail and descend a hill to a footbridge. Reach Rowley Rd. and turn right to continue toward Linebrook Rd., but before reaching the road turn left into the woods. After a short woods walk cross Linebrook Rd. The trail now passes through an area of eskers—long, flowing hills—before reaching Boxford Rd. (Rowley) at 9.7 mi. at the Georgetown–Rowley State Forest. Turn right and briefly follow Boxford Rd.; then leave the road left and ascend into the woods.

Descend an esker and cross a bridge before passing through an eroded area (use caution here). Turn left, paralleling I-95. In Georgetown turn right (11.2 mi.) before the I-95 fence, then cross I-95 on the Pingree Farm Rd. bridge at 11.5 mi.

Bear left (west) at a fork in the road, then right at a T-junction. Follow blazes carefully for the next 0.5 mi. as this section of the trail is being re-routed. Cross MA 97 onto Kelsey Rd., follow this road about 0.2 mi., and turn left (south) onto an old railroad bed. The trail now heads up an embankment to run parallel to Kelsey Rd. Turn left onto Hemlock Rd., right onto Ipswich Rd., and left onto Round Top Rd. Follow Round Top Rd., turning right onto Campground Rd. then left onto Chapman Way. Cross the inlet to Lowe Pond (caution: may be flooded by recent beaver activity) on a bridge at about 16.1 mi.

Turn right onto Boren La. and left at junction 49 to the entrance of Chapman Way, which leads to Boxford center. Take Chapman Way to Georgetown Rd. Turn left (south) onto Georgetown Rd. and follow it to Depot Rd. Continue south about 0.25 mi. to Boxford Center at 16.9 mi. In Boxford center turn left onto Topsfield Rd. (BCT sign), follow it for 0.5 mi., turn right onto Cahoon St. (BCT sign), then right again into Boy Scout Park. Follow blazes onto Dana Rd., turning right onto this road and entering Lockwood Forest at 18.2 mi. Follow the path to Fish Brook, turn left, and continue on the path with the brook on the right. Pass through a field and reach Lockwood La. at 18.8 mi. Turn right onto Lockwood La., then left just before a second bridge. Follow trail markers to Middleton Rd. Cross the road and reach Bald Hill Reservation at 19.5 mi.

Bay Circuit Trail: Prospect Hill (Rowley) to Middleton Rd. (Boxford)

Distances from Prospect Hill to
- US 1: 7.6 mi., 3 hr., 35 min.
- MA 97: 14.9 mi., 6 hr. 30 min.
- Bald Hill Reservation: 19.5 mi., 9 hr.

Section 3. Boxford to Andover (15.2 mi.)

From the entrance to Bald Hill Reservation continue straight through the gate and past a pond on the left. Just beyond the edge of the pond, bear straight (right) at junction 14 off the woods road, ascending through hemlock forest. The trail crosses a small stream and climbs uphill. Turn left at junctions 23, 22, and 21; then bear left again at a fork and pass junction 26. Turn right at the wooden gate at a Trail Closed sign, then right again at junction 8A, where the main woods road is rejoined. A side trail at junction 8A leads to the summit of Bald Hill (limited views when leaves are off). Rock cairns lead to Sharpner's Pond Rd. at 3.6 mi.

Turn right onto Sharpner's Pond Rd. and follow it for 0.8 mi., then turn right onto an old railroad bed. Leave left at the first BCT blaze and cross Salem St., then power lines at 4.4 mi. Bear right at the fork, then right again at the next junction (watch for potential reroute due to beaver flooding). Follow blazes to the road past the athletic fields, then turn left onto Berry Rd. Follow Berry Rd. to MA 114 at 5.4 mi.

Cross MA 114 to Harold Parker Rd. at the entrance to Harold Parker State Forest. The BCT enters the woods about 100 yd. down the road on the right. Be alert and follow blazes carefully for the next 1.25 mi. through the forest, especially at junctions. Note the relocation of the trail at about 0.9 mi. due to wet conditions. Cross Salem St. (parking) at 7.9 mi. (there is a picnic area on the right), then reach Berry Pond Rd. at 8.2 mi. Follow the road right for a short distance, then turn right onto a trail past old quarries to a footbridge. Cross Jenkins Rd. (parking) at 9.0 mi., reaching Skug River Reservation at 9.2 mi. Many trails in Skug River Reservation use white blazes; look for BCT logos at junctions.

After passing another recently flooded area at a glacial boulder, the trail passes an old mill site, then crosses an extended boardwalk before turning left onto Salem St. (parking here) at 10.0 mi. Follow Salem St. for the short distance to Hammond and Mary French Reservations. At 10.3 mi. the trail begins a long boardwalk section that crosses the Skug River twice and offers beautiful views of the wetlands. From the boardwalk continue to Korinthian Way, turn left and follow the road to Grey Rd., turn right onto Grey Rd., then almost immediately leave the road left through the woods to Tucker Rd. at 11.3 mi.

Quickly leave Tucker Rd. right, then bear left into Charles Ward Reservation. Continue along a grassy cart path along the edge of a field and into the woods. Gradually ascend through a field to a junction—follow the wide, level path to the top of Holt Hill, where there is a beautiful view of Boston and the Blue Hills to the south. Take a sharp left (BCT marker) and descend to a paved access road at 12.2 mi. Turn left onto the access road, then right onto the trail, and continue to Prospect Rd. Turn right onto Prospect Rd. at 12.8 mi. Cross MA 125 (caution: fast-moving traffic) and continue right, parallel to the highway briefly past a wetland, then enter the woods into the Phillip's Academy Sanctuary.

Follow a woods road and cross the field on the diagonal through a driveway to Salem St. Turn right onto Salem St., then immediately left onto Holt Rd., then right into the woods, passing athletic fields and tennis courts. Follow a driveway to Main St., where the trail turns right at a traffic light. Cross the street and continue north to Philips St. Turn left onto Philips St., cross both School St. and Central St., then turn left onto Lupine Rd. and reach Purdon Reservation at 15.2 mi.

Bay Circuit Trail: Boxford to Andover

Distances from Boxford to
- MA 113: 5.4 mi., 2 hr. 10 min.
- Tucker Rd.: 11.3 mi., 3 hr. 50 min.
- Purdon Reservation: 15.2 mi., 5 hr. 20 min.

Section 4. Andover (Shawsheen River) to Lowell (National Park Visitor Center) (11.7 mi.)

The BCT is unblazed in the town of Tewksbury. In Lowell the BCT coincides with the Merrimack River Trail, which uses similar markings to the white blazes of the BCT.

From Reservation Rd. at the south end of Indian Ridge Reservation, follow the road uphill 0.1 mi., turn right and follow the trail up an esker to the Alice Buck memorial stone, then climb a second esker that passes behind Andover High School. At 1.0 mi. follow a boardwalk to West Parish Meadow Reservation; here the trail crosses the meadow and proceeds down a boardwalk before turning right onto Reservation Rd. Follow the trail through West Parish cemetery to MA 133 at 1.8 mi.

Cross MA 133 and enter Doyle Link. Follow the trail to High Plain Rd., turn left (west), and follow the road about 1.4 mi., crossing over I-93 and I-495 along the way. (*Note: At 3.6 mi. a woods road leaves to the left; this is the beginning of the proposed portion of the BCT that would lead east into Tewksbury.*) The trail enters Harold Rafton Reservation at

4.6 mi.; watch for the BCT logo at trail junctions. At 5.3 mi. the BCT crosses a brook, then passes through a field before reaching the junction of River and Chandler Rd. (parking) at 6.3 mi. Turn left onto River Rd. and quickly turn right onto Launching Rd. to reach Deer Jump Reservation.

Follow the trail toward the Merrimack River, turning left at the junction and descending toward the riverbank. Follow the river trail for 2.5 mi. to the Tewksbury pumping station. At the pumping station follow the driveway to River Rd., turn right (west) past the cemetery, and continue to a junction with MA 133. Turn right onto Burnham Rd. and walk toward the river, then turn left at the river onto the public river trail that runs through Lowell. Follow the trail along the river (BCT and Merrimack River Trail). Follow the trail closely, as some abutters have infringed on the right of way, making passage more challenging. At 11.2 mi. reach the confluence of the Merrimack and Concord Rivers. Leave the trail, walk around the Lowell Memorial Auditorium, and turn right onto Merrimack St. Follow the Merrimack River Trail to the Lowell National/State Historic Park Visitor Center (11.7 mi.) on the corner of Market St. and Shattuck St. (parking). This is the end of the marked trail in this area; Lowell Parks and Conservation Trust are working to create the Concord River greenway that will likely be the eventual BCT route. When completed the BCT will leave the Merrimack River Trail near Middlesex Community College to access the greenway.

Bay Circuit Trail: Andover (Shawsheen River) to Lowell (National Park Visitor Center)

Distances from Shawsheen River to
- MA 133: 1.8 mi., 40 min.
- Harold Rafton Reservation: 4.6 mi., 1 hr. 55 min.
- National Park Visitor Center, Lowell: 11.7 mi., 4 hr. 15 min.

Section 5. Fawn Lake Conservation Area (Bedford) to Monument St. (Acton) (4.2 mi.)

This segment is a connecting route from Fawn Lake north of Bedford center to the main BCT trail. From the Fawn Lake Conservation Area parking lot, the BCT proceeds south on the rail trail, passing a hospital and the

York Conservation Area. At 1.3 mi., the trail turns right on Springs Rd. Cross the road at the crosswalk and continue through the Bedford historic district to the town center at the junction of Springs and Great Rds. (MA 4 and MA 225). Cross Great Rd. and proceed west to Mudge Way. Follow Mudge Way left past historic buildings, the library, and the high school and athletic fields to Winchester Dr.

At 2.5 mi., the trail exits Winchester Dr. and enters the Elm Brook Conservation Area. From the back right corner of the parking lot, it soon joins an old railroad bed which leads west past side trails and the water treatment plant. After crossing Hartwell Rd., the trail continues past the Webber Wildlife Preserve, reaching a parking lot on MA 62 adjacent a red school building at 4.2 mi. The railroad bed continues from MA 62 to Great Meadows Wildlife Sanctuary, joining the trail from Acton at Monument St.

Bay Circuit Trail: Fawn Lake Conservation Area (Bedford) to Monument St. (Acton)

Distances from Fawn Lake Conservation Area parking lot to
- Elm Brook Conservation Area: 2.5 mi., 1 hr. 10 min.
- MA 62: 4.2 mi., 1 hr. 50 min.

Section 6. Acton (MA 225–MA 27 Intersection) to Concord (Annursnac Hill Conservation Area) (6.2 mi.)

The Acton section of the BCT runs along the grade of an abandoned railroad line just southeast of the intersection of MA 225 and MA 27. Follow the railroad bed generally south, crossing MA 27 at 0.7 mi. opposite a gravel pit. The trail crosses Butter Brook, then Nashoba Brook at 1.1 mi. Turn left onto a driveway (permission to use the driveway has not formally been obtained) that leads to MA 27. Turn right (south) along MA 27 (Main St.) to Wheeler Lane on the left (east). Turn onto Wheeler Lane and follow it to the dead end, where a kiosk and parking area are located.

The trail soon enters Nashoba Brook Conservation Area and runs parallel to the brook. At 2.3 mi. cross a boardwalk, then cross Nashoba Brook on a wooden bridge. Turn left (east) at the junction and head uphill, entering Spring Hill Conservation Area. At 3.0 mi. come to a junction where the BCT splits into two routes, one going to Carlisle and the other to Concord. The Carlisle link is a proposed route at this time.

The Concord link begins by turning right (south) at the junction, traveling uphill, and crossing boardwalks at 3.7 mi. and again at 4.2 mi. The BCT now climbs through forest to the top of Strawberry Hill (4.6 mi.) with views to the south. The trail descends to Jay Lane (dead end) and out to Strawberry Hill Rd. (parking). Turn left (east) on a sidewalk, turn right (south) onto Pope Rd. at 5.2 mi., then turn left (east) onto Stoneymeade Way. Bear left and enter the Stoneymeade Conservation Area at 5.9 mi. At 6.2 mi. enter the area of a ruined wartime bunker and the Annursnac Hill Conservation Area.

Bay Circuit Trail: Acton (MA 225–MA 27 Intersection) to Concord (Annursnac Hill Conservation Area)

Distances from MA 225–MA 27 intersection to
- Nashoba Brook: 2.3 mi., 55 min.
- Strawberry Hill: 4.6 mi., 2 hr.
- Annursnac Hill Conservation Area: 6.2 mi., 2 hr. 55 min.

Section 7. Concord (Annursnac Hill Conservation Area) to Walden Pond (6.5 mi.)

The section begins at the Annursnac Hill Conservation Area on the Acton–Concord town line. The BCT crosses a brook and reaches Strawberry Hill Rd. (there is an information kiosk here) at 0.5 mi. Turn right (south) onto Strawberry Hill Rd. then quickly right (south) to College Rd., which in turn leads to Barrett's Mill Rd. Turn left (east) onto Barrett's Mill Rd., crossing Strawberry Hill Rd. and the ruins of the Barrett Mill (1.9 mi.). Cross Lowell Rd. and follow Barnes Hill Rd. as it merges into Eastabrook Rd. Cross Liberty St. (Muster Field on the right) and enter Minuteman National Historic Park and Visitor Center at 3.3 mi. (parking and restrooms).

Continue down a dirt track past the Minuteman statue and the Old North Bridge, where the "shot heard 'round the world" occurred at the onset of the American Revolution in 1775. Cross the restored bridge that spans the Concord River at 3.7 mi. Follow the trail to Monument St. and turn right (south), traveling about 0.25 mi. to an old railroad bed. Turn right, passing a lumberyard and crossing Mill Brook before reaching Lowell Rd. at 4.2 mi. Turn left onto Lowell Rd., cross Mill Brook once more, and reach Monument Square. Pass through the square, turn right onto MA 62 (Main St.), and continue down the road, turning left (south) onto Walden St. and left (northeast) onto Heywood. Cross Mill Brook and swing right onto the trail that enters Heywood Meadow at 4.9 mi.

For the next 0.6 mi. proceed cautiously, as traffic is often heavy. Turn right onto Lexington Ave., then quickly bear right onto the Cambridge Turnpike. Past the home of Ralph Waldo Emerson, cross the road to a sidewalk on the east side. Follow the sidewalk over the brook and re-cross the turnpike at 5.6 mi. (utility pole 26), then follow the trail into Hapgood Town Forest. The trail wraps around a hill, reaches Fairyland Pond at 6.0 mi., and continues around a portion of the pond. Turn left before crossing the pond's inlet and climb past a spring. At the crest of the hill turn right and descend to Walden St. Turn left onto Walden St., which leads shortly to MA 2. Cross MA 2 (again, use caution crossing this multi lane highway) and travel a short way down MA 126 to the entrance of Walden Pond State Reservation (6.5 mi.) on the right.

> **Bay Circuit Trail: Concord (Annursnac Hill Conservation Area) to Walden Pond**
> Distances from Annursnac Hill Conservation Area to
> - Barrett Mill: 1.9 mi., 50 min.
> - Haywood Meadow: 4.9 mi., 2 hr. 10 min.
> - Walden Pond: 6.5 mi., 2 hr. 55 min.

Section 8. Concord (Walden Pond) to Wayland (Great Meadows National Wildlife Refuge) (12.1 mi.)

The BCT enters Walden Pond State Reservation and on the right follows the path along the shore of Walden Pond, passing the replica of Henry David Thoreau's cabin and the railroad tracks on the right. Turn right and follow the Esker Trail past the Emerson's Cliff Trail, then turn right onto a fire road that leads out of the reservation and to MA 126 at 1.3 mi.

Cross MA 126, then follow beside the road (turn right, south) on a trail that parallels the highway. At the junction with Old Concord Rd. cross MA 126 to Old Concord Rd. and follow it 0.1 mi. to a dirt road on the left. Follow the dirt road into the woods and reach Mt. Misery at 1.4

mi. Follow the Kettle Trail (blazed blue) to an intersection where the BCT turns left on a path marked with blue bike blazes. The path continues past a small pond to the parking area at the end of the pond. Continue through the parking area to MA 117, then turn left and follow the trail (east) that parallels the road, reaching the canoe launch parking lot for Farrar Pond at 2.4 mi.

Cross MA 117 just past the parking area, go up a private driveway (numbers 17 and 19), and turn left through fences onto a trail that stays close to the fence line. The trail then reaches Farrar Pond, crosses a spillway, and heads uphill. Follow the trail, now pavement, to Birchwood La. and turn right into the woods at 3.3 mi. The trail exits the woods near Kettlehole Dr. at 3.9 mi. Turn right onto Kettlehole Dr., which soon reaches Oxbow Rd. at the Wayland town line.

Note: Through Wayland there are BCT logos at trailheads. The remainder of the trail is not blazed. Follow Oxbow Rd. to Campbell Rd., turn right, and continue to a water department access road on the right. Turn left onto the access road and continue a short way to a trail on the right before the pump house. Enter the Trout Brook Conservation Area at 4.4 mi. on a red-blazed trail that crosses the brook, then climbs uphill through an area with many kettle holes. Follow red blazes to the B junction, then follow yellow blazes (right turn) to the M junction. Continue on the yellow-marked trail to Sherman's Bridge Rd. and the main trailhead for the Trout Brook Conservation Area.

Cross Sherman's Bridge Rd. onto Alpine Rd. Continue a short distance to the Castle Hill Conservation Area and a colonial-style road on the left at 5.0 mi. The trail passes through wetlands east, then south, of Schoolhouse Pond and then east to MA 126. Turn right onto MA 126 and proceed to Moore Rd. This section of trail can be closed due to beaver activity flooding the trail. The bypass route is to travel 0.3 mi. east on Sherman's Bridge Rd., then right onto MA 126, and continue 0.75 mi. to Moore Rd., where the route rejoins the BCT.

At Moore Rd. turn right (northwest) and travel 0.4 mi. to a parking area for the Sedge Meadow Conservation Area on the right. Follow the trail through Sedge Meadow, passing fields and water company land along frequently wet paths. Pass Sedge Meadow Monument at 7.7 mi. before reaching Glezen La. near Black Cat Farm (parking). Turn right (west) onto MA 27 (there is parking to the left at Cow Common Conservation Area).

Cross MA 127 and enter the Cow Common Conservation Area at 8.5 mi. The BCT heads across a field, turns right (south) into the woods and over a stream, coming to some community gardens and reaching MA 27 at 9.4 mi. Turn right onto MA 27, then bear left onto Bow Rd. to Concord Rd. (MA 126). Turn right onto MA 126 and pass through the town center. Turn right (west) onto US 20, then follow Pelham Island Rd. southwest across the Sudbury River on a narrow bridge. Turn left onto Heard Rd. and follow this to its dead end (parking). The trail enters a field and loops around Heard Farm to Erwin Rd. Turn right onto Erwin Rd., then quickly left onto Pelham Island Rd., which passes Heard Pond and enters Great Meadows National Wildlife Refuge at 12.1 mi. This is the end of this portion of the BCT. It resumes in Sudbury at the Weisblatt Conservation Land.

Bay Circuit Trail: Concord (Walden Pond) to Wayland (Great Meadows National Wildlife Refuge)

Distances from Walden Pond to
- Mt. Misery: 1.4 mi., 45 min.
- Cow Common Conservation Area: 8.5 mi., 4 hr.
- Great Meadows National Wildlife Refuge: 12.1 mi., 6 hr. 5 min.

For a description of the Bay Circuit route from Sudbury to its southern end on the coast in Duxbury and Kingston, see Part VI—Southeastern Massachusetts and the Islands—beginning on page 336.

Dogtown

The Dogtown area of Cape Ann, which occupies approximately 3 sq. mi. of undeveloped land between Gloucester and Rockport, was once "common land" where each settler in the village at the southern end of the cape had rights for cutting wood and pasturing. When a village started to grow here in 1719, it was known as the Commons Settlement.

By the 1740s, 25 houses were at Dogtown, including those of several wealthy families. After the American Revolution, however, the more prosperous families began moving toward the harbor, where opportunities for trade were better, and Dogtown slid into decline. Some trace the name *Dogtown* to the packs of animals that poor women and widows kept for protection. Others insist that the origin is lost in history. Generations ago the upland plateau known as Dogtown resembled something out of the Sherlock Holmes novel *The Hound of the Baskervilles*, with rough moors and obtrusive boulders. Today the area is growing up into a thick coastal forest of oak and sumac, with the thorny tangles of greenbrier filling the swamps.

To reach Dogtown take MA 128 to the rotary in Gloucester (Exit 11). Turn left onto MA 127 toward Annisquam and continue 1.0 mi. to Reynard St., located on the right just after the Mill River crossing. Take Reynard St. east until it ends at Cherry St. Turn left (north) onto Cherry St. and drive for about 0.15 mi. to Dogtown Rd., the first right off Cherry St. Turn right to the parking area. The left gate is the continuation of Dogtown Rd.; the right gate is the entrance to the Cape Ann Sportsman's Club Rifle Range (gunshots are often audible).

The city of Gloucester owns much of the Dogtown area, and the described trails explore land open for public use. Avoid venturing onto private land, and do not walk on or cross the MBTA high-speed railroad tracks at the southeast end of Dogtown. Don't block the gates when you park. The trails in Dogtown can be divided into fire roads, main trails, and secondary paths. It is easy to get lost—follow the trails and markers carefully. The cellars are designated by numbers carved on nearby rocks. Be cautious when venturing onto secondary trails, as it is sometimes challenging to keep to the paths.

Dogtown Trail (City of Gloucester)

Follow Dogtown Rd. beyond the gate as it heads northeast. The Adams Pines Trail leaves left (north) for Common Rd. at junction 1. Dogtown Rd. continues past many cellar holes, each with a number chiseled on it for identification by Roger Babson, who made a directory of the families who once lived here. The trail reaches Dogtown Square, where a low rock on the right is marked D.T. SQ. Granny Day Swamp is to the left (northwest), with Wharf Rd. following the east side of the swamp to Common Rd. The Moraine Trail heads east from here. Dogtown Square is used as a common point to make circuits of the surrounding land.

Old Gravel Rd. (City of Gloucester)

This trail heads southeast from Dogtown Rd. near the south end of the gravel pit. It crosses over fairly level, easy ground and through a maze of glacial boulders, the rocky remains of a glacial moraine left behind as the ice retreated thousands of years ago. The path now descends, tapering to a rugged, often wet trail that leads to the northern tip of Babson Reservoir. Just east of the reservoir, at junction 22, the Babson Boulder Trail heads north toward Dogtown Square and the Old Gravel Rd. ends.

Babson Boulder Trail (City of Gloucester)

Roger Babson was a widely published financier and entrepreneur who helped found several universities. He literally left his mark on this Dogtown trail via a series of boulders with motivational words and phrases carved into them. From the Old Gravel Rd. junction the trail begins to ascend the ridge, reaching a boulder (Truth) just before a side trail leaves left. The Babson Boulder Trail continues uphill, passing Work and Courage. The path now crests the ridge and cruises through the woods before climbing to a marshy wetland with blueberries before the trail reaches relatively level ground. Near Uncle Andrew's Rock the trail reaches Dogtown Rd. very near Dogtown Square.

Common Rd. (City of Gloucester)

Common Rd. links Goose Pond Reservoir in the west to Squam Path Trail in the north. The trail begins off the service road, midway up the east side of the reservoir. From the Dogtown parking area it can be accessed by taking Dogtown Rd. to the Adams Pines Trail at junction 1, then turning left (north) onto the Adams Pines Trail to junction 2 just east of the trailhead. The trail passes through a swampy area with tangles of brier and summersweet. At junctions 4 and 5 Wharf Rd. leaves right (south) for Dogtown Square. Past the Wharf Trail is a large glacial boulder called Peter's Pulpit; then the path swings north and climbs over a small plateau. It then drops down to meet the Luce Trail at junction 16. Common Rd. coincides with the Luce Trail (orange dots) and reaches the signature feature of Dogtown—the Whale Jaw Boulder.

Whale Jaw is a huge glacial boulder split in such a way as to look like a tremendous whale, mouth agape, breaking from the ground in search of hiker snacks. Generations ago when Dogtown was open country the stark boulder was chillingly impressive. Today the oaks and brush seem to be swallowing the rock rather than the reverse. The trail continues with the Luce Trail until Common Rd. ends at Squam Path at junction 19 at the far northern end of the reservation.

Ravenswood Park

This 600-acre wooded reservation, located in the Magnolia section of Gloucester, was the vision of Samuel Sawyer, who began to acquire and preserve land in the 1800s. When he died in 1889 he left an endowment and instructions to a group of trustees to turn the then 26 parcels into a park named Ravenswood, from the *Bride of Lammermoor*, by Sir Walter Scott. Today the property consists of about 10 mi. of carriage roads and hiking trails, including a boardwalk through Great Magnolia Swamp where sweet bay magnolias grow. The park is located on MA 127 in Gloucester. From MA 128, take Exit 14 and follow MA 133 east for 3.0 mi. to MA 127. Go south on MA 127 for 2.0 mi.; the entrance and parking are located on the right.

The wide carriage roads are generally hard-packed and smooth enough to be used for wheelchairs. A broad carriage road (closed to vehicles) enters the park from the main entrance and is intersected by an extensive network of narrow woodland paths. New trail markers are now in place.

Old Salem Rd. (TTOR)

This trail begins on MA 127, about 0.3 mi. west of the main entrance. Because there is no parking here, most hikers approach this trail via Valley Rd. The trail enters the woods north of MA 127 as a narrow footpath, and soon crosses the Swamp Trail (to the left is the swamp, to the right is Valley Rd.). Shortly an unmarked link to the Swamp Trail is passed on the left. At 0.6 mi. the trail meets Valley Rd. and continues straight (northeast) on the carriage road. To the right Valley Rd. leads back to the main entrance. Also at this junction is another link to the Swamp Trail, leaving east past an old cellar hole.

Old Salem Rd. continues on the carriage road, past a trail junction where the northern end of the Swamp Trail leaves left and an unmarked link to Ridge Rd. leaves right. At 1.0 mi. another carriage road, Evergreen Rd., leaves on the right, followed shortly by an unmarked link to Evergreen Rd., also on the right.

At 1.6 mi. a stone with a plaque marks the former location of the old Hermit Shelter, once the home of Mason Walton, a naturalist who lived in a cabin here in the late 1800s. At this point the carriage road turns to the right and becomes the north end of Evergreen Rd. Old Salem Rd. reverts to a narrow path and continues straight. The Ledge Hill Trail departs to the right just before the Ravenswood property boundary. Old Salem Rd. continues off the property and ends at MA 127 a short distance north of Hough Ave.

Old Salem Rd.

Distances from MA 127 (Western Ave.) to
- Valley Rd.: 0.6 mi., 20 min.
- southern end of Evergreen Rd.: 1.0 mi., 30 min.
- northern end of Evergreen Rd.: 1.6 mi., 50 min.
- MA 127 (Western Ave.): 1.8 mi., 1 hr.

Swamp Trail (TTOR)

The Swamp Trail leaves on the left between two boulders, 0.2 mi. from the trailhead. After traversing huge flat ledges, it descends the western side of the moraine to a large swamp filled with ferns in spring and scarlet swamp maples in fall. After crossing the swamp the trail veers north for 0.5 mi. before rejoining Old Salem Rd. by an old cellar hole at 1.5 mi.. The swamp can be impassable in spring but can be avoided by taking a shorter trail that runs north along the western side of the moraine before rejoining Old Salem Rd. by the cellar hole (0.8 mi.).

Swamp Trail

Distance from Old Salem Rd. to
- Old Salem Rd. second junction: 1.5 mi., 40 min.

Ledge Trail (TTOR)

The Ledge Trail leaves Old Salem Rd. directly opposite the south junction with the Swamp Trail. It winds its way northeast past Otter Pond, around boulders covered with evergreen ferns, among tall hemlocks and oaks, and past views over a quarry and Buswell Pond. At 2.0 mi. it ends at the north end of Old Salem Rd. Farther up Old Salem Rd. is the forked entrance to Ridge Rd., which leads northeast to connect with Evergreen Rd.

Ledge Trail
Distance from Old Salem Rd. to
• Old Salem Rd. (north end): 2.0 mi., 55 min.

Halibut Point and Sea Rocks

Halibut Point in Rockport is Cape Ann's northernmost headland, originally called "Haul-about Point" by mariners heading to and from Annisquam to the southwest. The protected land on the point includes a 56-acre state park (DCR) and an adjoining 12-acre property of The Trustees of Reservations, and features a stretch of rockbound coastline similar to that found farther north in Maine. Universally accessible restrooms are available. Sea Rocks is a narrow stretch of rocky headland owned by the town of Rockport and open to the public. It is located just east of the tract owned by TTOR.

From MA 128 take Exit 9 to MA 127 and continue north 3.0 mi. to Rockport center. Turn left onto Railroad Ave. (MA 127) and continue 2.4 mi. to Gott Ave. Turn right to the entrance and a large parking area.

The state park is home to a large, abandoned quarry. In the early 1900s, stone blocks of up to 40 tons were moved from here with the aid of steam drills, four hoisting derricks, and a railroad system. The Great Depression, along with the shift in construction from cut stone to concrete, led to the end of quarrying in 1929. The main quarry is now flooded and the deep green water looks inviting, but swimming is strictly forbidden due to danger from submerged rocks and equipment. The visitor center is located in the old fire control tower at the edge of the Babson Quarry. Amazing views can be had from the top of the 60-ft.-tall structure. Most areas of the park are universally accessible, and assisted-listening devices are available for park tours.

Halibut Point offers short, well-marked footpaths that allow easy exploration of the rocky coast and overlooks of the Atlantic Ocean. Below the high-tide level, many tidal pools lie among the granite boulders; use caution, as the rocks can be slippery. A consistent ocean breeze blows over the point, and from the top of the "grout pile" (waste stone heap) a clear day offers a view extending to the Isles of Shoals in New Hampshire and beyond to Mt. Agamenticus in Maine.

Maudslay State Park

Once the elegant estate of the Moseley family, this 480-acre state park is a joy to visit. Located on the Merrimack River in Newburyport, the grounds are a blend of nineteenth century gardens growing near tangles of mountain laurel and azalea. Towering pines and woodlands offer hiking and biking trails. Some of the features accessible from the many trails include the punch bowl, kettle pond, beech grove, Italian rose garden, and Rhododendron Dell.

To reach Maudslay Park from I-95 (Exit 57), take MA 113 east for 0.5 mi. and turn left onto Noble St. Continue to a stop sign and turn left onto Ferry Rd. Bear left and follow signs to the entrance. From the west, take Exit 55 off I-495 to MA 110 east. Travel 1.0 mi. to Merrill St., turn right at the second light, and continue for 1.5 mi. on Merrill and Spofford St. At a stop sign turn right onto Ferry Rd. and follow signs to the entrance.

Merrimack River Trail (DCR)

The Merrimack River Trail traces a mostly east-west course across the northern perimeter of the reservation, following the south bank of the river. Its western trailhead is at the end of Curzon Mill Rd., which is accessed at the main entrance. The trail follows the edge of the river, passing a pair of scenic overlooks. It then turns left on the Mile Circuit multi use trail, then left again on the Laurel Walk Trail, which it follows briefly north before the trails split. The River Trail then bears right and continues on bluffs above the river, veering away briefly to follow the Castle Hill Trail. The trail then turns south and exits the reservation near Arrowhead Farm.

Merrimack River Trail

Distance from western trailhead at Curzon Mill Rd. to
  • eastern trailhead at park boundary: 1.5 mi., 45 min.

Parker River National Wildlife Refuge

The Parker River National Wildlife Refuge on Plum Island, in Newbury, Rowley, and Ipswich, is operated by the U.S. Department of the Interior's Fish and Wildlife Service. The headquarters is located at 6 Plum Island Turnpike in Newburyport.

The refuge encompasses a variety of coastal habitats, including a 6.3-mi. beach, dunes, shrublands, and fresh and saltwater marshes. The birdlife is outstanding; Parker River is a nesting site for many shorebirds, including the threatened piping plover. The area is managed primarily as wildlife habitat; recreational use is limited accordingly.

Beginning April 1, the entire 6.3 mi. of beach is closed to all public entry to protect the plovers and other birds such as least terns. Areas of the beach that are not being used by the birds may be reopened beginning July 1. The entire beach is usually reopened by mid-August. A one-day deer-hunt is allowed in fall, and at this time the area is closed to all other activities. Current information about closings can be obtained from the Fish and Wildlife Service (978-465-5753).

The Nelson Island area is accessible only by foot, and is closed during waterfowl hunting during the fall and winter. Biting insects are troublesome throughout the refuge during the warmer months. Mosquitoes, greenhead horseflies, and ticks are common.

Universally accessible restrooms can be found at parking areas 1 (seasonal) and 4 (year-round). Potable water is available only at parking area 1. To reach the refuge from the traffic light on MA 1A just south of Newbury center, turn right (northeast) onto the Plum Island Turnpike, continue 0.5 mi., and turn right (east) again. Proceed 2.3 mi. (passing the airport on the right) to a paved road on the right. Turn onto the paved road and enter the refuge in 0.5 mi. During warmer months the refuge fills to capacity quickly, and on busy days the entrance gate may close as early as 9 a.m. (*Note: The gate closing applies to cyclists as well as those arriving by car.*) Gate closings can last for several hours; an early arrival is recommended.

The refuge's 6.5-mi. (one-way) road is designed for scenic enjoyment and not fast travel. Roadside parking is prohibited along the entire length of the road, and the speed limit is 25 MPH throughout. The first 3.5 mi. of roadway are paved; the remaining distance is gravel. Various small parking lots provide access to boardwalks to the beach. The salt pannes, just after lot 2, attract numerous and varied shorebirds. At lot 4 the Hellcat Swamp Nature Trail, described below, traverses a series of habitats, and other short trails begin at lots 5 and 6. The road ends at Sandy Point State Park, which includes more beaches and a wooded hill. Public access in the refuge is limited to the road, the beach, and the marked trails. Off-limit areas are clearly indicated by blue-and-white signs.

Hellcat Interpretive Trail (USFWS)

This 1.4-mi.-long trail is comprised of two short trails, the Marsh and Dunes Trails, that fork from the trailhead near the parking area and lead through the refuge's diverse habitats on a series of boardwalks. This is considered one of the Northeast's finest birding trails, especially during spring migrations. An interpretive booklet provides information about the reservation's characteristic vegetation and habitats. To reach the trailhead, follow the auto road to lot 4.

The trail leads north from the parking area and splits at junction 1. Here the 0.8-mi. Marsh Trail bears left. At the start of the loop beyond interpretive post 2, bear left and follow the trail along the edge of a large freshwater marsh that was created during the 1950s to provide wildlife habitat. After post 5, bear left at a junction at the north end of the loop and continue to the trail's end at a wooden observation blind from which a variety of waterfowl and wading birds can be seen. Turn around and retrace your steps to the end of the loop, then follow either fork back to the split at junction 1.

The 0.6-mi. Dunes Trail continues right from junction 1. It passes oak woodlands and a small swamp before crossing the refuge road. From the refuge road, the trail loops over one of the refuge dunes on wooden stairs, with views of the various habitats and an overlook that provides a good perspective of this narrow barrier island. The loop ends as the trail returns to the refuge road; backtrack from the road to junction 1 and the parking area.

Hellcat Interpretive Trail

Distances from parking area trailhead to
- end of Marsh Trail loop: 0.8 mi., 30 min.
- end of Dunes Trail loop: 0.6 mi., 25 min
- cumulative distance from trailhead: 1.4 mi., 55 min.

Crane Beach

Crane Beach consists of 1,233 acres of white sand beach and dunes along both sides of Castle Neck, a finger of land extending into the sea. The area is one of the most important nesting sites for the endangered piping plover. An extensive pitch pine forest, carnivorous plants, and cranberries can all be found here. More than 5 mi. of marked trails explore the area, some on elevated walkways to protect the environment. The area is also known for its bird watching and fall foliage.

From MA 128 take Exit 20A and follow MA 1A north for 8 mi. to Ipswich. Turn right onto MA 133 east and continue 1.5 mi., then turn left onto Northgate Rd. Travel 0.5 mi., turn right onto Argilla Rd., and drive 2.5 mi. to the entrance at the end of the road (1,300 cars).

During peak season (Memorial Day through Labor Day) Crane Beach is a popular albeit expensive swimming beach. (Admission fees are lower for cyclists.) Summer weekends can be particularly crowded. Dogs are not allowed between April 1 and September 30, but are allowed on leash from October 1 to March 30.

Near Crane Beach is the Crane Wildlife Refuge (TTOR), which consists of 697 acres of islands, salt marsh, and intertidal environments. More than 3 mi. of trails explore this area, where over 200 species of birds have been observed.

Crane Beach Loop (TTOR)

Two trails start from the right side of the beach parking lot: a short, well-marked nature trail, and a longer, less well defined "low-impact" trail marked by posts in the dunes. Take a pleasant round trip of about 5.0 mi. by following the posts up and down the dunes until the path emerges on the bank of the Castle Neck River. (Exact location of the posts may change occasionally to minimize the impact of foot traffic.) At the river turn left and follow the riverbank around the point to the barrier beach, and then follow the beach back to the parking lot. (*Note: This area is ecologically fragile. The dunes, which prevent the land from being engulfed by the sea, are held together by the long, connected roots of plants. Stay on the marked trail and do not walk along the crests of the dunes, slide down the dunes, or step on the vegetation.*)

Crane Beach Loop
Distance from beach parking lot to
 • trailhead (circuit): 5 mi., 2 hr. 50 min.

Bradley W. Palmer State Park

Bradley Palmer was a high-powered lawyer in the first half of the twentieth century who counted among his clients Sinclair Oil (Teapot Dome scandal) and Woodrow Wilson (the Treaty of Versailles). His estate is now a 721-acre park located in the towns of Hamilton and Topsfield. The park includes old farm and pastureland that have grown up to woods extending south from the Ipswich River. Carriage roads run across the property and are often lined with rhododendrons, providing spectacular scenery in June.

A universally accessible trail begins near the parking area by the main entrance on Asbury St. and runs roughly along the course of the Ipswich River. It ends near the footbridge that spans the river and leads to the Ipswich Rd. parking area. Unmarked trails of various lengths total more than 20 mi. Horseback riders use them extensively, as do cross-country skiers and snowshoers. Willowdale Hill (196 ft.), known locally as Moon Hill, provides a good view north from its grassy top.

To reach the main entrance and park headquarters, follow Ipswich Rd. in Topsfield 1.25 mi. east from US 1 (state park sign) and turn right onto Asbury St. The park entrance is a short distance on the left.

Grassland Trail (DCR)

This trail begins on the paved road (closed to vehicles) leading northwest through a gate opposite the parking area. At 0.3 mi. the road curves left (heading toward the Ipswich River and the River Trail), while the Grassland Trail continues as a dirt road straight ahead. At a trail junction at 0.5 mi. the Willowdale Trail goes left (north) to a junction with the River Trail and the Fisherman's Trail, while the Bittersweet Trail goes right (south) toward Blueberry Hill. The Grassland Trail continues straight and shortly thereafter turns sharp right; the Winthrop Trail leads straight ahead from this junction to reach the Ipswich River in 0.3 mi. near Willowdale Dam and the remains of an old gristmill. (From the end of the Winthrop Trail, a return loop can be made via the Fisherman's Trail and the River Trail.)

Heading south, the Grassland Trail passes a short side trail to the right leading to the open field atop Willowdale Hill. Passing several other trail junctions but continuing straight, it ends near the recreation area at the eastern end of the park.

Grassland Trail

Distances from park headquarters to
- Willowdale Trail: 0.5 mi., 15 min.
- Winthrop Trail: 0.6 mi., 20 min.
- recreation area: 1.4 mi., 40 min.

Willowdale State Forest

This 2,400-acre forest in Ipswich is composed of three separate areas, each of which consists of mixed conifer and hardwood growth scattered amid swamps and meadows. The forest is traversed by 40 mi. of easily followed, but unmarked, woods roads. These travel on the ground that borders and separates the eastern and western sections of Willowdale Swamp, which occupies most of the central section of the area. Additional recreational opportunities exist at Hood Pond, a 100-acre lake within the forest. The eastern end of Willowdale also borders Bradley W. Palmer State Park along Ipswich Rd. Hikers at Bradley Palmer can walk across the footbridge near the end of the universally accessible trail, cross Ipswich Rd., and hike on the gravel carriage roads. The Bay Circuit Trail bisects the forest.

All three areas border on Linebrook Rd. in Ipswich, which crosses US 1 at a point 3.6 mi. north of the junction of US 1 and MA 97 in Topsfield. The smaller areas are on the right (north) and left (south) of Linebrook Rd., 1.5 mi. and 2.0 mi., respectively, west of its junction with US 1. The main entrance to the forest is through a gate on the right (south) side of Linebrook Rd., 0.8 mi. east of US 1 and 100 yd. west of Howe St. A woods road goes right (south) from the gate, reaches a fork at 150 yd., goes left, and continues to a second fork, where the Willowdale Circuit Walk begins. (A right turn at the first fork, continuing south at all intersections, leads to a point on Gravelly Brook Rd. a few hundred yards north of where Gravelly Brook Rd. joins Ipswich Rd. opposite the western entrance to Bradley W. Palmer State Park.) Refer to the USGS Georgetown quadrangle.

Willowdale Circuit Walk (DCR)

This walk begins 300 yd. south of the main entrance at the second fork. It turns left (east) along a woods road, passes a woods road on the left leading to Linebrook Rd., and, near a grove of red pines, turns right (south) along another woods road that follows along a glacial esker just north of Willowdale Swamp. The trail turns right (south) along a dirt road, continues through a cornfield, and crosses a causeway over a narrow neck of the swamp. After passing over Bull Brook at the swamp's northeast outlet, the trail continues east to a fork (the dirt surface ends here) and follows a woods road right (south). [Going left at the fork skirts the northern base of steep, twin-summited Bartholomew Hill (184 ft.) to end at Pine Swamp Rd., the eastern boundary of the forest.]

The trail continues south on the woods road and in 0.3 mi. descends a bluff to a woods road on the right. (This 0.4-mi. road connects the eastern and western parts of the circuit and can be used to shorten the walk by 1.5 mi.) The trail continues south from this junction, then turns right at a crossroads. (The woods road traveling northeast from here passes between the northern and southern summits of Bartholomew Hill. The woods road traveling southeast skirts the base of the southern summit. Both roads end at Pine Swamp Rd., 0.1 mi. apart.) The trail bears sharp right (west) along a 160-yd. causeway that crosses a narrow strip of swamp and Gravelly

Brook (the south outlet of Willowdale Swamp), which between this point and the Ipswich River forms the eastern boundary of the forest.

The trail proceeds right at a fork to a grassy triangle, makes a sharp right turn (northwest), and soon bears right (north) at a wide triangle. (A left turn leads south to Gravelly Brook Rd., which in turn goes south to Bradley W. Palmer State Park.) The trail follows the woods road north between the eastern and western sections of the swamp, crosses the narrow northwestern end of Gravelly Brook, passes through a gravel pit, and reaches the western end of the shortcut. The trail then crosses an unnamed stream via a bridge and slightly more than 0.3 mi. farther north returns to the beginning.

Willowdale Circuit Walk

Distance from second fork in woods road to
- second fork (circuit): 3.5 mi., 2 hr. 30 min.

Discover Hamilton Trail (DCR)

This 10.0-mi.-long, white-blazed loop trail begins and ends at the town hall in Hamilton's Historic District. It uses roads and trails to connect the many parks and reservations around the area, including Harvard Forest, Appleton Farms Grass Rides, Essex County Greenbelt Willowdale Mill Reservation, Bradley W. Palmer State Park, and Pingree Reservation. A summary description with approximate distances follows; for more detail refer to trail maps and information which are available at the Hamilton Town Hall on Bay Rd.

From the town hall, the trail follows Bay Rd. north for 0.25 mi., then turns left (southwest) on Cutler Rd., skirting the north edge of Cutler Pond and its associated wetlands. The trail arcs away from the road, then rejoins it shortly before crossing the Boston and Maine railroad tracks at 1.25 mi. The long loop begins just west of the crossing, and is described here as a clockwise circuit.

Turn left at the junction and follow the trail through the Black Brook watershed, passing Harvard Forest and the Pingree Reservation. The trail winds, then bears west to Highland St. at 2.8 mi. Turn right and walk northwest on Highland St., then follow the trail left into Bradley Palmer State Park. The trail crosses the park entrance road, then arcs west and winds over Blueberry and Willowdale Hills; the latter (196 ft.) is also known as Moon Hill and offers good views to the north.

The trail descends Moon Hill and turns sharp right near the east bank of the Ipswich River at 5 mi. The trail follows the river north through the Willowdale Mill Reservation, then turns right on Winthrop St. (parking available). It continues due east along Winthrop St., then turns left (north) on Highland St. at 6.7 mi. Follow Highland St. to the junction called Nancy's Corner (parking available), and turn right on Cutler Rd. The trail briefly follows Cutler Rd., then bears left off the road and enters the Appleton Farms Reservation (TTOR). The trail passes the stone bridge, Appleton Farms Grass Rides, and a granite monument that marks several of the farm's carriage paths. The trail continues southeast, completing the loop as it rejoins Cutler Rd. at 8.6 mi. Turn left (east) and retrace your steps to the historic district and town hall.

Discover Hamilton Trail

Distances from town hall to
- start of loop on Cutler Rd.: 1.4 mi., 45 min.
- right turn near Ipswich River: 5.0 mi., 2 hr. 20 min.
- junction of Winthrop St. and Highland St.: 6.7 mi., 3 hr. 10 min.
- town hall (circuit): 10.0 mi., 4 hr. 30 min.

Ipswich River Wildlife Sanctuary

This is Massachusetts Audubon's largest sanctuary, consisting of 2,267 acres of unspoiled forest, wetland, and meadows in Topsfield. In addition to 10 mi. of trails, the preserve also offers 8 mi. of canoeing on the Ipswich River. For MAS members only, camping is permitted on Perkins Island about 0.25 mi. upstream on the river, and a cabin is available for rent near the office. Part of the sanctuary was once an old arboretum; the boulders and exotic plants are explored along the sanctuary's Rockery Trail. Specific features to enjoy include Great Wenham Swamp, Hassocky Meadow, Rockery Pond, and the drumlin called Bradstreet Hill. Trails are well marked by numbered posts at junctions, keyed to a trail map available at the registration desk. Restrooms are available near the parking area and office.

From Boston and points south, follow I-95 north to Exit 50, turning onto US 1 north. At the junction of US 1 and MA 97, turn right onto MA

97 south (toward Beverly and Danvers). Take the third left onto Perkins Row. Continue on Perkins Row for 1.0 mi. to the entrance on the right.

From the north, take I-95 south to Exit 53 and follow MA 97 south to its junction with US 1 in Topsfield. Continue on MA 97 south and take the second left onto Perkins Row. Follow Perkins Row for 1.0 mi. to the entrance on the right.

Swamp Marsh Edge Circuit (MAS)

This circuit route combines parts of several different trails to provide an interesting and varied walk. Proceed south from the sanctuary headquarters and follow the Bunker Meadows Trail for 0.4 mi. along a stone wall, crossing the Drumlin Trail. To the right is a wooden observation tower that offers a nice view of the Bunker Meadows marshes, notable for their magnificent expanse of water lilies in summer. The Bunker Meadows Trail turns east to the Ipswich River. Continue northeasterly to junction with the South Esker Trail, which offers a resting bench with a view of Wenham Swamp and Fowler's Island. The South Esker Trail turns north through higher ground and ends at a wooden bridge. A few yards north a larger stone bridge with views of Mile Brook and Waterfowl Pond often offers sightings of painted turtles and colorful dragonflies. Follow the signs to Averill's Island, and take the Averill's Island Trail, which splits and comes together again, with both branches heading north.

Continue to the junction with the White Pine Trail, then go left and follow the White Pine Trail west to the Mile Brook Trail. Turn left (south) onto the Mile Brook Trail, following the edge of a privately owned swamp. (*Note: The Mile Brook Trail may be very wet. Several paths to the right lead to the higher North Esker Trail, which can be used as an alternate route.*) Both the Mile Brook and North Esker Trails go south through forest to reach the stone bridge. Cross the stone bridge and turn right onto the Innermost Trail, a boardwalk through marshy woods that leads to a wide grass path back to the sanctuary headquarters.

Phillips Academy Bird Sanctuary

This sanctuary in Andover is especially beautiful in May and early June when the azaleas and rhododendrons are in bloom. Wild ducks and Canada geese often land on the artificial ponds, and many birds inhabit the woods. The trails are well-maintained gravel roads. The sanctuary closes at 6 p.m. Dogs are not allowed in the sanctuary.

Circuit Trail (Phillips Academy)

This trail begins in Andover at the end of Chapel Ave., just beyond the Andover Inn at the parking area beyond George Washington Hall. The trail leads straight ahead on a continuation of Chapel Ave. past Phillips Academy dormitories on the left and George Washington Hall on the right. The trail passes Stimson House on the right (sign) and enters the Moncrief Cochran ornamental memorial gate. Soon after passing through this gate the trail leads through the right-hand door in the metal sanctuary fence. (*Note: Be sure that the gate is securely latched after you enter.*) The trail proceeds up a path among rhododendron bushes. At the crest of a rise it bears right at the fork.

A road soon enters left. This is the western end of a loop around two artificial ponds. The Circuit Trail continues straight ahead, crossing a bridge over a small brook in a short distance. It ascends a slight rise and passes the eastern loop road on the left. The trail continues straight ahead and soon reaches a log cabin at the crest of a hill. The trail continues on the road, which bears a sharp left downhill. It turns left at a fork at the foot of the first short descent, passes a trail on the right (a shortcut), and continues straight ahead. The eastern loop around the pond soon enters left. The trail then crosses a bridge over a pond outlet. Near the top of a steep rise, the western loop enters left. The trail bears right uphill and soon swings left, leading back to the crest of the rise.

Peggy Keck Reservation (AVIS)

Part of the eastern section of this 40-acre reservation is wetland, and the rest is hilly with rock outcrops. To reach the reservation, take I-93 to Exit 41, then follow MA 125 north for 2.9 mi. Park west of MA 125 at the intersection with Gould Rd. diagonally across from the State Police barracks. Rocky Hill Rd. (unpaved) runs off Gould Rd. diagonally across the reservation from southeast to northwest.

Two places in the reservation are especially worth visiting: some rocky cliffs and an interesting view of a deep valley. The main trail is an old woods road formerly known as Rocky Hill Rd., and there are trails that loop back to the main trail on both sides of the woods road (loop distance: 1.0 mi.).

Vale Reservation (AVIS)

Located between the commuter rail tracks and the Shawsheen River, this 45-acre reservation consists of hillocks and wetlands. To reach it, follow I-93 to Exit 42, then take Dascomb Rd. east. Turn right onto Clark Rd. and continue 0.5 mi. Turn right onto Andover St., cross the railroad tracks, turn sharp left onto Dale St., and continue to the end of the dirt road (no sign) where the reservation begins. Parking is available here.

The marked trail begins on the right (east) and continues to the Shawsheen River. After about 0.25 mi. the trail crosses over an elevated platform and splits. The right fork follows the Shawsheen River downstream and then rejoins the left fork. (The right fork may be impassable during wet weather.) The left fork heads north through woods and open fields into Shawsheen River Reservation. (Loop distance: 2.0 mi.)

Shawsheen River Reservation (AVIS)

This 30-acre reservation extends 0.5 mi. between the Shawsheen River and the railroad tracks. It is mostly grassy fields, with some wetlands along the river. Take I-93 to the Dascomb Rd. exit, then go east on Dascomb Rd. for 1.3 mi., turn left onto Andover St., and go 0.7 mi. to the Horn Bridge. Park just beyond the bridge in an open space on the right.

Walk under the bridge onto Central St. and enter the reservation on the right. The trail leads across a meadow. In 0.1 mi. a marshy brook traverses the field. Cross the small bridge near the railroad tracks, then follow the river past some large granite blocks. At 0.5 mi. a path diverges across the meadow (possible short loop) and the trail continues south to Vale Reservation.

Baker's Meadow Reservation (AVIS)

This bird sanctuary is remarkable for its migratory waterfowl. Its 59 acres include a marsh and pond along with a bordering strip of higher ground. The entrance is located on Reservation Rd., 0.8 mi. northwest of the Horn Bridge (where parking is available), opposite the exit from Indian Ridge Reservation and the Esker Trail. The marked, 1.3-mi. trail begins at a sign for Baker's Meadow. It passes through hilly woods and then skirts the edge of a pond. At 0.7 mi. a marked spur trail on the right leads 0.3 mi. to Argilla Rd. The main trail, bearing left around the pond, crosses a dam and continues around the pond for 0.2 mi. It then leaves the pond, running 0.1 mi. northeast to Reservation Rd. It continues 0.3 mi. northwest on the road to the beginning. (*Note: Heavy beaver activity in this area may cause sections of the trail to become flooded.*)

Four Reservations Trail (AVIS)

This trail traverses Vale, Indian Ridge, Baker's Meadow, and Shawsheen River Reservations. Begin at the southern end of Vale Reservation (see the Vale Reservation description for directions). The trail proceeds north along the Shawsheen River, leaves the Shawsheen River Reservation at the Horn Bridge, turns left under the bridge, then proceeds northwest on Reservation Rd. to the entrance to Indian Ridge Reservation. It continues through this reservation on the Esker Trail, emerging on Reservation Rd.

The trail crosses the road to the entrance to Baker's Meadow Reservation and continues through the reservation to Reservation Rd. Crossing the road, the trail follows the Indian Ridge Trail to the top of the slope. The trail then turns right and proceeds southeast to the entrance of the Indian Ridge Reservation. It turns left onto Reservation Rd. and continues southeast to the Horn Bridge. After passing under the bridge, it turns right into and through Shawsheen River Reservation and crosses town land into Vale Reservation.

Four Reservations Trail
Distance from Vale Reservation to
• Vale Reservation (circuit): 6.3 mi., 4 hr. 30 min.

Harold R. Rafton Reservation (AVIS)

This 226-acre reservation is bordered by High Plain Rd. on the west, I-93 on the east, and I-495 on the south and is bisected by a power-line right of way that runs west-east. Most of the terrain is rocky woodlands. The western section is high and hilly, while the eastern section is low, including a marsh through which Fish Brook passes from south to north. To reach the reservation, take I-93 to Exit 44, then take Lowell St. east for 0.3 mi. Turn left onto Greenwood Rd. and in 0.9 mi. turn left onto High Plain Rd. Cross over I-93 and I-495 and continue to the top of the hill. About 400 ft. beyond the top of the hill an AVIS sign is mounted high on a tree on the right. Parking is allowed on the roadside.

Harold's Path–Bay Circuit Trail

The Bay Circuit Trail follows a well-trodden path called Harold's Path for 1.9 mi. through Harold R. Rafton Reservation. It heads into the woods a few feet beyond the sign. At 0.2 mi. the trail turns parallel to a power line, continues through a stone wall, and divides. The left branch passes under the power line, enters the woods, and continues on fairly level ground. At 0.3 mi. it turns left, then descends about 1,200 ft. to a wide water-line right of way running north-south. Follow the water-line right of way to the intersection of Chandler Rd. and River Rd. (To return by road to the starting point, turn left onto River Rd., left onto Forest Hill Dr., left onto Cross St., and left onto High Plain Rd.)

Harold's Path–Bay Circuit Trail
Distance from parking area to
• intersection of Chandler Rd. and River Rd.: 1.9 mi., 50 min.

Deer Jump Reservation (AVIS)

This 160-acre reservation lies between River Rd. and the Merrimack River in West Andover. It contains two large wooded areas, each with a 0.3-mi. frontage on the river, connected by a relatively narrow strip of land along the shore varying from about 60 to 400 ft. wide and 2.3 mi. long. Some of the terrain is hilly, with several small gullies and brooks. It adjoins Spaulding Reservation on the west. Trails are blazed in white. The Merrimack River Trail, with white blazes similar to those used on the Bay Circuit Trail, follows the river along through the property.

To reach the reservation, take I-93 to Exit 45, then follow River Rd. west 1 mi. Turn right onto Launching Rd. and park in the small parking area just past the second cul-de-sac on the left.

Deer Jump Reservation Trail

The reservation's main, white-blazed trail makes a pleasant, easy loop through hemlock woodlands above the Merrimack River. This trail leads away from Launching Rd. (passing a junction with the Bay Circuit Trail, which it rejoins at the end of the loop) and descends easily toward Fish Brook as it flows to its confluence with the Merrimack River. Before reaching the brook, the white-blazed trail bears left and rises to follow bluffs above the river (to extend this outing, hikers also have the option of crossing the brook on a wood bridge and bearing left towards the pump house to join the Merrimack River Trail, which leaves the reservation and continues along the riverbank). The main trail then rejoins the Bay Circuit Trail; turn left and complete the circuit with a short walk back to the entrance.

Deer Jump Reservation Trail
Distances from parking area to
- circuit via Bay Circuit Trail: 0.7 mi., 35 min.

Charles W. Ward Reservation

This 695-acre reservation in Andover and North Andover is owned and administered by The Trustees of Reservations. It includes Holt Hill (420 ft.), the highest point in Essex County, Boston Hill (385 ft.), and Shrub

Hill, separated by Cat Swamp. The reservation has 17 mi. of stone walls that provide evidence of its agricultural past and is an excellent place to see club mosses, ferns, and other flora. Another feature is the ring of solstice stones, large blocks of cut stone arranged to mark the seasonal equinoxes and solstices. For the most part the reservation paths pass through wooded areas, but the hilltops have some viewpoints of Mt. Monadnock and the Temple Hills to the west, southern Kearsarge to the northwest, and Boston and Great Blue Hill to the south.

At the base of Holt Hill is Pine Hole Bog, an interesting quaking bog with an interpretive trail and 700 ft. of boardwalk. The reservation contains 14 mi. of hiking trails ranging from easy to moderate.. The majority of these trails are on the north side of Prospect Rd., opposite the visitor center.

To reach the reservation from I-93, take Exit 41, go north on MA 125 for 5 mi., then turn right onto Prospect Rd. Trail information and maps are available at the parking area.

Holt Hill via Bay Circuit Trail (TTOR)

These trails combine to provide a short route to the top of Holt Hill. From the parking area, cross Prospect Rd. and look for the trailhead on the right. Follow the path along the edge of the orchard, then past the edge of a field. The trail then meets the Bay Circuit Trail at a junction, then bears left and right and continues on a moderate grade through a clearing to the solstice stones at the summit, with its view to Boston and the Blue Hills.

Holt Hill via Bay Circuit Trail
Distance from parking area to
• Holt Hill summit: 0.5 mi., 20 min.

Sanborn Trail (TTOR)

The Sanborn Trail connects the Bay Circuit Trail from just below the top of Holt Hill to Old Chestnut St., which provides access to the reservation's western trails. This rocky path winds for 0.9 mi. along the base of Holt and Shrub Hills and the side of Cat Swamp.

Sanborn Trail

Distance from Bay Circuit Trail junction to
• Old Chestnut St.: 0.9 mi., 25 min.

Boston Hill Loop (TTOR)

From junction 14 on Old Chestnut St., follow the path east, following signs for Boston Hill. After a brief moderate climb, the trail arrives at the summit clearing and Elephant Rock in 0.5 mi. From the clearing, the trail continues downhill past junctions 12 and 11, rejoining Old Chestnut St. at junction 10.

Boston Hill Loop

Distances from Old Chestnut St. junction 14 to
• Clearing and Elephant Rock: 0.5 mi., 20 min.
• Old Chestnut St. junction 10: 1.0 mi., 30 min.

Bog Trail (TTOR)

A favorite of naturalists, this short trail begins at the parking area and quickly leads to a boardwalk, where an interpretive guide is available. The boardwalk leads through the bog before ending at a nice overview of Pine Hole Pond. Take time to observe the wetland's unique vegetation, which includes sheep laurel, leatherleaf, cotton grass, and swamp azalea, and watch for a variety of birds and dragonflies along the edge of the pond.

Bog Trail

Distance from parking area to
• boardwalk end at Pine Hole Pond: 0.3 mi., 15 min.

Bald Hill Reservation

Located in the towns of Boxford, North Andover, and Middleton, Bald Hill Reservation comprises three adjacent, protected properties: Boxford State Forest, the John Phillips Wildlife Sanctuary, and property owned by the Essex County Greenbelt Association.

To reach the forest, take I-95 to the Topsfield Rd. interchange. Follow Topsfield Rd. 1.3 mi. west to Boxford center and turn left onto Main St. Follow Main St. 0.3 mi. to Middleton Rd. Turn left onto Middleton Rd. and proceed 1.7 mi. to the Bald Hill Rd. entrance to the reservation.

A trail map is posted, and is also available from the Essex County Greenbelt Association, 82 Eastern Ave., Essex, MA 01929 (508-768-7241). Trail junctions are numbered and are keyed to the trail map. A volunteer group, Friends of Bald Hill Reservation, has been organized to assist with trail maintenance and land-use planning, and can be reached through the Greenbelt Association.

Sawyer Trail (ECGA)

This trail begins at trail junction 11 on the Bald Hill Rd. and proceeds generally south along a woods road to Peabody St. in Middleton. This woods road is referred to as Thomas Rd. on most maps and is a private drive into the Wissa Farm (formerly the Sawyer Farm) at the Peabody St. end. The trail is not marked but is obvious for its entire length. Those wishing to use the trail at the extreme southern end should request permission at the farm.

After leaving Bald Hill Rd. the trail passes a small burial plot on the left at 0.25 mi., passes a narrow trail left at 0.35 mi., and then continues through fairly dense woodland to a junction with a woods road on the right (dead end) at 1.0 mi. The trail continues straight ahead at this junction and passes another trail junction on the left at 1.3 mi. After passing through some partially cleared land, the trail reaches the Wissa Farmhouse and Peabody St., just west of the Ipswich River.

Sawyer Trail
Distance from Bald Hill Rd. to
• Wissa Farm (Peabody St.): 1.6 mi., 50 min.

Weir Hill Reservation

This 194-acre property in North Andover, belonging to The Trustees of Reservations, is bounded by Lake Cochichewick and Stevens Pond (Lake Cochichewick is a public water supply—public access is prohibited). Pronounced *wire hill*, the reservation consists of a double drumlin—a long hill formed by glaciers—rising about 300 ft. over the valley. There are beautiful views from the meadow of the Merrimack Valley, 1 mi. of lakeshore, and 4 mi. of moderate woodland trails. The property is an ideal spot for hiking, cross-country skiing, nature study, picnicking, and photography.

From I-93 follow MA 125 north (Andover bypass), merging with MA 114 west. At Merrimack College turn left (Andover St.), turn right at the traffic lights, bear right at the fork, and continue through North Andover center to Stevens St. Turn left onto Stevens St.; the entrance is 0.8 mi. ahead on the right. A detailed trail map is posted at the Stevens St. entrance as well as at many of the trail junctions.

Stevens Trail (TTOR)

From the parking area, follow the path northeast and bear right on the Stevens Trail, which leads to the hilltop meadow and scenic overlook at 0.3 mi. From the vista, the trail continues southeasterly, passing another clearing and reaching the reservation's southeast corner, where it ends at the junction with the Alewife Trail.

Stevens Trail

Distance from entrance to
- overlook: 0.3 mi., 15 min.
- junction with Alewife Trail: 0.9 mi., 35 min.

Harold Parker State Forest

This 3,400-acre forest located in Andover, North Andover, North Reading, and Middleton offers a wide range of outdoor recreational activities on 26 mi. of trails. Hardwood, hemlock, and white pine forests predominate. The waterways amid the wooded terrain, and the abundance of birds and wildflowers, make for scenic hikes.

Most of the 11 forest ponds are the result of dams built in the 1930s. Universal-access facilities include restrooms, camping, and beaches. A nature center is located in the campground off Jenkins Rd. during the season, and nature walks and programs are run from forest headquarters on Middleton Rd.

The state forest is accessible from a number of roads, including Middleton Rd. (where the forest headquarters is located), the eastern section of Harold Parker Rd. (which runs south from MA 114 in North Andover), and the western section of Harold Parker Rd. (which runs east from MA 125 in Andover).

Stearns Pond Trail (DCR)

The Stearns Pond Trail is reached from a short trail that begins on the east side of the eastern section of Harold Parker Rd., 0.3 mi. from MA 114 or 0.8 mi. from Middleton Rd. Limited parking is available at this end of the trail; no on-street parking is available at the other trailhead on Marblehead St.

The trail begins as a gravel road (closed to vehicles) that enters the woods, leads to a footpath that follows the bank of a pond, and then crosses a brook below a spillway dam. Shortly thereafter a second trail diverges left to a second dam.

The trail runs into a paved road, from which other roads lead to a large parking lot, a swimming beach, and park headquarters. The trail soon passes through another gate and reaches Middleton Rd. Turning left onto Middleton Rd., the trail reenters the woods in about 25 yd. (marked by a sign, Upper Salem Pond Rd.). The trail winds and climbs slightly until it reaches Salem Pond and crosses a small footbridge over a narrow channel between parts of the pond.

The trail now continues past another section of the pond on the left to a fork, where it bears left. In about 0.3 mi. Salem Pond Rd. (a.k.a. the Sudden Pond Trail) diverges left. The Stearns Pond Trail continues straight past this junction, winds and climbs for a short distance, then descends straight past Bradford Pond on the right to its end at Marblehead St. A side trail that circles Bradford Pond diverges from the Stearns Pond Trail just before Marblehead St.

Stearns Pond Trail

Distances from Harold Parker Rd. to
- Middleton Rd.: 1.2 mi., 45 min.
- Sudden Pond Trail: 2.5 mi., 1 hr. 15 min.
- Marblehead St.: 3.5 mi., 1 hr. 45 min.

Sudden Pond Trail (DCR)

This trail begins at the last fork in the Stearns Pond Trail, turning left at a sign marked Salem Pond Rd. The trail soon skirts the southern end of Salem Pond, crosses a bridge over the pond outlet, and bears sharp right. Shortly after crossing the pond outlet the trail bends left and almost immediately forks, with both forks leading quickly to Middleton Rd. The trail turns right onto Middleton Rd. and continues past the North Andover–North Reading boundary sign and the Forest Riding Academy (both on the left). It proceeds southeast on Middleton Rd. and turns left onto paved Sudden Pond Rd. just past the riding academy. This point is located about 1 mi. southeast of the forest headquarters.

The trail follows Sudden Pond Rd. briefly, then turns right off the paved road where the road turns sharp left. The trail follows a woods road leading north and soon crosses the pond outlet. It continues along the shore and soon branches right and then turns sharp left. Soon it turns left onto a woods road, then left again at a large rock. It follows this side path back to Sudden Pond Rd. (*Note: If you miss this path, just follow the shore of the pond and rejoin the trail on Sudden Pond Rd.*) Continuing west, the trail passes a path on the right and almost immediately passes between two posts and emerges on Middleton Rd. at a point a short distance southeast of where the Stearns Pond Trail crosses Middleton Rd.

Sudden Pond Trail
Distance from fork to
 • Middleton Rd.: 2.8 mi., 1 hr. 15 min.

Brackett Pond Trail (DCR)

The Brackett Pond Trail begins at the main parking lot on the western section of Harold Parker Rd., 0.3 mi. east of MA 125. From the parking lot, walk east along Harold Parker Rd.; Collins Pond will soon appear on the left, and Field Pond on the other side of the road. Fifty yards after passing the partially submerged fish-stocking structure below the Collins Pond dam, turn left into a smaller parking lot and head through the gate. This woods road leads along the eastern shore of Collins Pond and then Brackett Pond. About 200 yd. along this road a trail leaves to the left, crossing between the two ponds on a scenic route that leads almost directly back to the starting point.

For a longer hike continue north on the road along the eastern shore of Brackett Pond. Bear right at a fork leading away from the pond north on a woods road (Walker Rd.; a left at this fork leads around Brackett Pond then back to Harold Parker Rd.). Soon reach a second fork where a left turn leads to another pond, while a right turn leads another 0.5 mi. to the trail's end at the forest boundary.

Brackett Pond Trail
Distance from parking lot to
  • forest boundary: 1.4 mi., 45 min.

Reading Town Forest

The Reading Town Forest and Well Fields comprises 290 acres in the northwest portion of Reading under the supervision of the Reading Town Forest Committee; 100,000 red and white pines as well as spruce, balsam, and Scotch pines were planted by Boy Scouts and other townspeople beginning in 1930. The area includes several examples of hardwoods and many fine eskers, and the proximity of the Ipswich River makes it a good place for bird watching. The forest has vernal pools and is home to great horned owls, red foxes, and many varieties of wildflowers, including pink and showy lady's slippers. In winter cross-country skiing and snowshoeing are excellent. There are several forest roads and short trails that lead off these roads. Most are blazed and easy to follow. Camping is by permit only.

The forest can be accessed off Fox Run La. (off Franklin St.) and Strout Ave. (off Grove St.), with additional parking off Roma La.

Big Pine Trail (Town of Reading)

This trail uses unpaved roads and short trails marked with bright yellow blocks and arrows. It begins immediately behind the trail sign and follows the path along the ridge of an esker to an overlook of the Point One parking area (the Ipswich River is on the left). Here the trail doubles back (south) along a smaller esker (a road runs parallel below). After a short distance the trail drops to the road, crosses it, and continues south along another esker.. The trail drops down right to a road junction, then goes left (northeast) along the well-traveled dirt road. It continues past the Old Council Ring on the right and a pump house on the left, emerging from the pines as the road descends to a fork.

On the right the road continues to Scrub Oak Hill; ahead on the left is the Ipswich River and the site of an old swimming hole. However, the trail immediately cuts back into the pine woods to the southeast along a well-worn path. (Look carefully on the right for the two yellow arrows and the continuation of yellow markings.) After about 200 yd., just before reaching a woods path, the trail follows the Garden Club Trail left (east). It continues 30 ft., crossing a damp area, then goes right (southwest) at a fork on an esker until reaching its end. (Watch along the left of the esker for a wide variety of spring wildflowers and dogwood.)

From the esker the trail continues to be marked with yellow blazes. It goes through a wet area, then up another esker, following it until arriving at the top of a cliff overlooking the junction of the well-traveled road. The trail drops down to the road, turns right at the fork, and then turns immediately left at the next fork in the road. After about 0.1 mi. the road arrives back at the Big Pine Trail sign.

Big Pine Trail
Distances from Big Pine Trail sign to
- Garden Club Trail: 1.1 mi., 45 min.
- Big Pine Trail sign (circuit): 1.6 mi., 1 hr.

Willard Brook State Forest

Located in Ashby and Townsend, this 2,597-acre forest is hilly and rocky, with many large areas of mountain laurel. It is a scenic area, especially in the vicinity of Willard Brook. Trap Falls Brook, Trap Falls, and Pearl Hill Brook are other attractive features. Recreational activities include swimming, hiking, birding, and fishing.

The trails generally emanate from either the Damon Pond recreation and camping area or the Pearl Hill Brook Pond recreation and camping area. To reach Damon Pond from the junction of MA 119 and MA 124 in West Townsend, go 3.1 mi. west on MA 119 and turn left onto Hosmer Rd. To reach Pearl Hill, follow MA 119 west from West Townsend. Almost immediately after passing MA 123, turn left onto New Fitchburg Rd. and follow it 1.8 mi. to the recreation area. Parking, trail information, camping, swimming, and picnicking are available at both recreation areas; a parking fee is charged in season. Parking along the sides of the roads within the state forest is prohibited.

Willard Brook Loop (DCR)

From Damon Pond two main hiking trails are maintained by the DCR that can be combined into an interesting 3.0-mi. loop. The north trail leaves Damon Pond and follows the south side of Willard Brook through hemlock forests; Townsend Rd. (MA 119) follows the opposite bank. Leaving the brook, it climbs briefly, crosses two wet areas, and at 1.2 mi. reaches the Trap Falls Brook area and a gravel forest road a few hundred yards from the forest headquarters on Townsend Rd. From the road turn right (south) and follow the road past two intersections. Bear right each time. The road passes a small pond as it swings northwest. A south trail trailhead is about 600 ft. past the pond on the right. The path now climbs generally west, passing two connector paths that link to the north path. The trail passes a junction on the left that leads in about 0.2 mi. to Fort Hill Rd. The south trail ends as it reaches Hosmer Rd. just east of Damon Pond.

Willard Brook Loop

Distance from Damon Pond to
- Trap Rock Falls Brook: 1.2 mi., 40 min.
- Damon Pond (circuit): 3.0 mi., 1 hr. 40 min.

Gulf Brook and Heald's Pond

This is the most scenic area of Pepperell, lying in the western part of town and crisscrossed by a series of blue-blazed connecting trails. Refer to the USGS Townsend quadrangle. Several conservation areas offer trails that lead through woodlands, wetlands, and ravines. These reservations are connected by the 8.0-mi. long Jeff Smith Trail. The Jeff Smith Trail runs from Blood Brook Ravine on Jewett St. in Pepperell to Rocky Pond Rd. in Hollis, N.H. Because of several road crossings, the Jeff Smith Trail can be conveniently hiked in sections. The path connects several of the town's natural areas including Heald's Pond, Gulf Brook Ravine, Stewart Brook, and Nashoba Conservation Area. The Jeff Smith Trail is blazed with blue paint dots throughout.

Blood Brook Ravine Trail (Town of Pepperell)

This trail runs from Jewett St. to Shag Rock on the west shore of Heald's Pond over Pepperell Conservation Commission land. To reach the trailhead take MA 113 northeast from its intersection with MA 119 near Pepperell. In 0.25 mi. turn left onto Shattuck St. and continue past Harbour St. to its end on Jewett St. Turn left (west) onto Jewett St. and follow it 0.6 mi. to a wetland on the left draining through a culvert into Blood Brook on the right. The trail begins 200 ft. east of the culvert at a sign marking the Blood Brook Ravine Conservation Area. Watch carefully for the yellow blazes that mark the trail, as the footpath is not well worn. Most of the trail is clearly blazed with yellow triangles, except for a section along the shore of Heald's Pond, which is marked with a few faded blue blazes.

The trail passes the foot of the highest rock face in Pepperell and meets Heald's Pond at the mouth of Blood Brook. Here the trail turns left (north) and steeply upward to the face of Shag Rock, which slopes steeply down into the pond. Once over Shag Rock, the trail skirts the pond to its northern end on Heald St. (behind the Community Church on MA 113 in Pepperell center).

Blood Brook Ravine Trail
Distance from Jewett St. to
• Heald St.: est. 1.0 mi., 30 min.

Pepperell Springs Trail (Town of Pepperell)

This trail leads through a gulf or gorge, following the brook from Heald St. to Chestnut St. Although scenic, the trail has a few steep places and at one point crosses the brook at an old dam. Marked by blue blazes, the trail begins at Heald St. across from Heald's Pond—the end of the Blood Brook Ravine Trail. To reach the trailhead from the Pepperell Town Hall drive about 2.0 mi. on Heald St. to the ravine on the right. Parking is on the side of the road.

The trail follows a well-traveled cart path along the left (west) bank of the stream, which is littered with rocks and thick with beech trees. The cart path ends after several hundred yards, passing on the left the almost closed entrance to a pre-Revolutionary silver mine blasted out of solid rock. Several hundred yards farther on are the remains of a mill and dam in the middle of the gorge. The trail crosses the brook over the dam and continues at the top of the eastern side of the gorge. The trail generally follows the stream for almost a mile to a dirt road (Chestnut St). Turn left on the dirt road for a few hundred yards to reach Oak Hill Street. To pick up the trail on Heald Street, drive on MA 113 to a blinking light at the Pepperell Town Hall. Turn north onto Park Street and then quickly turn left onto Heald Street (behind the Community Church in Pepperell center). Parking is on the side of the road.

Pepperell Springs Trail
Distance from Heald St. to
  • Chestnut St.: 1.0 mi., 40 min.

Gulf Brook and Steward Brook Conservation Areas Trail (Town of Pepperell)

To pick up this trail on Oak Hill St., take MA 113 to a blinking light at the Pepperell Town Hall. Turn north onto Park St. and travel about ½ mile, bearing left on Oak Hill Street. The trailhead is at the bottom of a hill after the intersection with Maple St. and Lawrence St., across from the end of the Pepperell Spring Trail.

The trail heads north from Oak Hill St. through the forest and wetlands along Gulf Brook. At a stream below a broken beaver dam, use the fallen log to cross. Watch for blazes where the official trail makes several sharp turns. The trail crosses Stewart Brook (during low water times, it is possible to walk across on rocks, but hikers should be prepared to wade), then turns to the left and goes up a steep hill. At the top of the hill, there is a junction where the Jeff Smith Trail goes to the right, soon reaching Lawrence St.

Gulf Brook and Steward Brook Conservation Areas Trail
Distance from Oak Hill St. to
- Lawrence St.: 1.0 mi., 30 min.

Great Brook Farm State Park

This unique destination in Carlisle combines more than 20 mi. of recreational trails for hiking, canoeing, horseback riding, skiing, and mountain biking with a working dairy farm. The mosaic of open fields and woods separated by stone walls and old cellar holes is the epitome of New England scenery. And once the hikes are done there are barn tours and an ice cream stand. Universally accessible restrooms are available, and a nature center is also on the grounds. Some trails that offer good hiking include the multi use Pine Point Loop, the Woodchuck Trail, the Garrison Loop, and the Litchfield Loop Trail.

To reach the park take MA 128 to Exit 31B. Follow MA 225 west to Carlisle center, then travel north on Lowell St. to the entrance.

Woodchuck and Garrison Trails Loop (DCR)

The Woodchuck Trail begins at the trailhead on North Rd. opposite the canoe launch at the eastern end of Meadow Pond. This multiuse trail heads northeast, passing the Garrison Loop Trail on the right and the log cabin on the left.

Turn right (southeast) onto the Garrison Loop to return to the earlier junction with the Woodchuck Trail. The trail passes a historic site known as "the city," a cluster of cellar holes from colonial times. The trail curves left (west) and returns to the trailhead in 0.5 mi.

Woodchuck and Garrison Trails Loop
Distance from North Rd. to
- trailhead (circuit): 0.5 mi, 20 min.

Litchfield Loop (DCR)

The 1.0-mi.-long Litchfield Loop Trail, blazed with maple leaves, circles the main farm complex, offering varied views of the fields, pastures, barns, and adjacent woodlands as it explores the park. It also passes by the ice cream stand.

Litchfield Loop

Distance from North Rd. marker 27 to
• end of trail: 1.0 mi., 35 min.

Old Town Hill

This 509-acre reservation of tidal creeks and salt marsh surrounds a drumlin called Old Town Hill. Three miles of moderate hiking trails wander through the upland woods that grow on the hilly terrain above the Little River, which snakes through the marsh. Years ago the marsh was cut for its salt hay. The reservation is located off Newman Rd. in Newbury Old Town Hill. To reach Old Town Hill from I-95 take Exit 54 to MA 133 and travel east for 4.5 mi. Turn onto MA 1A north; just beyond the bridge over the Parker River turn left onto Newman Rd. The parking area and entrance are on the left in 0.2 mi.

Ridge Trail (TTOR)

From the parking area, the Ridge Trail ascends the west side of Old Town Hill (168 ft.), where the views include the Parker River National Wildlife Refuge to the east, Mt. Agamenticus in Maine to the north, and the Isles of Shoals off New Hampshire to the northeast.

Ridge Trail

Distance from parking area on Newman Rd. to
• overlook: 0.6 mi., 20 min.

Misery Islands

This 87-acre preserve in Salem Sound is much nicer than its name suggests. The preserve's two islands got their name when a winter storm stranded shipbuilder Capt. Robert Moulton for three days in the 1600s. Today a 2.5-mi. system of easy to moderate trails on Great Misery Island explores rocky shorelines, open grassy fields, and overlooks. Nearby Little Misery Island can be accessed during times of very low tide by walking the shallow channel between the two islands.

Access to Misery Islands is by canoe, kayak, or a rowed boat such as a dinghy. Landing sites are the three rocky beaches. Additional access is provided from Salem via Sun Line Cruises, which operates from Salem Willows Park. Public restrooms (composting toilets) are available.

Appleton Farms and Appleton Farms Grass Rides

Appleton Farms is a 658-acre working dairy farm with 4 mi. of easy trails over sweeping pastures and fields. The farm employs agricultural techniques that seek to work with the ecology of the area and demonstrate that dairy products can be produced in harmony with the environment. Some of the trails are part of the Bay Circuit Trail system; one path links Appleton Farms with nearby Appleton Farms Grass Rides. Offering more than 5 mi. of carriage paths lined by stately woods, Appleton Farms Grass Rides is unique because the carriage paths emanate from a central point, a clearing dominated by a granite obelisk once part of the Harvard Library. The name derives from the original use of the trails as bridle paths—so the intent was to ride the paths, not walk them.

To reach Appleton Farms and Appleton Farms Grass Rides from MA 1A in Hamilton, take Cutler Rd. to Highland St. Turn right onto Highland St., then quickly right again to reach the parking area.

Ayer Conservation Land

Walks may be started at Woodford of Ayer, the former Ayer Hospital on Winthrop Ave. (a brick building on top of the hill east of the village). To reach Woodford of Ayer from Main St. (MA 111), go north on Washington St., then east on Highland Ave. to its end, and proceed south on Winthrop Ave. Woodford of Ayer is on the left. These walks visit Chapel Hill, Pingrey Hill, Snake Hill, and Tophet Swamp, the last being a deep gorge presumed to have been formed during the glacial period. They do not follow marked trails, so follow the directions carefully. Interesting variations on the walks described are possible with the aid of the USGS Ayer quadrangle. Take care when crossing private property.

Chapel Hill Walk (Town of Ayer)

This walk begins in front of the Woodford of Ayer Nursing Home on Winthrop Ave. and ends at the corner of Old Ayer Rd. and Indian Hills Rd. in Groton. It goes north on Winthrop Ave. and continues generally north and uphill for 0.3 mi. through the woods to the Ayer water towers. The trail crosses the Ayer School grounds to the east, keeping right of all the buildings and left of the athletic field, then descends to Groton–Harvard Rd. The trail turns left onto Groton–Harvard Rd. (downgrade) and continues 0.3 mi. to the second power line. On the right an obscure path ascends the ledges on the left side of the power line. The trail follows this path about 500 ft., then goes left (leaving the power line) on a good path to a big hayfield with extensive views. (*Note: Do not cross the hayfield.*)

The trail goes northeast along the edge of the field next to the woods, then turns left onto Snake Hill Rd. and right onto Old Ayer Rd. It continues to the foot of the hill, turns right at the Chapel Hill sign, and continues 0.5 mi. to the top of the hill (views in all directions). The trail descends (no path) northeast to Indian Hills Rd. It turns left onto Indian Hills Rd. and continues a short distance to the junction with Old Ayer Rd.

Chapel Hill Walk
Distance from Woodford of Ayer Nursing Home to
• junction of Indian Hills Rd. and Old Ayer Rd.: 3.5 mi., 2 hr. 45 min.

Snake Hill Walk (Town of Ayer)

Follow the directions for the Chapel Hill Walk to Snake Hill Rd. This trail turns right onto Snake Hill Rd. then descends under a power line to the telephone company's underground cable. It turns sharp left and continues to the top of Snake Hill (view west). The trail follows the cable line 1.0 mi. to a woods road, turns right onto the road, and proceeds 50 yd. to Wright Rd. It turns right onto Wright Rd. and continues 0.5 mi., passing several driveways on the left that lead to cottages on Sandy Pond. At the end of Wright Rd. the trail turns right onto Snake Hill Rd., passes the Ayer Gun Club on the right, and continues to the power line. After crossing the power line the trail immediately turns left onto a path to re-cross the power line.

Following the path blazed with metal triangles through the woods, the trail continues 0.5 mi. to a brook, crosses on a broken-down dam, then bears left along a meadow and proceeds uphill past Balance Rock. It turns left onto a woods road, which leads to Groton–Harvard Rd. The trail turns left onto Groton–Harvard Rd., proceeds to the first house, then turns right onto a winding woods road. Ascending, the trail makes a sharp left to avoid another woods road on the right. Near the top of the hill this trail merges with the beginning of the Chapel Hill Walk. It passes a small swamp and turns right, then left onto Winthrop Ave., where the walk began.

Snake Hill Walk
Distance from Woodford of Ayer Nursing Home to
  • Woodford of Ayer Nursing Home (circuit): 3.0 mi., 1 hr. 30 min.

SUGGESTED HIKES

Easy Hikes

Bog Trail [rt: 0.3 mi., 0:15], page 273. A fascinating walk that includes 700 ft. of boardwalk to Pine Hole Bog, one of the reservation's treasures.

Hellcat Interpretive Trail [lp: 1.4 mi., 55 min.], page 259. Offering exceptional bird watching and fine views, this trail leads through several coastal habitats including marshes, dunes, and woodlands.

Moderate Hikes

Willard Brook Loop [lp: 3.0 mi., 1 hr. 40 min], page 280. A pleasant loop that includes a scenic section along the hemlock-lined banks of Willard Brook.

Strenuous Hikes

Bay Circuit Trail, Section 7 [rt: 6.5 mi., 2:55], page 248. A trip through Revolutionary War history, this hike passes the Minuteman statue and ends at the restored Old North Bridge.

Discover Hamilton Trail [lp: 10.0 mi., 4:3], page 264. This collection of paths links a number of parks and reservations in the town of Hamilton.

PART FIVE
Boston and Vicinity

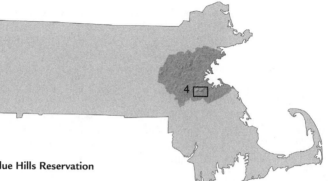

4

Map 4: Blue Hills Reservation

The area around greater Boston is framed by a number of interesting natural areas. To the west of the city is a string of parks, forests, and reservations that wrap around the boundary of the metropolitan area like a necklace of natural gems. Among these are the Blue Hills, Rocky Narrows, and Noanet Woodlands. The rugged coastal areas offer adventures like no other place in the state, and include such destinations as World's End Reservation and the Boston Harbor Islands. Interlaced throughout the region are natural areas, from marshes to riverside forests that are magnets for wildlife, including Neponset River Marshes Reservation and Great Meadows National Wildlife Refuge. These areas offer crucial habitat for hundreds of species of migratory song and shorebirds following the Atlantic Flyway. While the landscape in this region is largely suburban and urban in nature, many destinations make the city feel far away indeed.

Blue Hills Reservation

A surprisingly large oasis of wilderness, Blue Hills Reservation lies less than 10 mi. south of downtown Boston in the communities of Milton, Canton, Randolph, Braintree, Dedham, and Quincy. This mostly wooded, 7,000-acre reservation—under the jurisdiction of the Department of Conservation and Recreation (DCR)—is the largest open space located within the inner metropolitan area. I-93 bisects the reservation. The large, northern section includes a stretch of the Neponset River and the adjoining wetlands of Fowl Meadow; a series of wooded summits, the largest of which are Great Blue Hill (635 ft.) and Chickatawbut Hill (517 ft.); Houghton's Pond and several other smaller ponds; and the Quincy Quarries Historic Site, now a popular rock climbing locale. Ponkapoag Pond, the largest body of water in the reservation, is the principal attraction south of the highway.

The reservation offers many outdoor activities in addition to hiking. Picnicking, fishing, boating, horseback riding, swimming, mountain biking, and rock climbing are all permitted in various parts of the park. In winter there is alpine skiing at the Blue Hill Ski Area on the western side of Great Blue Hill, and cross-country skiing on many of the reservation trails and the Ponkapoag golf course, which is part of the reservation.

The Massachusetts Audubon Society operates two educational facilities within the reservation. The Trailside Museum (617-333-0690) on MA 138, 0.5 mi. north of I-93, is known for its outdoor enclosures that offer close-up views of native wildlife. The Chickatawbut Hill Education Center offers a summer camp and programs for organized groups. The AMC's Ponkapoag Camp, on the east shore of Ponkapoag Pond, has cabins available for rent. Reservations are required; contact the AMC's Joy St. headquarters (617-523-0655) or go online at www.outdoors.org for information.

For the hiker, the reservation offers 125 mi. of trails, woods roads, and old carriage roads that can be combined into trips of varying lengths. Trail difficulty generally ranges from easy to moderate. A large network of trails has been blazed. The blazing system uses circles to indicate a loop trail, with the color of the blaze—yellow, green, or red—indicating easier, moderate, or more strenuous terrain, respectively. The 9.0-mi.-long, blue-blazed Skyline Trail traverses the reservation, passing over several of the major hills, including Great Blue Hill.

Trail intersections are marked with four-digit numbers keyed to the DCR's Blue Hills Reservation map, which is posted at many trailheads. The map, which was updated in August 2008, is available at the Trailside Museum (see above) and at the reservation headquarters on 695 Hillside St., Milton, MA 02186, behind the state police station. Also refer to map 4, Blue Hills Reservation, included with this book.

Because of its size, there are a number of access points for visitors. To reach the parking area for the Great Blue Hill trails and the Trailside Museum, from combined I-93 and US 1 take Exit 2 and follow MA 138 north to the Skyline Trail parking area at 0.5 mi., and the Trailside Museum at approximately 1.0 mi. The MBTA Red Line and Canton-Blue Hills buses offer public transportation to the reservation.

Great Blue Hill Red Loop (DCR)

This 1.2-mi. loop trail (red circles) is the most popular route for climbing Great Blue Hill. It begins at the bulletin board behind the Trailside Museum and heads generally east and then southeast. After crossing paved Summit Rd. it becomes somewhat steeper and rockier. At the summit the

Eliot Tower offers views of the Boston skyline and the surrounding area. Descending, the trail heads northeast from the summit, takes a sharp left at marker 1082, and follows a pleasant woods path back to the museum.

Great Blue Hill Red Loop (map 4: C2)

Distances from trailside museum (250 ft.) to
- Great Blue Hill summit (635 ft.), 0.6 mi., 400 ft., 25 min.
- trailside museum (circuit): 1.2 mi., 400 ft., 50 min.

Great Blue Hill Green Loop (DCR)

This 2.8-mi. loop meanders through the Great Blue Hill section of the reservation. It generally follows the cols between the hills, never ascending to any of the summits.

The trail begins at the north parking lot at the Trailside Museum. Heading northeast, it soon crosses paved Summit Rd., then follows Wolcott Path, a dirt road which heads east through a stand of tall white pines. At marker 1085 the loop proper begins, with the return trail coming in from the right. Continue straight on the road for a few hundred feet to marker 1100, where the trail turns left onto Border Path and runs northeast along the edge of some wetlands.

At marker 1135 the trail turns right and heads southeast through the col between Wolcott Hill on the right and Hemenway Hill on the left. At marker 1141 it crosses a dirt road and the Skyline Trail. Continuing southward on Five Corners Path, the trail circles Wolcott Hill and turns north through Wildcat Notch on Wildcat Notch Path, which separates Wolcott Hill from Great Blue Hill. It passes two small swamps, and just after the second, the trail turns left and heads northwest to the dirt road (Wolcott Path) where the loop began. Turn left onto the dirt road to return to the parking lot.

Great Blue Hill Green Loop (map 4: C2)

Distances from Trailside Museum (250 ft.) to
- Trailside Museum parking lot (circuit): 2.8 mi., 200 ft., 1 hr. 20 min.

Houghton's Pond Yellow Loop (DCR)

This easy, 1.0-mi. trail is a popular walk for families with small children. The trailhead is at the main parking lot for the Houghton's Pond swimming area. Take Exit 3 north from I-93, turn right onto Hillside St., and turn right into the parking lot in 0.3 mi. There is supervised swimming here in summer.

The trail proceeds to the left (east) past the beach, bearing right just after the bathhouse. It joins a dirt road for a short distance around the eastern end of the pond, and then turns right off the road. The trail continues along the southern edge of the pond, crosses the pond's outlet at the western end, and heads north past a field. It then travels through a small swamp and bears left (east) up a hill past a pavilion to the starting point.

Houghton's Pond Yellow Loop (map 4: C3)
Distances from Houghton's Pond parking lot (150 ft.) to
• trailhead (circuit): 1.0 mi., 0 ft., 25 min.

Houghton's Pond Green Loop (DCR)

This 2.8-mi. trail begins at Houghton's Pond and circles (but does not ascend) Tucker Hill to the northeast of the pond. It begins at the Houghton's Pond beach parking lot and follows the yellow loop trail along the north shore of the pond. After passing the bathhouse, the green loop bears left from the yellow loop, then turns left and heads due north on an old carriage road. At marker 2070 the loop proper begins. Traveling clockwise, the trail leaves the road and continues north on Tucker Hill Path, crossing the Skyline Trail (which leads right up to the summit of Tucker Hill).

Circling the north end of Tucker Hill, the trail approaches (but does not meet) Chickatawbut Rd., then heads south through Dark Hollow on Dark Hollow Path, again crossing the Skyline Trail. At marker 2096 it turns right onto a dirt road and heads generally west back to the starting point of the loop. Turn left at this intersection to return to the trailhead.

Houghton's Pond Green Loop (map 4: C4)
Distance from Houghton's Pond parking lot (150 ft.) to
• trailhead (circuit): 2.8 mi, 150 ft., 1 hr. 35 min.

Ponkapoag Green Loop (DCR)

This 3.9-mi. trail starts at the small parking area just south of Exit 3 off I-93. It heads south for 0.3 mi. to a fire gate on the left where it splits, heading either east or west and returning to the same point. Traveling west (right), it follows a woods road (Redman Farm Path) for 0.4 mi. to the YMCA camp, where a map board and trail marker on the left indicate the entrance to the dead end Ponkapoag Bog boardwalk (a nice side trip). Ponkapoag Pond is slowly drying up, and the bog represents the first stage in the pond's gradual transition to what will eventually be dry land.

From the YMCA camp, heading left (south), the trail proceeds along the eastern edge of the Ponkapoag golf course for 0.6 mi. to the fire gate at the end of Maple Ave., the paved golf access road. Turning left, the trail follows Acton Path along the south shore of the pond for 0.8 mi. to Fisherman's Beach on the left, where there is a scenic view of Great Blue Hill. Continuing east through wetlands and then turning north, the trail passes the AMC's Ponkapoag Camp (reservations required). At marker 5343 the Ponkapoag loop continues west on a bluff above the pond back to its starting point.

Ponkapoag Green Loop (map 4: C4)

Distances from parking area (150 ft.) to
- Fisherman's Beach (150 ft.): 2.1 mi., 1 hr.
- trailhead (circuit): 3.9 mi., 100 ft., 2 hr.

Skyline Trail (DCR)

This trail, marked by blue rectangular blazes, is the longest in the Blue Hills Reservation, extending from Fowl Meadow in Canton east to Shea Rink on Willard St. in Quincy. The trail can be accessed from any one of four major streets: (1) MA 138, at a parking lot on the west side about 0.5 mi. south of the Trailside Museum. (2) Hillside St., at the reservation headquarters. (3) Randolph Ave. (MA 28), where the closest parking is about 0.25 mi. south of the trail crossing. (4) Willard St. at the trail terminus at Shea Rink.

Section 1. Little Blue Hill (DCR)

The westernmost portion of the Skyline Trail connects Green St. to MA 138 at the base of Great Blue Hill. The trail leads through open woods for 1.0 mi., passing the Cosmos and Mountain Paths as it passes below Little Blue Hill's 270-foot wooded summit. *Use caution crossing MA 138, and around highway construction at both ends of the trail.* ⚠

Skyline Trail: Green St. to MA 138 (map 4: C1)

Distance from Green St. (100 ft.) to
  • MA 138 (250 ft.): 1.0 mi., 150 ft., 35 min.

Section 2. Blue Hill Ave. (MA 138) to Hillside St. (DCR)

From the parking area on MA 138, the trail leads 0.5 mi. steeply up the southwest side of Great Blue Hill to the circular road and bridle path at the summit. From the top of Great Blue Hill, two routes—the North Skyline Trail and the South Skyline Trail—lead east, joining at the reservation headquarters on Hillside St. The longer, northern branch crosses Wolcott, Hemenway, and Hancock Hills, while the southern branch crosses Houghton Hill. Blue blazes mark both.

The North Skyline Trail begins at marker 1063, to the east of the stone tower on the summit of Great Blue Hill, at the north end of the stone bridge. It descends steeply to Wildcat Notch and the junction with Wildcat Notch Path and the Great Blue Hill Green Loop at marker 1092. It follows the green loop left about 50 ft., then turns right across low ground and ascends the ridge of Wolcott Hill (470 ft.). It continues over the summit and down to a hollow, where it bears right for 50 ft., then left up a rise to the top of the ridge.

The trail continues down the ridge to Five Corners Path junction (marker 1141) in the Wolcott–Hemenway col, where it crosses the other side of the Great Blue Hill Green Loop. The trail goes straight across the junction and ascends, first gently and then steeply, to a ridge on the south side of Hemenway Hill. At 1.8 mi. the trail turns right over ledges with good views ranging from southeast to northwest. At 1.9 mi. the trail bears left across some ledges, then in 225 ft. turns sharp right around a large boulder. It descends left to a small col, crosses Breakneck Ledge Path, and ascends a rocky grade to the ridge of Hancock Hill (510 ft.).

After crossing an old bridle path, the trail climbs a short rise to the summit of Hancock Hill. From the top, the trail descends more gradually near a ledge on the left (with good views) and crosses Hancock Hill Path to meet a woods road, which it follows left to a gate, passing near the horse stables and the reservation headquarters. The trail then follows the paved driveway to Hillside St. and ends at the junction with the South Skyline Trail.

At the summit of Great Blue Hill the South Skyline Trail leaves east from the circular summit drive at marker 1066, about 200 yd. south of the stone bridge. The well-defined trail passes over ledges, with good views east and south. It descends Shadow Cliff via a steep, rocky path and continues on the right side of a wet-weather brook to a brook crossing on large stones. Continuing on the left side of the brook, it soon passes between large boulders. Leaving the brook, it crosses Five Corners Path and Houghton Path, then ascends the slope of Houghton Hill. Crossing just south of the summit, the trail then turns right and descends steeply to Hillside St. Follow Hillside St. left (north) 200 ft. to meet the northern branch.

Skyline Trail: Blue Hill Ave. (MA 138) to Hillside St. (map 4: B2–B3)

Distances from Blue Hill Ave. (250 ft.) to

- summit of Great Blue Hill (635 ft.): 0.5 mi., 400 ft., 30 min.
- summit of Hancock Hill via northern branch (510 ft.): 2.2 mi., 700 ft.1 hr. 20 min.
- Hillside St. via northern branch (200 ft.): 2.5 mi., 700 ft. (rev. 300 ft.), 1 hr. 30 min.
- Hillside St. via southern branch (200 ft.): 1.9 mi., 700 ft. (rev. 200 ft.), 1 hr. 15 min.

Section 3. Hillside St. to Randolph Ave. (DCR)

This section of the trail starts at the junction of the North and South Skyline Trails at the marker on Hillside St. across from the DCR stables. It bears right onto Bugbee Path, a well-worn woods road, for about 400 ft., then turns left into the woods at marker 2054. It bears right up a slope, crosses Tucker Hill Path, continues to the west ridge of Tucker Hill (499 ft.), and proceeds through scattered pine trees (care is needed here) to a ledge with fine views to the west and south. It continues along ledges and down a steep, rocky trail to the bottom of Dark Hollow and the Dark Hollow Path. Next it bears left, then right; it crosses low ground and climbs gradually on a rocky trail, passing through a wooded section over the north ridge of Boyce Hill (404 ft.) and crossing the Doe Hollow Path. Continuing eastward, the trail ascends a steep, rocky grade to the ridge of Buck Hill (496 ft.). From the summit the trail plunges down a steep, rocky slope, crosses Buck Hill Path and Forest Path, then continues down the hillside to Randolph Ave. (MA 28).

Skyline Trail: Hillside St. to Randolph Ave. (map 4: C3–C5)

Distances from Hillside St. (200 ft.) to

- summit of Buck Hill (496 ft.): 1.9 mi., 300 ft. 1 hr.
- Randolph Ave. (MA 28) (200 ft.): 2.2 mi. 3,000 ft., (rev. 300 ft.), 1 hr. 10 min.

Section 4. Randolph Ave. to Willard St. (DCR)

After crossing Randolph Ave. the Skyline Trail quickly reaches a pipeline right of way, then follows an easy route to a hemlock grove, where it turns right onto a bridle path. It continues through the grove about 100 ft. to marker 3042, where it turns left and proceeds up Chickatawbut Hill (517 ft.) on a steep, rocky path. It bears right at the top of the ridge and turns left into the woods within 100 ft. Soon ascending another steep ledge, the trail bears right uphill.

At the top of the ledge the trail ascends gradually into the woods and over more ledges, passing a large puddingstone boulder on the left. The trail skirts the summit of Chickatawbut Hill, then descends into Slide Notch, climbs back up over Kitchamakin Hill, then heads down again over stone steps to Sassaman Notch. (Local rock climbers call the large boulder here the Grepon.)

From Sassaman Notch the Skyline Trail turns right for 50 yd., then turns left and follows the blue blazes up some stone steps. At the top of the steps the trail turns right, away from an intersecting trail, and ascends steeply to the ridge of Nahanton Hill, following ledges to the summit (480 ft.), where there are good views north and south. The trail bears right through scrub oak and over open ledges, some of which offer views of South Shore Plaza. The trail descends gradually through the Broken

Hills and across several cols with short, steep descents and ascents until it reaches a fence around Blue Hills Reservoir.

The trail follows the fence to the right some distance, then proceeds over more ledges to Chickatawbut Rd. It crosses the road at a trail marker post, and at the Wampatuck Hill marker post it goes right up the slope and over the ledges of Wampatuck Hill (353 ft.), providing views of Boston and the bay. The trail turns right along ledges south of the summit and continues along the rim of a cliff with views of South Shore Plaza and Great Pond. The trail descends into scrub oak at the end of the ledges and soon crosses a MWRA water supply pipeline.

After crossing the pipeline, the trail descends and bears to the left. After 40 yd. it turns right up a steep, rocky trail to Rattlesnake Hill; bear left to skirt a smooth ledge near the top of the rock. At the top the trail turns right and crosses a trail to the right that leads to the top of Rattlesnake Hill and many views. The Skyline Trail descends rock steps, crosses an old trail, climbs briefly, and continues over a ledge and boulders to an old quarry. It continues around the quarry to a gravel path, which it follows to the right for about 140 yd., then forks left. It soon forks left again into pines and oaks, and after some distance reaches an old woods road, which it follows to the right a short distance to Wampatuck Rd. Cross this road and follow the trail between the ponds to Shea Rink on Willard St.

Skyline Trail: Randolph Ave. to Willard St. (map 4: B5–B7)

Distances from Randolph Ave. (200 ft.) to
- summit of Chickatawbut Hill (517 ft.): 0.7 mi., 300 ft., 20 min.
- summit of Nahanton Hill (480 ft.): 1.3 mi., 450 ft. (rev. 150 ft.), 35 min.
- Chickatawbut Rd. (250 ft.): 2.1 mi., 500 ft. (rev. 50 ft.), 1 hr.
- Willard St. (100 ft.): 3.6 mi., 700 ft. (rev. 200 ft.), 1 hr. 45 min.

Stony Brook Reservation

This 400-acre DCR reservation is located between the West Roxbury and Hyde Park sections of Boston, and is crisscrossed by a network of easy—although generally unmarked—hiking paths. Although none of these paths can be considered a major hiking trail, Stony Brook is notable as a large, publicly owned, undeveloped forest preserve within the city limits. As such, it provides Bostonians with the chance to do some easy forest walking without traveling farther. Despite its location, Stony Brook is relatively unknown, and visitors are unlikely to encounter the crowds normally found at other urban parks.

Stony Brook Reservation is located on both sides of the Enneking Pkwy. (formerly the Turtle Pond Pkwy.). The section to the east of the parkway is the larger of the two, and includes such points of interest as Stony Brook itself, Turtle Pond, and some excellent examples of glacial drumlins. On the eastern side of the reservation is Bald Knob, a rock outcrop with good views of Hyde Park and the Blue Hills. At the northeast tip of the reservation, at the corner of Washington St. and the West Roxbury Pkwy., is Bellevue Hill, the highest point in Boston. At one time this summit afforded an excellent panoramic view, but in recent years the view has become all but obliterated by trees.

There is some limited parking along Enneking Pkwy., although the parking areas may be closed at times due to DCR budget cutbacks. There is always parking available at the recreation complex at the very south end of the parkway, although this requires a short walk to reach the undeveloped part of the reservation.

Boston Harbor Islands National Park and State Park

Boston Harbor Islands National Park and State Park consists of 34 islands in Boston Harbor, just 45 min. by ferry from Boston. The Massachusetts Department of Conservation and Recreation manages seventeen of the islands as Boston Harbor Islands State Park; six of these islands are staffed and open to the public during the warmer months. Recreational opportunities include island camping, hiking, fishing, and boating.

The harbor islands have experienced many commercial and public uses over the past 350 years, including forts, prisons, hospitals, lighthouses, sewage plants, a firing range, an airport, and even a glue factory. As some of these older enterprises faded, efforts began to convert some of the islands to recreational uses, which in turn led to the establishment of the state and national parks.

Most of the islands have easily followed walking paths, and many have interesting abandoned fortifications and historical ruins. Care should be taken, as these ruins, as well as the rubble left from other past uses, can create some hazards for walkers.

Most of the islands can be reached only by boat. Ferry service is available in season to Georges Island from Long Wharf at State St. and Atlantic Ave. in downtown Boston. Boston Harbor Cruises supplies the ferry service (617-227- 4321). Free water taxi (shuttle) service is available from Georges Island to other islands, including Lovells, Peddocks, Bumpkin, and Grape Islands. A shuttle schedule is available at Long Wharf and other departure points, including Hingham Shipyard off MA 3A.

Camping is permitted only on four designated islands: Grape, Bumpkin, Lovells, and Peddocks. Reservations are required, and a fee is charged. Potable water and food are not available. Campsite reservations on Grape and Bumpkin Islands can be made by calling 877-422-6762; for Lovells and Peddocks call 617-422-6762.

These islands can be accessed by ferry or shuttle service:

Lovells Island (62 acres) is separated from Georges Island by a waterway known as the Narrows. Just east of the Narrows is Bug Light. The shuttle from Georges Island docks at the pier on the southwest shore near Fort Standish. A trail leads from the pier past Fort Standish on the right, then traces a course northwest along the shore past a camping and picnic area.

Georges Island (28 acres) has a pier, restrooms, and ferry service to Boston. Trails diverge from the pier, with one heading north to Fort Warren at the northern end of the island, and the other exploring the south section. Fort Warren is constructed of granite and once housed prisoners during the Civil War.

Peddocks Island (113 acres). This large, elongated island is formed by five drumlins—large glacial hills. On the island are Fort Andrews (near the pier where the Georges Island shuttle docks), a camping area with eleven campsites (north of the pier), and a lighthouse northwest of the pier. A maze of short paths covers the north part of the island, with fewer but longer trails heading south through the narrow neck of land at the island's center to West Head at land's end on the southwest shore. A variety of birds, including black-crowned night herons, nest on the island. Restrooms are located on the south side of the island's north end.

Grape Island (50 acres) is due north of Hewitt's Cove and close to the ferry dock at Hingham Shipyard. It is covered with roses, wildflowers, bayberries, and many species of birds. There are ten campsites, including one group site, and picnic facilities. Easy walking trails cross the island.

Bumpkin Island (35 acres) in Hingham Bay is one of the more southerly of the harbor islands and offers slate beaches, ten individual campsites, and one group site. A trail leads to the remains of a hospital for children and the ruins of a stone farmhouse.

Islands without public boat service include:

Great Brewster Island (23 acres), one of the outer islands, has one of the highest hills (about 100 ft.) of the harbor islands, with vistas of Massachusetts Bay and the harbor. It was used for centuries to defend the harbor. Great Brewster Island is open for day use only. Visitor facilities include picnic tables, a self-guided trail, a composting toilet, and a small shelter for use in inclement weather.

Middle and Outer Brewster Islands (12 and 17.5 acres) were originally used for agriculture, but because of their impressive sea cliffs they have often been used for harbor defense.

Whitney and Thayer Woods Reservation

This property in Hingham and Cohasset comprises 824 acres of gently rolling glacial woodland with some marshy areas, brooks, and huge glacial boulders. More than 10 mi. of moderate cart paths and foot trails weave through a hemlock-pine-hardwood forest with scattered American holly trees. Clusters of azalea and rhododendron bushes bloom in spring next to wildflowers and ferns. A highlight of the property is the Milliken Memorial Path, created in the late 1920s by Arthur Milliken in memory of his wife, Mabel. Stone walls running throughout the woods mark much of the land as having once been farms and pasture. The property contains a stretch of Brass Kettle Brook and a portion of Great Swamp. Turkey Hill, a 187-ft.-high glacial drumlin with a view of Cohasset Harbor is co-managed with the towns of Cohasset and Hingham. The remains of a radar installation dating from the Cold War are atop the hill. The trails are open for hiking, cross-country skiing, and snowshoeing. The property abuts 3,500-acre Wompatuck State Park and is close to Boston Harbor Islands State Park.

The entrance to the reservation is on MA 3A opposite Sohier St. in Cohasset, 2 mi. south of the junction of MA 228 and 3A. Numbers in the descriptions below refer to numbered trail junctions. Detailed trail maps can be purchased at the service station across from the entrance on MA 3A.

Howe's Rd. (TTOR)

This cart path is one of the main trails through the south portion of the property. It starts at the north side of the MA 3A parking lot and goes southwest, crossing Brass Kettle Brook near the boundary with Wompatuck State Park. Bear right (west) at junction 19 onto the Milliken Memorial Path to head toward Turkey Hill via One Way Path. At junction 21 turn left (south) onto the Bancroft Trail, which loops past Rooster Rock (on the left) and Ode's Den on the right. Here Theodore Pritchard lived in a boulder cave when he lost his home in 1830. This loop returns to Howe's Rd. at junction 20, north of Brass Kettle Brook.

Howe's Rd.
Distance from parking area on MA 3A to
• Brass Kettle Brook: 0.8 mi., 50 min.

Whitney Rd. (TTOR)

This road exits right at junction 22 (northwest) from Howe's Rd., 0.5 mi. from the beginning of the latter. It passes several roads and trails, all of which are marked. The road ends at junction 15, Side Hill Rd., which can be followed north to MA 3A. Or follow Turkey Hill Lane northwest to Turkey Hill.

Whitney Rd.
Distance from Howe's Rd. (junction 22) to
• Side Hill Rd. (junction 15): 1.1 mi., 45 min.

Bancroft Trail (TTOR)

This white-blazed trail begins at the Nature Trail sign in the grassy field near the entrance on MA 3A. It travels southwest across the reservation, passing along ledges and intersecting Howe's Rd. at junction 2. It then proceeds west to junction 3 at Bigelow Boulder, a 200-ton glacial granite boulder with a nearby smaller boulder. Turning south, the path crosses Whitney Rd. at junction 4, then climbs steeply through giant hemlock and white pine woods, crossing Howe's Rd. at junction 21. Rooster Rock, a glacial boulder supported on one side by a small stone, is on the left. The trail descends through hemlock woods to Ode's Den. Swinging north, the trail crosses Howe's Rd. at junction 20, Whitney Rd. at junction 5, and Boulder La. at junction 6, then circles eastward to end at Bigelow Boulder.

Bancroft Trail

Distance from Nature Trail sign to
- Bigelow Boulder: 1.8 mi., 1 hr.

Milliken Memorial Path (TTOR)

This path, a continuation of Howe's Rd., begins at junction 19, 1.1 mi. from the parking lot. It continues to the junction of James Hill La. and Ayer La. at junction 18. Heavily used as a bridle path, it is popular because of its rhododendrons, azaleas, and other plants not commonly found in the area.

Milliken Memorial Path

Distance from Howe's Rd. (junction 19) to
- James Hill La. and Ayer La. (junction 18): 0.8 mi., 25 min.

Ayer Lane (TTOR)

Ayer Lane is a connecting link from the Milliken Memorial Path to Whitney Rd., and is often used as a bridle path.

Ayer Lane

Distance from Milliken Memorial Path (junction 18) to
- Whitney Rd. (junction 10): 0.4 mi., 15 min.

Thayer Trail (TTOR)

One of the main east-west trails, the Thayer Trail begins on Whitney Rd. at junction 8 and circles east, passing an abandoned well and turning west after Adelaide Rd. at junction 12. Continuing west, the trail crosses an abandoned railroad bed, and turns left (west) at a T-junction. It then winds through a magnificent American holly grove. The trail then crosses One Way Lane at junction 16 and ends at Turkey Hill La., southwest of Turkey Hill.

Thayer Trail

Distance from Whitney Rd. (junction 8) to
- railroad bed: 0.7 mi., 40 min.
- holly grove: 0.8 mi., 45 min.
- Turkey Hill Lane: 1.5 mi., 1 hr. 30 min.

Turkey Hill Trail (TTOR)

Starting at the intersection of One Way La. and the Thayer Trail, the Turkey Hill Trail climbs north on One Way La. to Turkey Hill La. (paved). The trail turns right and continues a short distance to pastureland on the left, from which there are views over Cohasset Harbor. Return via the same route, as the old Turkey Hill loop trail has been abandoned.

Turkey Hill Trail

Distance from One Way La. and Turkey Hill La. (junction 16) to
- pasture: 0.3 mi., 15 min.

World's End Peninsula

This 251-acre peninsula in Hingham was originally laid out by famous landscape architect Frederick Law Olmsted in 1889 and includes an interesting drumlin and beach. A number of cart paths snake through the reservation, with footpaths emanating from them to explore the meadows and hills. The peninsula is a large glacial drumlin roughly shaped like an hourglass; its "waist" is a slender neck of land about 500 ft. wide called "the bar." The surface is mainly grassy with occasional granite outcrops. The upper peninsula, called World's End, is traced by three loop trails. The Rocky

Neck section of the lower peninsula is laced with footpaths that explore Ice Pond and other natural features.

The pristine nature of World's End is now protected and managed by the Trustees of Reservations, but the land was once the proposed site of a nuclear power plant and before that was the intended location of the United Nations headquarters.

To reach the peninsula from MA 3A in Hingham, turn onto Summer St. and continue northwest to a four-way intersection with Rockland St. Continue straight onto Martin's La. and travel 0.7 mi. to the gatehouse and parking on the right. Parking is limited and often fills up, particularly on pleasant spring or fall weekends.

Cutler Park

This park on the Charles River encompasses 700 acres of marsh and woods in the towns of Dedham, Needham, and Newton. Home to the largest freshwater marsh on this portion of the Charles River, the park is known for its wide diversity of animal and plant life—especially birds, with more than 100 species. Popular activities include birding, hiking, canoeing, and fishing.

From I-95 take the Highland Ave. (Needham) exit, and turn left at the first light on Highland Ave. onto Hunting Rd., which parallels I-95. In about 0.5 mi. turn left onto Kendrick St., which immediately crosses the highway. The area shares a driveway with a Polaroid building at 140 Kendrick St. The Brook Farm Historic Site is best accessed from the parking area off Baker St. in Brookline. The marsh is at the south end of the property and can be accessed from Needham St.

Cutler Park Loop (DCR)

This interesting loop through the park circles Kendrick Pond to the south of the parking area on Kendrick St. An extension of the trail runs from the south part of this loop to Powell's Island. The path begins at the parking area and bears to the left of the pond, going east then swinging south through marshland. At 0.3 mi. it enters the woods and continues south, following the Charles River. At 0.5 mi. there is an open view of the opposite bank and a distant view of the Blue Hills. Also in view are some abandoned concrete bunkers, originally used by the DCR for water-control operations.

At 0.7 mi. the main path turns right and heads back toward Kendrick St. Heading north, the path passes a pond and side trail on the left. (This side trail ascends an esker for about 0.5 mi. and passes through a mature oak forest where lady's slipper orchids are abundant in early June. It then descends the esker and rejoins the main path about midway up Kendrick Pond.) The main path soon comes to another open view of the pond, including the Wells Industrial Park and the Gothic tower of the Gosman Jewish Community Center in Newton. The path finally ends back at the parking lot, having made a circuit of about 1.6 mi.

To reach Powell's Island, leave the main loop trail at 0.7 mi. and head southeast. The path descends into a boggy area and crosses a streambed 0.3 mi. from the main path. It then ascends to an oak forest that extends southeast in a strip about 350 yd. wide between the wetlands and I-95. At 0.7 mi. the path crosses a short stretch of marsh to Powell's Island, which still shows the scarred trunks and standing deadwood left from a forest fire in the late 1980s. (Powell's Island is actually what southerners would call a hammock, surrounded on three sides by the Charles River and separated from the mainland by about 100 yd. of marsh.) At 0.9 mi. there is a meadow, and at the far end a path begins that circles around the island. Turn left at the first fork, and for the next 0.3 mi. the path runs along the embankment above the river, dropping down twice for boat landings. The reviving forest is ideal bird habitat, and a bench along the path is a good place to watch and listen. At the next fork a triple-masted radio tower to the northwest serves as a landmark; here the right-hand path returns to the meadow in 0.1 mi. From there retrace the path to the main trail.

Cutler Park Loop

Distances from parking lot to
- Powell's Island cutoff: 0.7 mi., 20 min.
- marsh crossing: 1.5 mi., 45 min.
- island circuit and return to mainland: 2.5 mi., 1 hr. 5 min.
- return to main loop: 3.0 mi., 1 hr. 30 min.
- return to parking lot: 4.0 mi., 2 hr.

Neponset River Marshes Reservation

The Neponset River Reservation encompasses a variety of diverse natural habitats, including freshwater wetlands and extensive tidal marshes. The salt marshes were acquired by the state Metropolitan Park Commission in the late nineteenth century, and since that time an additional 750 acres of the watershed has been protected, including several former commercial sites that have been restored as parklands. To reach the reservation, follow US 1 south to Exit 12, then follow MA 3A south and merge on Gallivan Blvd. (MA 203). The marked main entrance is off of Gallivan Blvd., with additional access on Hallet St.

Lower Neponset River Trail (DCR)

This greenway trail, partially completed with other sections pending, follows the path of an abandoned railroad grade that runs along the banks of the Neponset River. The path is designed to link the Neponset area with other DCR trails in order to offer more and varied opportunities for recreation in the region. The trail presently includes a 2.2-mi. paved path that connects Pope John Paul II Park to Central Ave. in Milton, passing Granite Ave., the Neponset Marshes, and the Lower Mills along the way.

Eventual extensions of the trail will include a section from Port Norfolk to Commercial Point, designed to link with an existing trail that reaches to Castle Island, and from Central Ave. to Mattapan.

Lower Neponset River Trail
Distance from Pope John Paul Park to
 • Central Ave. (Milton): 2.2 mi., 1 hr.

Webster Conservation Area

This 113-acre wooded area in the Newton Centre and Chestnut Hill sections of Newton is owned and maintained by the city of Newton. Adjoining the Webster Conservation Area to the west of Hammond Pond Pkwy. is the 14-acre woodland owned by Temple Mishkan Tefila and 38-acre Hammond Pond Reservation (DCR). The reservation includes an easement granted by the DCR to the Mall at Chestnut Hill and the Chestnut

Hill Towers condominium, which provides vehicular access to these two establishments.

The trails through the Webster Conservation Area are short and easy to follow, but it is helpful to consult the map available from the Newton Conservation Commission (NCC). To reach popular Deer Park, park at the end of Suffolk Rd. (off Hammond St.) and walk along Lowell La. to the Deer Park gate, where the deer shelter, feeding station, and watering trough are located.

Blue Trail (NCC)

The Blue Trail meanders through Hammond Pond Reservation from the parking area at Hammond Pond, located just behind the Mall at Chestnut Hill on MA 9. Though the trailhead is unmarked, the Blue Trail is the largest and most obvious trail leading from the parking lot. The blue dots and directional triangles begin about 200 yd. up the trail, although they are at times difficult to follow.

At Hemlock Vale the trail continues across the culvert over Tarn Pond Brook, takes a sharp left just before the MBTA Green Line, and crosses Hammond Pond Pkwy. to the parking lot of the Temple Mishkan Tefila, where it follows the Temple Path. On the north side of the temple the trail turns right into the Webster Conservation Area woods, passes Cake Rock, and comes to Gooch's Caves, located on a high rock ledge. The trail then returns to Hammond Pond Pkwy., turns right along the fence (unmarked), and uses the same crossing and trail back to the parking lot.

Green Trail (NCC)

To reach the Green Trail park in the gravel lot west of Temple Mishkan Tefila, then follow the Temple Path to the Green Trail on the right. When the Green Trail reaches Gooch's Caves, it turns left and continues to the Elgin Path. At the intersection with the Elgin Path, the Green Trail turns sharp left and continues 150 yd., then turns to the right for 200 yd. to reach the fence at the MBTA tracks. At the fence the trail turns sharp left and goes a short distance past a spur on the right. The spur leads to a sign identifying the undeveloped Webster Playground land, near the intersection of Warren St. and Elgin St. The main trail continues another 200 yd. and turns left onto the Temple Trail, which returns to the temple parking lot.

Carlisle Path (NCC)

The Carlisle Path is accessible from the westbound lane of Boylston St. (MA 9) by turning right onto Langley Rd., then right again onto Madoc St. to reach the gate and trailhead. From the gate take the Madoc Path to its junction with the Carlisle Path. Turn left onto the Carlisle Path, which continues between the Charles Cohen Conservation Area (Webster Vale), Hammond Pond Reservation, and the Temple Mishkan Tefila woods to the junction with the Temple Path (right). A short distance north of this junction the Carlisle Path becomes the unmarked Elgin Path, which ends at a fenced Green Line right of way over which there is no legal access. At this point hikers can take the Green Trail (right) to Gooch's Caves and back to the Temple Path, or switch to the Orange Trail or the Blue Trail at Gooch's Caves and follow either of these to the Temple Path. Alternatively, take the Blue Trail to Hammond Pond Pkwy. and pick up any of the trails on the east side of the parkway.

Elgin Path (NCC)

The Elgin Path enters Webster Conservation Area from Hammond Pond Pkwy. (*Note: In the area north of the Green Line and west of the parkway, the DCR does not permit parking on the parkway berms or on the road. Parking is available, however, along the Houghton Garden frontage at the end of Suffolk Rd. To reach the Elgin Path, follow Suffolk Rd. 1 block to the intersection of Old England Rd. and Clovelly Rd., where a path enters the woods. Follow this along the north fence of Deer Park to Hammond Pond Pkwy. Cross the parkway and turn right to find the Elgin Path.*) The Elgin Path joins the Ledge Path (right), which skirts the base of some magnificent sandstone ledges and an old quarry area. The trail continues on log steps up to the ledges, runs along the rim of the ledges, then returns to the parkway.

Noanet Woodlands

Noanet Woodlands is a 695-acre tract of forest and hilltop in Dover. Named for a leader of the Natick Nation who once fished the waters of Noanet Brook, the reservation was the site of Samuel Fisher's profitable sawmill in the early 1800s. An iron company also once operated here—a 24-ft.-tall dam on the property is its most noticeable remnant. Today the peaceful woods are laced with 17 mi. of moderate hiking trails with some strenuous sections. One of the reservation's most popular features is the overlook on Noanet Hill, which provides a grand view over the forest to the skyline of Boston.

Visitors to Noanet Woodlands use the parking facilities at Dover's Caryl Park, which abuts the reservation. To reach the parking area from the center of Dover, follow Dedham St. 0.6 mi. east to the Caryl Park entrance on the right. Additional parking is available at the western end of the park.

Caryl Trail (TTOR)

From the parking area in Caryl Park, the yellow-blazed trail heads south, then turns right (west). It passes a trail on the left, turns left (south) at a second junction, and crosses a branch of Noanet Brook. The trail swings east, passing trail junction 2 before bending south and meeting the blue-blazed Peabody Trail at junction 3 (the red-blazed Larrabee Trail is just east of the intersection at junction 4). From the junction the trail climbs moderately to junction 6. To reach Noanet Hill turn left (southeast) and continue straight to the overlook at the top of the hill (387 ft.).

The path now heads west, turns left (southeast) at junction 7, and continues to the southern foot of Noanet Hill. The trail swings southwest, traverses a long level area, then traces a course between a low hill and a wetland. Turning left (east) at the southern property line, the trail then follows the boundary northeast. Turning north, the trail proceeds the short distance to the tri-junction of the Peabody and Larrabee Trails. The Caryl Trail ends at this junction. Both trails can be followed back to the Caryl Trail at junction 3 located about 0.5 mi. south of Caryl Park and the parking area.

Caryl Trail
Distance from parking area to
  • junction 3: 0.5 mi., 25 min.
  • Noanet Hill (387 ft.): 0.9 mi., 55 min.
  • Peabody Junction: 2.2 mi., 1 hr.

Peabody Trail (TTOR)

This blue-blazed path begins at junction 3 off the Caryl Trail, about 0.5 mi. south of the parking area at Caryl Park. From the trailhead the path climbs steadily, passes straight through a three-way junction, then follows the contour of the hill past junction 37 to reach another intersection just northwest of a small pond. The Old Mill site can be reached by following the side trail left (east) across the north shore of the small pond.

The Peabody Trail continues south past junction 36 and, passing to the west of a larger pond, traces a course between Noanet Brook and the foot of Noanet Peak. The path passes another small pond to the east as it continues down the Noanet valley. Just before junction 34 the path turns east as it follows the base of a low hill. It then turns southeast, crosses the brook, and ends at junction 18 where the Peabody, Caryl, and Larrabee Trails converge.

Peabody Trail
Distance from Caryl Trail to
  • junction 37: 0.3 mi., 10 min.
  • junction 18: 1.2 mi., 40 min.

Larrabee Trail (TTOR)

The third major trail of Noanet Reservation begins at junction 4, a short distance east of junction 3 and about 0.5 mi. south of the parking area at Caryl Park. To reach the trail follow the Caryl Trail south from the parking area to junction 3, turn left (east), and continue the short way to junction 4. The red-blazed Larrabee Trail heads north, descending toward the brook to reach junction 33, where the path swings southeast and begins to trace a course over the level ground of the valley. The trail crosses the brook just beyond junction 29, then continues south, passing close to the shore of a pond before swinging left (east) around the base of a hill. Turning south again, the path stays close to the top of a low ridge and easily descends to the southern terminus at junction 18, where it meets the Caryl and Peabody Trails.

Larrabee Trail
Distance from Caryl Trail to
• pond: 0.6 mi., 20 min.
• junction 18: 1.4 mi., 40 min.

Rocky Woods Reservation and Fork Factory Brook

These adjoining reservations in Medfield and Dover comprise 491 acres of beautiful woods, lovely ponds, and excellent views. Rocky Woods Reservation was once "common land," divided up into woodlots that were parceled to residents who didn't have enough fuel wood on their own properties. Today 6.5 mi. of trails explore the reservation's abundant woodlands, wetlands, ponds, and rocky cobbles.

To reach the reservation from I-95, take Exit 16B and follow MA 128 west for 5.7 mi., to Hartford St. Turn right on Hartford St. and proceed 0.6 mi. to the entrance on the left. To reach the reservation from the intersection of MA 109 and MA 27 in Medfield, follow MA 109 east to Hartford St. and turn left. The entrance is 0.6 mi. ahead on the left. There is a gatehouse and large parking area at the entrance. Farther up the road is a second parking area by the visitor center and restrooms. Trail maps are available at the visitor center.

Chickering Pond Trail (TTOR)

This short 0.5-mi.-long trail loops around Chickering Pond. Beginning at the visitor center the trail heads east, crosses the outflow brook, and then swings northeast. The path climbs a ridge to an overlook with a view of the pond. Nearby is junction 3, where the Noanet Trail leaves right (northeast). The trail now traces a path between the southern foot of Cedar Hill and the lake, reaching junction 4, where the Tower and Ridge Trails enter, at the north end of the lake. The trail now leaves the lake, bending west and reaching junction 5 with the Quarry Trail. Turning south, the path again approaches the lake, where the bridle trail leaves right. The path now stays fairly close to the shore as it returns to the visitor center.

Chickering Pond Trail
Distance from visitor center to
• trailhead (circuit): 0.5 mi., 20 min.

Cedar Hill Loop (TTOR)

A moderate loop can be made by combining the Chickering Pond, Noanet, Cedar Hill, and Tower Trails. Take the Chickering Pond Trail to junction 3 and turn right (northeast) down the Noanet Trail. At the Cedar Trail turn left (west) and ascend Cedar Hill to the Tower Trail. At this junction the Tower Trail leaves left (south), while the loop trail heads north, then west at a fork, and reaches an overlook on Cedar Hill (435 ft.). The trail steeply descends from the overlook to rejoin the Tower Trail. The Tower Trail continues down Cedar Hill to junction 4, where it joins the Chickering Pond Trail and heads back to the visitor center.

Cedar Hill Loop
Distances from visitor center to
• loop trail near overlook: 0.75 mi., 25 min.
• visitor center (circuit): 1.2 mi., 45 min.

Echo Pond Trail (TTOR)

This trail begins at junction 1 on the western side of the Loop Trail, which can be accessed from the lower parking area. The Echo Pond Trail initially heads west toward Echo Pond, reaches the east shore, then turns southwest and follows the shoreline. While the Echo Pond Trail continues straight to its end at the East West Trail, a side trail (the preferred route for scenery) makes a sharp right (west) turn and crosses the width of the lake on a footbridge. After reaching the far shore, the path follows the shoreline briefly, turns left (northwest), and joins a side trail to reach the Harwood Notch Trail south of junction 6.

Echo Pond Trail
Distance from Loop Trail Junction 1 to
- junction 6: 0.4 mi., 15 min.

Fork Factory Brook Trail (TTOR)

This property abuts Rocky Woods to the east of Hartford St. It is predominantly flat wetlands, with Mill Brook tracing a course through the property. A network of paths explores wetlands and low hilltops, eventually leading to an old mill site at the south end of the property. The single trailhead is on the east side of Hartford Rd., a few yards north of the entrance road to Rocky Woods.

For a loop along the outer perimeter, from Hartford Rd. follow the trail south to junction 1, and continue south along the wetland to junction 2. Bear right at this junction and continue south along the base of the hill to junction 3, where a side trail leads to an old mill site. Turn left (north) at junction 3 and continue to follow the trail right at junctions 4, 5, 7, and 8. The trail then returns to junction 1, and turn right to return to the trailhead.

Fork Factory Brook Trail
Distance from Hartford Rd. to
- junction 3: 0.5 mi., 20 min.
- trailhead (circuit): 1.25 mi., 40 min.

Rocky Narrows Reservation (TTOR)

This 227-acre property is situated in the southeastern part of Sherborn. Called the "gates of the Charles" for its tall cliffs, it consists of rocky woodlands on the banks of the Charles River. The reservation sports 7 mi. of hiking trails, including a section of the Bay Circuit Trail. There are two parking areas. One is off South Main St. (MA 27) just north of the junction with MA 115. This parking lot serves the portion of the reservation southwest of the railroad tracks and includes the Green Trail. Railroad policy forbids pedestrian crossing of the tracks. The other area is at the corner of Forest and Goulding Sts. at the north end of the property. A canoe landing is on the northeast portion of the reservation.

Red Trail (TTOR)

This red-blazed trail begins at the north parking area and heads south before turning slowly east to pass wetlands and upland hills. It then makes a sharp right (southwest) turn at junction 20 (0.6 mi.), followed shortly by a left (southeast) to reach junction 19 at 0.8 mi. From here, the canoe landing can be reached by a footpath that heads a short distance east to the river. The Red Trail continues west over level ground, then climbs to junction 18 nearly due west of the river narrows. The trail heads south along the ridge to reach the Narrows Overlook at 1.4 mi. From the overlook the path heads southeast past junctions 17 and 16, to reach junction 15 at 1.7 mi. A side trail leads from here to King Philip's Overlook. From junction 15 the Red Trail swings around the ridge and descends, approaching the railroad grade before turning northwest to pass between the tracks and the base of the hill. The trail follows an easy course north, then turns west at the northern end of the hill. The trail bends back north and continues on to the parking area at 2.7 mi.

Red Trail

Distances from north parking area to
- junction 20: 0.6 mi., 20 min.
- junction 19: 0.8 mi., 25 min.
- junction 15: 1.7 mi., 55 min.
- parking area: 2.7 mi., 1 hr. 30 min.

Sherborn Town Forest

This forest occupies several irregular contiguous and nearly contiguous tracts in the eastern and northern parts of Sherborn. It is mildly hilly and is bordered on the west by higher hills. The section of the forest just north of the junction of Goulding, Lake, Forest, and Snow St. (a triangle with a small house in the middle) has many trails of various lengths and conditions, but these trails, with the exception of the Town Forest Trail, leave the forest and traverse the surrounding area, including Mt. Misery and the woodlands west of the forest. Refer to the USGS Natick and Medfield quadrangles.

Town Forest Trail: Pine St. School to Lake St. (Town of Sherborn)

This easy hike passes near two wooded summits with limited views. The trailhead is located at the Pine St. School in Sherborn, just off MA 16 (Eliot St.) near its intersection with MA 27. Parking is allowed in marked spaces in the school lot from dawn to dusk on non-school days, but is not allowed on Lake St. The trail leaves the parking lot by the rear of the jungle gyms and is marked with single white blazes. Double blazes mark the frequent turns. The trail turns left in about 0.1 mi. and climbs quickly to the summit of Pine Hill, keeping to the right at a fork just before the summit. At about 0.2 mi. the trail bears right at a second fork, passing a horse-jumping field on the right. Turning right again, the trail follows a pipeline right of way down to Farm Rd.

The white blazes continue on the south side of Farm Rd., as the Town Forest Trail joins the white-marked Bay Circuit Trail. The trail bears left and returns to the pipeline track in about 0.1 mi., follows the pipeline for about 0.2 mi., and enters the woods to the right. When the Town Forest Trail bears left in about 100 yd., a short side trail to the right leads to the summit of Mt. Misery (279 ft.). The remainder of the trail winds through the woods down to Lake St., just north of the intersection of Lake, Goulding, Forest, and Snow St. A green metal gate marks this end of the trail.

Town Forest Trail: Pine St. School to Lake St.
Distance from Pine St. School to
  • Lake St.: 2.0 mi., 1 hr.

Broadmoor Wildlife Sanctuary

This Massachusetts Audubon Society sanctuary comprises about 624 acres off Eliot St. (MA 16) and South St. in South Natick and Sherborn and borders the Charles River. The area around Little Farm Pond in Sherborn (262 acres) was given to the Audubon Society in 1962 by Henry M. Channing in memory of Katherine Minot Channing. The Broadmoor property (South Natick and Sherborn) was donated by Dr. and Mrs. Carl Stillman in 1968.

The entrance to the sanctuary is at 280 Eliot St. (MA 16), 1.8 mi. southwest from South Natick. Trail maps are available at the nature center. The visitor center is a 1911-era horse barn renovated in 1983 that features composting restrooms, solar heating, and other innovative, earth-friendly features.

Broadmoor features 9 mi. of trails, including long boardwalks with excellent views of wetlands and wildlife, and forest paths. A number of well-marked trails leave from the parking area, including the Charles River Loop, a pleasant circuit which follows the riverbank and leads to a series of bedrock outcroppings.

Walden Pond State Reservation

Walden Pond and its surrounding woodlands, the site of Henry David Thoreau's retreat, were given to the state in 1922 with the provision that the public be allowed to swim, canoe, hike, and picnic there. During summer Walden Pond is a popular swimming and picnic spot. In the off-season visitors find the pond and its environs a tranquil escape. Maps of the extensive trail system are available at the park office or at the parking entrance. Trails include the Pond Path circuit, paths to the original site of Thoreau's cabin, a trail up Emerson's Cliff, loop trails west of the railroad tracks around the "Andromeda" ponds, and trails that connect to adjacent conservation land in Lincoln and Concord.

The reservation is located in Concord at the intersection of MA 126 (Walden St.) and MA 2. There is a parking fee from May through October (space for 350 cars). The lot may fill up on summer weekends due to the popularity of the pond's beach. Cars parked on the state highway will be towed. Dogs and mountain biking are not permitted. Park staff conduct year-round programs about Thoreau's life and his stay at Walden, and a small bookstore is located near the restrooms adjacent to the parking lot. A beach wheelchair is available for universal access to the swimming area. For more information, contact the park supervisor (978-369-3254).

Walden Pond Loop (DCR)

To reach the pond loop trail, cross MA 126 and follow the path downhill to the beach. The 1.8-mi. circuit follows the pond, offering continuous views from above the shoreline. A short side trail leads to the Thoreau cabin site. Near the pond hikers are asked to stay on marked trails and off the steep slopes, where bank erosion has been a problem in recent years.

Walden Pond Loop Path

Distance from beach trailhead to
- trailhead (circuit): 1.8 mi., 1 hr.

Great Meadows National Wildlife Refuge

Established to protect habitat for migrating birds, this 3,600-acre refuge is located 20 mi. west of Boston and encompasses 12 mi. of the Concord and Sudbury River watersheds. This freshwater marsh area is divided into two large units (Concord and Sudbury) that provide habitat for a great diversity of migrating and nesting birds, including waterfowl, shorebirds, and songbirds. More than 220 species of birds have been observed here; the Concord unit is known as one of the best birding areas in Massachusetts. Great Meadows offers opportunities for wildlife observation, hiking, photography, and nature study. For more information contact Great Meadows NWR, 73 Weir Hill Rd., Sudbury, MA 01776 (978-443-4661).

To reach the Concord unit follow MA 62 (Bedford Rd.) 1.4 mi. northeast of Concord center toward Bedford. After about 1.0 mi. turn left onto Monsen Rd. following the refuge sign, then continue to the refuge entrance at a dirt road on the left. Parking, photo blinds, and a seasonal comfort station are provided.

Trails in the Concord unit include the Dike Trail (2.7 mi.), a loop path that circles a pool in the marsh; the Black Duck Creek Trail (about 1.0 mi.); and the Timber Trail (0.5 mi.).

Concord Unit: Dike Trail (USFWS)

This popular trail, portions of which may be flooded during wet periods, offers excellent wildlife watching opportunities; in addition to the birds watch for a variety of colorful dragonflies and damselflies during warm months. The trail crosses a dike that divides two impoundments, then follows a portion of the Concord River before looping back to the trailhead.

Dike Trail
Distance from parking area to
• trailhead (circuit): 2.7 mi., 1 hr. 15 min.

Sudbury Unit: Weir Trail (USFWS)

For the Sudbury unit, proceed about 1.4 mi., and turn left onto Weir Hill Rd. (refuge sign), and follow signs to the visitor center. Follow US 20 west through Wayland and turn left onto Pelham Island Rd. Continue to a parking lot on the right side of the road, across from Heard Pond. The visitor center, a three-story building that hosts exhibits, the refuge headquarters, and facilities for seasonal interpretive programming, is open weekdays year-round and closed holidays and weekends. Parking, an observation tower, and restrooms are provided.

The unit's 0.75-mi. trail begins at the visitor center and weaves around marshes, woods, fields, a red maple swamp, and brooks.

Weir Trail
Distance from nature center to
• trailhead (circuit): 0.75 mi., 30 min.

Middlesex Fells Reservation

This reservation, lying in Stoneham, Medford, Winchester, Melrose, and Malden, is maintained by the DCR. It contains 2,575 acres of rough woodland, ponds, brooks, reservoirs, and granite outcrops traversed by fire roads, bridle paths, and footpaths. Stone towers on Pine Hill and Bear Hill, as well as numerous outlooks, offer good views. Middlesex Fells (*fell* is the Saxon word for "rocky place") is a very popular destination. Mountain biking is permitted on all fire roads as well as on the designated bike loop path (marked with red-and-white bike path markers). This loop circles the three reservoirs in the western tract and consists of mostly fire roads with some single-track. A map of the reservation is available from the Friends of the Middlesex Fells (to contact the organization, write to 4 Woodland Rd., Stoneham, MA 02180, or visit their website www.fells.org) as well as local bookstores and the AMC offices at 5 Joy St. in Boston.

From I-93 take Exit 33 to MA 28, travel north a short distance to South Border Rd., take a right onto the road, and proceed to the Bellevue parking area in the south portion of the western tract. To reach the reservation by Mass Transit take the Orange Line to Wellington Station, then MBTA bus 100 to Roosevelt Circle Rotary. From there walk south to the rotary and follow South Border Rd. (on the right) less than 0.25 mi. to Bellevue Pond.

Cross Fells Trail (DCR)

The blue-blazed Cross Fells Trail is a good connecting trail between the eastern and western sections of the Middlesex Fells Reservation, because it touches every major trail in the reservation. This trail follows sections of the Rock Circuit, Mini Rock Circuit, Virginia Woods, Skyline, and Spot Pond Trails. The eastern end of this trail is 0.6 mi. north of the Oak Grove terminal of the MBTA Orange Line. To reach the trailhead in the eastern section of the fells, follow Washington St. north to Goodyear Ave., then follow Goodyear Ave. west (left) to the trailhead in Melrose, near the Melrose–Malden line.

The trail climbs west along easy wooded grades to a high rocky ridge. Here it turns left (south) and follows the Rock Circuit Trail (white-blazed) and the Mini Rock Circuit Trail (orange-blazed) to Black Rock. The Cross Fells Trail continues some distance with the Rock Circuit Trail (but not with the Mini Rock Circuit Trail) before exiting right (west) to cross Black Rock Path (a bridle trail) and Fellsway East (paved). It continues west, skirting the south side of the high reservoir and picking up the Mini Rock Circuit Trail. Shortly the two trails come to the Virginia Woods Trail (red-blazed). The Mini Rock Circuit Trail exits right (north) with the Virginia Woods Trail, while the Cross Fells Trail continues west.

The trail crosses several bridle paths before passing south of Shiner Pool. It then rejoins the Rock Circuit Trail and crosses a swampy section before leaving this trail and crossing Woodland Rd. (paved) just north of the hockey arena. It next joins the Virginia Woods Trail, passing the southern end of Quarter Mile Pond and heading west over the hills. In 0.3 mi. the Virginia Woods Trail exits left (south) to Wright's Pond, while the Cross Fells Trail continues west to Fellsway West (MA 28). The trail follows Fellsway West and the Spot Pond Trail (yellow-blazed) a short distance to an underpass of I-93, then crosses Fellsway West.

The trail follows Brooks Rd. (dirt) to a junction with the Skyline Trail (white-blazed). Here the Cross Fells Trail turns left (south) to go partway up a small hill with the Skyline Trail. Soon the Cross Fells Trail turns right (west) to follow a ridge above Brooks Rd. The trail bends left (south) and picks up a series of bridle paths before turning left (east) into the woods to rejoin the Skyline Trail on the summit of Wenepoykin Hill.

The two trails then head south together to East Dam Rd. (dirt). Here the Cross Fells Trail continues south downhill to a brook and on to rejoin another section of the Skyline Trail. The two trails continue west until the Cross Fells Trail turns left (southwest) to pick up a group of bridle paths. After crossing S. Border Rd. (paved), the trail climbs a hill to the site of the former Lawrence Observation Tower. Descending the hill, the trail follows bridle paths to the reservation's Whitmore Brook entrance on Winthrop St. in Medford, across from Playstead Rd. (the end of the MBTA Sullivan Square–West Medford bus line).

Cross Fells Trail

Distance from Goodyear Ave. (Melrose) to
• Whitmore Brook entrance: 4.3 mi., 2 hr. 30 min.

Rock Circuit Trail (DCR)

This white-blazed trail affords the best views in the Middlesex Fells. Living up to its name, it is very rocky and offers rewarding but rugged hiking. A convenient approach to this trail is from Woodland St. in Medford, opposite the northern end of the hockey arena parking lot (south of New England Memorial Hospital in Stoneham). Follow a woods road east for a short distance to the crest of a hill to pick up the Rock Circuit Trail.

Turning right (south), the trail climbs a nearby ridge overlooking sections of Medford. Here it joins the Virginia Woods Trail (red-blazed) for a few feet, then goes south along the ridge before turning left (east) to another ridge. The trail goes north before turning sharp right (east) to drop into a valley, crossing a bridle path and a brook.

At the brook the trail turns left (north) and soon rejoins the Virginia Woods Trail, again for only a few feet. The Rock Circuit Trail crosses a bridle path and climbs southeast up a ridge. In 0.1 mi. the trail turns right (south) and drops into a valley. The trail then makes a long, gentle climb southeast to Boojum Rock, where it picks up the Mini Rock Circuit Trail (orange-blazed) for 0.1 mi. Leaving fine views of the Boston area, the trail drops sharply and heads east to cross a bridle path and then Fellsway East (paved). It rejoins the Mini Rock Circuit Trail and climbs Pinnacle Rock, from which there are more fine views. At Pinnacle Rock both trails turn north, almost doubling back on themselves, and pass a television tower enclosure, where the Mini Rock Circuit Trail exits.

The Rock Circuit Trail then follows a rough ridge north to Black Rock. At Black Rock, this trail combines first with the Cross Fells Trail (blue-blazed) and then with the Mini Rock Circuit Trail to surmount a fine viewpoint. The three trails continue north a short distance before the Cross Fells Trail turns sharp right (east) downhill to exit the fells. The two Rock Circuit Trails continue north along the top of the ridge to White Rock and Melrose Rock with many fine views.

At Melrose Rock the two trails separate, with the Rock Circuit Trail turning left (west) through the woods to re-cross Fellsway East (paved) and to skirt the eastern end of the high reservoir. The trail crosses Wyoming Path to enter some young tree growth and soon rejoins the Virginia Woods Trail and then the Mini Rock Circuit Trail. It ascends a ridge behind (east of) New England Memorial Hospital, from which there is a fine view north. The Virginia Woods Trail separates here, with the two Rock Circuit Trails turning left from the ridge. Soon the Mini Rock Circuit Trail exits left (south), and the Rock Circuit Trail goes right (west) through a fine pine grove to join the yellow-blazed Spot Pond Trail for 0.2 mi. while passing south of New England Memorial Hospital.

After leaving the Spot Pond Trail and crossing several bridle paths, the Rock Circuit Trail passes the northwest shore of Shiner Pool and soon joins the Cross Fells Trail to cross a swampy area. It then leaves the Cross Fells Trail, turning left (south) along a ridge adjacent to Woodland Rd. to complete the circuit.

Rock Circuit Trail
Distance from trailhead to
• trailhead (circuit): 4.0 mi., 3 hr. 30 min.

Mini Rock Circuit Trail (DCR)

The Mini Rock Circuit Trail is a shorter and smoother variation of the Rock Circuit Trail. This orange-blazed trail takes in the best high points of the Rock Circuit Trail and some fine sections of other trails but avoids many rough sections. On a clear day this trail affords spectacular views. The Mini Rock Circuit Trail is accessible from any of the other trails in the eastern section of the fells or from either of its two crossings of Fellsway East. For this approach follow the Cross Fells Trail (blue-blazed) from its eastern end on Goodyear Ave. in Melrose. The Mini Rock Circuit Trail turns right (north) from the Cross Fells Trail 0.1 mi. from Goodyear Ave.

The Mini Rock Circuit Trail goes along a ridge with the Rock Circuit Trail (white-blazed) over White Rock and Melrose Rock. The trails then turn left (west) and separate, with the Mini Rock Circuit Trail following a bridle path to Fellsway East (paved). After crossing Fellsway East, the trail winds gently west and ascends to a high rock behind (east of) New England Memorial Hospital, where it joins the Rock Circuit Trail and the Virginia Woods Trail (red-blazed). The latter separates almost immediately at a fine viewpoint. The other two trails descend and separate shortly, with the Mini Rock Circuit Trail going left (south) through the woods to rejoin another section of the Virginia Woods Trail.

These two trails soon come to Bent Rd. (dirt), which they follow right (west) until the fence on the left (south) turns left around the high reservoir. The trails also turn left, and in 0.1 mi. they leave the fence, heading right (southwest) to meet the Cross Fells Trail. Here the Mini Rock Circuit Trail leaves the Virginia Woods Trail and turns left (southeast) to join the Cross Fells Trail. The two trails work back to the high reservoir fence and continue down a ridge before separating. The Mini Rock Circuit Trail continues southeast a short distance along a fire road before turning right (southwest) to zigzag up a hill to rejoin the Rock Circuit Trail on Boojum Rock.

The Mini Rock Circuit Trail turns left (southeast), and the two trails soon reach an excellent viewpoint of Boston, its harbor, and the surrounding land. At the viewpoint the trails separate, and both head for Pinnacle Rock. The Mini Rock Circuit Trail bears left (northeast), crossing two bridle paths and Fellsway East (paved). The two trails remerge for a short distance at Pinnacle Rock and then almost double back. They go north, separating after passing a television tower enclosure. The Mini Rock Circuit Trail follows bridle paths north to Black Rock, where it joins the Rock Circuit Trail and the Cross Fells Trail at another fine viewing location. The three trails continue north a short distance to complete the loop for the Mini Rock Circuit Trail.

Mini Rock Circuit Trail

Distance from trailhead to
  • trailhead (circuit): 2.8 mi., 2 hr.

Skyline Trail (DCR)

This trail is located in the western section of the fells. Marked with white blazes, it circles the Winchester Reservoirs as it travels through Medford, Stoneham, and Winchester. A popular starting point is Bellevue Pond, off S. Border Rd. in Medford, a short distance west of I-93 (Exit 33) and MA 28.

Quarry Rd. (dirt) goes east (right) of Bellevue Pond. The Skyline Trail follows Quarry Rd. to the first blaze near the northern end of Bellevue Pond. The trail turns right up Pine Hill, at the top of which is Wright's Tower with commanding views of Boston, its harbor, and the Blue Hills. The trail continues north along a rocky ridge before turning west to drop into a valley. It climbs the ridge to the west and on top of the second ridge turns north for 0.3 mi., dipping once to cross a notch with a spur of Quarry Rd. (bridle path). At the northern end of the ridge is a good view north over I-93.

The trail descends northwest, passing the northern end of the next ridge before turning west and dropping into a valley. It continues west, descending a hill. Near the summit the trail turns right (north) and joins the Cross Fells Trail (blue-blazed) for a short distance to the summit. The Skyline Trail follows high land north over several hills, including Silver Mine Hill. Soon after Silver Mine Hill, the Skyline Trail rejoins the Cross Fells Trail for a short distance as it descends to Brooks Rd. (dirt). The Skyline Trail continues north over Gerry Hill and on to Chandler Rd. (dirt) along the Winchester Reservoir fence, which detours the Skyline Trail with the Reservoir Trail (orange-blazed) to the right (east) a short distance and then left (north).

Very shortly the Reservoir Trail exits left (northwest), while the Skyline Trail goes uphill to the Sheepfold picnic area. The trail passes the eastern end of the parking lot, skirts the east side of the picnic area, then crosses a former soapbox derby track on the way north to Winthrop Hill, where there is a fine view of the Winchester North Reservoir. From here it continues along a ridge toward Bear Hill. About 0.2 mi. north of Winthrop Hill the Skyline Trail turns sharp left (west) downhill at a trail junction. (*Note: Straight ahead—north—uphill is the short Bear Hill Connector Trail, which connects with the Spot Pond Trail at the Bear Hill observation tower.*)

The Skyline Trail crosses Dike Rd. (dirt), where it joins the Reservoir Trail to cross a brook and continue through a former meadow and a pine grove to another dirt road. Here the Reservoir Trail exits left (southwest) on the dirt road, while the Skyline Trail continues straight over Money Hill. On the west slope of Money Hill the two trails remerge and descend, crossing N. Border Rd. (dirt) into a ravine north of the Winchester North Reservoir dam.

The trails cross a brook (outflow from the reservoir), then soon bend left (south) a short distance before zigzagging up the west slope of the ravine to pass north of the old firehouse. They continue to paved Alben St., on to Reservoir St., and finally on to Hillcrest Pkwy., where there is parking and access to the trail. Both trails very shortly leave the paved roads and go south via the West Dam Path. After crossing a dirt service road, they soon separate. The Reservoir Trail exits right, while the Skyline Trail continues straight over a couple of minor hills. The Skyline Trail crosses the Reservoir Trail and soon climbs steeply up Nanapashemet Hill, where there are limited views.

The Skyline Trail continues south over numerous hills to merge with the Reservoir Trail at the Winchester South Reservoir standpipe. The two trails continue south, then east around town water supply land at the west reservoir dam. The trails almost reach S. Border Rd. before passing over a hill to the Middle Rd. Path. A dirt road on the right leads shortly to a parking area off S. Border Rd. and an access to the two trails. The trails soon bend left (north) to pick up the East Dam Path. They soon separate, with the Reservoir Trail going straight (north) and the Skyline Trail turning right uphill. At the top of the hill the trail bends right along a ridge before turning left to cross Middle Rd. (dirt) and soon joins the Cross Fells Trail for a short distance. The Skyline Trail turns right to head for Panther Cave, passing almost directly over the cave before dropping to cross the Red Cross Path and Straight Gully Brook. It then climbs Little Pine Hill on its way to Bellevue Pond, where it completes its circuit.

Skyline Trail
Distance from Bellevue Pond to
• Bellevue Pond (circuit): 6.8 mi., 5 hr.

Reservoir Trail (DCR)

This orange-blazed trail is a very pleasant circuit around the three Winchester reservoirs. Individuals using the trail should be aware that the adjacent reservoir lands are not for general public access and that the nearby No Trespassing signs should be observed. This trail avoids major hills and rocky terrain. The trail was designed to be a possible ski touring trail when snow is sufficient. It has many fine vistas.

The Reservoir Trail can be joined from several locations. It will be described here starting from the Sheepfold and going counterclockwise. The trail follows close to the fence on the southern and western boundaries of the Sheepfold picnic area. It leaves the fence, crosses the former soapbox derby track, and enters the woods on an old bridle path. Soon it leaves the path and winds under Winthrop Hill along gentle slopes to keep between the hill and reservoir property.

North of the municipal property the trail drops down to Dike Rd. (dirt). It follows this road north to meet the Skyline Trail (white blazes) coming down from the side of Bear Hill. Here the Reservoir Trail turns left (west) with the Skyline Trail, goes to Dike Brook, then goes straight ahead through a former meadow and a pine grove to a dirt road. The Skyline Trail goes over Money Hill, while the Reservoir Trail leaves left (southwest) down the road and then climbs to skirt Money Hill to rejoin the Skyline Trail. The two trails descend together to cross N. Border Rd. (dirt) and enter a ravine north of the North Dam.

The trails cross a brook formed by leakage from the reservoir. Shortly the trails bend left (south) a short distance before zigzagging up the west slope of the ravine to pass north of the old firehouse (which has water pumps in the basement) out onto Alben St. (paved) to Reservoir St./Hillcrest Pkwy. There is parking and access here for the two trails. The two trails very shortly leave the paved roads and go south via the West Dam Path. They cross a dirt service road and soon separate. The Skyline Trail goes ahead (south), while the Reservoir Trail goes right (southwest) to skirt a couple of marshes, crosses a brook, and then crosses the Skyline Trail before joining a dirt road southeasterly toward the Middle and South Reservoirs.

At the end of the road, the trail enters a bluff with fine views of the Middle and South Reservoirs and the causeway between them. The trail bends back and drops into a ravine. It crosses a brook and goes over one small hill and then over the shoulder of another hill to a dirt road. From here the trail goes south for nearly a mile, crossing Molly Spring Rd. (dirt), two brooks, and several stone walls and eventually rejoining the Skyline Trail adjacent to the South Reservoir standpipe. The two trails go south, then east around the municipal land near the reservoir's West Dam. The trails almost reach S. Border Rd. before going over a hill to the Middle Rd. Path. (The dirt road to the right leads shortly to parking off S. Border Rd.—an access spot for the two trails.) The two trails go straight, then bend left (north) to pick up the East Dam Path, where they separate. The Skyline Trail turns right (east) up a hill, while the Reservoir Trail goes ahead (north).

As the Reservoir Trail approaches the South Reservoir it leaves the road and heads northeast, not far from East Dam Rd. (dirt). Adjacent to the small East Dam the trail descends into a ravine, then ascends it and continues parallel to the patrol road going north. After going over Silver Mine Hill, the trail passes close to the sealed shaft of a silver mine. (Note the concrete posts of a former fence around the mine shaft.) The trail continues north with more views of the reservoirs, not far from the patrol road, until it reaches Chandler Rd. (dirt) with a fence on its north side. The trail goes right (east) along Chandler Rd., joins the Skyline Trail, and heads for the Sheepfold to complete its circuit.

Reservoir Trail (DCR)
Distance from Sheepfold to
  • Sheepfold (circuit): 5.5 mi., 3 hr.

Elm Bank Reservation (DCR)

This 182-acre property in Wellesley is a conglomerate of historic sites, period landscaping, and woods and fields surrounded on three sides by the Charles River. Listed on the National Register of Historic Places, this reservation is especially attractive for family outings, as the terrain and facilities are friendly to the needs of children.

To reach Elm Bank Reservation from Boston, take MA 9 west to MA 16 (Washington St.). Travel south along MA 16 through Wellesley and past Wellesley College. About 1.0 mi. beyond the college turn left onto the entrance road, which crosses the Charles River and then forks roughly north and south. Both roads take circuitous routes to the center of the reservation, where the parking area, ranger headquarters, and Massachusetts Horticultural Society are located. A hiking trail explores the river neck, which makes up much of the north and central parts of the reservation, and can be accessed by following the roads either north or west from the parking area. A canoe access is located northwest of the reservation entrance.

Breakheart Reservation (DCR)

The DCR's Breakheart Reservation, in Saugus and Wakefield, covers 640 acres of oak-hemlock-pine forest, with numerous hills, jagged rocky outcrops, two freshwater lakes, and a meandering stretch of the Saugus River. Several rocky hills provide views south toward Boston and north to New Hampshire. The swimming area on Pearce Lake (restrooms and first-aid station) is popular in summer, and fishing and birding are popular on both Silver and Pearce Lakes. To reach the reservation, take the Lynn Fells Pkwy. exit off US 1, then continue southwest 0.4 mi. to Forest St. on the right. Follow Forest St. to the parking area at the reservation headquarters. Trail information is available at the headquarters building.

A network of blacktop roads serves all areas of the reservation, although only Pine Tops Rd. is open to vehicular traffic. Pine Tops Rd.

makes a one-way counterclockwise loop through the center of the reservation. It heads north from the reservation headquarters on Forest St. to Pearce Lake, where swimming is allowed only when lifeguards are on duty. The road then turns south roughly parallels the shores of Pearce and Silver Lakes before returning to the reservation headquarters.

The other paved roads are Elm Rd. and Hemlock Rd., which connect to form another loop from Pine Tops Rd. near Pearce Lake. This loop heads around the west side of the lakes and back to Pine Tops Rd., about 200 yd. before the exit at the headquarters. Elm Rd. and Hemlock Rd. meet at the Wakefield Vocational High School gate, where parking is allowed. Vehicular access to the reservation is prohibited here. Finally, unpaved Flume Rd. runs between Pearce and Silver Lakes, connecting Hemlock Rd. to Pine Tops Rd. at fire gate 11 in the middle of the reservation.

In addition to the roads, an extensive series of hiking trails crisscrosses the reservation. The Fox Run, Breakheart, Saugus, and Lodge Trails are all marked with yellow blazes as well as wooden trailhead posts.

Fox Hill Trail (DCR)

This trail begins about 75 yd. north of the front gate and entrance onto Pine Tops Rd., after a wooden fence on the left. A gate and a wooden post mark the trailhead. It climbs steeply for a short distance and bears right (north) at a junction with the Breakheart Trail. The trail continues between the loop of Pine Tops Rd., then turns sharp left (southwest) at the junction with the Saugus River Trail. In about 100 yd. the path bends right toward an exposed rock ledge. It crosses a large rocky plateau overlooking Pearce Lake, and then descends steeply to the Pearce Lake swimming area at fire gate 9.

Fox Hill Trail
Distance from gate to
 • Pearce Lake swimming area: 1.0 mi., 30 min.

Saugus River Trail (DCR)

This trail begins at the first gate on the right after entering the reservation on Pine Tops Rd. It heads east toward the river and connects with a spur on the right, which leads to the somewhat buried remains of a stone dam built in the early 1800s. (*Note: If you take the spur, stay to the right after a large opening before a small picnic area; otherwise you will just get to a small stream.*) The main trail stays to the left and follows the river, eventually turning west and crossing Pine Tops Rd. The trail reenters the woods about 50 yd. to the right on Pine Tops Rd. Shortly after this point the trail bears left at a fork, continues straight, and intersects with the Fox Hill Trail.

Saugus River Trail
Distance from gate to
• Fox Hill Trail: 0.8 mi., 25 min.

Pearce Lake Trail (DCR)

This trail starts at the swimming area and circles Pearce Lake, hugging the shoreline, which varies from sandy beach to rocky outcroppings to dense hemlock groves. It is a well-traveled path marked with blue blazes, and passes the Flume Trail, which leads to the Silver Lake Trail. The trail heads south, leaving Pine Tops Rd. south of fire gate 9 and intersecting a dirt road on the left at a point nearly opposite Eagle Rock on the far shore.

The path then stays close to the lake, coming close to Hemlock Rd. as it swings around the south end of the lake. Heading north, the trail passes the Fern Trail on the left (north) and quickly comes to a jeep road and the Eagle Rock Trail, both of which leave left. The Eagle Rock Trail leads to Eagle Rock, which overlooks the lake, then rejoins the Pearce Lake Trail near the north bay. The Pearce Lake Trail continues to follow the shore, meeting the Eagle Rock Trail a short distance before reaching Elm Rd. Turn right (east) and continue the short way to the beach.

Pearce Lake Trail
Distance from Pearce Lake beach to
• Pearce Lake beach via Elm Rd. (circuit): 1.3 mi., 45 min.

Silver Lake Trail (DCR)

The Silver Lake Trail can be accessed from Flume Rd. south of fire gate 11 or from the dirt road that leaves Hemlock Rd. north of fire gate 18. From

Flume Rd. the trail heads east to where the path splits and the loop begins. Proceeding clockwise (east), the path travels southeast, roughly follows the shore, and passes through the narrow area between the lake and Pine Tops Rd. near fire gate 12. The trail then heads west along the shore before bending south to trace the contour of the southern cove.

Turning north, the path passes the dirt road on the left that leads to Hemlock Rd. Continuing north, the trail hugs the lake and closes the loop just east of Flume Rd. To return to the beginning, follow the shore of Silver Lake and continue past the Flume Trail, a short spur that connects the Silver Lake Trail to the Pearce Lake Trail.

Silver Lake Trail

Distance from Flume Rd. to
- Flume Rd. (circuit): 0.9 mi., 30 min.

Ridge Trail (DCR)

This trail, clearly marked with white blazes, begins on Pine Tops Rd. at fire gate 14 near the headquarters building. It initially heads southwest, then jogs left and right before turning sharp right (northwest). The trail crosses both parts of the Ash Path loop, a wide dirt road, and follows a series of ridges and valleys roughly parallel to Hemlock Rd. As the trail approaches a run of power lines, it passes a short spur trail on the left (west) that leads to the top of Castle Rock (good views). The Ridge Trail continues north and reaches the Spruce Path. Turn right (east) to reach Hemlock Rd. at fire gate 17.

Ridge Trail

Distance from trailhead to
- Hemlock Rd.: 1.7 mi., 50 min.

Lynn Woods

Located northwest of Lynn, this 2,200-acre woodland reservation is the second largest municipal forest park in the United States. The park is bisected by Walden Pond (not to be confused with Thoreau's Walden Pond in Concord). About one-quarter of the park (the wilder part) lies north of the pond, while the remainder lies south. The reservation is open to mountain biking, horseback riding, and hiking. Bikes are permitted only on official, blazed trails, and are not permitted on any trail marked Foot Traffic Only. Horses are allowed on the orange-blazed fire roads. Camping, fishing, all-terrain vehicles, and dirt bikes are not permitted within the reservation. Picnicking is permitted, but grills, open fires, and stoves are *not* allowed due to the fire hazard in the woods.

The main entrance is located at the south end of the reservation just west of Breed's Pond; take Walnut St. to Pennybrook Rd. and turn north. The east entrance is located just southeast of the eastern tip of Walden Pond; follow MA 129 (Lynnfield St.) to Great Woods Rd.

The trail network is based on a web of fire roads that spread throughout the woods. These blazed roads are linked by trails at frequent intervals, providing the opportunity to create many different routes through the reservation. The official trail map contains a grid that corresponds to trail intersections, which aids in navigating through the forest. This map is especially useful for first-time visitors and is available at the Lynn town hall. Sanctioned trails are marked with paint blazes. Unblazed paths are either closed or are bootleg trails that should not be used.

Burrill Hill Rd. Trail (Town of Lynn)

This fire road exits Great Woods Rd. 0.3 mi. northwest of the east entrance. It turns southwest and strenuously climbs Burrill Hill. After cruising along the crest of the hill, the road meets Dungeon Rd. at 1.1 mi.

Burrill Hill Rd. Trail
Distance from Great Woods Rd. to
• Dungeon Rd.: 1.1 mi, 40 min.

Mt. Gilead Trail (Town of Lynn)

This trail begins with Dungeon Rd. off Great Woods Rd., 0.8 mi. northwest of the east entrance. Veering away from Dungeon Rd., the trail climbs the hill along a wide gully near the top and reaches the stone observation tower at 0.3 mi. Past the tower, it continues along the western ridge of Mt. Gilead to rejoin Dungeon Rd. at 0.4 mi.

Mt. Gilead Trail

Distance from Dungeon Rd. to
- tower: 0.3 mi., 20 min.
- Dungeon Rd. second junction: 0.4 mi., 30 min.

Dungeon Rd. Trail (Town of Lynn)

This road begins off Great Woods Rd. 0.8 mi. northwest of the east entrance. It climbs the north face of Mt. Gilead to meet the Mt. Gilead Trail on the western ridge at 0.25 mi. It then descends the ridge, sweeping around the slopes to avoid the steepest places, and meets Pennybrook Rd. at 0.4 mi. Heading southeast, the trail regains the high ground and cruises over the ridges to meet Burrill Hill Rd. at 1.0 mi.

The trail then passes Dungeon Rock on the right. This rock cave is a colorful part of the reservation's history, as at one time pirates were believed to have hidden stolen treasures in a cave on a hill above Breed's Pond. In the mid–seventeenth century an earthquake closed the cave. A later treasure hunter wasted much time and effort reopening it in search of easy wealth. Of course there was no treasure, but today there is a sizable cave that descends into the rock and ends in a very dark rock chamber. The cave is open seasonally when a ranger is present. The trail then steeply descends to Breed's Pond. There it turns west and ends at Pennybrook Rd. at 1.9 mi.

Dungeon Rd. Trail

Distances from Great Woods Rd. to
- Mt. Gilead: 0.25 mi., 20 min.
- Burrill Hill Rd.: 1.0 mi., 30 min.
- Pennybrook Rd.: 1.9 mi., 1 hr.

Great Woods Rd. (Town of Lynn)

This city road exits west from MA 129 (Lynnfield St.) about 3.0 mi. east of its junction with US 1. It enters the reservation through a gate and becomes a reservation road with the same name. Immediately past this gate, a paved road exits sharp left uphill to the Happy Valley Golf Club. Great

Woods Rd. continues straight ahead to a parking lot with an athletic field on the right. This road (closed to automobiles) continues through a stone gateway at the far left corner of the parking lot. It runs parallel to the south shore of Walden Pond, but remains some distance away. Cooke Rd. enters left, and soon the Mt. Gilead Loop and Dungeon Rock Rd. enter left as well. Farther along is a picnic area on the right. Great Woods Rd. continues along the south and east shores of Walden Pond, parallels and then crosses Pennybrook, and ends at Pennybrook Rd.

SUGGESTED HIKES

Easy Hikes

Houghton's Pond Yellow Loop [lp: 1.0 mi., 0:25], page 293. This short path is a favorite among families with small children. The route circles the pond, passing a beach (swimming in summer) and a swamp along the way.

Chickering Pond Trail [lp: 0.5 mi., 0:25], page 312. This short path travels around Chickering Pond.

Dike Trail [rt: 2.7 mi., 1:15 hr], page 318. An exceptional trail for observing birds, dragonflies, and other wildlife, this trail passes a freshwater impoundment that provides habitat for a variety of waterfowl.

Moderate Hikes

Great Blue Hill Green Loop [lp: 2.8 mi., 1:20], page292. This hike explores the reservation's Great Blue Hill area, starting and ending near the Trailside Museum.

Cutler Park Loop [lp: 4.0 mi., 2:00], page 305. This trail meanders through marshes and past a hammock of land called Powell's Island.

Red Trail [lp: 2.7 mi., 1:30], page 315. Sections of this trail travel along the rugged shoreline of the Charles River, passing viewpoints from ledges above the water.

Strenuous Hikes

Skyline Trail [lp: 6.8 mi., 5:0], page 294. This hike runs across the Blue Hills Reservation from Blue Hill Ave. to Shea Rink on Willard Ave. Along the way the trail climbs numerous hills with views of Boston and the Bay.

Cross Fells Trail [rt: 8.6 mi., 5:00], page 320. This trail connects the east and west portions of the Middlesex Fells Reservation, and intersects many other trails along the way.

Rock Circuit Trail [rt: 4.0 mi, 3:30], page 321 This rugged and rocky trail offers the best views at the Middlesex Fells Reservation, including those from White Rock and Melrose Rock.

PART SIX

SOUTHEASTERN MASSACHUSETTS AND THE ISLANDS

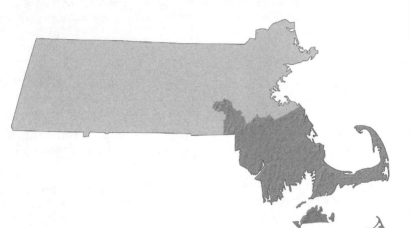

This chapter includes areas south and southeast of the Boston metropolitan area. It extends from the Warner Trail corridor in the west to Cape Cod and the islands in the east. The landscape is composed of low rolling hills and level plains of seacoast sands and clays. There are no significant mountains, although a few scattered ridges and hills stand out against the level terrain. The diverse habitats of the coastal region include pine-oak woodlands, sand dunes, freshwater ponds, and many miles of sandy shoreline, including the vast beaches that are protected by the Cape Cod National Seashore.

Ticks can be abundant along the coast, and hikers should be particularly alert to the dangers of tick-borne illnesses such as Lyme disease (see Trip Planning and Safety in the front of this book). Mosquitoes and a number of biting flies also frequent this area; bring the bug spray. Poison ivy is abundant in many areas, and there is some poison sumac in the swamps.

Warner Trail (AMC)

The Warner Trail offers delightful and varied outdoor experiences as it stretches more than 30 mi. from Sharon, Mass., to Diamond Hill State Park in Cumberland, R.I. The possibility of establishing a woodland trail connecting the south fringe of the Boston area with the trail system in Rhode Island was first envisioned by AMC members Charles H. Warner and John Hudson prior to World War II. With the energetic assistance of Ron Gower and a number of other AMC members, the trail was slowly put together, one section at a time, starting at the AMC Ponkapoag Camp. By 1947 it extended south to High Rock in Gilbert Hills State Forest. By the early 1950s the trail had reached Diamond Hill, R.I., but development soon resulted in the loss of the stretch from Ponkapoag Camp to the Canton Junction Rail Station. This spurred Mead Bradner, another AMC member, to form the Friends of the Warner Trail in 1994 to protect the trail.

The basic philosophy in the development of the trail was to maximize the challenges while at the same time providing the greatest amount of enjoyment. As a result, the trail wanders considerably from elevated viewpoints to swamp crossings, brooks, and reservoirs. It connects a number of state and town forests, Audubon Society land, conservation areas, and other public land.

The trail is maintained by the Friends of the Warner Trail and AMC volunteers from the Boston, Narragansett, and Southeastern Massachusetts Chapters. These individuals take care of blowdowns, marking, and relocations. If you would like to get involved in the stewardship of this trail, contact the Friends of the Warner Trail, P.O. Box 85, Mansfield, MA 02048. Maps and a guidebook are available by writing to this address. A small donation is appreciated with each request. Trail information can be obtained from the Moose Hill Audubon Sanctuary (781-784-5691) and the offices for the Gilbert Hills State Forest (508-543-5850).

The Warner Trail links many sections of public land with paths through private land. Public areas have varying rules and regulations regarding motorized and nonmotorized use of their properties, but only hiking is allowed on the Warner Trail when it passes through private property. No motorized vehicles or mountain bikes are allowed on these sections. This trail can be enjoyed as a series of day hikes, or it can be used for snowshoeing or to access paths to several lunch spots. Users are asked to respect the property of private landowners who have generously granted permission for the trail to cross their land.

The Warner Trail is blazed with an array of markers, including old-style 2-in. metal disks that have probably rusted, newer stainless-steel 2-in. disks, and white metal 2-in. disks. White rectangular paint blazes are occasionally used, as are white plastic triangles with a dark green hiker in the center and Warner Trail on the bottom. A change in direction is shown by either stacked blazes with the top blaze offset in the direction of the turn, or, by having the top of the plastic triangle pointing in the direction of the turn.

Section 1. Sharon (Dedham St.) to Moose Hill Audubon Sanctuary Headquarters (Sharon) (3.8 mi.)

To reach the northern end of the Warner Trail, leave US 1 south of Boston near the Norwood Memorial Airport or take I-95 (Exit 11) to Neponset St. Follow Neponset St. 1.2 mi. east into Canton, turn right onto Walpole St., and continue for 1.5 mi. Turn left onto Dedham St. and proceed uphill 0.2 mi. to a pull-off on the left. The trail begins at the woods across from the pull-off.

The first 0.5 mi. of trail weaves through driveways and woods. It crosses a bog bridge and passes through a wet area before crossing Beaver Brook on a wooden bridge at 0.3 mi. The trail then reaches a woods road junction at 0.5 mi. and turns left (southwest). The trail continues roughly southwest through a pine grove and reaches a power line (0.9 mi.). The trail turns right (north) and follows the power line on the service road to Mt. Fern St. Turning left (southwest) onto Mt. Fern St. (gravel changing to pavement), reach Bullard St. (1.1 mi.) and turn right, following Bullard St. (watch for potential relocation here) the short way to Norwood St. (MA 27) at 1.3 mi.

The trail turns right onto Norwood St., then quickly enters the woods and follows a bridle trail through tall red pines to reach a power line at 1.7 mi. It turns right (west) and follows beneath the power lines a short distance, then turns left onto Everett St. (gravel). Following Everett St. onto Audubon land, the road tapers to a cart path, passes a large rock outcrop (left), and turns right onto a woods road just past a vernal pool (right). The path heads uphill then over level ground, turns left before a boardwalk, and reaches Moose Hill Pkwy. at 2.9 mi. Within Moose Hill Sanctuary the Warner Trail is also marked with the letter A.

After turning right onto Moose Hill Pkwy., the path quickly turns left (south), leaving the road and entering the woods. The trail wanders through the sanctuary, passing close to Moose Hill St. and through an old parking lot to Moose Hill St. at 3.7 mi. Turn right onto Moose Hill St. and continue the short distance to the sanctuary headquarters.

Warner Trail: Sharon (Dedham St.) to Moose Hill Audubon Sanctuary Headquarters (Sharon)

Distances from Dedham St. to
- power line: 0.9 mi., 25 min.
- Norwood St.: 1.3 mi., 35 min.
- Moose Hill Pkwy.: 2.9 mi. 1 hr. 25 min.
- Moose Hill Audubon Sanctuary Headquarters: 3.8 mi., 1 hr., 45 min.

Section 2. Sharon (Moose Hill Audubon Sanctuary) to Foxboro (US 1) (9.5 mi.)

The trail (also marked with the letter "A" within the sanctuary) turns left through the parking lot gate and jogs slightly to the right to reach a gravel road passing between two stone posts. In about 50 yd. it turns right onto the Summit Trail, which it follows for 0.3 mi. to the fire tower atop Moose Hill. Proceeding left (southwest) from the fire tower, the trail comes out on a rocky knoll and drops down fairly steeply through the woods to a junction with a woods road. It turns right, then heads east on the Old Pasture Trail.

The trail now passes through an area with many side trails; watch for the Warner Trail blazes. Climb the northern slope of Bluff Head to the top, where there is a view to the south (1.5 mi.). The trail then heads southwest, descending several rocky ledges, making one brief sharp climb past the chimney on Allen's Ledge, and reaching a woods road near the bottom of the slope. Turn left to head downhill to Walpole St. at 2.1 mi.

The trail goes left down Walpole St. for a few yards, then crosses the road and enters the woods, and climbs to the top of Pierce Hill (350 ft.) at 2.3 mi., where there are good views south and west. It then descends steeply at times to Old Post Rd. (once a main road, now a woods road), which it follows south for 0.3 mi. The path now follows a driveway for 200 yd. to Pine St. It turns left onto Pine St., continues to S. Walpole St. turns right (southwest) and follows S. Walpole St., as it goes over the northbound and under the southbound lanes of I-95. Beyond the interstate it passes a cranberry bog and turns left at telephone pole 46. The trail now follows Dudley Hill Rd., a thin path that is often overgrown and frequently hard to follow. *Note: In this section the trail is intentionally left overgrown and poorly defined to discourage misuse of the private property.*

Take care to go around the end of a blocking fence without damaging the bushes (intended to discourage all but pedestrians). Keep right of the blocking fence, passing along the edge of a backyard (white house). At the back corner of the yard the path begins again, bending right at a fork onto a smaller path through wetlands, and reaches a berm. The trail passes over the berm and crosses the swamp on bog bridging.

The trail now passes close to several houses as it comes to Beach St. Watch closely for blazes and take care to follow the trail. Turn right onto Beach St., continue for 50 yd., then turn left (south) onto a right-of-way just beyond a large pin oak (lower branches droop downward) and a wooden fence. The trail continues through a row of large rocks then turns left onto an old gravel road used by off-road vehicles, which it follows a short distance to Edwards St. (parking) at 3.9 mi. *(Note: The gravel road section may be relocated in the future.)*

The trail turns right onto Edwards St., follows it for 0.6 mi., and turns left at telephone pole 27 to travel up an overgrown bank and through the woods to Camp Rd. (gravel). For the next 0.6 mi. take the following roads to Foxboro Conservation Property: McCasland Way (Whispering Pines), McKenzie La., and Munroe St. At the end of the cul-de-sac the trail reenters the woods onto Foxboro Conservation Commission land at 5.2 mi.

Heading to the south through open woods, the trail passes Neponset Reservoir on the left, then the dam at the reservoir outlet. It heads southwest to the railroad tracks, then runs parallel to the tracks over several bog bridges to Chestnut St. (parking). The trail turns right and follows the street through the Chestnut Green community. As the trail approaches the rotary, it turns left on North St. and continues to the traffic light. Crossing with the light toward the Dairy Queen, go left (south) on Main St. (MA 140), and proceed the short distance to the Foxboro Conservation parking lot (right) at 6.7 mi.

From the back of the parking lot, the trail follows a lane to the west, then turns right at a trail junction. Continue through the woods toward Lakeview Rd. Near the road the path swings left and descends toward a brook, then follows the brook out to Lakeview Rd. The trail turns left and crosses the dam for Lakeview Lake. It then turns right, following the conservation lane along the side of the lake (lake on the right) and continues west until it comes to Upper Dam Pond, where it crosses the dam and swings southeast around the pond to Messenger Rd. (gravel).

The trail turns right (southwest) onto the road and begins a long climb toward High Rock in Gilbert Hills State Forest. As the road nears the top, the trail forks right (there is an emergency bad-weather shelter here) onto an old woods road and climbs almost to a fenced-in old radar test station. Here the trail turns left at the foot of a large boulder (High Rock) at 9.1 mi. and follows a short path over the rise to a gravel clearing at the foot of a large microwave relay tower and base building. A paved road, maintained by AT&T, leads to US 1, 0.5 mi. south of its intersection with MA 140.

Warner Trail: Sharon (Moose Hill Audubon Sanctuary) to Foxboro (US 1)

Distances from Moose Hill St. (Moose Hill Audubon Sanctuary) (380 ft.) to
- Bluff Head summit (450 ft.): 1.5 mi., 35 min.
- Pierce Hill summit (350 ft.): 2.3 mi., 1 hr.
- Edwards Rd.: 3.9 mi., 1 hr. 30 min.
- Foxboro Conservation Property: 5.2 mi., 1 hr. 55 min.
- Foxboro Conservation parking lot: 6.7 mi., 2 hr. 30 min.
- High Rock: 9.1 mi., 3 hr. 10 min.
- junction of US 1 and MA 140: 9.5 mi., 3 hr. 20 min.

Section 3. Foxboro (US 1) to Wrentham (Wampum Corner) (9.9 mi.)

To reach the northeast end of this section from the US 1 and MA 140 junction, follow US 1 south for 0.5 mi. to High Rock Rd., then follow High Rock Rd. to the gravel parking area of F. Gilbert Hills State Forest. Park only on the gravel area; do not park on the AT&T paved parking area, and do not block the fire lane gate.

The trail leaves the eastern end of the parking area near the barrier gate. At 80 yd. it turns left and follows a winding path, dropping down and passing under an overhanging cliff (Goat Rock—look for the tree growing out of the rock). The path swings right over a number of large rocks and an underground stream to reach a trail junction. Proceed up a series of rock steps built by the CCC to the junction with the Acorn Trail (sign for Warner Trail). The Acorn Trail is a rugged feeder path leading 2.2 mi. to the state forest headquarters on Mill St. in Foxboro.

From here the trail goes south a short distance to the top of a large rock slab (excellent view west). The trail descends southwest to the base of the slab, and after a short distance turns right (north-northwest) on a woods road and follows it 0.4 mi. Pass two towers before turning left onto a path that leads to US 1 at 1.3 mi. The trail crosses US 1 and proceeds on Myrtle St. in Wrentham. It follows Myrtle St. a few yards, and then turns left just before a conservation area parking lot.

Following a path that parallels US 1 for a short distance, the trail jogs right and then left on a telephone-company-cleared way and into pine woods. It skirts a swamp and crosses over an extended bog bridge, eventually emerging on the cul-de-sac at the end of Davis Ave. The trail follows Davis Ave. one block to its end on Ames Ave., turns right onto Ames

Ave. for one block, then turns left onto Dunn Ave. After one block the trail turns right onto Thurston St. and continues briefly to Warner Trail Rd., onto which it turns left and proceeds 0.2 mi. to a cul-de-sac. The trail continues straight on a 10-ft.-wide conservation restriction, then bears left, circles through a notch to the remains of the sealed-over Wrentham land-fill, and passes through the gate to Madison St.

The trail crosses the street and enters Wrentham State Forest. It turns sharp left, and, after a short flat stretch, circles to the right and steadily climbs to the first of several peaks, with some views north to Boston. The trail descends to a woods road before making a short, steep climb to a ledgy crest, then proceeds over several other knobby peaks known as the Pinnacles. From the Pinnacles the trail descends to a woods road, turns right, crosses a dirt bike trail, then bears left onto a dirt bike path. The trail leaves the bike path, passes some large boulders, and continues over a level, rocky area. Next, climb to a cliff, cross a dirt bike trail, and turn right onto a woods road. The trail follows this road and bears right at the next two junctions. It then weaves through dirt bike trails, paths, and woods roads (watch for blazing), finally climbing Outlook Rock at 4.6 mi.

From Outlook Rock the trail descends, crosses the brook, then tra-verses a wet area before climbing to a cliff overlooking Minnehaha Pond. Below and to the right are the remains of an old dam. Descending to Min-nehaha Brook, the trail follows the eastern bank a short way before turning right (southwest) onto a woods road (the Red Fox Path). (A short bush-whack south about 200 yd. leads to the Minnehaha Falls rapids.)

The Warner Trail passes a number of trail junctions before winding un-der an impressive rock ledge to the right at 5.3 mi. The path passes more side trails, then follows a rutted dirt bike trail. After passing near some houses the trail emerges onto Taunton St. at 6.3 mi. and turns right (north).

After 0.1 mi. the trail turns left (west) into handsome pine woods and approaches the Wrentham Senior Center (parking). Cross the parking lot and reach the road that leads to the Wrentham Water Works and the Trout Pond Recreational Center. The trail follows a woods road roughly paral-lel to the Department of Public Works (DPW) road and reaches the bot-tom of an abandoned ski lift. It then ascends the steep slope to the sum-mit of Knuckup Hill at 6.9 mi. (extensive view north, including the Bos-ton skyline).

The trail continues, following the gravel road left and down the hill, then branching right on a path that avoids the brick building. At the paved road it turns right and follows the gravel road along Trout Pond. At the far end of the pond the trail turns right onto another gravel road that runs past a second pond and reaches Beech St. The trail goes left (southeast) onto Beech St., bearing right at 170 Beech St. after 0.2 mi. onto Bear Swamp Rd. This private woods road (stay on the trail) then enters Wrentham State Forest.

The trail follows the woods road, nears I-495, turns right, passes beneath the cliffs of Wampum Rock, and approaches the highway twice more before curving to the right (north) and climbing slowly. It turns left, and after a long descent followed by a short sharp climb, drops down to MA 1A (South St.). Turn right to reach Wampum Corner, at the junction of MA 1A and MA 121, at 9.9 mi.

Warner Trail: Foxboro (US 1) to Wrentham (Wampum Corner)

Distances from US 1 to
- Outlook Rock: 4.6 mi., 1 hr. 40 min.
- Minnehaha Cliff: 5.0 mi., 2 hr.
- Taunton St.: 6.3 mi., 2 hr. 35 min.
- Knuckup Hill: 6.9 mi., 2 hr. 55 min.
- Wampum Corner: 9.9 mi., 3 hr. 40 min.

Section 4. Wrentham (Wampum Corner) to Hancock St. (Wrentham) (2.9 mi.)

The trail leaves Wampum Corner on MA 121 (West St.), heads southwest for about 100 yd., then climbs a steep bank (left) and follows an old railroad grade for the next mile. The railroad bed passes under I-495 in front of the Wrentham Premium Outlet Mall, and by a pond on the left. It then leaves the railroad bed to the right, follows a bike path, and climbs an embankment. The trail runs along some wetlands to the right, then turns sharp right before some power lines. It climbs to a mound above the mall, then descends to the mall's gravel emergency road. Turn left onto the emergency road and continue toward the cell tower, reaching Green St. at 1.8 mi.

Turn right onto Green St. then quickly turn left onto a gravel road used by dirt bikes and all-terrain vehicles. Follow this worn track, ignoring the many side trails, until the trail reaches a junction about 0.4 mi. from Green St. Turn right here, continue to another junction, and turn left to climb to the top of a ledge. The trail climbs 0.1 mi. to another outcrop, which affords limited views of Providence to the south. The trail continues over Red Brush Hill to a power line, where it jogs right 20 yd., then turns left into the woods. It proceeds to Sunset Rock, which offers excellent views west and southwest toward Diamond Hill in Rhode Island. Continuing southwest, the trail descends the ledge through the woods and soon emerges on Hancock St. at a point 0.7 mi. east of MA 121 in Sheldonville (a part of Wrentham).

Warner Trail: Wrentham (Wampum Corner) to Hancock St. (Wrentham)

Distances from Wampum Corner to
- Green St.: 1.8 mi., 35 min.
- Hancock St.: 2.9 mi., 50 min.

Section 5. Hancock St. (Wrentham) to Diamond Hill, R.I. (5.6 mi.)

Note: The Warner Trail between Hancock St. and Rhodes St. is closed until it can be relocated around the Wentworth Hills Golf Club. Follow the alternate route directions below until the relocation is completed.

Warner Trail Alternate Route: Turn right onto Hancock St., and follow it as it bears left at the fork. Continue about 0.5 mi. to Burnt Swamp Rd., turn left, and travel about 1.6 mi. on Burnt Swamp Rd. to Reservoir Rd. and the Warner Trail.

Follow Reservoir Rd. southwest to Camp Ker-Anna, then turn right onto a path a short distance beyond the camp sign. For the next 2.4 mi. the trail cruises through the woods, circling Diamond Hill Reservoir on a woods road, and passing a brief cutoff to the left and another woods road. The trail continues generally west to a small brook, where it turns left (south) and goes through a swampy area. It then winds along the side of the reservoir, sometimes coming within a yard of the water. Climbing up to the right, the trail follows the side of a hill for about 0.5 mi. It then climbs west to a rocky ledge with an open crest and views of Diamond Hill Reservoir.

The trail goes generally south down the slope of the ridge, proceeds onto a woods road, and just before the road goes underwater and turns right onto a path that leads up and over a rise. In 0.1 mi. the trail turns left (southwest) through some heavy brush, crosses a small stream, and climbs up a sharp rise. Descending the other side, the trail bears left (south) onto a woods road. It then bears right onto a path through many muddy, narrow spots along the side of the reservoir until it comes to Fisher Rd.

The trail turns sharp right and proceeds up the remains of the old road. The road becomes paved and enters Ski Valley Condominiums. Continue on the paved road for about 0.3 mi.; then turn left onto a well-worn path up a slope and zigzag to the summit of Diamond Hill (481 ft.), where indistinct remains of the old ski operations can be seen. On the east side, below the summit, the Boston and Providence skylines are visible in good weather.

From the large cement block at the top of the hill, the trail passes a large water tank and wanders south along the ridge, passing several viewpoints and sheer drops, before finally coming to a steep drop off on the right. At this point the trail descends to RI 114 in Cumberland (there are many unmarked trails through here). The trail continues, keeping the cliffs to the left. The trail travels north through woods at the bottom of an abandoned quarry, continuing straight ahead to reach the Diamond Hill parking lot.

Warner Trail: Hancock St. (Wrentham) to Diamond Hill, R.I.

Distances from Hancock St. to (approx.)
- Diamond Hill summit: 4.5 mi., 2 hr. 5 min.
- Diamond Hill parking lot: 5.6 mi., 2 hr. 45 min.

Bay Circuit Trail (Southern Sections)

An overview of the Bay Circuit Trail and descriptions of the northern sections are presented in Part 4 of this guide, beginning on page 238. Described below are the sections of trail located in the southeast region, including the trail's southern terminus at Bay Farm. The trail is blazed with vertical white rectangles supplemented with BCT logos at junctions, trailheads, and other locations where more clarity is required.

Section 9. Sudbury (Weisblatt Conservation Land) to Southborough (Pine Hill Trail) (9.4 mi.)

From the Weisblatt Conservation Land parking area of the Sudbury Conservation Commission follow the Salamander Trail to where it loops left; the BCT continues straight (BCT blazes begin here), entering the Nobscot Boy Scouts Reservation at 0.4 mi. Follow along a ridge and climb to Tippling Rock (426 ft.), a great split boulder at the south end of the ridge. The trail now descends the hill, following white blazes to Nobscot Conservation Land and reaching Brimstone Lane at 2.0 mi.

Cross the road and pass through a low wetland before climbing the hill to Wittenburg Woods in Framingham. Weave through the woods and over a stone wall to enter the Sudbury Valley Trustees' (SVT) Gross Tract property. Head downhill and cross a stream, reaching Wayside Inn Rd. Cross the road and enter Henry's Hill (SVT). Continue on the trail to again reach Wayside Inn Rd. Head south on Wayside Inn Rd., turn right onto Edmands Rd. at 3.7 mi., and continue to Welch Reservation (SVT). Follow the trail through the Welch Reservation, climbing the hill to Callahan State Park and reaching Edmands Rd. at 5.0 mi.

From the road climb the hill, following the Backpacker Trail up Gibbs Mtn. (504 ft.). Descend and reach Beebe Pond on the Pine Tree Trail and cross the dam at the south end of the pond. The trail joins the Bear Paw Trail and crosses a field. Continue to Nourse St., turn left (southwest) onto an abandoned road, and enter Sudbury Reservoir. After winding through the woods the trail emerges at Parmenter St. at 7.0 mi. Cross the road and follow the trail through pine and hemlock forests (DCR). The Pine Hill Trail ends at a gate by Nicholas Rd. and Clemmons Rd. at 9.4 mi. This is the effective end of the BCT in this section. The next section of trail (disregarding walking along roads and highways) begins at Ashland Town Forest in Ashland.

Bay Circuit Trail: Sudbury (Weisblatt Conservation Land) to Southborough (Pine Hill Trail)

Distances from Weisblatt Conservation Land to
- Brimstone Lane: 2.0 mi., 50 min.
- Edmands Rd.: 5.0 mi., 1 hr. 55 min.
- Pine Hill Trail: 9.4 mi., 4 hr. 35 min.

Section 10. Ashland (Ashland Town Forest) to Sherborn Town Line (7.8 mi.)

From the entrance of the forest (parking) follow the Turnberg Trail (white blazes) until it reaches Winter St. at 3.0 mi. Turn right (west) onto Winter St. and at 3.4 mi. turn left into the woods (this is private property; stay to the right of the hill). Follow the trail through a DPW yard and along Ponderosa Rd. to the Riverwalk. Turn left onto the Riverwalk and follow it downstream for 0.5 mi. At 4.3 mi. the Riverwalk ends at Sudbury and Birch La. Take consecutive right turns onto Birch La., Birch Hill Rd., Pine Hill Rd., and Mill Pond Park (parking). Cross Myrtle St. and rejoin the Riverwalk for a short distance. Continue straight onto Concord Ct., then make consecutive rights onto Concord St. and Front St. From here follow Main St. and Homer Ave. to MA 135. Cross MA 135 and continue on Chestnut St. to Wildwood Cemetery on the left at 5.6 mi.

Pass through the cemetery, staying far left, to an old cart path that reaches Cadorette Rd. Descend a hill to Grover St.. Turn left onto Grover St., cross Cedar St. onto Mulhall Dr. and then Wenzell Rd., reaching MA 126 at 7.3 mi. Turn right (south) on MA 126; then after the fifth telephone pole bear left at a break in the guardrail onto the dike. The dike continues for 0.5 mi. east across a swamp and beaver pond to the Sherborn town line at a stone wall.

Bay Circuit Trail: Ashland (Ashland Town Forest) to Sherborn Town Line

Distances from Ashland Town Forest to
- Riverwalk: 3.7 mi., 1 hr. 50 min.
- MA 126: 7.3 mi., 2 hr. 45 min.
- Sherborn town line at end of dike: 7.8 mi., 3 hr. 30 min.

Section 11. Sherborn (Elevator Rock) to Medfield (Charles River) (12.3 mi.)

This section, marked with BCT blazes at trailheads and white blazes elsewhere, begins at the Sherborn town line at the end of the dike. The trail turns right, then left before the outcropping known as Elevator Rock, then exits the woods at the Conrail railroad yard. Use Whitney St. to safely cross the tracks. Return to the trail, which is near a rock ledge. It now passes through wetlands and beneath power lines, then swings south and reenters the woods. Cross Western Ave. at 2.7 mi. and follow Stevens St. to Harrington Ridge Rd. Turn right onto Harrington Ridge Rd., then left onto Oldfield Rd., left again onto Dexter Dr., and finally right onto the trail. Follow the trail across private land to Sherborn Conservation Land. Cross a brushy field and head north, crossing Brush Hill Rd. and following the trail through the woods to Perry St.

Cross the road and follow a pleasant woodland trail that explores Sherborn Town Forest before reaching and following a pipeline. The trail now climbs up and over Brush Hill and crosses the railroad tracks before reaching MA 27 (N. Main St.). The path passes the Sherborn Highway Department and continues to follow the pipeline to MA 16 (Eliot St.) at 6.8 mi. Cross the road and pass through woodlands before reaching Pine Hill School. From the school the trail skirts Pine Hill Cemetery and follows the ridge uphill along an ancient fault line atop Pine Hill. The path descends the ridge to Farm Rd., which it follows to Farm Rd. Cross the road, remaining close to the pipeline, and make a series of road walks to Rocky Narrows Reservation at 9.1 mi. Rocky Narrows Reservation is rugged and beautiful. Stay on the trail, as it is easy to get lost. The trail passes through woodlands and by the picnic and canoe area on the bank of the Charles River. It then ascends to a rocky ledge and on to King Philip's Overlook, with a stunning view of the river. Return to the parking lot. From the parking area follow Forest St. southwest, and then take consecutive left turns onto Snow St. and MA 27. Pass the MA 27 parking area for Rocky Narrows Reservation, and cross the Charles River into Medfield at 12.3 mi.

Bay Circuit Trail: Sherborn (Elevator Rock) to Medfield (Charles River)

Distances from Elevator Rock to
- MA 16: 6.8 mi., 3 hr.
- Rocky Narrows Reservation: 9.1 mi., 4 hr. 5 min.
- Charles River: 12.3 mi., 5 hr. 5 min.

Section 12. Medfield (Charles River) to Walpole town line (10.8 mi.)

Beginning at the Charles River, cross at MA 27 (parking) and travel east on MA 27 about 0.4 mi., then turn left (southeast) onto Hospital Rd. The trail leaves the road to the right, descending to a large field then climbing a hill past baseball fields before reaching West Mill St. Turn right onto West Mill St., then left onto Adams St., continue for 0.4 mi., then turn right onto West St. Follow West St. for a short distance to a dirt road along railroad tracks past a large landfill and the Medfield DPW garage, reaching MA 27 at 3.2 mi. Turn left onto MA 27, then left onto Dale St., then left again into a cemetery. Pass through the cemetery (the trail may have very few blazes here) to MA 109.

Turn right (southwest) onto Causeway St. and follow this for 1.6 mi., turning left (east) onto Noon Hill Rd. at 5.5 mi. Follow Noon Hill Rd. past the north end of Holt Pond and into the Noon Hill Reservation. The trail now loops through the reservation to again meet Noon Hill Rd., turns right (east) on the road, crosses a brook, and reaches South St. at 6.7 mi.

Turn right (south) onto South St., then left (east) onto Rocky La., left onto Henderson Way, left onto Granite St., right onto Forest St., and right onto MA 27 (High St.). Cross the road and proceed to the trail on the left before some power lines. The trail parallels the power lines, then turns off into the woods, passing along access roads of town water wells. Continue along athletic fields near Wheelock School and follow the road to Elm St. Turn right (east) onto Elm St., reaching the Walpole town line at 10.8 mi.

Bay Circuit Trail: Medfield (Charles River) to Walpole Town Line

Distances from parking area on MA 27 to
- Noon Hill Rd.: 5.5 mi, 2 hr. 35 min.
- Walpole town line: 10.8 mi., 4 hr. 15 min.

Section 13. Walpole Town Line to Sharon (US 1) (8.2 mi.)

The BCT crosses into Walpole and turns right onto a power-line path that blends into the Old Indian Trail, an undulating path that traverses an esker and follows Mine Brook. At the end of the trail turn left past the water treatment plant, then right onto Leonard Rd. and follow it to the end, taking the woods path south to Robbins Rd. Turn right onto Robbins Rd., then left onto MA 27 (Elm St.), then right on Glenwood Ave. to Main St. at 3.7 mi.

Cross Main St. and continue to Memorial Pond opposite the town hall. Follow the trail around the south end of the pond, turn right onto Diamond St., then turn left onto Stone St. Continue to the Clark Pond Conservation Area at 4.5 mi. Follow the trail around the west side of the pond, briefly follow Lake St. southwest, and pass through the parking lot of Walpole High School.

At the back of the school pick up the trail that enters the Walpole Town Forest. Follow this river trail, which parallels the Neponset River, passing a waterfall and old dam site. The well-marked BCT continues through the forest, passing a short spur trail to Duffy Point. Follow the path up a Department of Public Works driveway, then cross Washington St. onto a trail that leads to the town forest at 6.4 mi. The trail heads south through varied terrain, reaching a gravel cart path. Continue southeast to the power lines, then turn left and follow the path beneath the wires to reach US 1 at 7.5 mi. Turn right on US 1 and continue along the grass strip to the traffic light; then cross US 1 to Pine St. and travel about 0.3 mi. to the Sharon town line.

Bay Circuit Trail: Walpole Town Line to Sharon (US 1)

Distances from Walpole town line to
- Clark Pond Conservation Area: 4.5 mi., 2 hr. 5 min.
- Sharon town line: 8.2 mi. 4 hr.

Section 14. Sharon (Pine St.) to Borderland State Park (Sharon) (11.5 mi.)

Pine St. becomes South Walpole St. in Sharon. Cross I-95 on South Walpole St. and follow the Warner Trail (triangle blazes) to Old Post Rd. Take a left onto Old Post Rd. and ascend Pierce Hill, descending on the northeast side. Cross Walpole St. and enter the Moose Hill Wildlife Sanctuary. The BCT and Bluff Head Loop trails coincide as they ascend to Bluff Head. Continue following the Cistern, Old Pasture, and Summit Trails to the 534-ft. summit of Moose Hill (3.6 mi.), then descend steeply at times to the visitor center via the Summit and Billings Loop Trails.

From the Moose Hill Sanctuary Visitor Center (parking, restrooms) the BCT follows the Kettle Trail south from the overflow lot, then follows the Trillium, Kettle, and Hobbs Hill Trails before continuing straight to the Moose Hill Pkwy. Turn right onto the paved road, which soon reaches the railroad tracks of the high-speed Acela Express train. *(Note: Approximately the next mile of trail runs parallel to and crosses active railroad tracks used by high-speed trains. In places the visibility up and down the tracks is poor.)* It is advisable to pick up the trail again at Deborah Sampson Park (6.35 mi.) on South Main St. (parking).

Cross the park in an easterly direction, passing between old school buildings and through woodlands to Beach St. At Beach St. turn left and pass around the north end of Lake Massapoag to a five-way junction. Follow Massapoag Ave. south (east sidewalk) as it takes a course along the shore of the lake. Just before reaching Mansfield St. take the trail on the left that enters the trail system of Borderland State Park. (The entrance to the park is approximately 1.0 mi. farther down Massapoag Ave.) The BCT then successively follows the Morse Loop, Ridge, Northwest, French, West Side, and Pond Walk state park trails to the visitor center at 11.5 mi. Restrooms and parking (small fee) are available at the visitor center.

Bay Circuit Trail: Sharon (Pine St.) to Borderland State Park (Sharon)

Distances from Pine St. to
- Moose Hill summit: 3.6 mi., 1 hr. 30 min.
- Deborah Sampson Park: 6.4 mi., 3 hr.
- Borderland State Park visitor center: 11.5 mi., 5 hr. 25 min.

Section 15. Borderland State Park to MA 138 (Sharon) (10.4 mi.)

From the visitor center, the BCT follows the Pond Walk across Poquanticut Brook to the Rockland St. Trail, which leads to Rockland St. in 1.5 mi. Turn left (east) on Rockland St., then shortly right on a new trail that ends at a utility road. The trail follows power lines across Poquanticut Ave., then leaves the clearing and meets the Fox Mtn. Trail at 2.5 mi. The trail leads through Beaver Brook Woods before crossing a brook and reaching a parking lot on Poquanticut Ave. at 3.4 mi. Turn left on Poquanticut Ave., then right on Roundtable Rd., then left on a footpath that leads through the Old Pond area, passing a wetland and pine grove en route to the dam and parking area at 4.5 mi.

From the parking area, the trail follows Foundry St. (MA 106) through the Furnace Valley Historic District. Turn right on South St., crossing two brooks to Highland St., then turn left on Highland St. and continue to Bay Rd. Turn right on Bay Rd. and follow it to the Wheaton Farm access road; then go right again on the access road and continue past a field and gate to an old cart path at 6.0 mi. Turn left and follow the path south past a kettle pond; then at a junction follow the farm trail across the Ward's Pond–Hammond Reservoir dike to a large parking area. Walk down the driveway to Bay Rd., passing the Wheaton Farm barn at 7.1 mi.

The BCT turns left on Prospect St. and continues to a power line. Turn right on the maintenance road, then cross an old railroad bed. The trail follows the power line southeast, passing through the Hockomock Swamp and reaching MA 138 at 10.4 mi.

Bay Circuit Trail: Borderland State Park to MA 138 (Sharon)

Distance from Borderland State Park visitor center to
- Old Pond parking area: 4.5 mi., 2 hr. 5 min.
- Bay Rd.: 7.1 mi., 3 hr. 20 min.
- MA 138: 10.4 mi., 5 hr.

Section 16. MA 138 (Sharon) to Spring St. (East Bridgewater) (6.5 mi.)

From MA 138, the BCT continues to follow the power line south through Hockomock Swamp Wildlife Management Area, passing the West Bridgewater town line at 0.6 mi. At 1.3 mi., the trail turns on a utility access road, with the Hockomock River to the left. Cross the river on a stone bridge, then turn left on Old Maple St. (unpaved) and continue straight to a gate and parking area.

At 1.8 mi. the blazed section of the BCT ends temporarily. From Old Maple St. turn left on Pleasant St., then right on South Elm St. after the MA 24 overpass. Follow South Elm St. for 1.2 mi., then turn right on River St. and continue to the junction with Forest St. at 3.6 mi., where there's a good view of the Town River, a stone bridge, and historic buildings.

The trail continues on River St. for 0.4 mi., then follows Arch St. past the War Memorial Park. Cross a bridge, then turn left on Bryant St. and continue through a residential area. The trail crosses MA 28 and continues on Ash St, passing Reynolds Landing on the left. It then turns left on MA 28 and reaches the Bridgewater town line at 5.7 mi.

The short segment of the BCT in Bridgewater is also presently unblazed. Continue on MA 28 south, then turn left on High St. at the traffic light and continue to Ironworks Park at 6.5 mi. From the park follow High St. to MA 18, then MA 18 north to a left on Spring St. Parking (4 cars) is available on the shoulder of Spring St. at an old railroad crossing.

Bay Circuit Trail: MA 138 (Sharon) to Spring St. (East Bridgewater)

Distances from MA 138 to
- utility road at Hockomock River: 1.3 mi., 40 min.
- Forest St.: 3.6 mi., 1 hr. 45 min.
- Ironworks Park: 6.5 mi., 3 hr.

Section 17. Spring St. (East Bridgewater) to East Bridgewater–Hanson Town Line (5.8 mi.)

The BCT in East Bridgewater is marked with periodic white blazes. From the Spring St. parking area, the trail follows Spring St. northeast. Cross MA 18 at the traffic light, then go southeast on Central St, then bear right on Plymouth St. at the town common. At 1.5 mi., the trail crosses the Satucket River, then turns left on Bennett La. and enters the Satucket River Conservation Area. The BCT follows the river for 0.5 mi., passing other trails and crossing a brook just before the marker for the Phillips Wildlife Area. It passes a pine grove and cranberry bog, then bears right, passes through a fence, and leads uphill, exiting the conservation area onto Susan Pl. at 2.7 mi.

Follow Susan Pl., then bear right on Rolling Hills Dr. Where Rolling Hills Dr. goes left, continue straight to Bridge St. Turn left on Bridge St. near Johnson Memorial Park *(large parking area),* then at 3.7 mi. go right on Crescent St. Follow Crescent St. across Washington St. to the water supply station access road on the right at 5.2 mi., just after Deer Run Dr.

The trail turns right on the access road, then continues through shrubby growth to a sandy road at a power line. Turn right on the road; then follow the blazes left on a shady trail that leads to a footbridge over Poor Meadow Brook. [Note: The area at the end of the bridge may be flooded. An alternate 3-mi. detour is *to return to Crescent St and turn right. Making right turns at each intersection, follow Crescent to Cedar St (becomes Franklin St), to Main St (MA 27), to Elm St, to the parking area at entrance to Burrage Pond Wildlife Management Area.* An extension of the bridge to the town line is planned.] The trail continues near the brook, passing the East Bridgewater/Hanson town line at 5.8 mi.

Bay Circuit Trail: Spring St. (East Bridgewater) to East Bridgewater–Hanson Town Line (5.8 mi.)

Distances from Spring St. parking area to
- Satucket River Conservation Area: 1.5 mi., 45 min.
- Bridgewater–Hanson town line: 5.8 mi., 2 hr. 40 min.

Section 18. East Bridgewater–Hanson Town Line to Maquan Rd. (Hanson) (7.8 mi.)

From the East Bridgewater/Hanson town line, this segment of the BCT continues near Poor Meadow Brook, then follows power lines uphill to Elm St. Parking is allowed on the Smith-Nawazelski property along the cart path (do not block the road). At 0.6 mi., the trail enters the Burrage Pond Wildlife Management Area (parking for three cars; do not block the gate or road) and runs parallel to power lines, passing cranberry bogs and crossing over the historic Indian Crossway to a proposed section of the trail (here there is presently a gap in the dedicated route).

At 2.0 mi., the trail resumes at Crooker Pl. near the Light Control property. Continue up Crooker Pl., then go left on MA 27 (Main St.), then right on Robinson St., which becomes Pierce Ave. Turn right off Pierce Ave. on High St., then follow the blazes on utility poles to a right on MA 58 (Liberty St.), passing the town hall (parking available) and Wamputuck Pond. A BCT kiosk is situated by the boat ramp. The trail follows Liberty St. right past the Nathaniel Thomas Mill, then bears right on Indian Head St. (still MA 58).

At 5.2 mi. the BCT enters the Hanson Town Forest, makes a brief loop, then rejoins Indian Head St. At 6.3 mi., the trail turns left and enters Camp Kiwanee, passing the gatehouse and parking area for Cranberry Cove Beach, where another BCT kiosk is located. The BCT passes behind the gate house and through the woods, following cart paths to Maquan St.

(MA 14) at 7.4 mi. Turn right on Maquan St., which reaches the Hanson–Pembroke town line at 7.8 mi.

Bay Circuit Trail: East Bridgewater–Hanson Town Line to Maquan St. (Hanson)

Distances from East Bridgewater–Hanson town line to
- Hanson Town Forest: 5.2 mi., 2 hr. 30 min.
- Hanson–Pembroke town line: 7.8 mi., 3 hr. 35 min.

Section 19. Hanson–Pembroke Line to Pembroke–Kingston Line (6.2 mi.)

From the town line, the BCT follows Maqain St. southeast past a large cranberry bog to the right. The trail turns right on Mattakeetsett St., then left on Philips Rd., passing Great Sandy Bottom and Furnace Ponds. Bear right on Ridge Ave and cross a small stream. At 1.5 mi. follow the trail left at the intersection with Glenwood Rd. and bear left at a fork, then left again at the top of the hill onto a dirt road which crosses Sandy La. Near the brick school, follow the path to the left, then turn right at the intersection and follow utility poles behind the elementary school. At the bottom of the hill, turn right and follow the road, which curves to Center St. (MA 36).

Walk to the far left side of the opening onto the street by the mailbox. Cross Center St. and enter the paved driveway. In about 20 ft., step off onto the dirt path on the right *(note: Stay within the marked path here, as the public way closely skirts private property).* The path passes rocky outcroppings and makes a couple of sharp turns as it goes over the hill and down to Tubb's Meadow, a wildlife-rich area of old cranberry bogs and ponds.

At 2.7 mi., the trail turns left on the bog road and skirts the perimeter of an open area, passing a stone directional ring. Watch for many species of birds here, including waterfowl and great blue herons. After crossing a cement culvert, turn left and follow the main trail south past a pump house. Bear left at three successive junctions, then right and continue down the hill to the parking area for Tubb's Meadow Preserve at 3.7 mi.

The BCT exits the parking area right onto Monroe St., then turns left on School St. (MA 27). At 4.3 mi., it turns right at two white posts into the Veteran's Commemorative Town Forest. The trail follows the top of an esker, then descends sharply right to its base. Turn right, then left at successive T-junctions, then bear left at a Y-junction (a short side trip right leads to a overlook of Silver Lake). Follow the trail over rolling terrain past several more intersections to the town forest parking lot at 5.3 mi.

A temporary trail from here to the Kingston town line (reached at 6.2 mi.) has been blazed along School St. (MA 27) *(Caution: periodically heavy traffic).* The Pembroke BCT Committee is presently working to establish an off-road trail.

Bay Circuit Trail: Hanson–Pembroke Town Line to Pembroke–Kingston Line

Distances from Hanson–Pembroke line to
- Tubbs Meadow bog road: 2.7 mi., 1 hr. 15 min.
- Veteran's Commemorative Town Forest: 4.3 mi., 2 hr. 10 min.
- Pembroke–Kingston town line (MA 27): 6.2 mi., 3 hr.

Section 20. Pembroke–Kingston Town Line to Bay Farm (BCT Southern Terminus)

From MA 27, use Barse's La. to access the Silver Lake Sanctuary (large parking area). The BCT leads east from the shore of Silver Lake, crossing two brooks and the Jones River at 0.5 mi. (caution: this area may be flooded in spring). Turn left at a bench and follow the path up a hill, around a building and retaining walls, and along the hillside with Forge Pond on the left. At 1.0 mi., the trail turns left on Lake St., crosses the high school athletic fields, and bears left on a power line. Bear right on a woods road, leaving the power lines, and follow the road past cranberry bogs, a pond, and a pumping station.

At a storage barn and house, the trail turns right on a dirt access road, passes through a chain gate at 2.1 mi, then bears left on a woods road that shortly leads to Grove St. Turn left on Grove St. and continue east to a right on Foxworth La. At 3.0 mi. the trail bears left at a fork, then right onto a power line, then quickly left on a footpath. After crossing three bridges over the Jones River, the trail enters the Hathaway Preserve and follows the blue-blazed trail to the yellow trail, then follows the yellow trail to its end. Turn left on a woods road, which soon reaches MA 106 at 3.8 mi.

The BCT turns left on MA 106 (caution: heavy traffic), passes four houses, then turns right at a hydrant, passing between a barn and house. Continue through a field, cross a brook on a railroad bridge, then bear left at three successive forks. At 5.7 mi., the trail turns left at the Elm St. bridge (parking and a picnic area can be found here), then right after passing the Kingston Water Department pumping station. Bear left along the riverbank on a small trail that follows the side of a hill with the river to the right, climbing to an area with numerous side paths. The trail then bears right through trees and a field to the paved Meadow Crest housing driveway. Follow the driveway to the entrance, then stay straight on Hillcrest Rd. to its junction with MA 3A at 6.25 mi.

The trail turns left on MA 3A (caution: heavy traffic), then immediately right on Linden St., then left on Landing Rd., which passes under a railroad bridge and the MA 3 overpass. After the overpass, turn left on a discontinued road and continue through cedar trees to Park St. at 7.0 mi. The trail turns right on Park St., then left as it returns to Landing Rd. Follow Landing Rd. to the entrance and parking area at Bay Farm, then continue through the fields to the BCT's southern terminus at the shoreline of Kingston Bay.

Bay Circuit Trail: Pembroke–Kingston Town Line to Bay Farm (BCT Southern Terminus)

Distances from Pembroke–Kingston town line to:
- MA 106: 3.8 mi., 1 hr. 45 min.
- MA 3A, 6.25 mi., 3 hr.
- BCT southern terminus at Kingston Bay: 7.6 mi., 3 hr. 55 min.

Section 21. Pembroke (Valley Rd.) to Duxbury (Bay Farm) (7.0 mi.)

From the Pembroke–Duxbury town line at Valley St. the BCT heads southwest on a cart path through woods, meadows, and a small marsh to reach Summer St. (MA 53) at 1.1 mi. The trail crosses Summer St. and enters the Trout Farm Conservation Area. The trail system here has numbered junctions. Turn right at junction 11, left at 10 and 9, continue straight at 8, cross the brook at 7, pass 6, cross the brook again at 5, then go left at 4 to reach Union Bridge Rd. at 2.1 mi. Turn right and follow the road briefly before crossing the street and entering the woods. Travel through woods, over a footbridge, and reach King Philip's Path (paved) at 2.3 mi. Cross the road, through the woods along a footpath, then a cart path, and reach Vine St. at 3.1 mi. Turn left and follow Vine St. to Chandler St., turn left onto Chandler St. and proceed to Mayflower St., and then turn right onto the cart path.

The BCT now passes along a dam and small pond, then past a cranberry bog to the east. Turn left onto East St. (4.4 mi.), cross over MA 3 at 4.9 mi., and follow cart paths until the trail approaches Mayflower St. The path turns right (there are both white and yellow blazes here) and runs to the east side of Round Pond. Follow the blazes as the trail wraps around the pond and comes to a cranberry bog. Continue between the cranberry bog and a small pond to a dirt road and Elm St. at 5.9 mi.

Cross Elm St. and proceed south on School St., which merges with Oak St. Cross MA 3A at 6.4 mi. and continue south on Park St., turning left onto Loring Ave. at 6.8 mi. Follow the mowed path left around the perimeter of Bay Farm meadow to a granite ledge (7.0 mi.) on the shore of Kingston Bay. This is the very beautiful end of the BCT. Pragmatically, the trail continues to the right toward the parking lot for Bay Farm, but enjoy the view first.

Bay Circuit Trail: Pembroke (Valley Rd.) to Duxbury (Bay Farm)

Distance from Valley Rd. to
- Summer St.: 1.1 mi., 25 min.
- Union Bridge Rd.: 2.1 mi., 50 min.
- Vine St.: 3.1 mi., 1 hr. 15 min.
- MA 3: 4.9 mi., 2 hr. 5 min.
- Elm St.: 5.9 mi., 2 hr. 35 min.
- southern terminus at Bay Farm and Kingston Bay: 7.0 mi., 3 hr. 10 min.

Ashland Town Forest

This town-maintained forest occupies a 2-sq.-mi. section of northeastern Ashland. It is bounded on the west by Oak St., on the north by Oregon Rd. and Salem End Rd. (the latter in Framingham), on the east by Myrtle St. and Badger Rd., and on the south by Winter St., on which the main forest entrance is located. To reach the entrance, start from the intersection of MA 135 and Main St. in Ashland. Go north on Main St. for about 0.5 mi. and bear right onto Myrtle St. After about 100 yd. turn left onto Pine Hill Rd. At the road's end turn left onto Winter St. In about 200 yd. a roofed sign on the right says Ashland Town Forest. There is parking at an adjacent lot for four cars, and at the trailhead for four cars. Map kiosks are located at several points along the trails.

White Trail (Town of Ashland)

There is one main trail from this entrance, marked by white blazes, which is a section of the Bay Circuit Trail. The well-maintained White Trail bisects the town forest for 1.5 mi. from Winter St. to Oregon Rd. (also a trail-head, with limited parking for two or three cars). The trail has many turns on slightly rolling terrain, rising gradually for its first two-thirds and then descending gradually to Oregon Rd. It crosses three small brooks. Several marked and unmarked side trails branch off of from the main trail. The Red Trail leads to Cowassock Woods in Framingham, a property owned and maintained by the Sudbury Valley Trustees. Although these side trails are maintained, some are rockier with steeper sections, particularly the yellow trail, so caution should be used. Side trails branching west from the main trail are generally less strenuous, although some are steep in places. Some of the trails branching east pass interesting rock formations and converge on top of Wildcat Hill (436 ft.). Refer to the USGS Framingham quadrangle. The two main trails are excellent for cross-country skiing.

White Trail

Distance from Winter St. to
  • Oregon Rd. trailhead: 1.5 mi., 50 min.

Ashland State Park

This 470-acre state park in Ashland includes 157-acre Ashland Reservoir. Perhaps the most notable aspect of the park is its well-developed network of universally accessible (UA) recreation opportunities. These include UA swimming, beaches, picnicking, trails, restrooms, and an accessible boathouse. A trail map is available.

To reach Ashland State Park from I-495, take Exit 21A and travel east on MA 135 to the entrance on the right.

Ashland Reservoir Trail (DCR)

This trail, which skirts the reservoir's wooded shore, offers interesting views of the water and shore as well as distant views of Ashland and the surrounding hills. It is well worn and easy to follow. The trail begins right of the park bathing beach, follows the shore south for a short distance, then cuts through a wooded area to the Ashland Girl Scout Camp. It crosses the camp area to the left of the main camp building and continues south, staying close to the shore until it reaches a dirt road at the southern end of the reservoir. The trail then follows the dirt road left (east) across a bridge over an inlet to a boat launching area, passes to the right of a small bathing beach, and continues north beside an old wire fence to within sight of the reservoir dam. The trail goes west across the top of the dam, turns left, and follows the shore south to the starting point at the beach.

Ashland Reservoir Trail
Distances from park bathing beach to
- Girl Scout camp: 0.5 mi., 20 min.
- inlet bridge: 1.2 mi., 35 min.
- dam: 2.5 mi., 1 hr. 20 min.
- park bathing beach (circuit): 3.2 mi., 1 hr. 45 min.

Moose Hill Audubon Sanctuary

This 1,984-acre sanctuary is the oldest property operated by the Massachusetts Audubon Society. Located 25 mi. from Boston, its diverse terrain, vegetation, and geology includes mixed woods, open fields, and wetlands. A red maple swamp, traversed by a boardwalk, is especially beautiful as the leaves turn in late summer.

Highlights include the summit of Moose Hill (534 ft.), with a panoramic view from its fire tower; Bluff Hill and Bluff Head (450 ft.), with precipitous granite ledges and spectacular views to the south and west; and geological formations, including drumlins, a kettle hole, a bog, and granite ledges and outcrops.

A network of trails and woods roads makes much of the property accessible. The Warner Trail (marked by white markers) passes through the sanctuary and over the summits of Moose Hill and Bluff Hill (see the description of the Warner Trail). The Bay Circuit Trail also passes through the sanctuary. Trail maps are available at the information shelter by the sanctuary parking lot or at the sanctuary office.

To reach the sanctuary from the intersection of US 1 and MA 27 in Walpole, go east on MA 27 for 2.0 mi. and turn right onto Moose Hill St. The sanctuary is 1.5 mi. ahead on the right.

Summit Trail (MAS)

This trail travels north from the sanctuary headquarters, crosses a gravel road (Billings Way) in about 100 yd., then turns northwest and follows a fairly straight course. After crossing an old woods road, it continues to the summit of Moose Hill, where there is a fire tower with views in all directions. For most of its distance it coincides with the long-distance Warner Trail.

Summit Trail
Distance from parking lot (380 ft.) to
- summit of Moose Hill (534 ft.): 0.5 mi., 20 min.

Bluff Hill (MAS)

This route is a combination of three separate trails and provides the most direct access to Bluff Hill from the sanctuary parking lot. From the parking lot, start on the Billings Loop Trail, and then bear right onto the Bluff Head Trail. This leads through pine woods, past a wall of rocks on the right. Continue uphill past an old water cistern and a couple of small ponds to the summit of Bluff Hill.

Bluff Hill
Distance from parking lot (380 ft.) via Billings Loop and Bluff Hill Trails to
- Bluff Hill summit (450 ft.): 1.5 mi., 45 min.

Stony Brook Wildlife Sanctuary

This 122-acre reservation in Norfolk includes large areas of marsh, open fields, and woods. Highlights include Stony Brook; three interconnected ponds known collectively as Stony Brook Pond; adjoining marshes; and a narrow, wooded isthmus centrally located amid the three ponds. The northernmost and largest pond is called Kingfisher Pond.

The Stony Brook Nature Center, which includes the park's offices, is located a short distance south of the junction of North St., Pond St., and Needham St. in Norfolk. From Norfolk center follow MA 115 south for 1.0 mi. to North St. Turn right onto North St. to reach the sanctuary entrance on the right. Maps are available at the nature center.

Pond Loop Trail (MAS)

This loop trail starts from the rear (west) of the nature center. It leads west between stone walls and crosses a bridge between Stony Brook Pond on the right and Teal Marsh on the left. Muskrat houses are visible in the distance in Teal Marsh. The trail then climbs along the southern flank of a forested glacial knoll to the beginning of a long boardwalk. The boardwalk passes between Kingfisher Pond and Teal Marsh, provides great views all along the way, and ends at a small island forested with beech trees. At the western end of the island is an observation platform, where great blue and green herons, swans, and a number of other birds can be viewed.

The trail loops around the island, then returns across the boardwalk. At the glacial knoll the path turns left and passes a boulder field called Rock Hollow. The trail continues to the north end of the knoll, crossing a bridge and wandering through woods of maple, birch, and dogwood to reach Stony Brook. The trail crosses the brook on a bridge; the ruins of an old mill and millrace are nearby. The trail then heads south across an open meadow and past a butterfly garden to return to the starting point at the nature center.

Pond Loop Trail

Distance from Stony Brook Nature Center to
• Stony Brook Nature Center (circuit): 1 mi., 30 min.

Borderland State Park

This 1,600-acre state park was purchased in 1971 from the estate of Blanche Ames and includes wooded hills, ponds, and open fields. The name, given to the property by the Ames family, refers to the Easton–Sharon border on which the park lies.

Interesting features of the landscape include the many dams constructed in an attempt to transform swampland into ponds. The Ameses created a forest and wildlife preserve on the majority of the estate, while developing the land's potential for outdoor recreational activities such as hiking, canoeing, skating, and skiing.

The park contains a number of hiking trails, most of which are easy to follow and suitable for hikers of all abilities. There is a lovely trail over the Long Dam, which separates Lower and Upper Leach Ponds. Farther to the east lie more ponds and, at Mountain St., the historic Colonel Israel Tisdale House, which was destroyed by fire in 1983.

More difficult trails include the Lower Granite Hills Loop and Upper Granite Hills Loop, both of which lie to the north of Upper Leach Pond. These interconnecting trails (a total of 3.0 mi.) wend their way through oak forests and large granite outcrops.

The ponds are great for fishing and non-motorized boating, and are most easily reached via the park road that leads in from the Bay Rd. entrance on the east side of the park. No open fires are allowed, and a strict no-alcohol policy is enforced.

To reach the park from Sharon center (MA 27 at N. Main St. and Depot St.), go south via Pond St. and Massapoag Ave., passing Lake Massapoag, for 4.4 mi. From the east, south, or west, use MA 106 or MA 123, which combine in this part of Easton. Opposite the Belcher Malleable Iron Co., turn north onto Poquanticut Ave. Follow this for 1.5 mi. to the second left, then turn northwest onto Massapoag Ave. and continue 2.0 mi.

Myles Standish State Forest

At more than 14,000 acres, Myles Standish State Forest in Plymouth and Carver is one of the largest reservations in the Massachusetts state park and forest system. The forest offers universally accessible restrooms, five camping areas (Fearing Ponds 1 and 2, Charge Pond, Barrett's Pond, and

Curlew Pond), and sixteen ponds. A portion of Charge Pond is set aside for equestrian camping. There are 15 mi. of cycling paths, 35 mi. of equestrian trails, and 13 mi. of hiking paths (blazed with blue triangles) that venture deep into this unique area.

Myles Standish State Forest contains some of the largest areas of pitch pine–scrub oak forest in New England. The forest is also well known for its kettle ponds, created as huge chunks of glacial ice became partially embedded in the ground and then melted when the ice ages ended. The holes left behind filled with water and became round ponds. There are many fragile natural areas in the forest, such as the shores of the kettle ponds, and these are marked with signs—please stay on the trail in these areas. In summer interpretive programs include explorations of cranberry bogs, trips to ponds, and visits to fire towers.

In addition to hiking, the recreational opportunities here include camping, bicycling, canoeing, and swimming. The terrain is excellent for mountain biking, which is very popular here. Myles Standish State Forest is closed to all all-terrain vehicle and off-road vehicle use.

To reach the forest from the north, take MA 3 south to Exit 3. Turn right (west) onto Long Pond Rd. and travel about 3 mi. to the entrance on the left. Park headquarters is located on Cranberry Rd. To reach the headquarters from the west (I-495), take Exit 2 (South Carver) to MA 58. Turn north onto MA 58, continue straight on Tremont St. where MA 58 bears left, and proceed for a little less than a mile to Cranberry Rd. on the right.

Easthead Trail and Bentley Loop (DCR)

The Easthead Trail is a scenic and easy 3.0-mi. loop that circles the Easthead Reservoir. In 1991 the 4.5-mi. Bentley Loop was added at the northern end of the original loop. Both the original trail and the Bentley Loop are clearly blazed with blue trail markers or blue paint slashes and are well maintained.

The Easthead Trail begins on the north side of Cranberry Rd., about 150 yd. east of park headquarters, at a sign that indicates the entrance to the Easthead Nature Trail. Entering the woods, the trail proceeds north, roughly following the eastern side of the reservoir, where a variety of waterfowl and wading birds may be observed. In about 1.4 mi., the trail turns left onto a well-used bridle path that follows a gas pipeline. In a short distance the trail reaches two junctions. At the first, the original Easthead Trail loop turns left to begin its return to the starting point via footpaths along the reservoir's western shore

To continue on the Bentley Loop, walk a few yards right onto a paved road. Follow the paved road a short distance, then turn onto the first dirt road on the left (with a metal gate numbered 75). The trail continues a short distance along this dirt road and then turns right onto a woods road. At the end of this road, just before a meadow, is a trail junction where the Bentley Loop heads both left and right.

Turn left at the junction and follow the well-blazed trail. (Use caution, as there are many unmarked paths that cross the trail in this section. If no trail marker is seen after a short distance, retrace the route to the last intersection.) The trail skirts the edge of New Long Pond, bears right then left, and passes Three Cornered Pond on the left. Beyond the pond the trail traverses the first of several meadows. It proceeds almost straight across this meadow (there is a 5-ft. post in the middle), then turns left just before a second meadow and heads north toward College Pond.

The trail turns left at another meadow and continues some distance along its left edge. The path turns left into the woods at another marker and quickly reaches its northernmost point at a junction. The path heading north leads to the College Pond parking area, while the Bentley Loop turns right and proceeds south.

After about 50 yd. the trail turns left and descends the hill, turns sharp right, and comes to a meadow (the first since turning south). Traverse the meadow and exit left at the far end. Soon College Pond Rd. is visible on the left. The trail skirts the edge of a parking lot, then turns right into the woods. Cross another meadow and the trail enters into the woods for a short time before proceeding straight across yet another meadow at the bottom of a hill. From here the trail takes a very winding course to arrive back at the loop's starting point.

To return to the Easthead Trail, walk down the woods road, turn left at the dirt road, and proceed to the gate at the paved road. Turn right onto the paved road, follow it to the bridle path, turn left onto the bridle path, and then make a quick right to continue on the second portion of the Easthead Trail. Follow it for about 1.5 mi. around the reservoir back to the starting point. At one point along this section, the trail follows the road for about 100 yd. and then reenters the woods.

Easthead Trail and Bentley Loop

Distances from Cranberry Rd. trailhead near forest headquarters to
- start of Bentley Loop: 1.5 mi., 45 min.
- Easthead Reservoir circuit without Bentley Loop: 3.0 mi., 1 hr. 30 min.
- end of Bentley Loop: 6 mi., 3 hr.
- Cranberry Rd. (circuit): 7.5 mi., 3 hr. 45 min.

Stony Brook Valley

An interesting network of trails is located in the town of Brewster, on property belonging both to the town and to the Cape Cod Museum of Natural History. These trails are in the valley of Stony Brook, which flows down from a series of freshwater ponds, becomes a tidal estuary merging with a salt marsh, and has its outlet in Cape Cod Bay. There are 300 acres of town-owned conservation land abutting the museum, including Wing's Island on the north side of the shore road and many acres of salt marsh and beach. The Cape Cod Museum of Natural History owns an additional 80 acres, including marshland and beech woods.

Three nature trails traverse salt marsh, sandy scrub, and woodland, with views over Cape Cod Bay. All of the trails are well marked and easy to hike. Parking and access to trails is at Drummer Bay Park, which is roughly 1/8 mi. from the museum parking lot on MA 6A, 1.7 mi. west of the junction of MA 6A and MA 137. The museum parking lot is limited to museum visitors and members only. Maps are available at the museum, which offers many exhibits and interpretive programs.

John Wing Trail (CCMNH)

From the museum, the John Wing Trail leads north, soon reaching a boardwalk across a marsh to Wing Island. The trail then continues through a mixed coastal forest, then passes an old field with solstice stones. Bearing left at the junction beyond the field leads to the beach and views of Cape Cod Bay. The main trail makes a short loop along the island, passing nice views of the marsh associated with Paine's Creek and a side trail with another view of the bay. Return to the parking area via the boardwalk.

John Wing Trail
Distance from museum parking area to
• parking area (round trip): 1.5 mi., 50 min.

Nickerson State Park

This 1,900-acre state park contains 420 camping sites, an 8-mi.-long bike path that connects to the 25-mi.-long Cape Cod Rail Trail paved recreational path, and more than 15 mi. of excellent hiking trails. Universally accessible facilities include fishing, beaches, camping, picnicking, and restrooms. The park is also within walking distance of Cape Cod Bay. Eight kettle ponds lie within the bounds of the reservation, surrounded by characteristic coastal scrub oak-pitch pine woodlands.

The park entrance is located on the south side of MA 6A in Brewster, about 1.5 mi. west of Exit 12 off the Mid-Cape Highway (US 6). The main parking lot is on the right just inside the entrance to the park. An easy access to some of the trails is at the end of Flax Pond Rd., the first road on the left after entering the park. Follow it to a parking area between Big Cliff Lake and Little Cliff Pond, where there is a boat ramp. Trail access may also be gained at the end of Long Nook Rd. and at Fishermen's Landing, which can be reached by following the main park road 1.8 mi. to the parking lot on the left. Park maps are available at the entrance gate; also refer to the USGS Harwich and Orleans quadrangles.

Cliff Pond Trail (DCR)

The reservation's longest hiking trail makes a scenic circuit around Cliff Pond, which lies southwest of the park entrance. From the trailhead near the boat ramp, the blue-blazed path leads northwest along the pond's north shore, passing small sand beaches and the cove known as Fisherman's Landing. It then continues to follow the edge of the pond south, then east, passing two more coves and a marshy area. Complete the loop by swinging left (north) through a narrow stretch of land between Cliff and

Little Cliff Ponds (stay on the main trail, as a path also leads around Little Cliff Pond).

Cliff Pond Trail
Distance from boat ramp to
- Fisherman's Landing: 1.1 mi., 40 min.
- trailhead (circuit): 3.25 mi., 1 hr. 55 min.

Lowell Holly Reservation

This 135-acre Trustees of Reservations property in Mashpee and Sandwich holds an array of attractions, all linked by a 4-mi.-long trail system. Two knolls overlook Mashpee Pond and Wakeby Pond, and offer fine views of the water. The donor of the property, Abbot Lawrence Lowell, planted many rhododendrons and mountain laurels, as well as more than 50 species and varieties of holly. During June, this is one of the most beautiful floral displays in Massachusetts. The trails range from footpaths to historic carriage roads.

To reach Lowell Holly from US 6 (Exit 2) follow MA 130 south for 1.5 mi. Take a left on Cotuit Rd., continue for 3.4 mi., turn right onto S. Sandwich Rd., and proceed for 0.1 mi. to parking on the right.

Sandy Neck Barrier Beach

Sandy Neck is a 6-mi.-long barrier beach bordering Cape Cod Bay. Managed by the town of Barnstable, it provides habitat for several endangered species, including piping plovers, diamond-backed terrapins, and spadefoot toads. The dunes are covered with wildflowers, wild cranberries, and hardwood trees. A network of trails and crossovers offers options ranging from a 1.6-mi.-long nature walk to a hike of more than 13 mi. along the protected marsh and 100-ft.-tall dunes to the open waters of Cape Cod Bay.

To reach Sandy Neck from US 6 (Exit 5), head north on MA 149, turn left onto MA 6A, then right onto Sandy Neck Rd. Follow Sandy Neck Rd. to the parking lot at its end. A fee is charged for parking in season. Four-wheel drive vehicles are allowed in certain areas, and hunting is permitted during the appropriate season. Mileage is posted at all intersections. Check tide charts, as low-lying areas on the marsh side may be flooded at exceptionally high tides, especially in the area adjacent to the start of the Marsh Trail.

The circuits below are described counterclockwise, but they can be walked in either direction. Hikers are not allowed to enter private property or areas marked Erosion Control and must stay off the dunes, crossing over only on designated trails. Because of the exposure, be sure to bring adequate water and sunblock; allow time for slow going in soft sand.

Sandy Neck Circuit (Town of Barnstable)

This circuit begins on the Marsh Trail, the trailhead for which is located in the parking area opposite the check-in booth. The trail initially passes through an area of red pine and scrub oak, then opens up by the great marsh. Large square blue boxes line the marsh—these are traps to control the green fly. The dunes to the left obstruct the view of the ocean. Stay on the sandy trail to avoid ticks and poison ivy, and to avoid destroying the beach grass and other fragile dune plants. At 0.5 mi. a junction is reached. A left turn here leads 1.1 mi. back to the parking lot via the beach. Alternately, continue straight ahead to signpost 2 at 1.5 mi. Poverty grass displays its yellow blooms in early June, and pale purple patches of sea lavender grow prolifically along the trail.

As the trail approaches crossover 2, Scorton Creek comes into view, meandering near the bay. Turn onto crossover 2 to return to the trailhead and complete a 4.7-mi. hike. For a 9.0-mi. hike continue straight to signpost 4 (there is no 3). Along the way is a dune cottage with no less than twenty swallow houses. Watch for horseshoe crab molts and deer and coyote prints. The historic cottages on Beach Point and of the decommissioned Sandy Neck Light come into view as the trail approaches signpost 4. Turn left at crossover 4 to return to the parking area and to complete a 9.0-mi. hike, or continue straight for another 1.5 mi. to crossover 5 and turn left for a 13.0-mi. hike.

A horse trail intersects trail 5. Cross straight over it to reach the shore. Private land lies between the path here and the tip of Sandy Neck. To extend the hike, continue east along the beach to the lighthouse before retracing the route and returning to the parking lot along the shore. Be aware that a trip to the lighthouse extends the mileage by a couple of miles.

> **Sandy Neck Circuit**
> Distances from parking area to
> - circuit via crossover at post 1: 1.6 mi., 1 hr.
> - circuit via crossover at post 2: 4.7 mi., 2 hr. 50 min.
> - circuit via crossover at post 4: 9.0 mi., 5 hr. 30 min..
> - circuit via crossover at post 5: 13.0 mi., 8 hr.

Monomoy National Wildlife Refuge

Encompassing 2,700 acres at the elbow of Cape Cod, the Monomoy National Wildlife Refuge is one of the most spectacular wildlife areas of the New England coast. The refuge's beaches, forests, sandbars, and islands—which are constantly reshaped by erosion from coastal storms—are home to great flocks of shorebirds, as well as colonies of harbor and gray seals, which are staging a remarkable population recovery here. While the majority of the refuge is only accessible by boat, the portion on Morris Island, which is accessible by car, includes the headquarters, a nature trail, and a section of beach.

Contact the refuge (508-945-0594) for more information; the Cape Cod Museum of Natural History, Wellfleet Bay Wildlife Sanctuary, and local boat operators offer tours and access to the offshore portion.

Interpretive Trail (USFWS)

This trail can be walked as a short, easy circuit, or combined with a walk along the beach for a longer outing that provides a good sampling of the refuge's diverse habitats, with fine views across the water. The trail begins at the parking area adjacent the headquarters, and shortly leads to a pair of overlooks with fine views from atop ocean cliffs. It then descends to the beach on wooden stairs, and follows the shore southwest for 100 yd. *(Caution: High tides may make the beach inaccessible here.)* The trail bears right off ⚠ the beach and leads through low woods and shrubs to a salt marsh, then rejoins the beach at Morris Point (post 10). From here, either turn left and return along the beach to the steps (0.75 mi. round-trip), or turn right and continue along the beach as it arcs to the refuge boundary, then backtrack to the trailhead (approximately 1.5 mi. round-trip).

Interpretive Trail
Distances from trailhead at refuge headquarters to
  • trailhead via Morris Point loop: 0.75 mi., 35 min.
  • trailhead via beach extension: 1.5 mi., 1 hr. 10 min.

Wellfleet Bay Wildlife Sanctuary

The Wellfleet Bay Wildlife Sanctuary, operated by the Massachusetts Audubon Society, is an 1,100-acre preserve situated on the east shores of Wellfleet Bay, opposite the Great Island peninsula. The mixed habitats here include pine woodlands, ponds, creeks and brooks, tidal flats, marshes, and an uncommon heath land; this variety is reflected by the 250 species of birds that have been recorded on the grounds. The sanctuary's abundant and often visible wildlife and 5-mi. network of easy walking trails, all of which are well-marked, makes it an excellent destination for explorers of all ages looking to sample a wide range of Cape Cod's nature. The sanctuary's marked access road is located on the west side of MA 6 near the Wellfleet–Eastham town line, just north of the Wellfleet drive-in theater. A modest admission fee is charged for non-MAS members.

Bay View–Fresh Brook Pathway (MAS)

This trail explores several habitats in the northern portion of the sanctuary. From the visitor center, follow signs for the Bay View–Fresh Brook Pathway. The trail follows the edge of the expansive salt marsh, then makes a brief detour into the woods to a T-junction with the short loop connector on the right (this trail offers a shorter, 1.0-mi. loop through a large open shrubland with a view of the bay). The main trail bears left at this junction and continues along the marsh. Watch for a variety of birds here, including wading birds and sandpipers along the mudflats.

The trail then leads into the woods at the upper junction with the short loop. The Fresh Brook Pathway soon branches left and winds easily over a knoll with a view of Fresh Brook and its associated wetlands. The trail then leads through grassy pitch pine forest as it parallels Rte. 6. After passing the sanctuary campground, the trail ends at the open fields near the visitor center and parking area.

Bay View–Fresh Brook Pathway

Distance from nature center to
- Circuit via short loop: 1.0 mi., 25 min.
- Circuit via Fresh Brook Pathway: 1.6 mi., 45 min.

Goose Pond–Try Island Boardwalk Trail (MAS)

This popular trail offers a variety of outstanding wildlife viewing opportunities. From the trailhead at the nature center, bear left, following signs for the Goose Pond–Try Island Trail. The path passes Silver Spring Pond, where painted turtles are easily observed, and the Silver Spring Trail (an optional 0.6-mi. loop through tall oaks and pitch pines along the pond), then soon leads to a bird blind and short boardwalk at nearby Goose Pond. In addition to birds, cottontail rabbits, frogs, and peepers are frequently seen along this path. After passing an observation deck with an overview of the salt marsh, the trail splits at post 33, where the Try Island loop leaves right.

Bear right and follow the trail as it rises through a small hummock of mature forest, then winds to an overlook on the right and descends from the woods to the boardwalk. Here great numbers of fiddler crabs pop in and out of holes in the mudflats, which are also frequented by shorebirds. The boardwalk leads to a picturesque area where Hatches Creek meets the bay *(Caution: watch the tides when exploring the shoreline here)*. Complete the ⚠ Try Island loop by following the boardwalk and path along the edge of the marsh back to post 33, then backtrack to the visitor center.

Goose Pond–Try Island Boardwalk Trail

Distance from nature center to
- end of boardwalk: 0.8 mi., 30 min.
- trailhead: 1.6 mi., 1 hr.

Cape Cod National Seashore (NPS)

Established in 1961, the 45,000-acre Cape Cod National Seashore is maintained by the U.S. Department of the Interior's National Park Service. The seashore includes six beaches—Coast Guard and Nauset Light Beaches in Eastham, Marconi Beach in South Wellfleet, Head of the Meadows Beach in Truro, and Race Point and Herring Cove Beaches in Provincetown—plus extensive inland areas of oak and scrub pine, salt marsh, and freshwater wetlands.

There are two visitor centers—Salt Pond Visitor Center on the corner of Nauset Rd. and MA 6 in Eastham and Province Lands Visitor Center on Race Point Rd., about 1 mi. from Provincetown off MA 6. The Province Lands Visitor Center has an observation deck with a 360-degree view, movies, and ranger-guided activities. The Salt Pond Visitor Center has a ranger-guided museum, films, a bookstore, and expansive views of Nauset Marsh.

There are many hiking paths and nature trails in Cape Cod National Seashore. Most are well marked and relatively easy to hike.

Great Island Trail (NPS)

The National Seashore's longest trail is the spectacular Great Island loop, which explores a peninsula that juts into Cape Cod Bay near Wellfleet Harbor. Great Island is open only to hikers and boaters; no vehicles are permitted. To reach the beginning of the Great Island Trail from the town pier in Wellfleet, keep the bay on your left and follow Chequesset Neck Rd. to the marked parking area. The trail begins at the parking lot at the end of the road. The Great Island Trail is a scenic but, because of its length and sections over loose sand, somewhat strenuous loop that leads through woods, dunes, and swamps and finishes with a long walk along bay beaches. (*Note: The sections of trail along the marshes might be wet during high tide, especially during fall and winter.*)

From the parking lot the trail heads east on a sand path. Winding through a pitch pine forest, the trail heads toward the marshy neck of land known as the Gut that connects Great Island to the mainland. The loop begins on this neck of land. On reaching the island, turn left and proceed east-southeast, skirting the marshes and dunes along the northern edge of

Great Island. At a junction a short connecting path turns right (south) off the main trail; taking this trail cuts approximately 1.3 mi. from the hike's distance.

The main trail continues east to the northeast corner of Great Island, then swings abruptly west near the site of an old tavern and leads to the center of the island, where it rejoins the connecting path.

The trail now winds through the woodlands that cover the interior of Great Island, heading generally west and south. Passing by marshland, the trail heads to the south, and crosses over Great Beach Hill. At the southern end of Great Island is a trail junction, where a spur trail leads south along a sand spit toward Jeremy Point, which is inaccessible at high tide *(Caution:* ⚠ *watch the tide carefully here).* The Great Island loop returns to the north, following the bay beaches for approximately 3 mi. along the western edge of the peninsula, passing towering dunes and excellent views across Cape Cod Bay to Provincetown. Ascending over dunes via stairs and a board-walk, the trail returns to the neck of land between Great Island and the mainland. Turn left to return to the parking lot.

Great Island Trail

Distance from parking lot to
- sharp right near tavern site: 1.75 mi., 1 hr.
- junction with spur trail to Jeremy Point: 4.3 mi., 2 hr. 15 min.
- parking lot (circuit): 7.5 mi., 4 hr. 15 min.

Fort Hill–Red Maple Swamp Trail (NPS)

These trails combine to form a scenic and diverse loop that offers fine views of Nauset Marsh and a coastal red maple swamp that is especially at-tractive as the leaves change color in late summer and autumn. To reach the trailhead from MA 6 in Eastham, turn onto Governor Prence Rd. (brown sign for Fort Hill), and follow the road to its end at the parking area and trailhead. The boardwalk portions of the Red Maple Swamp Trail are uni-versally accessible and can be reached via Hemenway Landing at Fort Hill, which is one block north of Governor Prence Rd. off MA 6.

At the trailhead, there's a sweeping vista across Nauset Marsh. Here the Fort Hill Trail leads north past open meadows and woodlands to an-other overlook and interpretive shelter at Skiff Hill. The trail follows the paved path past another vista, then reaches the junction with the Red Maple Swamp trail. Follow the Red Maple Swamp trail boardwalk, which makes a short loop through the heart of the swamp, then follow the trail out of the swamp over wood steps. Turn right at a junction and make a short walk east to the lower parking lot. Across the street here is the historical home (ca. 1867) of Edward Penniman, a prominent whaler and sea captain. The trail continues behind the house and soon returns to the Fort Hill parking area.

Fort Hill–Red Maple Swamp Trail

Distance from parking area at Fort Hill to
- start of Red Maple Swamp Trail: 0.8 mi., 20 min.
- trailhead via Penniman House (circuit): 2.0 mi., 1 hr.

Nauset Marsh Trail (NPS)

This easy 1.2-mi.-long path begins at the Salt Pond Visitor Center and explores the edge of Nauset Marsh and Salt Pond, passing excellent views along the way. The trail leads away from the visitor center and descends to Salt Pond, a coastal kettle pond that is connected by a channel to the nearby Nauset Marsh. It then crosses a dike and rises easily through the adjacent to an open area with a fine overview of Nauset Marsh. From the overlook, the trail then continues through woodlands as it loops back toward the visitor center. Near its end, it crosses the paved recreational trail and joins the Buttonbush Trail (a specially designed trail for the visually impaired) before emerging at the parking area.

Nauset Marsh Trail

Distance from visitor center to
- visitor center (circuit): 1.2 mi., 45 min.

Doane Loop Trail (NPS)

This trail is a paved, universally accessible path on Doane Rd., located about 1 mi. from the Salt Pond Visitor Center (where directions are available). The trail wanders through a pine-oak forest and views of Nauset Marsh, passing two unique features—Doane Rock and the site of the Doane Homestead. Doane Rock (a.k.a. Enoch's Rock) is a large glacial erratic and the largest exposed boulder on Cape Cod. Deacon John Doane settled here in 1644 along with six other Pilgrim families; the site of his home is marked by a granite marker just off the path.

Doane Loop Trail
Distance from Doane Rd to
• trailhead (circuit): 0.5 mi., 20 min.

Atlantic White Cedar Swamp Trail (NPS)

This moderate 1.2-mi.-long trail begins at the Marconi Site and descends through pine-oak forest into a mature woodland. The path then comes to a boardwalk that winds through a regionally uncommon swamp of beautiful Atlantic white cedar. From the boardwalk the path heads uphill and returns to its start via "Wireless Road," a path of loose sand that can be tiring. To reach the trailhead from the Salt Pond Visitor Center, travel 6.0 mi. north on MA 6 to Wellfleet; watch for signs for the Marconi Site.

Atlantic White Cedar Swamp Trail
Distance from parking area to
• parking area (circuit): 1.2 mi., 50 min.

Pamet Trail (NPS)

The Pamet Trail combines several paths that explore a glacial hill, kettle pond, and section of beach and dunes near the site of an abandoned cranberry bog in Truro's Pamet River Valley. To reach the trailhead, from MA 6 in Truro, take the Pamet roads exit and follow North Pamet Rd. for 1.6 mi. to a small parking area on the right (2-hr. time limit). The trail begins across the road and rises easily through an open heathland on Bearberry Hill. A short side trail forks right to the top of the hill, which offers a 360-degree view that includes the ocean, dunes and a kettle pond below. The main trail descends the hill to the junction with the Old King's Highway, a wider path on a sandy fire road. Bear left and follow the Old King's Highway north, passing several unmarked side trails. At 0.5 mi., the trail descends to the beach, with fine views of the surrounding high dunes.

After exploring the beach, backtrack along the Old King's Highway to the junction with the Bearberry Hill path. Those wishing to bypass the climb over the hill can continue straight on the Old King's Highway, which passes a fire road gate and leads to a close view of the kettle pond. Turn right on the paved road and make the short walk to the parking area.

Pamet Trail

Distance from parking area to
  - beach via Bearberry Hill and Old King's Highway: 0.5 mi., 25 min.
  - parking area via Old King's Highway: 1.1 mi., 50 min.

Pilgrim Heights (NPS)

The Pilgrim Heights area in Truro features a pair of short loop trails over easy rolling terrain that lead to historic sites and overlooks with sweeping vistas. To reach the trailhead, from MA 6 in Truro, continue north past the Highland Lighthouse exit and look for the prominent signs for Pilgrim Heights on the east side of the highway. Follow the road through the large parking area to the trailhead at a small shelter and picnic area.

From the shelter, the Small Swamp Trail leads through an old farm site in a glacial kettle hole, then passes a pair of scenic overlooks with panoramic views across the dunes to the ocean. After 0.75 mi., it returns to the shelter, where the Pilgrim Spring loop also begins. The Pilgrim Spring Trail leads to another overlook, then descends to the site where the Pilgrims first drank fresh water after landing nearby in 1620 (the High Head bike trail is the paved path near the spring). The trail then climbs back through pitch pine woods to the parking area.

Pilgrim Heights

Distances from interpretive shelter at parking area to
  - Small Swamp (circuit): 0.75 mi., 20 min.
  - Pilgrim Springs (circuit): 0.75 mi., 20 min.
  - Small Swamp and Pilgrim Springs combined loop: 1.5 mi., 40 min.

Beech Forest Trail (NPS)

Located south of the Province Lands Visitor Center, this excellent birding trail passes a large pond and wetland and leads through a rare coastal beech woodland. To reach the trailhead, from MA 6 in Provincetown, turn north on Race Point Rd. and continue 0.6 mi. to the parking area on the left (the visitor center is farther north along Race Point Rd.). From the parking area, the trail begins on a short boardwalk, with views of Beech Forest Pond to the left. It continues north to a cutoff path that allows the option of a 0.75-mi. loop that bypasses the beech grove. From the junction, the main trail leads through the tall forest for 0.25 mi., climbing wood steps to a nice perspective of the knoll before descending to rejoin the Pond Loop. Bear right at the junction and follow the trail along the pond as it returns to the parking area; a short side trail on the right leads to a viewing platform that overlooks the wetland.

Beech Forest Trail
Distance from Race Point Rd. trailhead to:
- circuit (Pond Loop only): 0.8 mi., 25 min.
- circuit (Pond and Beech Forest Loops): 1.0 mi., 40 min.

Cape Poge Wildlife Refuge

This 516-acre barrier beach is on the east shore of Chappaquiddick Island on the eastern side of Martha's Vineyard. The beach runs for 7.0 mi. from Wasque Point to the Gut beyond the Cape Poge Lighthouse. To the west of the beach, a series of sand dunes covered in rugosa rose and beach pea separate the ocean from Cape Poge Bay. Managed by The Trustees of Reservations, the Cape Poge Wildlife Refuge includes 14 mi. of moderate trails. Portions of the refuge may be closed seasonally to protect nesting birds.

To reach the refuge from Martha's Vineyard, take the Edgartown–Chappaquiddick Ferry to Chappaquiddick Island, then travel east on Chappaquiddick Rd. for 2.5 mi. to Dike Rd. Continue on Dike Rd. (dirt) for 0.5 mi. to reach the Dike Bridge and parking area.

Cape Poge Beach (TTOR)

The refuge's main trail follows the beach along the east side of Chappaquiddick for 6.0 mi. to the Cape Poge Lighthouse. The trail begins at the Wasque Reservation as a boardwalk to the beach, then heads north along the shore, passing by Pocha Pond and Cape Poge Bay. Because of the soft sand and exposure to sun and wind, the full 12.0-mi. round trip is a strenuous hike; those looking for a less involved outing can walk a shorter portion of the beach before doubling back.

Cape Poge beach
Distance from Wasque Reservation to
  • Cape Poge lighthouse: 6.0 mi., 3 hr. 30 min.

Menemsha Hills

This 211-acre reservation on Martha's Vineyard overlooks Vineyard Sound and offers about 3 mi. of trails across open bluffs and through oak and beech forest. The view from Prospect Hill encompasses the village of Menemsha, Gay Head Lighthouse, and the Elizabeth Islands. From the bluffs overlooking the sound is a view of the Great Sand Bank. The Harris Trail offers a pleasant walk through diverse plant communities.

To reach Menemsha Hills from West Tisbury, follow North Rd. west for about 4.7 mi. to the reservation entrance. Parking is just beyond Tabor House Rd.

Coskata–Coatue Wildlife Refuge

This 1,117-acre refuge, managed by The Trustees of Reservations, protects a spectacular stretch of beach and rolling dunes on Nantucket Island. Jutting out into the waters of Nantucket Sound, the property is famous for its world-class fishing. More than 200 acres of dunes support varied plant communities, including bayberry, cedar barrens, and stunted oaks. About 16 mi. of trails offer a unique hiking experience. Harbor and gray seals are common at Great Point, and seasonal tours allow exploration of Great Point Lighthouse. Portions of the refuge may be closed seasonally to protect nesting birds. Contact the gatehouse at 508-228-0006 for information about the trails and access.

To reach the refuge from the Nantucket town rotary travel east for 6.0 mi. on Polpis Rd., then turn left onto Wauwinet Rd. and follow it to its end.

Great Point OSV Trail (TTOR)

The reservation's main trail, which is primarily an over-sand vehicle trail and follows soft sand, leads north from the gatehouse and leads to the outer beaches and Great Point. Please respect the private residences north of the gatehouse. At junction 1 at 1.2 mi., a side trail leads west toward the outlet of Coskata Pond, while bearing right leads to the shore. The trail continues past junctions 2 and 3, then crosses the narrow neck below Great Point. It reaches the lighthouse at approximately 5.5 mi.

Great Point OSV Trail
Distance from gatehouse to
  • Great Point lighthouse: 5.5 mi., 4 hr.

SUGGESTED HIKES

Easy Hikes

Summit Trail [rt: 1.0 mi., 0:35], page 376. This short trail ascends to the spectacular views atop Moose Hill.

Pond Loop Trail [lp: 1.0 mi., 0:30], page 363. Boardwalks, ponds, marshes...a fascinating walk for the whole family with excellent wildlife viewing opportunities.

Nauset Marsh Trail [lp: 1.2 mi., 0:45], page 387. This easy path travels by the Nauset Salt Marsh and pond. Grand views await.

Pilgrim Heights [lp: 1.5 mi., 0:40], page 378. The Small Swamp and Pilgrim Spring Trails are a pair of pleasant loops that lead to historical sites and several panoramic overlooks.

Goose Pond–Try Island Boardwalk Trail [rt: 1.6 mi., 1:00 hr.], page 373. Offering wildlife viewing ranging from shorebirds and fiddler crabs to turtles and cottontail rabbits, this route traverses a variety of coastal habitats.

Moderate Hikes

Fort Hill–Red Maple Swamp Trail [rt: 3.0 mi., 1:30], page 385. A charming trail with views of the Atlantic Ocean and the Nauset Marsh.

Sandy Neck Circuit [lp: 4.7 mi., 4:40], page 370. This circuit visits beautiful coastal environments. Turn onto crossover 2 for the 4.7-mi. loop.

Strenuous Hikes

Bay Circuit Trail, Section 20 [ow: 7.6 mi, 3:55], page 358. This hike covers the southernmost section of the Bay Circuit Trail, ending at Bay Farm by beautiful Kingston Bay.

Easthead Trail and Bentley Loop [lp: 7.5 mi., 4:40], page 374. A long hike past ponds and through forests and meadows.

Great Island Trail [rt: 7.5 mi., 4:15], page 374. This hike crosses a narrow neck of land to explore Great Island, then follows the beach along Cape Cod Bay back to the parking area. There are excellent views of the various habitats throughout.

APPENDIX: CONSERVATION AND RECREATION ORGANIZATIONS AND AGENCIES

Listed below are various organizations that maintain open space and hiking trails in this region, or can provide information about hiking and recreational activities. Many of the publications and maps produced by these organizations are also available at outdoor recreation suppliers and bookstores, as well as at the AMC's Joy St. headquarters (please see the overview of the AMC and the Massachusetts chapters on pages 400 and 402).

The Appalachian Trail Conservancy

The Appalachian Trail Conservancy (ATC) is a private, nonprofit volunteer organization dedicated to the preservation, maintenance, and promotion of the Appalachian Trail. It is a membership-based organization partnered with 31 clubs (including the AMC) that maintain designated sections of the trail. The ATC holds general meetings every other year.

Various periodicals and books about the Appalachian Trail are available from the ATC. Among these is a series of 11 guidebooks, with maps, covering the entire length of the trail. *Appalachian Trail Guide to Massachusetts/Connecticut, Eleventh Edition*, published in 2000, covers the AT in Massachusetts.

P. O. Box 807
799 Washington St.
Harpers Ferry, WV 25425-0807
Phone: 304-535-6331
Fax: 304-535-2667
www.appalachiantrail.org

Bay Circuit Alliance

Since its founding in 1990 the Bay Circuit Alliance (BCA) has developed a partnership of volunteers and other organizations to realize the goal of completing and sustaining the Bay Circuit Trail, a long-distance hiking trail around the perimeter of metropolitan Boston. Presently about 150 mi. of trail are open with another 50 mi. yet to be completed. Updated trail information is available on the BCA website.

> 3 Railroad Street
> Andover, MA 01810
> Phone: 978-470-1982
> *www.baycircuit.org*

Berkshire Natural Resources Council

Headquartered in Pittsfield, the Berkshire Natural Resources Council (BNRC) is a natural resource advocacy organization that works to preserve threatened lands in the Berkshires of western Massachusetts. The group presently owns and maintains more than 7,000 acres with an additional 9,200 acres protected by conservation restrictions. The hiking trails constructed to allow public enjoyment of these lands have a reputation of being both well maintained and environmentally responsible. The BNRC publishes a number of high-quality maps for regions in the Berkshires, including Yokun Ridge, Mt. Greylock, and the South Taconic Range. Maps are available from the organization's headquarters in Pittsfield or online at their website.

> BNRC Headquarters
> 20 Bank Row
> Pittsfield, MA 01201
> Phone: 413-499-0596
> Fax: 413-499-3924
> *www.bnrc.net*

Cape Cod Trails Conference

The Cape Cod Trails Conference is an informal organization of hiking enthusiasts that strives to improve the hiking experience on Cape Cod. Their website has information on many trails in the Cape Cod area.

www.cctrails.org

Housatonic Valley Association

The Housatonic Valley Association (HVA) is a river conservation group dedicated to preserving and protecting the Housatonic River watershed from source to sea. The organization partners with businesses and the community to increase access to the river and waterside lands as well as improve the overall health of the watershed. Projects include greenway hiking trails, water quality monitoring, stream team surveys of the river, and storm drain awareness.

The Berkshire office of HVA is located at:

1383 Rte. 102
South Lee, MA
Phone: 413-394-9796
Fax: 413-394-9818
www.hvatoday.org

Williams Outing Club

An organization of Williams College in Williamstown, the Williams Outing Club (WOC) is dedicated to making the outdoors more accessible to Williams students, as well as to others desiring to hike the trails maintained by the club. The WOC publishes a guide to northern Berkshire Trails complete with maps.

Williams College
Williamstown, MA
Phone: 413-597-2317
Fax: 413-597-4742
wso.williams.edu./orgs/woc

Williamstown Rural Lands Foundation

The Williamstown Rural Lands Foundation (WRLF) is a nonprofit, member-supported land trust that works with and within the community to protect lands around Williamstown in northern Berkshire County. Since its founding in 1986 the organization has helped protect more than 3,500 acres of land and maintains a number of trails in the northern Berkshires on land it owns or helps manage.

671 Cold Springs Rd.
Williamstown, MA 01267
Phone: 413-458-2494
www.wrlf.org

Midstate Trail Committee

This organization maintains and administers the Midstate Trail, a 92-mi.-long hiking trail bisecting the state. The Midstate Trail Committee operates under the auspices of the Worcester chapter of the Appalachian Mountain Club. The work of the committee is augmented by a large group of volunteer trail maintainers. The organization's website has updated trail information.

www.midstatetrail.org

Massachusetts Audubon Society

The Massachusetts Audubon Society (MassAudubon) manages 33,000 acres of land in 45 sanctuaries throughout the commonwealth. Dedicated to conservation, education, and research, this member-based organization is supported by 100,000 members and annually reaches 250,000 children and adults through educational programs. Many of the sanctuaries have trail networks, nature centers, and interpretive educational programs. Hours that the trails are open varies and some locations charge a modest admission fee.

208 South Great Rd.
Lincoln, MA 01773
Phone: 781-259-9500 or 800-AUDUBON
www.massaudubon.org.

Massachusetts Department of Conservation and Recreation

The Massachusetts Department of Conservation and Recreation (DCR) includes the Massachusetts Division of Parks and Recreation and the Division of Urban Parks and Recreation.

251 Causeway St., Ste. 600
Boston, MA 02114-2104
Phone: 617-626-1250
www.mass.gov/dcr/

Division of State Parks and Recreation

The DCR's Division of State Parks and Recreation (formerly the Massachusetts Department of Environmental Management) operates the nation's sixth-largest system of state parks and forests, encompassing more than 250,000 acres. Many of the parks and forests have extensive recreational facilities, including a number that are universally accessible. Admission fees are charged at some locations. Many forests and parks have extensive hiking opportunities, and many of the state's long-distance trails, such as the Appalachian, the Metacomet–Monadnock, and Midstate, pass through DCR properties.

Main Office and Region 6 (Greater Boston)

251 Causeway St.
Ste. 600/700
Boston, MA 02114-2104
Phone: 617-626-1250
Fax: 617-626-1351

Region 5 (Berkshires)

740 South St.
P.O. Box 1433
Pittsfield, MA 01202
Phone: 413-442-8928
Fax: 413-442-5860

Region 4 (Connecticut River Valley)

40 Cold Storage Dr.
P.O. Box 484
Amherst, MA 01004

Phone: 413-545-5993
Fax: 413-545-5995

Region 3 (Central)
Rte. 110
P.O. Box 155
Clinton, MA 01510
Phone: 978-368-0126
Fax: 978-368-0217

Region 2 (Northeast)
817 Lowell St.
P.O. Box 825
Carlisle, MA 01741
Phone: 978-369-3350
Fax: 978-369-1965

Region 1 (Southeast)
194 Cranberry Rd.
P.O. Box 66
South Carver, MA 02366
Phone: 508-866-2580
Fax: 508-866-7736
www.mass.gov/dcr/forparks.htm

Division of Urban Parks and Recreation

The DCR's Division of Urban Parks and Recreation (formerly the Metropolitan District Commission) is a Massachusetts state agency that manages and maintains parkland and recreational facilities in the metropolitan Boston area. It was established in 1893 to oversee and maintain the Metropolitan Park System. The agency now manages about 20,000 acres as well as a 120,000-acre watershed that supplies water to 2.5 million people. The division's properties are divided into four districts.

20 Somerset St.
Boston, MA 02108
Phone: 617-727-5114 (General Information)
617-727-5114 ext. 501 (Charles and Neponset Districts)
617-727-5114 ext. 504 (Mystic and Harbor Districts)
www.mass.gov/dcr/metroboston.htm

Massachusetts Division of Fish and Wildlife

The Massachusetts Division of Fish and Wildlife, known as MassWildlife, was founded in 1866 in response to the decline of salmon populations. Since its inception the agency has been dedicated to the protection, restoration, and management of the animals and plants of Massachusetts. The lands protected by MassWildlife are kept as wild and undeveloped as possible to serve as areas for wildlife restoration. These properties, called Wildlife Management Areas (WMAs), total over 100,000 acres across the state. Past restoration successes include the wild turkey and bald eagle; the redbelly turtle, peregrine falcon, and piping plover are some of the present projects. The recreational opportunities offered on MassWildlife lands include hiking and birding, as well as hunting and fishing. Hikers using these areas should be aware of open hunting seasons and take appropriate precautions.

www.mass.gov/dfwele/dfw/

Contact the following District Offices for the most up-to-date WMA information.

Western Wildlife District
400 Hubbard Ave.
Pittsfield, MA 01201
Phone: 413-447-9789
Fax: 413-442-0047

Connecticut Valley Wildlife District
90 East St.
Belchertown, MA 01007
Phone: 413-323-7632; Fax: 413-323-9623

Central Wildlife District
211 Temple St.
West Boylston, MA 01583
Phone: 508-835-3607; Fax: 508-792-7420

Northeast Wildlife District
68 Harris St.
Acton, MA 01720
Phone: 978-263-4347; Fax: 978-635-0292

Southeast Wildlife District
195 Bournedale Rd.
Buzzards Bay, MA 02532
Phone: 508-759-3406; Fax: 508-759-0381

National Park Service
Cape Cod National Seashore

The National Park Service (NPS) operates a huge expanse of beaches and dunes along the Atlantic shore of the Cape. Their website provides extensive updated information on the many features and recreational opportunities on Cape Cod National Seashore.

99 Marconi Station Site Rd.
Wellfleet, MA 02667
Phone: 508-771-2144 (Headquarters), 508-255-3421 or
508-487-1256 (Visitor Information)
Fax: 508-349-9052
www.nps.gov/caco

The Trustees of Reservations

The Trustees of Reservations (TTOR) is a member-supported nonprofit organization founded in 1891 by landscape architect Charles Eliot. The organization preserves for public use exceptional landscapes and special places across the commonwealth. TTOR presently protects over 25,000 acres on 99 reservations around the state. Four of the reservations are designated National Historic Landmarks, one is a National Natural Landmark, and eight are listed on the National Register of Historic Places. Combined the reservations have 270 mi. of trails. Sixteen properties contain links to long-distance trails, including the Appalachian Trail, Bay Circuit Trail, Metacomet–Monadnock Trail, Midstate Trail, and Tully Trail. Maps and guides are free at many reservations.

www.thetrustees.org
Headquarters: 978-921-1944 (Beverly)
Northeast: 978-356-4351 (Ipswich)
Southeast-Cape Cod: 781-821-2977 (Canton)

Islands: 508-693-7662 (Vineyard Haven)
Central: 978-840-4446 (Leominster)
Western: 413-298-3239 (Stockbridge)

New England Cartographics

This private company publishes a series of excellent, full-color trail maps covering the major hiking areas of central and western Massachusetts, including Mt. Greylock, the Mt. Holyoke Range, Mt. Tom, Mt. Toby, the Quabbin Reservoir, and Wachusett Mtn.

P.O. Box 9369
N. Amherst, MA 01059
Phone: 888-995-6277
Fax: 413-549-3621
www.necartographics.com

New York–New Jersey Trail Conference

This organization, a federation of 85 hiking clubs and environmental organizations (including the Appalachian Mountain Club) with a total membership of about 10,000, is dedicated to constructing and maintaining hiking trails in the New York–New Jersey area, including the South Taconic Trail of southeastern Massachusetts and eastern New York. The conference also publishes an excellent waterproof, tear-resistant map covering the trails in the South Taconic region of Connecticut, Massachusetts, and New York.

156 Ramapo Valley Rd. (Rte. 202)
Mahwah, NJ 07430
Phone: 201-512-9348
Fax: 201-512-9012
www.nynjtc.org

Town Conservation Commissions

Only a few towns have the resources to maintain municipal open space large enough to support trail systems. Where they exist, however, the recreational opportunities are often excellent. For information on trails and open space properties maintained by cities and towns, contact the conservation commission, in care of the appropriate city or town hall. Many of these commissions also provide maps of their properties, either free or at a minimal charge.

INDEX

Trail names written in **bold type** indicate that a detailed description can be found in the text.
Where multiple page references appear, **bold numbering** indicates the main entry for the trail or feature.
[Bracketed information] indicates which of the six maps displays the feature and where, by section letter and number.

Appalachian Mountain Club

Founded in 1876, the AMC is the nation's oldest outdoor recreation and conservation organization. The AMC promotes the protection, enjoyment, and wise use of the mountains, rivers, and trails of the Northeast outdoors.

PEOPLE

We are nearly 90,000 members in 12 chapters, 16,000 volunteers, and over 450 full time and seasonal staff. Our chapters reach from Maine to Washington, D.C.

OUTDOOR ADVENTURE

We offer more than 8,000 trips each year, from local chapter activities to major excursions worldwide, for every ability level and outdoor interest—from hiking and climbing to paddling, snowshoeing, and skiing. We teach people the skills to be safe outdoors and to care for the natural world around us through programs for children, teens, and adults, as well as outdoor leadership training.

GREAT PLACES TO STAY

We host more than 150,000 guest nights each year at our AMC Lodges, Huts, Camps, Shelters, and Campgrounds. Each AMC Destination is a model for environmental education and stewardship.

CARING FOR TRAILS

We maintain more than 1,700 miles of trails throughout the Northeast, including nearly 350 miles of the Appalachian Trail in five states.

PROTECTING WILD PLACES

We advocate for land and riverway conservation, monitor air quality, and work to protect alpine and forest ecosystems throughout the Northern Forest and Highlands regions.

ENGAGING THE PUBLIC

We seek to educate and inform our own members and an additional 2 million people annually through AMC Books, our website, our White Mountain visitor centers, and AMC Destinations.

JOIN US!

Members support our mission while enjoying great AMC programs, our award-winning AMC Outdoors magazine, and special discounts. Visit www.outdoors.org or call 617-523-0636 for more information.

THE APPALACHIAN MOUNTAIN CLUB
Recreation • Education • Conservation
www.outdoors.org

ABOUT THE AMC IN MASSACHUSETTS

The Appalachian Mountain Club has four active chapters in Massachusetts: Boston, Southeastern Massachusetts, Worcester, and Berskhire. Each offers a range of activities from rock climbing and backpacking to local walks, skiing, paddling, and cycling. Each chapter also offers social and young member events. AMC's Worcester Chapter maintains the Midstate Trail. AMC's Berkshire chapter maintains the Massachusetts sections of the Metacomet-Monadnock and Appalachian trails.

To view a list of AMC activities in Massachusetts and other parts of the Northeast, visit: trips.outdoors.org.

AMC BOOK UPDATES

AMC BOOKS STRIVES to keep our guidebooks as up-to-date as possible to help you plan safe and enjoyable adventures. If we learn, after publishing a book, that trails are relocated or route or contact information has changed, we will post the updated information online. Before you hit the trail, check for updates at www.outdoors.org/publications/books/updates.

While hiking or paddling, if you notice discrepancies with the trail description or map, or if you find any other errors in the book, please let us know by submitting them to amcbookupdates@outdoors.org or in writing to Books Editor, c/o AMC, 5 Joy Street, Boston, MA 02108. We will verify all submissions and post key updates each month.

AMC Books is dedicated to being a recognized leader in outdoor publishing. Thank you for your participation.

AMC BOOKS & MAPS

EXPLORE THE POSSIBILITIES

More Books from the Outdoor Experts

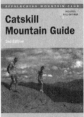
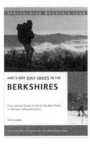
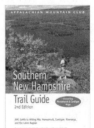